The
Vision
of
Jean Genet

The
Vision
of
Jean Genet

by *RICHARD N. COE*

❥✦❧

GROVE PRESS, INC., NEW YORK

For Joan and Vivian

CONTENTS

Author's Note   vii

Introduction

1   All Done with Mirrors   3

The Novels

2   Head down, Feet up (*Our Lady of the Flowers*)   31

3   Traps and Allegories (*Miracle of the Rose*)   66

4   The Golden Legend of a Professional Burglar
    (*The Thief's Journal*)   99

5   Love Thine Enemy (*Pompes Funèbres*)   135

6   Murder and Metaphysics (*Querelle of Brest*)   170

The Plays

7   The Small Boy Who Was Night
    (*Deathwatch* and *The Maids*)   213

8   Anarchy in the Brothel (*The Balcony*)   251

9   Politics without Platitudes
    (*The Blacks* and *The Screens*)   282

Bibliography   321

Thematic Index   337

ACKNOWLEDGMENTS

I should like to thank the following for their kind permission to quote from the works of Jean Genet : Editions Gallimard for their overall permission to quote from the French text of Genet; Messrs. Faber & Faber Ltd. and Grove Press, Inc. for the plays : *The Maids, The Screens, The Blacks, Deathwatch* and *The Balcony*, all translated by Bernard Frechtman; Messrs. Anthony Blond Ltd. and Grove Press, Inc. for the novels : *Our Lady of the Flowers, Miracle of the Rose, The Thief's Journal*, all translated by Bernard Frechtman, and *Querelle of Brest*, translated by Roger Senhouse; Grove Press, Inc. for *The Funambulists* translated by Bernard Frechtman, and published in *Evergreen Review*, No. 32; Editions Jean-Jacques Pauvert for 'Lettre à Pauvert sur *Les Bonnes*'. For other works the following must be thanked : Editions Gallimard for J.-P. Sartre's *Saint-Genet Comédien et Martyr* and Messrs. W. H. Allen & Co. and George Braziller Inc. for their English edition, *Saint Genet*; Messrs. Calder & Boyars Ltd. and Grove Press Inc, for *The Unnamable*, the third part of Samuel Beckett's trilogy; Editions Gallimard for J.-P. Sartre's *Les Mouches*, and Messrs. Hamish Hamilton Ltd. and Alfred Knopf Inc. for their English edition, *The Flies*, translated by Stuart Gilbert; The Clarendon Press, Oxford, for *Helvétius: A Study in Persecution* by D. W. Smith; Editions Gallimard for Ionesco's *Victimes du Devoir*, and Messrs. Calder & Boyars and Grove Press, Inc. for their translation, *Victims of Duty*, translated by Donald Watson; Miss Sonia Bronwell, Messrs. Secker & Warburg Ltd. and Harcourt Brace & World Inc. for George Orwell's *Keep the Aspidistra Flying*.

R.N.C.

AUTHOR'S NOTE

This book is *not* a biography of Jean Genet; it is a study of his ideas, his art, his imagery and his dreams—in short, his vision of the world—as he has chosen to give them to us in his poems, plays and novels. To attempt a serious biography of a living writer without his co-operation would be worse than a risk; it would be an unpardonable impertinence.

On the other hand, Genet has chosen to present at least two of his novels, together with the *Thief's Journal*, in the first person singular, and it is well-nigh impossible to refer to the omnipresent 'I' who forms the subject of these books other than as 'Jean Genet'. It is essential, however, to remember that *this* Jean Genet—the Jean Genet of *Our Lady of the Flowers* and of *Miracle of the Rose*, not to mention the *Thief's Journal*—while he *may* have roots in the real Jean Genet's emotions and experience, is essentially imaginary. Like the 'Marcel' of Proust's *Remembrance of Things Past*, the being who says 'I' in Jean Genet's novels, poems, plays and essays is as much a fictional character as Harcamone or Mimosa half-IV, as Stilitano or Clément Village. Nothing that Jean-Genet-the-Writer says about this character is necessarily false; but neither is it necessarily true.

Jean Cocteau, who was one of Genet's earliest champions, once uttered a famous paradox: *Il faut mentir pour être vrai*. This phrase should stand in letters of gold at the head of every chapter in this study.

* * *

Notes on the text are to be found at the end of each chapter. These include the English source of reference, followed by the original French text, followed by the French source of reference. Except where otherwise stated, French quotations from the novels have been taken from the definitive text as printed in the *Oeuvres Complètes de Jean Genet*, Paris (Gallimard), vol. ii (1951) and vol. iii (1953). Quotations from J.-P. Sartre, *Saint-Genet Comédien et Martyr* are also taken from this edition, vol. i (1952). For details of the sources of other quotations taken from Genet, reference should be made to the *Bibliography*, where the text used is indicated by an asterisk in each case.

The *Atelier d'Alberto Giacometti* is published in an unpaginated edition. For convenience of reference, I have introduced a provisional pagination (pp. 1-88), beginning at the title-page and including the illustrations.

All major quotations have been translated in the text, except for those taken from *Pompes Funèbres*; owing to copyright difficulties no translation of this has been permitted, and the original French appears in the text. I have used wherever possible the published translations by Bernard Frechtman, and in the case of *Querelle of Brest*, that by Roger Senhouse.

Certain difficulties arise when providing translations for quotations taken from Genet's dramas, since, frequently, the published French and English texts do not correspond. This is not only because Mr Frechtman has, quite rightly, aimed to produce good acting dialogue in English, rather than a word-for-word literal rendering; but also because the translations were often made from versions other than those which have since become definitive in French. Wherever possible, I have used the published English texts, even when the correspondence is not exact; and I have only substituted my own literal version, either when the precise point that I wished to make was obscured, or else, more frequently, when the passage quoted was missing altogether from the English edition.

The following abbreviated titles should be noted :

Balcon—C. J. L. Bal. Article : 'Comment jouer *Le Balcon*', which precedes the text of the play.

Bonnes—C.J.L.B. Article : 'Comment jouer *Les Bonnes*', which precedes the text of the play.

E.R. The Funambulists in *Evergreen Review*, No. 32, April-May 1964

Giacometti. L'Atelier d'Alberto Giacometti

Journal. Journal du Voleur

Miracle. Miracle de la Rose

Notre-Dame. Notre-Dame des Fleurs

Our Lady. Our Lady of the Flowers

Paravents—Q.I. Article : 'Quelques Indications', which precedes the text of the play.

Pauvert. 'Lettre à Pauvert sur *Les Bonnes*'

Q. of B. Querelle of Brest

Quevelle. Quevelle de Brest Rose. Miracle of the Rose

S. Genet. Sartre, *Saint Genet: Actor and Martyr*

Saint-G. Sartre, *Saint-Genet Comédien et Martyr*

Thief. The Thief's Journal

Introduction

1

ALL DONE WITH MIRRORS

The thief is a solitary creature. He knows little of normal human relationships. At liberty, his aim is to lose himself in the crowd, to pass unnoticed, unobserved by policemen and store-detectives, to cultivate anonymity almost to the point of non-existence. Caught and convicted, he is once again absorbed into a herd of dehumanized beings, all dressed alike, all moving in mechanical obedience to orders, all reduced to numbers and statistics in a card-index. He is alone, a nameless particle is a sea of namelessness; or else he is alone—literally—in his cell. And Jean Genet,[1] who has been both a thief and a convict, is obsessed with solitude. Such intimate realities as family, or friendship, or the comradeship of labour are abstractions to him; they appear as mere 'functions' of a complex social pattern, pleasanter perhaps, but ultimately no different in kind from the necessary functional interdependence of criminal and victim, or of prisoner-at-the-bar and magistrate-on-the-bench.[2] For Genet the only truly significant relationship is that of a man with himself.

Solitude, then, with its complexities, its rewards and its terrors, is Genet's main theme; it dominates the novels, it informs the early plays, it is constantly felt even behind the crowded tapestry of moving figures that constitutes *The Screens*. Genet is the poet of solitude. From the first, however, the poet, with his emotional responses of anguish, despair and visionary mysticism, has been accompanied by the philosopher, determined to discover a more or less rational

3

solution to the mystery of human loneliness. For the poet, 'Solitude is sweet. It is bitter. One might think that the head should be emptied there of all past entries (precursory practice of purification) . . .'[3]; but for the philosopher, the anguish of solitude lies rather in the fact that the being who is *totally* isolated—allowing this to be conceivable—has no way of knowing himself, of conceiving his own identity, and therefore no way of *being* himself in the plenitude of his own awareness. Like Pascal, Genet is haunted by a sense of his own imperfection—not by his social or moral shortcomings which, after all, offended only society, and society showed him fairly promptly that it was well able to look after itself in this respect— but by his incompleteness, his failure to realise himself (in the Sartrian sense) as a *being*, since the being can only lay claim to a real *identity* in so far as it is completely and immediately conscious of itself existing. Genet, the *'brillant de belle taille'* that jewellers call 'solitaire',[4] never came to know himself in the normal, fairly haphazard manner of the average, integrated being growing up in a society of which he feels himself a part : first accepting from his friends and parents certain simplified, ready-made notions about himself, then gradually comparing these notions with what he feels to be the inner reality, *his* truth, modifying and discarding as the years go by, until a working picture is formed of an apparently *real* and stable personality—an identity that *I* know as *myself*. This, as Jean-Paul Sartre has so brilliantly demonstrated,[5] was not Genet's way.

For Genet was an illegitimate child, born of an unknown father, and of a mother who was a prostitute and who abandoned him to be brought up by the public authorities. As a child, he lived with foster-parents in the country. Not *his* country, for in Paris he was born, and to Paris he has always belonged; nor *his* parents. From his very first moment of consciousness, everything was alien : between *himself* and *others*, there was a gap, an impassable abyss. And when these Others found words to describe him as he seemed to them, Genet possessed no well-adjusted subconscious mechanism to redress the balance. Between the conflicting internal and external awareness of that being known for reference as 'Jean Genet', there was no point of contact. Either the boy had to reject *everything* that he learned about himself from others (and how should a child do that?), or else he had to accept it all, and learn to see and feel himself—in short, to *be* himself—entirely as others said he was. And soon, the Others began to say he was a thief. So Genet *was* a thief. He lived thief, and acted thief, and felt thief. Jean Genet had no awareness of Jean Genet in terms of anything other than thief, which was what his foster-parents and his neighbours called him.

Yet there remained an awareness, precisely, of the fact that there was no other awareness : a sense of something missing, a consciousness of a Nothingness that had usurped the place of what Jean Genet ought to have known himself to be, but could not. At the centre of his being there was a Void—a *Néant*. He, as himself, could know nothing about himself because he, in himself and for himself, *was* nothing.

Hence the haunting sense of imperfection and incompleteness which pervades every line that Genet has written. Other, more fortunate people, can be-what-they-are; Genet can only be what the Others made him—and in a desperate attempt to achieve some sort of balance within himself, he one day took the momentous decision which, in *Our Lady of the Flowers*, he attributes to the child Culafroy, and which, in Sartre's view, marks the beginning of his authentic existence in this world :

> He did not want to disappoint. He joined in the rough stuff. With a few others of a small band that was as tightly knit as a gang, he helped commit a petty theft inside the home. The Mother Superior [. . . .] asked Lou why he had stolen. All he could answer was : 'Because the others thought I was a thief.'[8]

In other words, Genet is a classic case of existentialist schizophrenia. He possesses two distinct personalities, or rather, two distinct identities : the first, that which he presents to Others, the second, that which he really is within himself. Normally, we assume that the personality which I know and think of as myself is the ultimate reality, whereas that which Others see and upon which they pass their damning and categorical judgements in something superficial : it is not really me, but me-as-I-appear. Genet's schizophrenia, however, consists in this, that he invariably looks at himself with the eyes of others : he sees and judges himself as others see and judge him—and yet, at the same time, he is dissatisfied. He is obscurely aware that this Self, observed in such a manner from an alien point of view, is *not* himself. It is an appearance, an illusion, a reflection, nothing more or less, of something else, something that *is* himself, yet which, precisely because it *is* the perceiver, cannot be perceived. In Sartrian terms, the source of perception *(le pour-soi)* can never perceive itself; for, as soon as it has knowledge of something, that something, by definition, becomes not perceiver, but the object of perception *(l'en-soi)*. In short, Genet, by his own confession, is the ideal illustration of all those ontological conundrums that Sartre explores with off-beat, Germanic perserverence in the dense, interminable paragraphs of *Being and Nothingness*.

For Sartre, dispassionate observer and philosopher, the fact that

perception and perceived can never coincide—that I can never
know myself, save in terms of that which I am not—is a proposition
to be recorded, elaborated, and (with due academic moderation) considered as a source of nausea or anguish. For Genet, unprepared by
Husserl, unfortified by Heidegger, unschooled by the rigorous discipline of the rue d'Ulm, the same experience has to be lived through
as a blind temptation to madness, a chaos of despair and degradation, an urge towards the brink of suicide. For Genet's tragedy is
that he is a *lucid* schizophrenic—a schizophrenic who is incessantly
aware of the nature of his own disease, and who knows that it is
incurable. In Sartre's analysis, perceiver and perceived can only
realise themselves as a single unity in God; for Genet however,
this unity *must* be realised, somehow, here and now, in himself. He
is faced with an insoluble problem, yet cannot accept the fact that
is it insoluble. He—like every other being in this existentialist universe—is an irreconcilable duality; yet only unity is tolerable, and,
as a mystic, nothing can satisfy him for an instant, except the
Absolute.

All Genet's novels are concerned with a search for the Absolute—
whether for an Absolute Good or an Absolute Evil is, in the long
run, essentially indifferent, and indeed, in those ultimate domains
of thought, beyond time and space, to which he eventually leads us,
the one becomes indistinguishable from the other. The only way,
however, in which the being who is-what-Others-make-him can, in
any Absolute sense, be himself, is to abstract himself from the importunate gaze and knowledge of Others, and to confine himself for ever
in solitude—in 'singularity'. Yet even this is not salvation. For if, in
the completeness of his solitude, he were to achieve his ideal, his
Absolute, of being-what-he-is, then he would become like the bed in
his cell, or like the wall of the prison itself, an insensitive, unknow-
ing, unperceiving object, which likewise is-what-it-is, without a
chink in the armour of its absoluteness. He can only *know* himself
for what he is by taking up a position outside himself, and, in a
figurative sense, by looking at himself . . . but as soon as one part
of him takes a stand apart, and becomes aware of the other part
of him—that is, as soon as knowing emerges as something separate
from being—then he is no longer exclusively and absolutely what
he is. He is what he is but he is also himself aware of what he is—
not one person, but two, no longer Jean Genet in total and metaphysical solitude, but Jean Genet in the company of another : himself, his own double.

Outside the Self, of course, there are other phenomena which,
to a greater or lesser degree, affect its destiny and modify its self-
awareness. There is the world of inanimate objects which should,

ideally, just be what they are, yet which, more often than not, seem to possess some sort of awareness—a hostile awareness, in conflict with Genet's own. There is God, who may, or may not exist, but who, even if He is only a magnified projection of the Self—or rather, *especially* if He is a projection of the Self—provides an extra dimension with which the Self must reckon; for God has certainly created Hell, even if Heaven is rather more problematical. There are the Others, whose awareness and whose judgement of the Self constitute the perpetual danger, and at the same time the perpetual temptation. And finally, there is the Void.

For Genet, the Void may simply be death; or (rather worse) a continued existence from which life, in the full sense, has already withdrawn; or perhaps again merely the equivalent in the outside world of that Nothingness which is Genet's own self-awareness that has abdicated in favour of the Others' awareness of his own identity. Whatever its ultimate reality, the Void is constantly present in Genet's novels, and makes itself felt through countless symbols : the blank eyes of statues, or the transparency of glass, or the eyes of murderers, '. . . blue and vacant like the windows of buildings under construction, through which you can see the sky from the windows of the opposite wall'[7]—and which, adds Genet, '. . . hypnotize me as much as do empty theatres, deserted prisons, machinery at rest, deserts . . .'[8]—or, more significantly still, the Void is like two mirrors placed one in front of the other, each reflecting an eternal emptiness in infinite repetitions of Nothing. For the mirror is the most obsessive symbol in Genet's thought. God is a mirror that magnifies : the Other, a mirror that distorts; Good is the mirror-opposite of Evil, and darkness the mirror of light; while if the Self that is awareness wishes to observe the Self that is-what-it-is (and at the same time to observe itself observing), it has but to look in the mirror. For if, in the world of three-dimensional reality, the Self is complex and elusive, in the mirror it literally is-what-it-is and nothing more; it is pure appearance and, as Sartre argues with dogmatic optimism, while Genet, looking on in despair and anguish, agrees, 'what is reality, if not that which *is apparent*?'[9]

But the mirror is not merely the somewhat disquieting illustration of a problem in existentialist metaphysics; it is the symbol of the whole of Genet's world—a world in which there is no certain or tangible reality, but only appearances and voids : reflections alternating with panels of plain glass, both equally baffling and impenetrable. In *The Thief's Journal*, Genet describes how, at the Fun-Fair in Antwerp, he once watched Stilitano—the Serbian pimp and petty gangster who was his lover, slave-driver and tyrant before World War II—struggling quite literally to escape from one such labyrinth

of insubstantialities, a Hall of Mirrors; and this simple fair-ground
attraction emerges as a grotesque distortion of Plato's vision of man
forever tantalized by the dancing shadows on the rear wall of his
cavern :

> Stilitano, and he alone, was trapped, *visibly* at a loss, in the glass corri-
> dors. No-one could hear him, but by his gestures and his mouth one could
> tell he was screaming with anger [. . . .] Stilitano was alone. Everyone had
> found the way out, except him. The universe became strangely overcast.
> The shadow which suddenly covered things and people was the shadow
> of my solitude in the face of this despair. . . .[10]

In this remarkable passage, the emphasis is on the frustration of
the human situation : Stilitano is cut off from all contact and communication by invisible walls of glass, and his only direct experience
of reality lies in bumping up against his own reflection. Yet this is
only one aspect—and the most rational and encouraging aspect at
that—of man's eternal conflict with the shadows of his own identity.
From earliest times, in folk-lore and fairy-tale and occult literature,
the mirror has been credited with mystic or magic properties—sometimes purely symbolic : the 'Mirror of Perfection', or of Truth, the
Mirror that is Wisdom, the reflection of the power of God, 'the
glass of fashion and the mould of form'—sometimes involved in the
deployment of more sinister forces : the broken mirror that brings
bad luck, the speaking mirror that answers the Queen's questions,
the mirror that steals away the reflection that is confided to it, for
the powers of evil can rob a man of his reflection as easily as they
can rob him of his shadow, and with similar consequences.[11]

No less complex and sinister is the use that Genet makes of this
same symbol : the mirror betrays, robs, multiplies, distorts or lies;
it comes to life with a power of malice all its own, and yet contrives to remain a prosaic and impervious piece of furniture. In the
mirror, Genet the metaphysician merges with Genet the poet, and
the poetry is never far removed from the realms of magic and the
occult. In every sense, the balance between reality and reflection is
a delicate one : for if the basis of reality is appearance, then the
pure appearance of the object in the mirror is in the end more real
than the object which causes it. And being more real, it attracts
to itself all those attributes of existence which normally we attribute
to three-dimensional beings : life, independent actions, past and
future, identity. Darling (Mignon), for instance, in *Our Lady of the
Flowers*, has no future, save what the mirror knows better than he :

> . . . he continues by fits and starts the gestures of the drama which he is
> unaware he is acting out [. . . .] Finally he gets up and, in front of the
> little twopenny mirror nailed to the wall, he pushes aside his blond hair
> and, without realising what he is doing, looks for a bullet-wound at his
> temple.[12]

—whereas the Sailor of *'Adame Miroir* 'has no past' until the ballet starts, and for Genet 'his life begins' with the beginning of his first dance—that is, with the multiplication of his appearance in the wall of mirrors that forms the limit of his universe and the arena of the stage.[13]

Genet's solitary ballet, *'Adame Miroir* (1947) is one the most explicit pieces of symbolism that he has produced, and there is no more immediate or illuminating introduction to his strange, poetic universe of shimmering evanescences than this little scenario, with its sharp outlines, its stylisation and its insubstantial puzzles of identity. The very title, *'Adame Miroir*, with its shifting patterns of symbolic suggestion, is characteristic of Genet's preoccupations; for, around the central image of the mirror, 'Madame'—the female element in a sophisticated society—merges imperceptibly into 'Adam'—the male principle, the primitive, the first Original—while at the same time the clear classical French of Genet's prose ('madame') is reflected as in a glass darkly, and becomes the vague-outlined *argot* of Belleville with its elided 'm' (' 'adame')—an *argot* which is half the mystery of Genet's poetry. In the mirror, the image has no life : it is therefore Death—yet it is not, for it is alive with the life of the Dancer, and with its own life too, since it dances even when he is still. 'It is not Death,' comments Genet himself, 'But who? The author cannot tell.'[14] If Genet could have given a neat, clear answer, he would probably never have needed to write the ballet— nor, for that matter, any of his plays or novels. For none of them finds the real solution. They merely continue to ask the question.

'Adame Miroir, then, is a symbolic excursion into the inconceivable realms of ultimate identity. At first curtain-rise, the Sailor, imprisoned like Stilitano in his Hall of Mirrors, simply fails to find his reflection altogether. The mirrors show nothing but their own eternal emptiness. At first he is puzzled; but soon he comes to accept the miracle, not as something frightening, but as a freedom, an overwhelming liberation, a unlooked-for surge of joy. He taunts the mirrors, treating them, says Genet, 'with great familiarity'—for what are they now but Voids, whereas *his* reality, compared with that of the Nothing, liberated by the Nothing, is assured. He is himself . . . until suddenly, in one delirious turn, he bumps into a mirror, swings round—and sees himself. Immediately, the whole world changes focus. Wildly he rushes from mirror to mirror round the stage, but always the Image is there before him, granite-like, imperturbable, stronger than he. 'Maddened . . . exhausted . . . he falls to the ground'[15]—in front of the great central mirror that dominates the stage. While he is still on the ground, however, his Image begins slowly to rise of its own volition. Hypnotized, the

Sailor rises also; but when he begins to gesture in front of the Image, *the* Image becomes merely *his* image, and dutifully gestures back, identical with himself. Exasperated, the Sailor strikes the Image on the jaw—and half-knocks it out. As it recovers, the Image—which is still *his* image for all that—steps out of the Mirror to join its Master (or slave, or cause, or effect : the relationship constantly shifts and changes), and they dance. And the mirrors (logically, for once) cease to reflect.

Between the Sailor and his Image, there now follows an erotic dance, leading towards the impossible union—the mystic union of lover with beloved, of two-in-one, of Saint with Deity, of Self with Knowledge-of-Self—when suddenly the dancers are interrupted. From a hidden mirror leaps the Domino, selects the Sailor and rejects the Image; stabs the Sailor (the Image now looking on with bored indifference) and Hamlet-like 'lugs the guts into the neighbour room'. Now the Image alone is alive—yet maddened with loneliness, for his life is a life-in-death, a reality which is at the same time an impossibility : which, after all, is what a mirror-image is. The Domino returns, and violently tries to drive the Image back into the mirror, where he belongs. But the Image can only reflect the Sailor, and now the Sailor is dead. The only figure left to reflect is that of the Domino . . . the Domino, therefore, removes his sari-like costume and winds the Image in it. For a second they are confused, inextricable, half-Sailor-half-Domino; then they separate, and now the Image is the Image-of-the-Domino, but the Domino, stripped of his mask and robes, is now the Sailor.

But appearance *is* reality. Now that the Image *appears* to be the Domino, the Image *is* the Domino; likewise the Domino *is* the Sailor. The Sailor (ex-Domino) tries to leap back into his mirror; but the mirrors are resistant glass, and will not even reflect : The Domino (ex-Image-of-the-Sailor) chases the Sailor : in panic, the Sailor knocks once more at the door of the mirror, and this time the mirror relents and admits him, but refuses the Domino who tries to follow. Now the Domino and the Sailor are on opposite sides, with all the world and death between them. They fight, and their gestures reflect each other exactly—for at bottom, they *are* each other's reflection, for all that one is violet-robed and masked, the other still the Sailor. The Domino backs away from the mirror : the Image (both his, yet at the same time not-his) backs away simultaneously—and disappears. The Domino charges like a maddened bull against the mirror, but this time crashes up against his *own* reflection—his real own, in mask and violet robes. The Sailor has gone for good; now in every mirror there dances yet another Domino. They dance and dance until finally a mirror opens, the Domino is admitted back into reality—and so the ballet ends.

Although this scenario was written at the same time—or probably slightly before—the Stilitano episode in *The Thief's Journal*, its symbolism is vastly more complex. Almost all the major themes that dominate Genet's novels and plays are suggested in this sequence of dances, much as Samuel Beckett manages to condense all the essentials of his philosophy into the forty minutes of *Krapp's Last Tape*. There is the metamorphosis of identity, the interchange of appearance and reality, the longing to attain an ultimate mystic union with the Totality through erotic experience—which experience, however, being homosexual, is doomed to lead only to the embittered frustration of Querelle, in *Querelle of Brest*, when 'it seemed to him that he was pressing his face against a mirror that gave back his own image'[16]—the themes of murder and indifference, the idea of the Mask, the figure of the Sailor . . . all these we shall meet again and again. Meanwhile, however, we must set aside the poet and return to the Existentialist philosopher, in order to follow further the implications of the symbol of the mirror.

Critics have wondered at the strange phenomenon of *Saint Genet: Actor and Martyr*—one of the longest books of criticism ever to be devoted by an eminent philosopher to a controversial and at the time almost unknown contemporary. Yet it is not hard to understand why Sartre should have produced a treatise almost as long and as dense as the famous *Being and Nothingness* in honour of our delinquent poet with his passion for mysteries and mirrors. Remembering that, in *Being and Nothingness*, Sartre describes the basic structure of consciousness as *'un reflet-reflétant'*,[17] the link is already apparent. Genet not merely illustrates the Sartrian thesis in a series of brilliant images, but in fact takes the argument into regions where Sartre, too precisely trained in the rigorous exactitudes of philosophic dialectic, dare not venture.

For Sartre, the universe consists of two distinct elements : that which exists, and that which perceives. Obviously these two elements are interdependent to a large extent, since that which exists can only be said to be what it is when it is perceived; whereas that which perceives depends upon that which exists in order to have an object of perception. In this fashion, each is the mirror-image of the other, and the process of consciousness is reflection-reflecting.

For Sartre however, as for the Buddhist, that which exists, exists in an undifferentiated mass, as 'fullness', *until* it becomes the object of perception. Within the totality, there are no separate identities until the mirror is there to pick them out. Only a mind (the mirror of consciousness) can distinguish between, say, a cabbage and an

onion, an inch and a mile, green and violet, and it does so by apply-
ing negatives. It determines 'green' by eliminating all the colours
that are *not* green; it defines an object by postulating all around
it a space which is not-that-object, and therefore limits its extension
and gives it precise contours. Only the mind can say 'Peter is not
there'—in a *massive*, undifferentiated universe, the statement is an
absurdity. Absence is a mental concept, not a fact. There are no
negatives in nature.

Consciousness is the imposing of a negative on a positive—a process of *néantisation*. The dual character of the cosmos, therefore,
can now be defined rather more precisely : one aspect of it is positive, the other negative. All that massively exists (*l'être*, or *l'en-soi*)
is positive, while consciousness, which organizes that which exists, is
negative (*le néant*, or *le pour-soi*). Logically therefore, the *pour-soi*
(the negation which is consciousness) must lie outside all being; only
that 'which is not' is able to understand that which is. The *pour-soi*
is not Being; the *pour-soi* 'is its own Not-Being'.[18]

If this is true whenever I perceive a chair, say, or a tree, it is
also true when I perceive myself—that is, when I consider my own
identity, whenever I say 'I'. 'I' am both positive and negative, existent and non-existent. The 'I' that I can know about—my face, my
acts, my past, my memory, in a word, my whole identity—is an
object of perception : it exists, it 'is-what-it-is'. But it is *not* the
I-that-perceives. The I-that-perceives, which is my ultimate and
real identity, is negative and therefore lies for ever out of reach.
I can know myself as a *thing*, an alien object of my own perception;
but I can never know myself as a subject.

But what about the Image in the Mirror? As an object of perception, as an element having a real existence in the outside world,
it is-what-it-is, it exists *en soi*—yet at same time, it is-what-it-is-
not—which is precisely the definition of the negative element that
is consciousness. As a reflection, it is *not* the object reflected. My face
in the shaving-mirror has all the characteristics of the face which
I am trying to shave, yet, although I have a far more accurate knowledge of it than I have of my real face, which I cannot see, I have
the knowledge precisely because it *is not* what it purports to be. Moreover, not only does the mirror reflect 'me'; it also (whenever I look
at it carefully) reflects 'me' being conscious of 'me'. I see my eyes
looking at my eyes In the mirror, simultaneously, 'I am what I
am' and 'I am what I am not'. In the mirror, I am that Total Being
whom Sartre defines as God.

But there is still a further element to take into account. Over and
above my identity *(l'en-soi)* and my consciousness (what 'I' am not :
le pour-soi), there is also what-I-am-for-others' *(le pour-autrui)*.

My consciousness organizes the world for me by imposing negatives on everything that exists in terms of myself : the primary definition of 'this table' is that it is 'not-me'; and on this initial distinction all subsequent definitions depend. Whatever forces may restrain my acts, my perception is the manifestation of a monstrous egoism, of an unlimited freedom—I cannot so much as open my eyes without automatically organizing all spatial relationships in terms of myself. Once I am observed by the Other, however, the whole position changes. *I* become an object-in-space, and in someone else's space at that. *My* freedom, *my* egoism, are reduced to the most abject slavery; my very existence depends upon the Other's good pleasure— or even upon his absolute indifference, provided only that he continues to watch me. 'The other appears [. . . .] as the radical negation of my experience, since he is the one for whom I am, not subject, but object,' argues Sartre in *Being and Nothingness*; and a few pages later he sums up the predicament of the Self absorbed and destroyed by the Other in one of the most striking images in the book : 'It seems as though a sink-hole has been drilled in the middle of my Being, and that I am perpetually swilled away through this hole.'[19]

Hell, then—in this purely ontological sense—'*is* other people.' But, once again, what about the mirror? 'My' face in the mirror is observed by 'my' eyes : I am the Other for myself—I am my own sink-hole through which my own consciousness is swilled, only (presumably) to flood straight back in again through the taps. The mirror is the perpetual-motion machine of the existentialist universe—but it is also God, the Trinity, the Three-in-One : the *en-soi*, the *pour-soi* and the *pour-autrui* in a one-and-only indissoluble totality. In any theory of perception, but particularly in a phenomenological context, the mirror is an insurmountable stumbling-block; but fools rush in . . . and the poet-fool Genet has indeed chosen to rush in, to fling himself headlong precisely into that abyss where angel-philosopher Sartre dithered and hesitated cautiously on the brink.

For obviously Sartre too was tempted. There is no mention of mirrors in *Being and Nothingness*; but the stories and novels are full of them—or of their even more significant absence. In the Second-Empire Hell of *No Exit*, the one characteristic *objet d'art* that one would expect to find—the mirror—is missing (just as it is missing at Genet's Mettray, and with the same result) : Estelle is forced to make up her lips by relying on Inès' directions, and so the consciousness of the Other replaces that convenient fusion of Other/Self which is the looking-glass.[20] By contrast, Roquentin (in *Nausea*), Lucien (in the story 'The Childhood of a Leader'), and above all Daniel in *The Age of Reason* (the first volume of *Les Chemins de la Liberté*)—Daniel who is the clearest symbolic incarnation of Sartre's theory of *'le regard'*[21]—are constantly preoccupied and disturbed by the phenomenon of their own reflection. Sartre, in fact, is clearly aware of the problem, but fails to draw the conclusions; for Genet, the mirror is not only a symbolic starting-point for his philosophy and poetry alike, but he develops every implication in infinite detail.

We know too little about the intimate evolution of Genet the man to be able to decide whether his resolve to 'be what he was'— *i.e.* a thief—did in fact determine the whole of his early life; but this passion for authenticity is the unmistakable hallmark of his characters: Divine and Our Lady in *Our Lady of the Flowers*, the narrators of *Miracle of the Rose* and of *Pompes Funèbres*, Querelle and Nono and even Madame Lysiane in *Querelle of Brest*— all are concerned first and foremost to realize their existence and their identity 'as it is'. Certainly none of them is satisfied with anything less than the Absolute; for one of the few rewards of solitude is the opportunity to strive towards this elusive and ideal coincidence with oneself. But the 'complete man', in order to 'be what he is', has also, simultaneously, to 'know what he is', and this already involves a split in personality, like the birth of a double: every being is both observer and observed. Even this, however, is not the solution, for if the 'complete man' consists necessarily of the couple observer-observed, yet a third facet of personality is required to *perceive* the fact of this completeness . . . and so on *ad infinitum*. If I am only the total unity of myself when I observe myself in the mirror, then it requires another observer—or another mirror—to reflect and contain my totality. Thus the mirrors multiply, as in the Fun-Fair at Antwerp, or as on the stage in *The Balcony*. Even in the opening scene of *The Maids* there are, quite inconspicuously, three mirrors on the stage: the looking-glass on the dressing-table, the hand-mirror, and the reflection that 'Claire' sees in 'Madame's' shoes as she polishes them. There are also suggestions of this sequence of multiple reflections in the dramatic structure of *The Blacks* and *The Screens*. On the whole, however, the dominating structural feature (both metaphysical and technical) of Genet's plays and novels is a three-point relationship: a trio which, in one way or another, is destined to resolve itself into that unity which, at bottom, it always was—with this rider, that an absolute Unity may also be a *néant*, a total Void.

This characteristic structure, with its implications of a mirror-identity, is most clearly apparent in the early plays, *Deathwatch* and *The Maids*. In *Deathwatch*, the three characters are all to some extent reflections of each other; but one, Green Eyes, is already as good as condemned to death, while, during the action of the play, Lefranc, in a desperate attempt to *become* Green Eyes, deliberately murders the third character, Maurice, and thus launches himself likewise on the direct road to solitude and annihilation : 'I really am all alone',[22] is the line on which the play closes. Similarly in *The Maids*, the sisters Claire and Solange are not only mirror-reflections of each other, but both are reflected in Madame, whom they in their turn reflect alternately. All three are interchangeable, because all three are facets of a single identity. As the play proceeds, Claire as it were absorbs into herself both her sister and Madame, and thus in death becomes a unity; while Solange likewise remains alone, another total solitude, another unity embracing all three of the reflections. And once again, it is the solitude of the Void of death, for there is no more 'life' in Solange as the play finishes than there is in Phèdre as the curtain falls on Racine's tragedy.

There is no need to stress the fact that a concept so fundamental as the mystery of the Three-in-One will have religious as well as existential implications. Genet's religion—or perhaps mystic atheism might be a better word for it—is complex, and we shall see more of it later; it is fatalistic, and it is never very far from some form of primitive animism. But for Genet, the unattainable ideal, the inconceivable objective towards which he is forever striving in his 'pursuit of the Impossible Nothingness',[23] is a unity with himself, a unity in total solitude. Not so much, perhaps, the traditional mystic's longing to lose himself in God, but rather its mirror-counterpart : to lose God in himself. This seems to be one of the many implications of that strange, and at first sight grotesquely incongruous term 'sanctity' *(la sainteté)*—'the most beautiful word in human language', observes Genet in *The Thief's Journal*[24]—which permeates *Our Lady of the Flowers* and to a lesser extent the other novels, the *Journal*, and even plays as late as *The Balcony*. For the relationship of man with God is also triangular. God is man's own face made visible in the transcendental mirror of the infinite (remembering that God, for being man's reflection, is not for that reason any less real, any more than the image in the looking-glass is less real for being pure appearance)—but in addition to the Figure and the Divine Reflection, there is always, necessarily, a third element, whose function is to perceive and contain the initial duality. This third element is sometimes, in a more-or-less theological sense, Grace (as in some episodes in *Our Lady of the Flowers*, and particularly in *Deathwatch*); sometimes the Divine-Human double-image reflected in the consciousness of the Other. All Genet's murderers are, in this sense, 'Saints' in revolt. In their overpowering urge for the Totality of the One, they kill : by killing, they destroy—or rather, as in *Pompes Funèbres* and *Querelle of Brest*, they absorb into themselves—the Image of the Other; and in the same instant they destroy and absorb the Image of God. Thus, at the last, they are alone, in the absolute solitude of the Self; and then, relentlessly, the guillotine proceeds to annihilate the Self, and so the Three will be dissolved into the Total One, which is the Void.

As often as not, this triangular metaphysical structure reveals itself in the simplest of everyday actions. Again and again, for instance, one character, instead of looking directly at another, will watch him through the intermediary of a mirror, or even observe him in the reflections of a ditch or a puddle. In *The Balcony*, this indirect vision becomes one of the most curious aspects of the technique of the play : during the first three *Tableaux*, an unseen room is reflected on-stage by means of mirrors, only to appear as the main setting ('Irma's room') in *Tableau* V. In *Pompes Funèbres*, instances of this indirect vision occur five times, in *Querelle of Brest*, four : Dédé, in the mirror, studies the room where he lives[25]; Georges Querelle smiles indirectly at Lt Seblon[26]; Madame Lysiane watches Robert Querelle undress[27]; and finally, Georges Querelle himself, in a situation identical[28] to that of his brother Robert in an earlier episode, reaches one of the critical decisions of the novel.

That this indirect vision is not merely accidental, nor yet an ingenious but meaningless bit of technique borrowed from one or other of the great painters—Velásquez, for instance, or Vermeer— is demonstrated in a dozen different ways, when an indirect relationship is deliberately preferred to a direct one. In *Our Lady of the Flowers*, for instance, the child Culafroy discovers by accident that his mother's maiden name, Picquigny, was one of the great and noble names in mediaeval French history; his first reaction is to wonder why he himself does not enjoy the occult privileges of an ancient nobility; but immediately afterwards, he realizes that the experience of eternity, or of the 'sacred' world of the supernatural, resides in *indirect* participation,

> . . . just as many persons are more pleased to be the favourite of a prince than the prince himself, or a priest of a god than the god, for in this way they can receive Grace.[29]

—in fact, the primary condition of a mystical experience, for Genet and his characters, is that something or someone should intervene between the worshipper and his Divinity, whether that something be the mantle of coal-dust that half-conceals Querelle's body from the eyes of Lt Seblon, or Ernestine who intervenes between Culafroy and the Divine Grace of ancestry, or a simple mirror that comes between the German stormtrooper and the blush that stains the cheeks of Riton.[30]

To be-what-one-is, therefore, is not possible, save ultimately in terms of the Void of death and annihilation; or alternatively, in terms of a double (a reflection, an observer/observed duality), to which, in addition, yet a third independent consciousness must be adjoined, to contain the totality of the other two. To be-what-one-is without this process of metaphysical multiplication is—in Genet's terms—literally 'miraculous'. The inanimate universe, therefore, *is* miraculous in the inconceivable self-sufficiency of its existence, and this, in fact, is one of the primary significances that Genet gives to the term 'a miracle'. Not that the miracle is necessarily something pleasant—on the contrary, it is, more often than not, a manifestation of the powers of darkness and of evil. It is transcendental, but above all it is *inhuman,* and therefore terrifying. At the *human* level, only the greatest, the most god-like of living beings, those who have passed beyond the furthest boundaries of normal experiences—Harcamone for instance—can be what they are. Their realm is no longer that of humanity : they belong to the kingdom of the gods and evil spirits, they walk on air, they are Kings among men, their fetters turn into garlands of roses, their hearts are secret caverns of mirrors, they are to be feared, loved, and worshipped. They are taboo, for they are sacred. At times—at Mettray, for instance— even flowers may acquire something of this quality of satanic inhumanity : their scent, their colour, their beauty is what it is, and thus acquires a menacing, daemonic power of its own, threatening death and terror to the unwary observer :

> I continued on my way among the same flowers, among the same faces, but I sensed, from a kind of uneasiness which came over me, that something was happening. The scents and colours of the flowers were unchanged, yet it seemed to me that they were becoming more essentially themselves. I mean that they were beginning to exist for me with their own existence, with less and less the help of a support: the flowers.[31]

These flowers, in other words, came suddenly to possess, or rather to manifest, an absolute existence of their own, whose sign was beauty; and beauty, for Genet, becomes something progressively more evil in consequence, more inhuman, miraculous, satanic, independent and devastating. It has no place in that narrow human world of half-realities and mirrors, which is the only area where man can feel comparatively safe. It is dangerous. It is to be destroyed.

But normally, for the living being, an absolute identity represents an ideal well beyond the bounds of achievement. With the rarest of exceptions, to be-what-one-is means to be like (to be the reflection of) something else. This is what lies at the root of that imitative idealism which dominates Genet's people, from Jean Genet himself with his striving to 'be like' Stilitano, or Armand, or Harcamone, to Green Eyes who wants to be like Snowball (the condemned murderer who haunts, but never appears in *Deathwatch*), or the young delinquents of Mettray who want to be like the hardened gaol-birds of Fontevrault. On the other hand, since mind, as Descartes would argue, is superior to matter, the mirror-image which symbolizes the Self-that-knows is superior to the real Self that merely exists; the reflection in the glass is not simply an irrefutable fact of existence, but the object of an intense emotional relationship, which is at the same time love and hate : love, because the Image is, when all is said and done, oneself, the essential element without which no self-knowledge would be conceivable (thus, in *Miracle of the Rose*, Genet loves his mirror-image, the criminal Divers); hate, because the double is indispensable to the Self, and, at the same time, in its quality of conscious Otherness, superior—thus Georges Querelle hates his double and twin-brother, Robert, while Solange detests her sister Claire. Man is imprisoned, enslaved by the need for his own image; he is fascinated by it, obsessed, and yet tortured. If he could destroy it and still survive, he would do so—and so Querelle and Robert fight with knives, while Solange accepts without demurring the death of Claire, and, in one of the most memorable scenes of *Pompes Funèbres*, Erik, the Nazi officer, draws his revolver and lets loose hysterically at his own image in the mirror :

> *En rentrant au château, les glaces du vestibule renvoyaient d'étincelantes images de guerriers allumés par le vin. Le premier soir, Erik, ivre de vin, ivre d'être en face de lui-même, se regarda curieusement dans le vestibule [. . . .] Il se recula un peu. Dans la glace, son image s'écarta de lui. Il tendit le bras pour l'attirer à soi, mais sa main ne rencontra rien; il sentait bien, malgré l'ivresse, qu'il lui suffirait d'avancer pour faire venir à sa rencontre son image renversée, mais il sentait aussi que, n'étant qu'une image, elle devait obéir à ses désirs. Il s'impatienta [. . . .] Machinalement, c'est-à-dire selon un chemin beaucoup plus savant et plus sûr que s'il eût été apparemment concerté, il se campa, une jambe tendue, tendant elle-même le drap noir du pantalon, la main gauche relevant les mèches sur la tempe gauche, et la main droite s'appuyant, se reposant sur l'étui à revolver de cuir jaune. Le geste commencé par Erik, l'image le continua les yeux fixes. Sa main gauche ouvrit l'étui et tira le revolver, le braqua contre Erik et fit feu. Un éclat de rire éclata avec la détonation. C'étaient les cinq copains qui rentraient. Une salve retentit. Tous les cinq tirèrent sur leurs images.*[32]

In this passage, there is a typically Genetian symbol : a 'will to act' is transferred from Figure to Image in the middle of a sentence by means of a gesture which the one begins and the other finishes :

'Le geste commencé par Erik, l'image le continua les yeux fixes.'
Nothing could stress more vividly the inseparable relationship of
Existence and Reflection, which together make up the total Being.
Yet, although they are inseparable, Figure and Image are none the
less distinct : the Figure is-what-it-is, but cannot perceive itself without the Image; the Image, on the other hand, both is-what-it-is (a
two-dimensional pattern of form and colour), and is-what-it-is-not
(*i.e.* the Figure). In so far as it is *not* what it is, it is 'false' : a fake, a
pure-appearance which is a deception and an unreality; yet—as
we have seen—because it is also (on account of its very negativity)
the principle of perception or the *pour-soi*, it is superior to what it
reflects. Thus Genet gives a neat but devastating twist to Sartre's
fundamental argument in *Being and Nothingness*, and contrives to
demonstrate that once you distinguish (as you must, in existentialist
dialectic) between an *en-soi* which is positive and a *pour-soi* which
is negative, then logically you must conclude that falsehood is
superior to truth, the fake to the genuine, imposture to honesty,
hypocrisy to plain-dealing and treachery to good faith.

And it is precisely such a demonstration which, to the horror of
all right-thinking people, forms the vital sub-structure of Genet's
plays and novels. It is a skilfully-developed dialectic of anti-logic,
closely allied to that of Ionesco; but because its conclusions go
straight to the heart of our most sacred conventions (sex, property,
religion, patriotism, etc.) instead of remaining dialectical abstractions, Genet's arguments are profoundly shocking, whereas Ionesco's
rarely do more, at least on first acquaintance, than exasperate or
amuse. For Ionesco, Aristotelian non-sequiturs become 'pataphysical
syllogisms; for Genet, moral vices become metaphysical virtues . . .
once you look at them in the mirror. Appearance *is* reality, argues
Sartre. Appearance is *more* real than reality, counters Genet : the
mask is more real than the face; to pretend to act, or to act a pretence, is more essential than sincerity—in a word, all reality is
theatre, and the subtleties of showmanship are the *ne plus ultra*
of integrity. That which is, is a duality of true and false, with the
false as the fundamental condition which allows the true to exist.
'Don't complain about improbability,' protests Genet, as he tells the
tale of the two juvenile delinquents who escaped from Mettray disguised as nuns—an escapade which caused a passing sheepdog to
kneel down, cross itself and pray for the remission of sins :

> What's going to follow is false, and no one has to accept it as gospel
> truth. Truth is not my strong point. But 'one must lie in order to be true'.
> And even go beyond. What truth do I want to talk about? If it is really
> true that I am a prisoner who plays (who plays for himself) scenes of
> the inner life, you will require nothing other than a game.[33]

Truth and lies, then, have a reciprocal functional relationship to each other : that which, like the mirror-image, is-what-it-is-not engenders its own dynamic contradiction, and at bottom it is this inherent contradiction at the heart of 'reality' which generates the undeniable power of Genet's writing. At least three of Genet's major plays—*The Maids, The Balcony* and *The Blacks*—owe their entire dramatic tension to this violent opposition between false and true : the true Blacks play at being false Whites—but then, with the entry of Newport News (Ville de Saint-Nazaire), the true Blacks playing false Whites are themselves revealed, on another level, as Blacks acting Blacks acting Whites, while the authentic action of the true Blacks takes place off-stage. As in Spinoza, 'all determination is negation' : every positive implies a negative, and vice-versa. Positive and negative, Figure and Image, are inseparable, and all reality is the simultaneous co-existence of the two. Every Judge implies a Criminal, every Bishop a Sinner to be forgiven; and if there were no Sinners, then Bishops would cease to exist, their function having vanished. In order that the Good may exist, Evil must exist also : Evil is Good reflected in the mirror, Evil is the all-powerful reflection by which Good may know itself to exist; and reality, once again, is the synthesis of the two. '*J'aime le mal,*' asserts Genet in *Pompes Funèbres* : '*Mais si je montre tant de passion pour sortir du bien, c'est que je lui suis lié passionnément.*'[34] In *Querelle of Brest*, not only are Georges and Robert mirror-reflections of each other, making up between them a single unity-in-reality, but Mario, the Chief of Police, and Nono, the petty gangster and brothel-keeper, are dynamic opposites whose functions are complementary and interdependent. Nono, as an informer, fulfils in part at least the functions of the police, while Mario, in order to understand, and therefore to catch criminals, has to some extent to be a criminal himself—each, as it were, putting out a hand towards the mirror and continuing the gesture into the reflection, just as we saw Erik surrendering the continuation of his gesture to his Image. On a larger scale, man's gestures are projected and continued into the mirror of Heaven, which is God, only to return again, reflected back into that same mirror whence they originated.[35] Similarly, male is reflected and continued in female, female in male; and the two irreconcilable opposites oscillate like electric currents at such speed between their poles of negative and positive that—in the case of Divine and the other '*tantes*', but also in the case of Genet himself—the resulting total reality (as with Ionesco's anti-logic) goes beyond the power of normal language to express it, and invades the domain of symbolism, mythology, and above all *poetry* :

In order to think with precision, Divine must never formulate her thoughts aloud, for herself. [. . . .] Her femininity was not *only* a masquerade. But as for thinking 'woman' completely, her organs hindered her. To think is to perform an act. [. . . .] If, to define a state of mind that she felt, Divine dared use the feminine, she was unable to do so in defining an action which she performed. And all the 'woman' judgements she made were, in reality, poetic conclusions.[36]

For Genet, all reality (including sexual reality) is a synthesis of dynamic opposites. Miracles appear as truly miraculous only in so far as they are fake; crime is inseparable from punishment, and the criminal—like Our Lady—endures an anguish of unreality until he is tried and condemned. In one sense, Genet's plays and novels conform to the tradition of the best Victorian novelettes for young ladies : all his criminals—with the exception of Village, who is 'acting' his murder, and Querelle, who is a special case—are either caught, or else confess; for their crimes are not 'real' crimes, and therefore they themselves cannot be-what-they-are, even as criminals, until the act is completed with its opposite, which is punishment. By contrast, there are no innocents in Genet; even Lt Seblon, who alone confesses to a crime he has not committed, is, in his own mind, already guilty. The punishment of an innocent would upset the whole balance of the cosmos and reduce to absurdity the whole logic of human existence; it would annihilate in its very principle the whole concept of reality by which man lives. 'Nothing is more repugnant,' comments Genet, 'than an innocent man in prison. He has done nothing to *deserve* jail.'[37] By contrast, the genuine criminal, convicted and imprisoned, is the complete man, the total man, in whom Figure and Image at last have coincided, effect corresponding to cause, and cause producing its logical effect. God's in his heaven, and all's right with the world—or at least, with that world-within-a-world which is Prison.

The convicted murderer is one of those rare beings who is-what-he-is; his existence, in that short, intense period between sentence and execution, is absolutely authentic. But not everyone can be a convicted murderer. Even Genet, although a reasonably accomplished burglar, never achieved this supreme degree of authenticity, which, moreover (as Lefranc discovers in *Deathwatch*) is not to be attained merely by an act of will. The total fusion of Self with Image and Observer into the final unity is normally only to be realised in death, or at least in the inescapable imminence of death. There is, however, another way by which some semblance of

authenticity may be attained : namely, by separating oneself violently from one's own Image, by becoming, like Peter Schlemihl,
a 'man without a shadow'. This is the road of solitude and of hopelessness. 'I understood the loneliness and despair of the traveller
who had lost his shadow'[38] notes Genet in *The Thief's Journal*. It
is less mystical and less rewarding than the path of Total Unity;
but it is more practical and more immediate. If, as Genet argues,
the mirror-image is the positive element in human existence, then,
by stressing the negative, it *might* be possible to break away and
to become, as it were, an absolute negative, independently of all else.
This is the path which Genet's characters refer to broadly as
'singularity'. It leads to a world of abjection and nausea, of violence
and deliberate evil, of revolt and humiliation and homosexuality.
In the first argument, there were two complementary worlds to be
united; now, there are two irreconcilably hostile worlds to be
divided—to be separated by a gulf so wide that no reconciliation
is conceivable. There is Jean Genet's world of pimps and male
prostitutes, of Negroes, Arabs and juvenile delinquents, of dope-
runners, traitors and fifth-columnists, of kitchen-maids and waiters
and aging slaveys—the world of the submerged tenth, the people
without a future, the underprivileged and the undernourished, the
outlaws and the outsiders. And against this, there is *our* world,
yours and mine, '*votre* monde' sneers Genet,[39] compared with which
his own is not a 'monde' but an 'immonde'.[40] This is the world of
right-thinking citizens, of critics and readers of the *Times Literary
Supplement*, of householders and rate-payers, of politicians (with the
remarkable exception of Adolf Hitler who, notoriously, belonged to
the other camp) and patriots—in a word, of the bourgeoisie : the
world of those worthy holiday-makers who volunteered to block
the highways with their cars and shine their headlights in the ditches,
so that the police might round up every member of the herd of
terrified children who had escaped from the penitentiary of Belle-
Île, and send them back to that hell where they were 'horsewhipped
until they stopped screaming from sheer exhaustion, or died'.[41]
Genet had been one of these children—not at Belle-Île or at Eysses,
but at Mettray, which was only a degree or two better, and his
world is theirs, not ours; ours is the world of legality, his of the
untouchable, the taboo : 'a forbidden universe.'[42]

This search for an authenticity by opposition—by forcible separation of the Self from all the conventional beliefs and dictates that
surround it—is another of Genet's fundamental attitudes. It is
present from his earliest writings, although in *Our Lady of the
Flowers* and *Miracle of the Rose* it is to some extent overshadowed
by the search for a unity that comes through the fusion of opposites.

similar reasons, rejects the ideal of beauty as the province of *'la mauvaise foi'* and the last refuge of a sophisticated *'salaud'*. 'The result is treason of the worst sort : betrayal by beauty,' argues Sartre in 'Le Séquestré de Venise'—his extraordinary essay on Tintoretto.[46] 'The result is betrayal, the highest form of Beauty', in effect counters Genet.

This, then, is the general context of ideas against which the specific problems of Genet's plays and novels are set. If the mirror is the most characteristic of all Genet's symbols, it is because it is the meeting-point of the two most dynamic forces—themselves irreconcilable mirror-opposites—in the world of paradox and abjection which he has created. On the one hand, a densely-argued existentialist dialectic, which closely parallels and sometimes seems even to parody the arguments of *Being and Nothingness*; on the other, a kind of primitive animism, where poetry fuses into religiosity, where the Virgin Mary works miracles in sky-blue and baby-pink, and where 'An angel sobs entangled in a tree'.[47] It is not easy to appreciate both : one or the other must necessarily appear slightly absurd, if not obscene. For Sartre, the angels and the 'sanctity' are so much *bondieuserie* and balderdash, whose only significance is 'to allow men of bad faith to wallow in false logic'[48]; for Georges Bataille on the other hand, the animism relates to the deepest subconscious erotico-mystic experience of the human race, while the dialectic has 'je ne sais quoi de frêle, de froid, de friable'[49] and is a mess of second-hand, pretentious childishness. Yet *both* are Genet; and he stands or falls by the synthesis, and not by the separation, of these irreconcilables. They belong with each other, even if they distort and torment themselves in their reciprocal reflections, even if the Sailor is reflected as the Domino, even if both are void, or meaningless, or dead. For the image in the mirror *is* the Image of Death : it is death which is still, by some inexplicable mistake or 'miracle', endowed with the appearance of life. But Genet—the 'real' Genet—died when he was ten years old and when some right-thinking person branded him 'a thief'; and *he* is not deceived by these appearances of life : 'I am therefore dead. I am a dead man who sees his skeleton in a mirror.'[50]

NOTES

1 See *Author's Note* at the beginning of this book.
2 Cf. *Balcony*, p. 19 ('The Judge and the Thief'). (*Balcon*, p. 38)

3 *Our Lady*, p. 177. 'La solitude est douce. Elle est amère. On croit que la tête doive s'y vider de tous les énregistrements passés, usure avant-courrière de purification.' (*Notre-Dame*, p. 83)

4 *Pompes Funèbres*, p. 81.

5 The informed reader will notice many ideas in this study which can also be found in Sartre's *Saint-Genet Comédien et Martyr*. To indicate each reference would be pedantic and monotonous. I hereby acknowledge my general debt to Sartre, even when I disagree with his conclusions, and I shall henceforward indicate the source only when I have borrowed an important part of my own argument from *Saint-Genet*.

6 *Our Lady*, pp. 221-222. 'Il ne voulait pas décevoir. Il prit part aux coups durs. Avec quelques autres d'une petite brigade scellée comme une bande, il aida à commettre un petit vol à l'intérieur du patronage. Madame la supérieure [. . . .] demanda à Lou pourquoi il avait volé, il ne sut que répondre : "Parce que les autres me croyaient un voleur".' (*Notre-Dame*, p. 112)

7 *Our Lady*, p. 63. 'bleus et vides comme les fenêtres des immeubles en construction, au travers desquelles on voit le ciel par les fenêtres de la façade opposée.' (*Notre-Dame*, p. 10)

8 *Ibid*. 'm'hypnotisent autant que les théâtres vides, les prisons désertes, les machineries au repos, les déserts.' (*Notre-Dame*, p. 10)

9 Sartre, *Being and Nothingness*, tr. Hazel E. Barnes, London (Methuen) 1957, pp. xlv-xlviii; *L'Être et le Néant*, Paris (Gallimard) 1947, pp. 11-14.

10 *Thief*, p. 237-239. 'Stilitano, et lui seul, était pris, *visiblement* égaré dans les couloirs de verre. Personne ne pouvait l'entendre, mais à ses gestes, à sa bouche, on comprenait qu'il hurlait de colère. [. . . .] Stilitano était seul. Tout le monde s'en était tiré, sauf lui. Etrangement l'univers se voila. L'ombre qui soudain recouvrit toutes choses et les gens, c'était ma solitude en face de ce désespoir. . . .' (*Journal*, p. 282)

11 Among innumerable instances, see Chamisso's *Peter Schlemihl*, or Hofmannsthal's *Die Frau ohne Schatten*.

12 *Our Lady*, pp. 261-262. 'Il continue par saccades les gestes du drame qu'il s'ignore jouer. [. . . .] Enfin, il se lève et, devant ce petit miroir d'un franc cloué au mur, il écarte ses cheveux blonds et à sa tempe cherche sans le savoir une plaie par balle.' (*Notre-Dame*, pp. 138-139)

13 *'Adame Miroir*, p. 40.

14 *Ibid*. 'Ce n'est pas la Mort. Mais qui? L'auteur l'ignore.'

15 *Ibid*. 'Affolé . . . épuisé . . . il tombe par terre.'

16 *Q. of B.*, p. 231. 'Il lui semblait se cogner le visage contre un miroir réfléchissant sa propre image.' (*Querelle*, pp. 305-306)

17 Sartre, *Being and Nothingness*, pp. 173-174; *L'Être et le Néant*, pp. 221-222.

18 *Ibid.*, p. 23. (*L'Être et le Néant*, p. 59)

19 *Ibid.*, pp. 228 and 256. 'Autrui se présente [. . . .] comme la négation radicale de mon expérience puisqu'il est celui pour qui je suis non sujet, mais objet. [. . . .] Il semble qu'il s'est percé un trou de vidange au milieu de mon être, et que je m'écoule perpétuellement par ce trou.' (*L'Être et le Néant*, pp. 283 and 313)

20 Sartre, *Huis Clos*, in *Théâtre I*, Paris (Gallimard) 1947, pp. 135-138. See also pp. 123, 147.

21 There are striking resemblances between Sartre's Daniel and Genet's Gabriel in *Notre-Dame*. Both are homosexuals, both are nicknamed 'Archangel', both are fascinated with mirrors, both embody a deliberate will to evil. However, it is difficult to be specific about 'influences' either way. According to publication dates, *L'Âge de Raison* (1945) appeared after *Notre-Dame* (1944); in fact, however, Sartre appears to have written his novel in 1940-41, *i.e.*, earlier than Genet, who composed *Notre-Dame* in prison in 1942.

22 *Deathwatch*, p. 40. 'Je suis vraiment tout seul.' (*Haute Surveillance*, p. 135)

23 *Thief*, p. 94. 'poursuite de l'Impossible Nullité.' (*Journal*, p. 100)

24 *Ibid*, p. 191. 'le plus beau mot du langage humain.' (*Journal*, p. 227)

25 *Q. of B.*, p. 63. *Querelle*, p. 205.

26 *Ibid.*, p. 304. *Ibid.*, p. 341.

27 *Ibid.*, p. 201. *Ibid.*, p. 287.

28 *Ibid.*, p. 312. *Ibid.*, p. 346.

29 *Our Lady*, p. 206. 'Comme à beaucoup il plaît d'être le favori d'un prince plutôt que le prince lui-même, ou le prêtre d'un dieu plutôt que le dieu, car ainsi il peut recevoir la Grâce.' (*Notre-Dame*, p. 102)

30 *Pompes Funèbres*, p. 146.

31 *Rose*, p. 107. 'J'avançais toujours entre les mêmes fleurs, entre les mêmes visages, mais je devinais, grâce à une sorte de malaise qui s'emparait de moi, qu'il se passait quelque chose. Les parfums et les couleurs des fleurs ne se transformaient pas, cependant, il me sembla qu'ils devinssent plus essentiellement eux-mêmes. Je veux dire qu'ils commençaient à exister pour moi de leur existence propre, avec de moins en moins le secours d'un support: les fleurs.' (*Miracle*, pp. 262-263)

32 *Pompes Funèbres*, p. 141.

33 *Our Lady*, p. 225. 'Ne criez pas à l'invraisemblance. Ce qui va suivre est faux et personne n'est tenu de l'accepter pour argent comptant. La vérité n'est pas mon fait. Mais "il faut mentir pour être vrai". Et même aller au delà. De quelle vérité veux-je parler? S'il est bien vrai que je suis un prisonnier, qui joue (qui se joue) des scènes de la vie intérieure, vous n'exigerez rien d'autre qu'un jeu.' (*Notre-Dame*, p. 115)

34 *Pompes Funèbres*, p. 136.

35 *Our Lady*, p. 150. (*Notre-Dame*, p. 66)

36 *Ibid*, p. 235. 'Pour penser avec précision, Divine ne devait jamais formuler à haute voix, pour elle-même, ses pensées. [. . . .] Sa féminité n'était pas qu'une mascarade. Mais, pour penser "femme" en plein, ses organes la gênaient. Penser, c'est faire un acte. [. . . .] Si, pour définir un état qu'elle éprouvait, Divine osait employer le féminin, elle ne le pouvait pas pour définir une action qu'elle faisait. Et tous les jugements "femme" qu'elle portait étaient, en réalité, de conclusions poétiques.' (*Notre-Dame*, p. 121)

37 *Rose*, p. 27. 'Rien n'est plus répugnant qu'un innocent en prison. Il n'a rien fait pour *mériter* la tôle.' (*Miracle*, p. 205)

38 *Thief*, p. 205. 'Je compris la solitude et le désespoir du voyageur ayant perdu son ombre.' (*Journal*, p. 243)

39 *E.g. Rose*, p. 42. (*Miracle*, pp. 215-216)

40 *Journal*, p. 91. An untranslatable pun. 'Monde' = world. 'Immonde' = filth; but also, by implication, a 'not-world'.

41 In 1933. See Simone de Beauvoir, *La Force de l'Âge*, Paris (Gallimard) 1960, pp. 221-222 and 302. See also Jacques Prévert's poem, *Chasse à l'Enfant*:

> 'Il avait dit J'en ai assez de la maison de redressement
> Et les gardiens à coups de clefs lui avaient brisé les dents
> Et puis ils l'avaient laissé étendu sur le ciment. . . .'

(in *Paroles*: Paris, Gallimard, 1949, pp. 101-102)

42 *Thief*, pp. 7-8. 'un univers interdit.' (*Journal*, p. 10)

43 *Q. of B.*, p. 308. (*Querelle*, p. 343)

44 *Rose*, p. 20. (*Miracle*, p. 200)

45 *Ibid*, p. 264. '. . . osait détruire une beauté visible et établie pour obtenir une beauté—ou poésie—résultat de la rencontre de cette beauté brisée avec ce geste barbare. Un Barbare souriant au sommet de sa statue abattait autour de lui les chefs-d'œuvre grecs!' (*Miracle*, p. 375)

46 'The Venetian Pariah' in *Essays in Aesthetics* (London, Peter Owen; New York, Philosophical Library), p. 51. 'Reste la plus grande trahison: la Beauté.' ('Le Séquestré de Venise,' in *Les Temps Modernes*, vol. XIII, No. 141, Nov. 1957, p. 756). Countered by Genet, 'Reste la trahison, la plus grande des beautés.'

47 'Le Condamné à Mort', in *Poèmes*, p. 11. 'Un ange sanglote accroché dans un arbre.'

48 Sartre, *S. Genet*, p. 203. 'est de permettre aux hommes de mauvaise foi de raisonner faux.' (*Saint-G.*, p. 192)

49 Bataille, G., *La Littérature et le Mal*, Paris (Gallimard), 1957, p. 218. ('Something indefinably frail, cold, crumbly'.)

50 *Rose*, p. 32. 'Je suis donc mort. Je suis un mort qui voit son squelette dans un miroir.' (*Miracle*, p. 209)

The Novels

2

HEAD DOWN, FEET UP

(Our Lady of the Flowers)

Alle Romane, wo wahre Liebe vorkommt,
sind Märchen—magische Begebenheiten.
Novalis

Towards the beginning of *Our Lady of the Flowers* there is a remarkable passage in which Divine, from the depths of her abjection
in Paris, conjures up memories of the village where 'she' lived
when 'she' was still a child—memories of processions on Rogation or
Corpus-Christi Day, made up of choir-boys and little girls in white
dresses, of women in stiff black and of men

> . . . gloved in black, holding up a canopy of oriental cast that was plumed
> with ostrich feathers, under which walked the priest carrying a mon-
> strance. Beneath the sun, amidst the rye, pines, and clover, and inverted
> in the ponds, with their feet to the sky.[1]

Of all the many variations of the mirror-symbol in Genet's imagination, this is one of the most significant: the image of man reflected head downwards in a pool or ditch which also reflects the
sky and the stars, so that, to reach the stars and perhaps even that
which lies beyond the stars, the wretch that is man must move, not
upwards but *downwards*, ever lower, plunging into the surface of
the water, and then groping blindly among the broken bottles, slime
and old perambulator-wheels that lie hidden beneath—beyond the
reflection of Heaven. In Genet's vision of the universe, it is the

rivers, not the sky, which are full of stars[2]; and, in a different context, the marching columns of Nazi stormtroopers, crushing France
beneath the iron indifference of their tread, 'hammer the azure of
the heavens with their hobnailed boots'.[3]

In Genet's world, the lowest and the highest meet, and to descend
into the limbo of horror and abjection is to ascend into the region
of saints and angels. In some passages, the very words 'up' and
'down', 'rise' and 'fall' seem interchangeable; humiliation is glory—
'Oh, that's my decorations!'[4], says Querelle of the spittle-marks that
stain his clothes; to which Solange adds bitterly: 'My spurt of saliva is
my spray of diamonds'[5]—and abjection is sanctity. For Genet, the
most abject of all creatures is his mother, whom he never knew
and perhaps never forgave, neither her nor any other woman, for
having abandoned him at birth; and when, in his dreams, he meets
her, together they undertake a journey in search of the Absolute:

> . . . We would have pursued together the ascension—though language
> seems to call for the word 'fall' or any other that indicates a downward
> movement—the difficult, painful ascension which leads to humiliation.[6]

The pursuit of the Absolute—as we have seen—is the key to the
world of Genet's imagination; for only when the Fall is complete
does it become the equivalent of an Ascension. If God is the All-
Highest, then the Image-of-God is the All-Lowest; in between lies
nothing but the banality and the senselessness of the mediocre. The
traditional pattern of Christian cosmology is changed: it is no longer
God at the vortex, and Hell, presided over by Satan, the fallen angel,
at the nadir; but rather Heaven is at the summit and the reflection
of Heaven is in the abyss, while Hell lies in between. Hell is simply
reality: the reality of objects—of prisons, corridors, carpets, curtains, candelabra, flowers even—and of men, who are never quite
evil, or cruel, or inhuman enough; Hell is what *appears* to be our
world—the underside of our world, as Genet knew it, where starv-
ing children at dawn hunt for food and are happy with 'crusts
covered with hair . . . found in garbage cans'.[7] Sartre sees Hell as a
Second-Empire drawing-room; Dostoievsky as 'a bath-house full of
spiders'; Nathalie Sarraute as 'a face seen from inside'. All these
concepts are familiar to Genet:

> Infernal horror does not lie in an unwontedly, spectrally, inhumanly,
> deliberately fantastic setting. It accepts the setting and the ways of every-
> day life. A mere detail or two transforms them (an object that is not
> in its right place, or that is upside down, or that can be seen from inside),
> takes on the very meaning of that universe, symbolizes it, revealing that
> this setting and these ways pertain to hell.[8]

Hell is the Paris of Divine and Our Lady; for if they have fallen,
they have still not fallen far enough.

In such a context, obviously, the Christian concept of the Fall
changes in significance. (Genet's childhood religion was that of a
highly-coloured Catholicism, the Catholicism of Saints and incense
and angels in primitive colours; and it has remained with him,
although some of its concepts, like the objects in Hell-reality, 'are
no longer in their place'.) The sensation of falling is common to all
Genet's characters—Divine, Harcamone, Bulkaen, all have the same
experience; and the great prisons of France, notes Genet, are filled,
not only with fallen men, but even with a day-to-day vocabulary
based on 'la Chute'.[9] But in the mirror-world, to fall *down* is also to
fall *up* : 'the lead weight' is synonymous with 'the sickening lightness
of cork'.[10] The fall is not towards Hell, but towards the Absolute,
'le désespoir' : a fall into oneself, into timelessness; and he who falls
far enough and fast enough—even if he starts from an aeroplane
and finishes up crashing through the glass roof of a prison[11]—still
carries remnants of stars caught up in his clothing, like stray sequins
on the tights of a falling trapeze-artist. And the speed of falling is
in itself a part of the mystery of the Fall. Never quite certain of his
own reality, feeling himself transparent, like glass, or ghost-like, only
half-visible, a shadow that any passer-by can walk through, or else
a two-dimensional image, having no solidity, Genet finds in the
very speed of his fall into abjection, not only the kind of vertigo that
the mystic finds in contemplating God, but also that missing dimension of reality that enables him at last to be-what-he-is.

Abjection, to be effective, must be absolute : it must be the
equivalent of damnation. The Fall must lead, not merely into Hell,
but into the Hell-beyond-Hell which is a state of Divine-Satanic
'Grace'. For, if Christ promises Redemption, how, in mirror-logic,
shall there be Redemption, unless there is first damnation? If Christ
has chosen to be 'le Rédempteur', Genet chooses to be 'the Being
through whom Redemption may not come'.[12] If there were no
damned, Christ's mission on earth would have been gratuitous, and
God would have been wasting his time. Hence Divine—the name
is not fortuitous—exists to justify the acts, if not the existence, of
God.

Genet's first novel, *Our Lady of the Flowers*, was written in 1942,
in F- nes prison, and is still, in the eyes of many critics, his finest
achievement. It is a patchwork of dreams and fragments and memories, of grotesque and unforgettable episodes, a kaleidoscope of
shame and degradation, yet illuminated with poetry and imagery,
and inspired with the conviction that the most desperate sinner
is nearer to God than the clergyman or the company-director.
Whether this last attitude is a *sincere* conviction—as one might
argue it was with Dostoievsky—or whether it is merely a verbal

(*i.e.* literary) device, seems to be irrelevant. For what are 'thoughts', if not 'words'. 'I am what the words make me,' says Beckett's *Un-namable* : and Genet :

> I tear my words from the depths of my being [....] and these words [....] will re-create the loathsome and cherished world from which I tried to free myself.[13]

Words create thoughts, ideas, images; perhaps they create them wrong, distort and disfigure, like the burial of Jean Decarnin in *Pompes Funèbres*,[14] but there is no other way. If Genet's sanctity is made of words, so is his sincerity; sincerity and literature are equally unreal : but neither is more unreal than the other. Divine is what he says he is, there is nothing else he can be; and if Divine is what the words make him (or 'her'), so is Genet's 'I'—since the 'I' who writes is, to the reader and perhaps also to the writer, just as much and just as little a fiction as the 'I' that calls itself Divine, or Culafroy. For the 'I' who, in *Our Lady*, writes from prison, grew out of the Divine who was a *'tante'*, a male prostitute and petty criminal in Paris before the war; and Divine in turn emerged from Culafroy, who was once a boy in a country village in the Morvan.

Because Genet's first two novels, *Our Lady of the Flowers* and *Miracle of the Rose*, are in part autobiographical—because the actual process of writing them was, for their author, a way of liberation, of escape from anonymous degradation, sexual abjection and possibly madness and death—their structure is as complex as life itself. *Our Lady of the Flowers* covers three periods in time, each of which is both a past and an instantaneous present, and each of which is both dream and reality at once. How Culafroy *became* Divine, how Divine became Jean-Genet-in-prison, is not told (few things interest Genet less than a coherent narrative in time, with a beginning, a middle and, dutifully, an end); the episodes are super-imposed one on top of the other, absorbed into each other, so that the beginning is the funeral of Divine, and the end is the death of Divine, and both are interwoven with the voice of Genet, who *is* Divine, and who is dead and yet alive. Yet the central figure is always Divine, who, in 'her' precious dialect of a painted and decaying pansy, reveals 'her' passion for the Absolute :

> 'I really am, sure sure sure, the Quite-Profligate.'
> 'Oh, Ladies, I'm acting like such a harlot.'
> 'You know (the *ou* was so drawn out that that was all one noticed), *yoouknow*, I'm the Consumed-with-Affliction.'
> 'Here, here, behold the Quite-Fluff-Fluff.'
> One of them, when questioned by a detective on the boulevard :
> 'Who are you?'
> 'I'm a Thrilling Thing.'

> Then, little by little, they understood each other by saying: 'I'm the Quite-Quite', and finally: 'I'm the Q'. Q'.'[15]

Divine's most terrifying characteristic is her *purity*, for hers is a daemonic chastity, born where Good and Evil meet, the purity of that Hell which lies beyond Hell, and which consequently drags all those who cannot follow 'her' as far down into the depths as 'she' herself has plunged, towards death and perdition. 'Her' lovers are caught, one by one, in the toils of 'her' sanctity, and annihilated: Darling is pinched shop-lifting, condemned and imprisoned; Gabriel, the soldier, is killed in the Nazi advance; while Our Lady, the adolescent murderer, becomes possessed—almost in the Biblical sense—with the spirit, or rather with the gestures of Divine, and confesses to his crime, gratuitously and needlessly—'needlessly' in practical terms, in terms of bourgeois values, yours and mine, but *necessarily* in the context of Divine's world, where the Figure has no reality without its Image, nor the criminal without his punishment, and where damnation is essential to justify the ways of God to man. For confession is not repentance—in fact, the opposite. If the Image-of-God lies downwards, below the stars, if God is infinitely high above man exactly in proportion as man is infinitely far below God, then the evil must be *willed*, and with the evil, the punishment; then, and only then, are the two halves joined and the cycle completed. To repent is not only to destroy the function of the crime, but to distort the whole significance of the punishment; for the punishment of a repentant sinner is, to all intents and purposes, the punishment of an innocent, and this, as we have seen, is the gap in the dyke by which chaos will enter and subvert the order of the world. So Genet's criminals may dream, or die, or despair, but never repent—and Our Lady, having strangled an aged householder for a few hundred francs, goes to the guillotine with one of the most cynical and indecent phrases ever invented on his lips: 'The old guy was washed up. He couldn't even get a hard-on.'[16]

The young murderer, Maurice Pilorge, whom Genet had known, and whom, after his death, he loved retrospectively and made his idol among all *'les beaux assassins'*, reached similar heights of inhumanity and absolute moral insensibility—a humourless Til Eulenspiegel of the underworld, who, having thumbed his nose at the executioner,[17] served perhaps as model for *Our Lady of the Flowers*.

The violent effect that *Our Lady of the Flowers* produces on the ordinary reader stems from the fact that the dynamic opposition of evil and sanctity is not only stated, but presented in a series of vivid images : the highest and most untouchable concepts of the Christian religion—the most untouchable precisely because they are the most conventional : the Virgin with her 'apron as blue as a sailor's collar'[18]—are directly associated with the most degraded and degrading forms of sexual experience, described in the language of the barrack-room, the doss-house and the brothel. Ernestine, Culafroy's mother, 'saw God [while] gulping down an egg',[19] just as later the priest of *Pompes Funèbres* will have his vision of the Sacred Heart of Jesus while seated in the latrines.[20] The cowardice and cruelty of Darling are associated with the Holy Stigmata of Christ,[21] and infamy is conceived as the most ancient and glorious of honours.

To make Divine and Our Lady candidates for canonisation can only be, in the world of day-to-day business and sound moral principles, an absurd and untenable paradox, or else pure pornography. Yet Genet is not merely a pornographer : he is an erotic writer, granted, but that is not quite the same thing. The commonplace pornographer cajoles his reader, allowing him to enjoy in the imagination experiences that he would like to enjoy, but dare not, in real life; the erotic writer does violence to his reader, hurts him deliberately, leaves him nauseated, leads him along paths which, if he were to follow in reality, he could only do so at the price of self-disgust and self-destruction. For Genet's criminals are only in a very secondary sense offenders against society, or against the rational laws of discipline and property. It is notable, for instance, that although Genet himself was a burglar, the crime of burglary (essentially a crime against property) is of little interest to him, and is never described except by Genet himself in the first person—in which case he contrives to give his acts an occult significance which has nothing to do either with reason or with society. Divine, in the strict sense of the word—except when 'she' allows the child to fall to its death off the high balcony—is not a criminal : yet her life is infinitely more degrading and evil than that, say, of Gil Turko, who is. In other words, what transforms Genet's anti-heroes from studies in psychiatric case-histories, or instances from a criminologist's note-book, into symbols of a metaphysical reality, is the fact that they violate not laws, but *taboos*.

And because they violate taboos, they strike straight at the heart of our most primitive and instinctive vetoes. The Freudian, of course, might argue that it is *because* such temptations are within us that we build up defences against them; that Genet reminds us of subconscious temptations that we had carefully repressed; and that our immediate reaction, in consequence, is to strengthen our defence-mechanism . . . and have *Our Lady* forbidden by the censor. Be that as it may, what emerges clearly from *Our Lady* is that the less rational the taboos which are broken, the more violent is the reaction that the description of this violation produces in the reader. To describe the eating of excrement is more violently offensive than to describe the stealing of an old lady's handbag, although *rationally* the latter is more dangerous to the peace and order of society. A passive homosexual does less evil (in the context of social justice) than a drunken driver; yet the latter is acceptable in polite circles which would hound the latter off the premises. Genet, at bottom, is not really concerned with criminals at all, but with the violaters of taboos; not with evil-doers (who break the law), nor even with sinners (who go against the commandments of a personal God), but with *transgressors* (to use Georges Bataille's term[22]) who violate instinctive and irrational decrees without suspending their validity.

Of course, certain taboos are also embodied in the form of rational laws. 'Thou shalt not kill' is both law, divine commandment and taboo. But Genet's murderers—Our Lady, for instance—are 'sacred' in so far as they transgress against an indefinable ordinance; the fact that they are also, strictly speaking, criminals detracts rather than adds to their symbolic significance. The very fact that Divine's murder of the child[23] would be, in law, a less clear-cut offence than Our Lady's strangling of the old man, brings Divine nearer to the 'sacred world' than the vicious thug who is her lover. For to break the law merely leads one into a hygienic and human prison; to violate the taboo lifts the violator right out of the world of 'Union . . . brothers . . . Marx . . . capital . . . beefsteak . . .'[24] into that of tragedy and transcendence. The grotesque episode, for instance, when Divine extracts her false teeth and uses them as a royal crown, is in no way criminal : it is the more cruel, tragic and horrifying as a result. The concepts : sacred, sacrilege, sacrifice all have the same root and the same supra-rational implications; and these—not larceny, or dope-running, or pimping—are Genet's real themes. At the opposite pole from the horror-comic writers, who offer violence, murder, sex and sadism *ad nauseam*, yet observe the familiar taboos with the severity of a Rotary Club, Genet uses crime and violence only in so far as they serve to reinforce his assault on those barriers which humanity has set up to contain its most primitive and superstitious fears. And one of these fears is death; another is God.[25]

All Genet's crimes belong to a greater or lesser degree to the category of sacrilege—it is we, the readers, who acknowledge this whenever we shudder with nausea at Genet's perversions, obscenity or cynicism. Yet there *can* be no sacrilege unless there is something sacred : we, the readers, are affirming this when we shut the book in anger; and Genet, by stating that, through sacrilege, his characters penetrate into the realm of the sacred is merely confirming a fact that we have already, by implication, admitted.

But the sacred has other branches besides those of totem and taboo : it is the domain of all that is mysterious and supra-rational, from plain superstition through poetry to the ecstasy of the mystic and the highest concepts of the Divinity. In the mirror-world, the contrast is not between good and evil, but only between the Sacred and the Profane. The Profane embraces all that is *not* sacred—the bourgeois world of commercial values, honest effort and practical achievement. By contrast, all aspects of sacred experience belong essentially to the same order, no matter whether they are technically noble or base; and for Genet, the most abject perversions of sex, provided always that they are conceived as the irrational violation of an irrational taboo, are of the same order as the Meditations of St Theresa or the sacrifices of St Vincent de Paul. Hell—the Hell of the profane—lies once more in the middle : the two extremes ultimately mingle and lose their identity in each other.

Christianity, the most rational of religions, has given the world many benefits; but there is one thing that it has destroyed : it has destroyed our power to touch and experience the sacred through limited and controlled transgression. For the older religions, the Bacchanalia, the ritual sacrifices of men and animals, the ecstatic eroticism of temple-prostitution, were acknowledgements of the fact that certain civil crimes *might* be sources of spiritual wonderment and worship. Christianity has identified all transgression with the notion of the *Profane*, and called it sin : the Christian saint can only hope to acquire his sanctity through virtue. In this, Christianity has proved itself to be extremely humanitarian, if not always very wise or very profound. Divine, on the other hand, is certainly religious, and in fact positively thinks of herself as a saint; but her ecstasies have nothing humanitarian or virtuous about them, and her religion is much nearer to the primitive cults of Africa or of the Aztec empire, than to the more civilized and sophisticated religion of Christ. Yet even Christianity—in spite of Renan and Albert Schweitzer, Tolstoy and the worker-priests—is still a *religion*, that is, a codification of the symbols of the Sacred; and so these symbols come as naturally—and as appositely—to Divine as all the other symbols that compose her world. In a word, Divine uses the conventional language of one religion to describe her experiences in another; and the shocking incongruities of *Our Lady* are at bottom the incongruities that arise from two conflicting attitudes towards religious experience.

Divine's hold on the world of the Profane is slender; by contrast, she is plunged head-downwards into the maelstrom of *le sacré* :

and *le sacré*, by definition, is that which is incomprehensible, terrifying and dark. Which does not mean that Divine is necessarily close to God. It is indeed by no means certain that God exists (and even if He does, He may just as likely be a first-principle of evil as of good). *Le sacré* is an aspect of *human* experience, just as reason is an aspect of human experience; neither necessarily presupposes or excludes the existence of a Divinity. 'Art, religion, love [are the things] which are enveloped in the sacred,' muses Genet, as he considers Ernestine, Culafroy's mother,

> . . . for at the sacred, which is called, alas, the spiritual, one neither laughs nor smiles; it is sad. If it is that which touches upon God, is God therefore sad? Is God therefore a painful idea? Is God therefore evil?[26]

Ernestine is afraid of this dark underside of existence, and avoids it as much as possible.[27] But Our Lady and above all Divine are less timid. For them, the experience and ecstasy of *le sacré* is the supreme purpose and meaning of life, and of death likewise; and *le sacré* is reached, firstly through any experience of the Absolute— of cruelty, evil or degradation, but equally of beauty, poetry or light—and secondly through the violation of taboos : the taboo of murder, the taboo of sexual perversions, the taboos that forbid the desecration of churches,[28] corpses or human dignity. Moreover, the violator of taboos is himself taboo, in primitive societies; he is untouchable, a being apart; he is possessed, the demon is within him. But, as Genet understands the function of art, the same is true for the poet. In both cases, the victim is inspired, he is breathed through by a dark force from outside which does not depend upon the control of his own will—just as Darling, in the act of shoplifting, is 'breathed through' by Divine :

> He was at the mercy of the will of 'another', who stuffed his pockets with objects which, when he got to his room and put them on the table, he did not recognize.[29]

Thus Genet's people possess the essential gift of poetry, not in spite of the fact that they are pimps, prostitutes and criminals, but precisely *because* they are these things : because they are transgressors. The Christian religion—in our own time, at least—is largely made for man, adapted to his social needs and individual weaknesses. Divine's religion is far more primitive, fearful and exigent : man is made for it; man is the victim, the sacrifice, the puppet of the gods, who use him for their own ends, and reward him at one and the same time with ecstasy and extermination.

Consequently, one of the most disturbing features of *Our Lady of the Flowers* is its inextricable muddle of abjection and religious

inspiration—an inspiration which makes no distinction between
sentimental religiosity and severe theological dogmatism, between
'the rank sweat of an enseamed bed' and the mystery of the Mass,
between Catholicism, fatalism, animism and plain pagan superstition.
All Genet's characters are superstitious; but all recognize superstition as merely the fringe, the first outpost of something infinitely
greater and more dangerous. Even the taboo against lighting three
cigarettes with a single match is a chink through which the unknown
may flood in and annihilate the known : 'One starts with a little
superstition, and then falls into the arms of God.'[30]

In Genet's world, *all* images relating to the sacred are more or
less interchangeable. Darling comes into Divine's room, '. . . and the
wall bursts open just as a sky tears apart to reveal The Man, like the
one Michelangelo painted nude in *The Last Judgement*'.[31] Divine,
arrested for being drunk and disorderly, sings the wedding-canticle,
Veni Creator, and all the passers-by are transformed into 'little
married couples who kneel on tapestried prayer-stools'[32]; in Culafroy's village, the most beautiful woman is Marie, and Genet notes
of Marie's mother, Joséphine, that '. . . her situation was akin to
that of the Mother of Jesus among the women of the Galilean
village'[33]; while even the pimps and thugs of the Paris underworld,
boasting of a job that has come off successfully, finish their tale
with the ritual phrase, half-magic spell, half-Biblical reminiscence :
'Go, thou art healed.'[34]

None of this is parody, in the normal sense. Genet occasionally
does parody certain aspects of official or institutional religion—the
visiting Bishop at Mettray,[35] for instance, or the prison-chaplain
with his vision in the latrines[36]—but never religion itself. The language and imagery of Christianity are often distorted, or used in
circumstances where the sacrilegious merges with the grotesque, as
when Divine sips tea with Darling 'like the Holy Ghost in the form
of a Dove',[37] or when the imprisoned burglars at Fontevrault pray
to their absent house-breaking kit : 'Oh my solid, oh my fierce, oh
my burning one ! Oh my Bees, watch over us !'[38] Yet this strange
invocation, this *bouffonnerie*, comments Genet, 'in spite of its nature
remained *profoundly* grave'.

'Gravity' strikes a characteristic note in Genet's universe. Genet
himself is almost utterly devoid of humour, and all his characters
who have been touched with the breath of the Sacred are *'grave'*—
they move 'with the pitiless gravity of forests on the march'.[39]
Querelle is 'grave', and Gil Turko,[40] and Dédé,[41] and Harcamone,
for 'as facing his death was a grave act, he did it with gravity'.[42]
None of them laugh (except Divine, who has 'strident laughter,
festive or mad'),[43] for laughter, more than anything else, is destruc-

tive to the sacred world, and one outburst of hilarity can shatter the whole delicate structure of the supernatural and send it cascading into dust and fragments. Their love-making is as joyless and as humourless as their religion, and both belong ultimately to the sacred rituals of death. The funeral element is never long absent, and particularly in *Pompes Funèbres* the eroticism of Riton and Erik, and Erik and the Headsman, takes on the gruesome rhythm of a *danse macabre*. Not that this is unexpected, for, in the imagery of all intense and primitive eroticism, the sexual act is associated with the dissolution of life : the discontinuity of the individual is sacrificed to the boundless continuity of a fusion outside time and space. Sex and death are hedged about with the same taboos, rape and murder offer the same types of temptation, in dreams, or even in the factual reports of the Assize Courts. And both, when society allows a violation, are surrounded with a solemn religious ritual : the ritual of funerals, murder-trials, death-sentences, regimental colours, firing-squads; the ritual of courtship and weddings, of bride-bed and baptism.

Genet is not interested in the profane world of well-motivated acts and rational psychology. As his people cross the border from the profane world into the sacred, every act becomes a gesture, every movement a step in a symbolic ballet, every pose has the formal significance of sculpture, every situation the solemn and severe dignity of a ritual. Darling draws on his white rubber burglar's gloves as though for some elaborately formal occasion,[44] and with the same careful intensity as that with which Village, the Negro murderer, goes to the latrines.[45] Genet as a juvenile delinquent remembers bed-time at Mettray as a 'complicated ritual'[46]; Genet as an adult burglar stylises each movement in terms of a choreography as full of symbolic or superstitious significance as the gestures of the priest as Mass. 'I respected the superstitions',[47] he recalls in *Miracle of the Rose*; and elsewhere he describes the actions of breaking and entering as

. . . rites, the more important as they are inevitable and are not mere adornments of an action whose essence is still mysterious to me.[48]

The very name 'Riton', the hero of *Pompes Funèbres*, is symbolic of the main theme of the novel : the solemn acts of love and death, whose motivation lies invariably in an inherited and traditional mystery of symbols, never in the individual's immediate desire or need. As a burglar, Genet recounts that he very nearly destroyed the whole sacred significance of his transgression by using gestures dictated by his own intelligence instead of following the time-honoured ritual handed down by generations of house-breakers, and forming a part therefore of a common human subconscious[49]; and of the child placing a jar full of flowers at the foot of the tree where his lover, Jean Decarnin, had been shot by the *Milice*, he complains : *'Je refusais à quiconque le droit d'inventer, hors des rites polis et coutumiers, ces hommages indélicats.'*[50]

The sacred world is the world of religion, sexual union or violation, and death; consequently the rituals in terms of which the ballet of life is conceived are essentially those of the Church, marriage and murder—sometimes separately, sometimes in inextricable symbolic confusion. Querelle makes the sign of the Cross before killing Vic[51]—and *watches* himself make it, since the significance of the gesture lies in the gesture itself. Similarly Ernestine, before trying to kill Culafroy, puts on all her jewellery.[52] In *The Thief's Journal*, Genet describes his whole life, in retrospect, as 'merely one long mating, burdened and complicated by a heavy and strange erotic ceremonial'.[53] But this ritualism reaches its height in the symbols of the wedding and the funeral. *Our Lady of the Flowers* begins with the funeral of Divine, the solemn *cortège* and the corpse wrapped in a white lace sheet.'[54] *Pompes Funèbres* opens with the funeral of Jean Decarnin, closes with that of the Little Skivvy's dead child. The wedding-ritual is even more prevalent—possibly because its symbolism is even more complex. Its ritualistic white is the mirror-opposite of the black of death; its orange-blossoms belong to Genet's vast symbolic array of flowers, its veils link it with the poet's deepest awareness of beauty[55]; and Christ also is present at the marriage-bed. In dream and symbol, Genet himself is wedded to Riton,[56] Rocky to Bulkaen[57]; *The Thief's Journal* tells of the *'noces de deux Légionnaires invisibles'*,[58] while one of the most fantastic episodes in the *Miracle of the Rose* is the wedding of Genet and Divers at Mettray. And if Divine, humiliated and handcuffed between her two towering *flics*, sings the *Veni Creator* to the jeering crowds, it is because the boy Culafroy that she once was had similarly felt the magic of the solemn nuptial hymn—the magic of incense and orange-flowers and all the mystic ceremonial of marriage.[59]

If every situation is a ritual, every act is a gesture. It is certain that Genet is extremely sensitive to the beauty and poetry of certain gestures—particularly characteristic male gestures, such as lighting a cigarette, or hitching both thumbs between belt and trousers; but this purely instinctive awareness of the artist-paederast he transforms into a complex network of ideas and symbols which relate to the very basic patterns of his imagination. 'For, to Our Lady,' he observes, 'a gesture is a poem and can be expressed only with the help of a symbol which is always, always the same.'[60] In the Gesture, the world of mysticism and ritual merges with the world of existentialism and dialectic, continuity with discontinuity, and the individual with the archetype.

Sartre, in his brilliant analysis of the Gesture, inevitably stresses its dialectical significance. The ordinary man who acts, he argues, acts in order to perform, to achieve; but Genet, whose reality lies in the mirror, or in the words of Others, acts not in order to perform, but in order to *be*. 'The evil-doer wants evil for evil's sake. Genet commits evil in order to *be* evil.'[61] Thus every one of Genet's gestures creates a pure appearance; it produces an image, it is an unadulterated aesthetic *form*, devoid of function. 'It evokes the idea of work, while remaining none the less totally ineffective and gratuitous [. . . .] It is the choreographic stylization of human transcendency.'[62] Yet at the same time, the Gesture, having no purposive function of its own, achieves a symbolic significance, (*i.e.* it is recognized as having some specific designation) by referring back to an earlier repetition of itself. As an illustration, the gesture of thumbing one's nose at an enemy does not, *in itself*, perform any purpose as an act; it acquires its significance because it is recognized, from having been used on previous occasions, as a symbol of impertinent defiance. Thus every individual gesture gets its meaning by reference to an *archetype* : either to a Great Originator, or else to a Platonic essence, an abstraction. But, because the essence of the Gesture lies in its repetition, it belongs also to the category of religious ritual—the Mass, for instance, whose significance derives from the fact that it is a series of symbolic gestures repeated countless times though history, and leading back eventually to Christ himself. The Gesture, therefore, concludes Sartre, belongs to the realm of the irrational and the sacred : it eliminates time, the individual disappears before the essence, and yet remains related to it by '*le geste*'.[63]

This is an admirable analysis, as far as it goes; but Genet also develops other implications, especially in *Our Lady of the Flowers*. The gesture, which is *pure appearance* without purpose, *i.e.* without reality, begins as the Image. Only when the Image is in movement, that is, in time, does it become a gesture. Thus most of Genet's characters, at some point or other, are described *out of time*, as three-dimensional images : as statues, as pure sculpture.[64] Divine is a 'frozen statue', [65] she 'felt herself emerging from a rock carved by Michelangelo in the form of a slave',[66] she struggles 'just as Laocoön seizes the monster and twists it!'[67] Darling 'stands there solid and motionless, as if he were Andromeda's monster changed to a rock in the sea'[68]; Seck Gorgui stands 'in the pose which, you will recall, Lou discovered Alberto (Colossus of Rhodes). . . .'[69] Our Lady is equipped with a 'pedestal of cloud',[70] while a juryman possesses eyes 'hollow, like those of statues'.[71] These examples could be multiplied a dozen times from the other novels.[72] Genet's people exist first and foremost as objects of static beauty; they are appearance without movement and without purpose. They 'are what they are'. They exist outside the continuity of time. Darling's one moment of bliss comes when he lies motionless on the bed of his cell, smoking a cigarette : 'It is a moment of happiness, made up of Darling's delightful aptitude for being that which, by virtue of his pose, is profoundly that, and which this essential quality makes live again there with its true life.'[73]

But sooner or later, Genet has to give his statues movement.[74] What happens then? Time, which had hitherto been contiguous— that is, an infinite succession of present-instants, each unrelated to the next—now becomes a continuity : a phenomenon which, to Genet, is in itself a miracle, and belongs to the domain of the inexplicable, the sacred. The creatures start to transform one pose into another. But since the *value* of the original pose lay entirely in its plastic beauty, the mere intervention of time as a continuity will not alter this basic value. The significance of the act resides still wholly in its aesthetic qualities, never in its purpose. Every act is a gesture, and every series of gestures tends towards the ballet, for ballet is the one art which prolongs the aesthetic values of time-as-contiguity into the domain of time-as-continuity. Darling is likened to Nijinsky[75]; and, in one of the finest and most haunting episodes of the book, Culafroy, dancing at night among the sheets drying on his mother's wash-line, moves like an arrow from pose into gesture, from gesture into dance, and from dance straight into the sacred world of dream, ecstasy and levitation :

> If he ceased to touch the ground, save by an illogical movement of his taut instep, this movement might have made him take off, leave the earth, might have launched him into worlds from which he would never return, for in space nothing could stop him.[76]

In a gesture, therefore, man is-what-he-is. In a subconscious, and especially in a vulgar gesture, the crust of inauthenticity is broken, and 'through the crevice, which is as lovely as a smile or an error, we glimpse a patch of sky'.[77] But in so far as reality *is* appearance, and a pose or a gesture is a stylized symbol of appearance, then man literally *is* what his gestures make him. Theoretically, then, by willing or by inventing a gesture, a man can actually *become* what the gesture designates. In fact, however, the process is not quite so simple, because, as we have seen, the gesture belongs to the domain of the sacred; it refers back to the past, the essence, the archetype; it does not depend on the decision of a rational will. A gesture is *given*, like God's Grace to the Calvinist; it cannot be asked for or earned. It can be dictated by the physical beauty of the subject, as it is in the case of Erik,[78] or by subconscious reflexes and instincts[79]; or it can be inspired by imitation of the same gesture seen in another. But the one origin which is denied to the great, the archetypal gestures is that of 'ponderous reflection and decision'.[80]

On the other hand, once the gesture exists, then it is-what-it-is— it is its own supreme value, not only ethical (in which case, the *beauty* of the gesture ennobles its origins, however infamous these may have been in themselves[81]) but also psychological. A gesture cannot be spontaneous, it must have a cause, an origin; but once it has come into being, then it can discard its origins, and become symbolic of some totally *different* psychological motivation, which might have expressed itself in the same symbolic gesture. Thus Culafroy, climbing out of the window at night, '. . . would step over the railing—gesture of a lover, burglar, dancer, somnambulist, mountebank—and jump into the vegetable garden. . . .'[82] By the *fact* of his gesture, Culafroy could have been any of these things. The choice is his. Thus there are almost infinite possibilities of metamorphosis in any given identity at any given moment. Alternatively, by imitating the specific gesture of a model, one can *become* that model : one can take on his identity, feel what he feels, *be* what he *is*. Or else, working the trick backwards, once the gesture is established, one has a choice of motives, or essences, to tack on to it; and once the motive is identified retrospectively with the gesture, the reality of the gesture then substantiates the reality of the motive. Thus a motive may be inspired instinctively by fear; but if the *same* gesture could also be attributed to ferocity, then, simply by thinking of that gesture in terms of ferocity, its motive does in fact *become* ferocity . . . and Genet is transformed from the cowardly Divine into the pugnacious Querelle of Brest :

> With a slight shift, the signs of my confusion could all become signs of a splendid anger. I had only to transpose. I clenched my teeth and moved my cheekbones. My face must have taken on a fierce expression. I let myself go. My trembling became the trembling of . . . anger.[83]

On the whole, however, this substitution of motives within a given identity is a fairly rare phenomenon in the novels. Most of Genet's characters become what-they-are by imitating the gestures of an archetype—that is, literally, by *becoming* somebody else. And the more remote and awful the Great Original, the more power and magic reside in the gestures descended from him. Hence Culafroy's

passion for genealogy,[84] or Genet's own dream of finding himself
to be the last descendant of an ancient line of noble ancestors—his
fascination with heraldry and mediaeval grandeur which at first
sight suggests an affinity with Proust and his passion for the dynasty
of the Guermantes, but which in fact has a totally different origin :
a search for the most sacred and illustrious ancestor, not of a line,
but of a way of bending one's head to get into a car, a way of raising one's hat, a way of walking upstairs :

> Nobility is glamorous. [. . . .] Titles are sacred. The sacred surrounds and
> enslaves us. It is the submission of flesh to flesh.[85]

But if the Guermantes go back to the Middle Ages, the ancestry
of the underworld is no less illustrious. After all, Villon lived in
the fifteenth century, no less assuredly than did Bayard. And so
the *macs* have their own genealogy, each inheriting from his predecessors a set of gestures, and with it an identity which, belonging
as it does to the domain of ritual, is as sacred as the ceremonies of
courts or basilicas. Darling in his style of dress and walk, imitates
Pierrot-du-Topol, holding his head and shoulders

> . . . so as to resemble Sebastopol Pete, and Pete holds them like that so
> as to resemble Pauley the Rat, and Pauley to resemble Teewee, and so on ;
> a procession of pure, irreproachable pimps leads to Darling Daintyfoot,
> the double-crosser. . . .[86]

Identities are submerged in gestures, and gestures are transmitted
from generation to generation, and the sum-total of all these gestures
symbolizes a sacred act—an act of transgression. So that, in the end,
there is no longer a procession of thieves strung out across the centuries, but rather all the separate thieves rejoin the Ultimate, the
Essence; and Genet likewise, from having been *a* thief, surrenders
his identity to the ballet of gestures. Like Darling before him, he
becomes *the* Thief, and his gestures assimilate him to the Eternal
Archetype.

Divine has her room high up beneath the roofs of Paris, 'suspended like a cage between heaven and earth',[87] and overlooking
the Cimetière Montmartre. To reach it, Darling, Gorgui and Our
Lady must climb the never-ending staircase which winds from floor
to floor, and, as it rises, '. . . it dwindles and darkens until, at the
top, it is no more than an illusion blending with the azure'[88]—while
beyond Divine's retreat, beyond the roof itself (who can tell?) it
probably leads ever onwards, further and further, 'on steps of blue
air, up to heaven'.[89] And this is as it should be. Genet's world is full

of staircases : at Fontevrault, at Mettray, in hotels and garrets, even
in Culafroy's village where the treads 'squeak like violins being
skinned alive'[90]—for all his people live suspended, half-way between Heaven and earth. Their gravity—their immersion in the
sacred—drags them downwards, below the surface of the river
of stars; but their transcendence, their gestures which are their
participation in the Archetype or the Essence, give them a 'sickening lightness', an unreality which lifts them upwards towards the
empty sky. The exact equipoise between the two forces, the heavi-
ness of the Sacred, and the 'buoyancy'[91] of transcendence, annihilates the world of reality; and, like Ionesco's Amédée, or Choubert,
or Bérenger in Le Piéton de l'Air, all Genet's people, from Divine
and Our Lady to Querelle or even Madame Lysiane, tend to float
upwards towards the empyrean.[92] Even the title Journal du Voleur
holds the suggestion of a levitational pun ('Voleur', meaning both
'thief' and 'flier'). Of Divine, Genet notes that she always seemed
to be floating above both herself and her lover[93]; of the Little Skivvy
of Pompes Funèbres, that 'elle volait. Elle enseignait à voler'[94] : and
of himself, in a strange but characteristic passage, that the great
temptation of espionage—a transgression of unusual gravity—was
'. . . as if to anchor me to your soil where loneliness and poverty
made me not walk but fly. . . .'[95]

This half-way world, suspended between the stars and their
reflection, is, of course, the poet's world of dream and vision and
unreality : but it is something more than a gratuitous piece of
imagery. In so far as Genet is a mystic—that is, experiences the
world of the spirit as something more real than the world of materiality—the sensation of spiritual ambiguity (neither in Heaven nor
on earth : but also neither man nor woman) lies at the very root
of his sensibility, his perception of the meaning and nature of
existence. Nor is that experience always pleasant—as with other
experiences belonging to the sacred world, ecstasy is never very
far from nightmare. Sometimes, in this ambiguous situation between two orders of existence, he feels himself transparent, as
though he were made of glass, or smoke (Divine watches the ghosts
in the cemetery from her eyrie under the sky : '. . . the sly ghosts
torn by the sun'[96]); but more often his imagination gives this tortured
ambiguity the symbolic outlines of an angel.

Genet is haunted by angels. They are beautiful, they are evil,
they are 'neither mind nor matter'[97]—i.e. they are the diametrical
opposite of Genet's ideal in his search for an absolute of authenticity—they are nightmarish and sacred and incomprehensible. They
hover. Traces of the creatures appear even in the names that Genet
gives to his characters : Angel-Sun (Ange-Soleil), the Negro mur-

derer, or the Solange of *Our Lady* who reappears as the sister of
Claire in *The Maids*. Nor are angels of light *('Soleil', 'Claire')* in
any way necessarily less hostile than angels of darkness: it was the
Archangel Gabriel who appeared in brightness and cruelty, with a
flaming sword; fallen angels are more merciful. 'And I, more gentle
than a wicked angel . . .'[98] muses Genet, thinking of the occult
powers of these inhuman phenomena. For angels are a snare and
a delusion, but none the less dangerous for that. To them, God has
delegated all his will to evil, all his cruelty and indifference, all his
hypocrisy. They have the forms of men and of beauty (yet have
they teeth? Have they sexual organs?). They are abject, the supernatural *tantes* of the vault of heaven; they betray; they promise
the absolute and exterminate before they grant it. For Divine, they
are the force that transforms her acts into gestures,[99] dissolving
her existence in an unreality of essence, robbing her of her identity,
yet granting her no more than the illusion of sanctity. They are
'white, filmy and frightening',[100] like ghosts; they are vicious, they
are the spirits of violence and the souls of murderers (Harcamone,
the condemned murderer, the presiding genius of *Miracle of the
Rose*, is also known as 'Archangel')[101]; they are chaste, they are terri-
fyingly pure, as pure as Death, for they are God's messengers of
death—yet they fornicate with women, and from this vile union
spring war, magic, and all the evil, supernatural arts.[102] In a word,
they are that beauty which, by definition, is betrayal; they are
appearance which has murdered reality, the mask which has eaten
away the face. They are the poetry which springs from the destruction of perfection by brutality; like God, they exist and yet do not
exist . . . they are devilish by the fact of their non-existence, for, if
one could catch one by the wing-tip and fling it in a ditch among
the nettles and the water-mint,[103] it would cease to be elusive and
lose its magic. For the angel *is* a thing of magic, of primitive superstition; it animates the knife in the murderer's hand and turns it
against himself; it is the emissary and plenipotentiary of gods we
have forgotten, but who exist none the less; it superimposes one
reality on another, it is a lie more powerful than truth, a lie co-
existent with the truth, the mirror-image, the negative that simultaneously completes and destroys the positive; the annihilator, the
generator of the Void, the Nothing . . . the angel is a *miracle*, and
there is nothing that Genet and his characters find more obsessively
terrifying than miracles.

Like Bunyan on his pilgrimage, Divine in her progress towards
sanctity must encounter many obstacles; and of all these, the most
forbidding is the *Miracle*. Miracles take many forms in Genet's
world, from the vision of roses which gives the title to *Miracle of*

the Rose to the vision of the Sacred Heart in *Pompes Funèbres*, from the praying sheepdog in *Our Lady* to the resurrection of Si Slimane in *The Screens*. And they all have this in common : that, like God and his angels, they both are, and are not, at the same time; and if their reality is a first miracle, their non-reality is a second; and the two together are a nightmare, a final miracle of horror.

Obviously, this extremely unusual conception needs some clarification. To begin with, it is important to realize that Genet's characters—and Genet himself—feel themselves to be the object of a fatal conspiracy; they are beings predestined for damnation, not by a personal God, but by the very natural order of the universe. They belong to the Elect, but they are chosen to be plunged headlong into humiliation and evil. Admittedly, the paranoiac suffering from persecution-mania shares a similar delusion, although usually with less evidence to support it. Sartre, moreover, has argued that Genet, being the victim and elected scapegoat of a capitalist society, merely identifies the massed ranks of his bourgeois persecutors with the totality of the universe, and concludes—mistakenly, but again with a fair show of evidence—that he is the victim of a hostile cosmic will. Be that as it may, Divine believes that the entire natural order of the universe is specifically aimed at her destruction and, like the typical Romantic hero, the Byronic *âme damnée* outlawed and exiled by the whole of creation, feels that this selectivity, which has ordered the very stars in their courses in such a way as to accomplish the downfall of one single being, raises her so far above the common run of humanity that she is Queen, Archangel and Saint rolled into one : the Elect among the Elect, for whom all miracles are possible. Not only possible, but necessary, and quite literally natural. Since the entire natural order of the cosmos is specifically conceived and pre-ordained to be the instrument of her destruction, then every particular part of that general order is similarly aimed at her. Consequently, it does not require a miracle to *break* the natural order : the natural order is itself the miracle. It is quite enough for any one phenomenon simply to be-what-it-is, for it to be miraculous. More : for if, by deliberate act of God, the natural order of the universe were *disturbed*, it could only be in her favour; where the law condemns absolutely, an exception to the law—a miracle—can only be a relaxation of severity. But Divine's uniqueness—her sovereignty, her sanctity—depends upon her being singled out for opprobrium by the *whole* creation; once exceptions creep in, her uniqueness diminishes, her sanctity is tarnished, and she is but one among a million other down-and-outs. To be sacred, her damnation must be absolute. And so, for Divine, the very concept of a miracle in the normal sense—the exceptional, inexplicable infringement of the natural order—is abhorrent :

> I would be horrified if I were to be pointed at by God, singled out by Him; I know very well that, if I were sick, and were cured by a miracle, I would not survive it. Miracles are unclean. . . .[104]

The ultimate miracle—the only true miracle—for Genet is that the world simply is-what-it-is. The transcendental domain of the sacred is superimposed upon the profane world of objects, which remain exactly what they were in substance, yet *in significance* are totally transformed.

The miracle, then, is simply this : that the one category of reality is superimposed upon another, both existing simultaneously, some-times utterly indistinguishable one from the other, but sometimes (although rarely) so transformed that they *appear* to be of different natures. To distinguish between these two co-incident realities is the precise function of Jean Genet as a poet : it is the miracle of the *symbol* (and all Genet's art is composed of symbols) to make visible the sacred or essential reality of a phenomenon, while leaving its profane reality intact underneath. It is Stendhal's process of *crystal-lization* in reverse : the miracle is not that the twigs in the Salzburg salt-mines are transformed into glittering constellations of crystals (or Harcamone's chains into garlands of roses), but that *beneath* the miraculous glitter (or the beauty of roses) they are still plain twigs (or chains). Symbolically, the convicts of Fontevrault are aura'd demigods; in reality, they are verminous and disease-ridden cretins; the latter is the miracle, the former is merely the symbol. The same is true of the dream-world in which Genet and his creatures move : the dream is an immediate intimation of the sacred; but the sacred is never more than an extra dimension of profane reality. Genet's dreamers always dream awake. Arriving at Fontevrault, Genet suddenly perceives his Black Maria as a state coach leading him into exile : but he never loses his 'clear vision of a thing',[105] and the splendour—the miracle—of the vision is that the vehicle is never at any point anything else *but* a sordid Black Maria. This, I believe, is the sense of that strange scene when Culafroy dances among the drying sheets : his curious arena is *both* an '*irréelle mer-veille*' *and* a wash-line. The dream is the Image-in-the-mirror; the miracle is that, independently of the Image, the original Figure still is-what-it-is :

> When I write that the meaning of the setting was no longer the same, I do not mean that for Culafroy—and later for Divine—the setting was ever any different from what it would have been for anyone else, namely, wash drying on wire lines. [. . . .] Nothing had moved, and this indifference of the setting better signified its hostility. Each thing, each object, was the

result of a miracle, the accomplishing of which filled him with wonder. Likewise each gesture. He did not understand his room, nor the garden, nor the village. He understood nothing, not even that a stone was a stone. . . .[106]

This passage gives us an insight into the core of Genet's poetic vision of the universe. Moreover, take this vision to its logical conclusion, as Divine does constantly, and Darling too when he goes to Mass, and there follows one of Genet's most disturbing paradoxes : that the most miraculous of miracles is the *fake*. Later, when we discuss Genet's attitude towards the reality of God, it is a paradox that we should bear in mind, for it is of the same nature as that proposed by Samuel Beckett, when he argues that the only valid evidence of God's existence is evidence that He does not exist.[107] It is, incidentally, the sort of conclusion which follows logically from Sartre's proposition that the root of consciousness is negative, but which Sartre, good Calvinist that he is (especially in *Saint Genet*) signally fails to draw.

However, to return to the reality of miracles, the splendour of symbols lies in the fact that they have existence simultaneously in two totally different dimensions, two irreconcilable domains of experience, the sacred and the profane. The miracle lies in the simultaneity and in the transition. Bread and wine, to the believer, are the symbol of the body and blood of Christ : they *are* the body and blood of Christ. Yet they remain, under any form of chemical analysis, merely bread and wine : a complex pattern of carbohydrates : If the bread and wine were actually and literally (chemically) transmuted in the ceremony of the Mass, this would indeed be a miracle in the ordinary sense, but the reverse of a miracle in Genet's sense. It would be a miracle by which the whole natural order of the universe would be destroyed, the sort of miracle that, for Genet, represents the unbearable horror, annihilating all that he is. On the other hand, while the bread remains bread and the wine, wine, their transubstantiation into the sacred Body and Blood implies at one and the same time a spiritual miracle and a chemical imposture, or fake. For the believer, the miracle lies in the spiritual (sacred) experience of the Body of Christ, *in spite of* the bread remaining bread; for Genet, *the miracle consists in the fact of the bread remaining bread*, in spite of the spiritual experience. So powerful are the mysterious forces of the supra-rational world that, when the sacred and the profane come into contact, the greatest of wonders is that the profane survives at all : that its power to be-what-it-is should be strong enough to brand the miracle—in its own terms—as an imposture; for when the gods came into conflict with men, men need a miracle to save them.

Genet's paradox, then, is not that of the rationalistic unbeliever—
on the contrary, it is because his perception of the reality of the
symbolic and the supernatural is so intense that the fake becomes
evidence of the miracle. *Our Lady of the Flowers* is a long paean
of exultation, inspired by the vision of this reversed, this mirror-
miracle; for when the plaster statue takes the form of Christ (since
appearance *is* reality) it *is* Christ; and yet, miraculously, the plaster
somehow contrives to remain plaster. The believer is bewitched,
the sacred has him in its dark and sometimes damnable power; the
plaster alone is saved.

Thus Culafroy, when he wanders through the pine-forests, forever watches the swaying branches, expecting to see 'a miraculous
virgin, who, so that the miracle might be total, would be made of
coloured plaster'[108]; and Divine, herself a symbolic transformation
out of her own childhood, for whom the child Culafroy, and not
herself, is the miracle, 'fears the Saints in heaven . . . not [. . . .] because they are terrible [. . . .] but because they are made of
plaster'[109]—and when Notre-Dame was guillotined, the Veil of the
Temple was *not* rent :

> And nothing happened. What would be the point? There is no need for
> the veil of the temple to be ripped from top to bottom because a god
> gives up the ghost. All that this can prove is the bad quality of the cloth
> and its deterioration. Though it behoves me to be indifferent, still I would
> not mind if an irreverent scape-grace kicked through it and ran off
> shouting, 'A miracle!' It's flashy and would make a very good frame-
> work for the Legend.[110]

The failure of the miracle is the core of the miraculous. The
perverse obstinacy of things persists right into the heart of the Sacred
and the perception of a fake, for Genet, is not only evidence of
something more miraculous than most of the legends of Antiquity,
but it is also the root of poetry. Poetry, in one of Genet's definitions,
springs from the point where the visible is transformed into the
invisible—that is, from the meeting-point of sacred and profane—
and the miraculous imposture is precisely such a point. In the
later novels, and in *The Thief's Journal*, this original notion will be
broadened and developed to form a whole theory of imposture; if
the fake is evidence of the miracle, then Genet himself, by transforming himself into an imposter, is well on the way to realizing
the miracle of his own existence. Again and again, he notes his
'passion for imposture'.[111] And if the genuine were to be disguised
behind a fake so identical in every way that only Genet himself
could tell which was truth and which was lie, then he would hold
in his hands the secret power of the gods to make the miracle
function either way : for if the symbol is a fake, then the profane

object is miraculous; but if the object is a fake, then the miracle lies in the symbol! Only Jean Genet could then—perhaps—tell which was which. The miracle of the mirror is complete.

Symbols and miracles; impostures and ecstasies; abjection and humiliation; gravity and levitation . . . all milestones on Divine's— and Genet's—road towards the Absolute, towards becoming '*la Toute-Toute*' . . . towards sanctity. That the inconceivably degraded Divine should think of herself as a Saint is a paradox that has upset many critics, including Jean-Paul Sartre; but Dostoievsky would have understood, and probably Marcel Jouhandeau, and perhaps St Theresa. Conceivably also George Orwell, whose hero Gordon Comstock follows, albeit less success-fully and less radically, a similar path :

> He wanted to go down, deep down, into some world where decency no longer mattered; to cut the strings of his self-respect, to submerge him-self—to sink, as Rosemary had said. It was all bound up in his mind with the thought of being *underground*. He liked to think about the lost people, the underground people, tramps, beggars, criminals, prostitutes. It is a good world that they inhabit, down there in their frowzy kips and spikes. He liked to think that beneath the world of money there is that great sluttish underworld where failure and success can have no meaning; a sort of kingdom of ghosts where all are equal. That was where he wished to be, down in the ghost-kingdom, below ambition.[112]

Divine dives much further beneath the surface of ambition than ever Gordon Comstock dreamed of doing. For Genet, to be a Saint is to exchange the profane world—which is the world of the relative—for the absolutes of the sacred world; and to accomplish this exchange *before* the moment of death, since, in death, the pro-fane world is abandoned willy-nilly, and the sacred invades all. The profane world is the world of acts and intentions; the sacred, the world of symbols—and so Divine 'did what she thought fitting : she made gestures'.[113] The profane sinner accomplishes some evil, when he can, and breaks the laws that the community has seen fit to decree; the Saint is *below* (or alternatively *above* : the outcome is identical) ambition, and every deed and every thought is a trans-gression, not against the law, but against the instinctive fears of man. The conventional saint abandons the world for the sake of Christ; Divine abandons the world, not for the sake of Christ,[114] but for the sake of God—a radical distinction. Christ (from Divine's point of view) is not God; Christ is the Son-of-God, the incarnation of the goodness and the mercy of God. But God-without-Christ is by no means good or merciful. God is the sum-total of the sacred world; and the customary virtues are of very little relevance. The paradox of Divine's sanctity is not so much factual as linguistic; for Divine is not very intelligent (nor is Darling, still less Our Lady), and her language is conventional. To express the idea of God, she uses the tritest of Christian terminology (after all, she may be a poet, but she was never trained as an anthropologist); consequently, she expresses her longing for union with the God-Absolute in terms which derive from the God-of-Mercy. The clash between the two concepts is sometimes startling, as when Our Lady, the most vicious of adolescent murderers, appears for trial : 'I shall make so bold as to say that all eyes could read, graven in the aura of Our Lady of the Flowers, the following words : "I am the Immaculate Conception".'[115] The violence of this contrast is reinforced by the fact that, once the concept of virtue is eliminated, the two Gods—Christian and primitive—are still gods : sacred, mysterious and awful; and therefore Divine, in her quest for sanctity, can still follow (apparently) in the steps of her more conventional predecessors. *They* found God in solitude : so does Divine. They were cast out from among men : so is Divine. They were despised and humiliated : so is Divine. They preferred their nearness to God to the good opinion of men : so does Divine.[116] But then, of course, Divine's God is *not* that of Bernadette Soubirous. The question that Genet raises—and it is a tricky one to answer—is whether the Christian concept of God may not be wishful-thinking. Have we not unwittingly created a God in our own image, endowing Him with *our* ideal social virtues : a sort of celestial projection of President Kennedy? The question is not new—Voltaire and Diderot asked it over and over again—but it has rarely been stated in such disquieting terms as by Genet. Why should *one* specific social ideal of God prevail over and condemn all others? Why should Divine's 'road to Salvation' be less acceptable than that of St Teresa?

> We must realize that Divine does not live with gladness of heart. She accepts, unable to elude it, the life that God makes for her, and that leads her to Him. But God is not guilt-edged. Before His mystic throne, useless to adopt artful poses, pleasing to the Greek eye. Divine is consumed with fire.[117]

In a sense, there is more grandeur and more tragedy in the martyrdom of Divine than in that of St Stephen—'Stephen-the-Deacon', to whom Genet refers on more than one occasion. St Stephen, at the moment of his death, trusted in the mercy of God, just as Polyeucte had confidence in His justice; Divine has no such childlike faith to buoy her up, and moves, like Phèdre, towards an eternity of terror. Divine's 'union with God'—her experience of the sacred—'did not occur without difficulty (pain) on both sides'[118];

she struggles to avoid the Hand of God, she changes shape a thousand times, she darts and wriggles and dances 'like some maddened tragedy-queen' to avoid the terror of that clutching grasp : 'Nobody was aware of what was going on and of Divine's tragic moments as she struggled against God.'[119] For God's first act, in relation to Man, his creation, was to expel him from the paradise of Eden, and set a curse upon him. And Divine, unlike most Christians, remembers the curse, and fears it. God is a God of malediction. And yet Divine *dares* to be a Saint. Because of her longing for the Absolute, she is prepared to pass through the mirror and enter the dominion of God, even when God is the totality of all that man fears and trembles at. 'For,' comments Genet in *Miracle de la Rose*, 'this in effect is saintliness, which is to live according to Heaven, in spite of God.'[120]

Underlying Divine's tormented journey along the road to Calvary, there is a serious, almost a Calvinistic view of the meaning of the universe—in fact, the closer one comes to Genet's thought, the more evidence there is of a desperately ascetic temperament at work somewhere in the background, and the obscenities of *Our Lady*, even more so those of *Pompes Funèbres*, reveal a lurking horror and disgust at the antics of the human body which are closer to the visions of Grünewald than to the frivolous titillations of popular pornography. Divine discovers what the boy Culafroy did not yet know

> . . . that the importance of any event in our life lies only in the resonance it sets up within us, only in the degree to which it makes us move towards asceticism.[121]

Genet's own homosexual experiences (as he recounts them) may be humiliating, painful, exalting, mystic, disastrous—they are never 'gentle'. 'Gentleness' *(la douceur)*, particularly in the later works, almost invariably has disgraceful, even disgusting connotations. The ideal happiness, in so far as happiness can be conceived—and only a child can conceive it at all—is arid, sharp-contoured and desolate, like a desert of blue sand.[122] The symbols of sexuality are hardness and purity : glass, granite, marble, the bright, pitiless steel of the knife. Characteristically, intercourse usually takes place in the most uncomfortable positions : at dawn, against the rugged bark of a tree, or on a roof-top among the chimneys, during a squalid night of street-fighting. To this inherent asceticism, the paradoxical purity of Divine, and more particularly of Our Lady, seems to belong.

But if the symbolism and the sanctity of *Our Lady of the Flowers*, in this interpretation, reveal a genuine and deep-rooted view of the human situation, this does not exclude elements of a violent and bitter satire. Jean Genet has seen too much of the evil, cruelty and contempt of so-called Christians to have much confidence in the gentle teachings of Christ. For him, the Church of Christ is staffed by thorough-going representatives of the *bourgeoisie*—and he, the thief, the pre-ordained criminal, is the predestined scapegoat of a *bourgeois* ethic. And in so far as the representatives of Christ on earth are his personal enemies and persecutors, so Christ is also tainted by the vices of his servants. Unquestionably, Jean Genet gets a vitriolic and malicious pleasure from associating the sacro-sanct-sentimental images of the Sunday-School with the obscenest episodes between Darling and Divine—Divine who thinks of her lover's sexual organ as 'Jesus in His Manger'[123]—the sort of comparison which, as Genet himself notes elsewhere, is deliberately intended to set the reader's teeth on edge.[124] In any case, if the primitive gods of paganism are cruel and terrifying, the gentle God of Christianity—from all available evidence—is a hypocrite and a liar : in any event, neither Genet nor Divine has the slightest reason to love either. Whatever He is, and whether He exists or not, God— like all possibilities of transgression—is both dangerous and fascinating : the urge to find God belongs to the same category of urges as those of the classical Freudian subconscious—the urge to murder one's father and to rape one's mother, the urge to desecrate, destroy and kill that which one reveres. In the experience of Divine and Culafroy, there is a far greater sacrilege than that of masturbating on the Holy Altar : the sacrilege of living *in spite of* God.

Which brings us back to the irritating and almost insoluble problem : does Genet—or Divine, for that matter—believe in God? There is no straightforward answer. 'Does he believe in God?' asks Beckett's Bom of his victim, Pim. Reply : 'Yes.' Question : 'Every day?' Answer : 'No.'—which is probably about the most honest answer that most thinking people could give. Ernestine, the mother of Culafroy, is only slightly more cynical :

> As at other times, the days of big flush and gush, days of mystic debauch, she would say to herself : 'Suppose I played at believing in God?' She would do it until she trembled.[125]

That Jean Genet has—or has had—a constant and durable experience of the supra-rational (what poet has not?) is indubitable; but God is only one aspect of the supernatural, and here the experience is far less reliable, far more intermittent. Sartre's analysis of the problem,[126] based largely on one important but rather exceptional passage in *The Thief's Journal*,[127] is perhaps a bit too sceptical—or rather, it is one-sided : it takes account only of Genet in his more rational moments, it excludes the 'days of mystic debauch'. And, as far as we can tell, it seems to have been precisely on such days that Genet wrote—at top speed and in a few short weeks—his novels. Thus, for his characters, in so far as they are projections of himself, such days are the rule much rather than the exception.

In Sartre's interpretation, the concept of God is the categorical moral imperative of any given society. The preservation of society is envisaged as *the Good*, and so God will be good in so far as He embodies the rules which ensure that preservation. But Genet is society's scapegoat : and therefore this same goodness of God, which reassures the right-thinking citizen, is responsible for Genet's condemnation. In order to justify this condemnation (and thus to justify the existence of God), Genet did in fact *become* a criminal, the purest incarnation of evil that he could envisage; but, remembering himself as a child, he cannot help but realize that he was not *always* evil. At some point, therefore, God's (society's) condemnation *preceded* the crime for which he was condemned. If, now, Genet believes unremittingly in God, he must believe that God condemned him as an innocent child—and, as we have seen earlier, the convicted innocent, to Genet, is not merely intolerable, but evidence that the universe is returned to utter chaos—*i.e.* that God does not exist. In other words, a belief in God's existence leads straight to the proof that God cannot exist. To escape from this impossibility, argues Sartre, Genet prefers to half-believe : 'he plays at believing'[128]; sometimes he thinks of God as an Absolute; at others, of God as the projection of himself among the 'invisible and maybe dangerous constellations'[129]; at others again, of himself *as* God, containing God, and eternally creating and re-creating the universe in terms of his own boundless-divine ego.

All three of these attitudes are certainly to be found in Genet, but the first probably has more importance than Sartre allows it. The notion of God as a metaphysical—or perhaps almost literal—projection of the Self belongs especially to *Miracle of the Rose*, where God is to a greater or lesser extent symbolized as the luminous figure of Harcamone, whose exploit 'transpired in Heaven, that is, in the highest region of myself'[130]; although Harcamone himself has his 'prolongations' which project like searchlights into the night-sky of infinity. In this context, if God does *not* exist, then the Figure casts an Image which is never reflected, since there is no mirror to reflect : a God-less infinity—exactly like a prison-cell without a mirror—is torment, since perception, perceiving only the Void and never itself, can never know its own existence. Hence God becomes the direct consequence of Genet's own horror of the infinite :

If we are free—available—and without faith, our aspirations escape from us, as light does from the sun, and, like light, can flee to infinity, for the physical or metaphysical sky is not a ceiling. The sky of religions is a ceiling. It ends the world. It is a ceiling and screen, since, in escaping from my heart, the aspirations are not lost; they are revealed against the sky, and I, thinking myself lost, find myself in them, or in the images of them projected on the ceiling.[131]

By contrast, the perception of God as a totality contained *within* the individual belongs rather to *Pompes Funèbres* and to *The Thief's Journal*, although there are traces of it already in *Our Lady of the Flowers*. This is much closer to the traditional mystic's longing to contain the Totality, the cosmos, in his own being, yet at the same time to be contained as an indistinguishable atom within the Totality of the cosmos. 'Nothing [. . . .] will ever console me for not containing the world'[132] is a characteristic lament of the slightly peevish Buddhist whom we meet in the *Journal*—but then Genet, more often than not, does tend to peevishness when confronted with the Image of God. In *Pompes Funèbres*, the longing to contain/be contained by the world, and thus to absorb the Totality into oneself, is illustrated by a grotesque symbolic pattern of primitive cannibalism— Jean Genet devouring the dead flesh of Jean Decarnin, his lover, his beloved, his Totality, his God.[133]

But, on analysis, what is the implication of this gruesome and nauseating rite, if not—in rather more horrifying realistic terms— precisely that which the devout believer accomplishes at each repetition of the Mass : the devouring and digesting of the symbolic body of Christ in the ritual of Holy Communion. All that Genet has done is to consider, rather more lucidly than is usual among Christian believers, the precise implications of devouring 'the Body of my Love who is Christ', and to recognize for what it is, the shadow of an ancient cannibalism implicit behind the reverberating symbolism of the Vatican. In *Our Lady of the Flowers*, the image of 'absorbing God' is everywhere. Divine and Darling go to Mass and take communion from a 'mean-looking priest'[134]; and the symbolic thread that runs from this to the moment when Mimosa II (another pansy, the deadly rival of Divine) swallows a photograph of Our Lady, 'the way one swallows the eucharist',[135] is not far to seek. But if Christ is the Beloved, and if, to possess the Beloved and the world, the Beloved must be eaten, then the Beloved must first of all be dead—is Christ then also dead?—and consequently it may be imagined that the veritable magic power behind the ritual lies not so much as the swallowing as in the death. The ceremonial killing of the victim, the mystery of sacrifice, the sacred transgression of the taboo of death . . . we are back where we started from, with the notion that, in order to cross the barrier that separates the profane from the sacred, the way lies through transgression, murder and violence. And this in fact is the central paradox of *Our Lady of the Flowers*, that Our Lady, the murderer, is sacred, and to him, just as aptly as to Divine, the aura of beatitude and sanctity is attached. By taking a life, Our Lady has *absorbed* a life; a life is in him that is not his own, and he is on the road to becoming God.[136]

But although both these different concepts of God—the God within the Self, the God who is a projection of the Self—have an important part to play in Genet's novels, the poet's essential vision is neither of these. More often, it is of a God who is an Absolute, the sum-total of all the forces of the sacred world, and who is profoundly hostile to man. Or rather: so strong is the temptation for Genet, the poet and the mystic, to surrender his profane reality and to lose himself for good and all in the unreality of the supernatural (which, perhaps, is simply what ordinary people would call madness), that God, who is the symbol of this temptation, becomes—in Christian terms—the Tempter. Genet's obsession—psychological or existential, no matter—is to contrive somehow to be-what-he-is, and to perceive himself to be-what-he-is. But God is tempting him to let go of this reality—to let himself be absorbed into the Divinity, to become his own reflection—in short, to be-what-he-is-not. And Genet refuses. If he ventures into the world of supernatural reality it will be on *his* terms, not God's. He will be like the plaster Virgin, which remains plaster in spite of the miracle; and this is miraculous. Jean Genet will remain Jean Genet in spite of God's miracles: and this will be *his* miracle. He will be like the King of a ruined country, 'who, when confronted with a miracle, had the nerve to oppose it and thwart God'.[137]

'Thwart God. . . .' Here we have the key to Genet's attitudes, and, through them, to the significance of Divine and Darling and Our Lady. They are at death-grips with God, because God offers them sanctity and salvation on *His* terms. And they are tempted—but they will not be bullied. They are human beings, and they have one inalienable right: to be-what-they-are. God would take away from them this right—and so they defy God. If they are destined for sanctity, they are resolved to go there in their own way, not God's; they will plunge head downwards, feet pointing at the stars. Their abjection is their dignity; their degradation is their ultimate authenticity. God has sided with society, therefore God has betrayed them; not for that, though, will they renounce God's kingdom, but they will get there by diving head foremost into the mirror-image of Heaven. And if they emerge from the sludge, they may or may not in the end have haloes; but at least they will have dodged God in the process :

Mon Dieu, mon Dieu, mon Dieu, je fonds sous votre regard. Je suis un pauvre enfant, Gardez-moi du diable et de Dieu.[138]

NOTES

1 *Our Lady*, pp. 154-155. '. . . gantés de noir soutenant un baldaquin oriental d'allure, empanaché de plumes d'autruche, sous lequel le prêtre se promenait en portant un ostensoir. Sous le soleil, parmi les seigles, les pins, les luzernes, et se renversant dans les étangs, les pieds au ciel.' (*Notre-Dame*, p. 69)

2 *Ibid*, p. 80. (*Notre-Dame*, p. 21). (The English text uses a different image in this passage.)

3 *Ibid.*, p. 97. '. . . martèlent l'azur du ciel.' (*Notre-Dame*, p. 32)

4 *Q. of B.*, p. 233. 'Mes crachats . . . ça c'est mes décorations.' (*Querelle*, p. 307)

5 *Maids*, p. 16. 'Mon jet de salive, c'est mon aigrette de diamants.' (*Bonnes*, p. 34)

6 *Thief*, p. 81. '. . . avec elle nous eussions poursuivi l'ascension—encore que le langage semble vouloir dire le mot déchéance ou tout autre indiquant un mouvement vers le bas—l'ascension, dis-je, difficile, douloureuse, qui conduit à l'humiliation.' (*Journal*, p. 97)

7 *Our Lady*, p. 104. '. . . quelques croûtons mêlés de cheveux dans les poubelles.' (*Notre-Dame*, p. 37)

8 *Rose*, p. 210. 'L'horreur infernale ne réside pas dans un décor d'un fantastique inhabituel, hirsute, inhumain, délibéré. Elle accepte le décor et les manières de la vie quotidienne; seul un détail ou deux les transforme (un objet qui n'est pas à sa place, ou qui est à l'envers, ou qu'on voit du dedans), prend le sens même de cet univers, le symbolise, révélant que ce décor et ces manières relèvent de l'enfer.' (*Miracle*, p. 337)

9 *Ibid.*, pp. 70-71. (*Miracle*, p. 236)

10 *Ibid*, p. 70. '. . . l'écœurante légèreté du liège.' (*Miracle*, p. 236)

11 *Our Lady*, p. 263. (*Notre-Dame*, pp. 139-140)

12 This translation has been omitted in the English version of *Q. of B.* (*Querelle*, p. 333)

13 *Rose*, p. 34. 'C'est du plus profond de moi que j'arrache mes mots [. . . .] et ces mots referont le monde détestable et adoré ·dont j'ai voulu m'affranchir.' (*Miracle*, p. 210)

14 *Pompes Funèbres*, p. 10.

15 *Our Lady*, p. 122.
    '— Je suis bien sûr, sûr, sûr, la Toute-Dévergondée.
    —Ah! Mesdames, quelle gourgandine je fais.
    —Tu sais (le *us* filait si longtemps qu'on ne percevait que lui), *tussé*, je suis la Consumée-d'Affliction.
    —Voici, voici, regardez la Toute-Froufrouteuse.
    L'une d'elles, interrogée sur le boulevard par un inspecteur :
    —Qui êtes-vous?
    —Je suis une Emouvante.

Puis, peu à peu, elles s'étaient comprises en se disant :
—Je suis la Toute Toute.
Et enfin :
— Je suis la T'T' !' (*Notre-Dame*, pp. 48-49)

16 *Ibid.*, p. 299. 'Le vieux était foutu. Y pouvait seument pu bander.'
    (*Notre-Dame*, p. 163)

17 *Ibid.*, p. 61. (*Notre-Dame*, p. 9). Maurice Pilorge, to whom Genet's poem,
    'Le Condamné à Mort' is dedicated, was executed on 17th March
    1939 at Saint-Brieuc.

18 *Ibid.*, p. 180. '. . . tablier bleu comme le col des marins.' (*Notre-Dame*,
    p. 85)

19 *Ibid.*, p. 310. '. . . voit Dieu en gobant un oeuf.' (*Notre-Dame*, p. 170)

20 *Pompes Funèbres*, pp. 126-127.

21 *Our Lady*, p. 91. (*Notre-Dame*, p. 28). (The image is changed in the
    English text.)

22 Bataille, G. *L'Erotisme*. Tr. Mary Dalwood, London (Calder) 1962,
    p. 36.

23 *Our Lady*, pp. 307-8. (*Notre-Dame*, pp. 168-169)

24 Beckett, S. *No's Knife*, London (Calder) 1962. ('La Fin', in *Nouvelles
    et Textes pour Rien*, Paris (Minuit) 1955, p. 111)

25 Many of the ideas in this chapter are adapted from Georges Bataille :
    less, however, from his essay on Genet in *La Littérature et le Mal*,
    which seems, all in all, to miss the point, than from his remarkable
    general study, *L'Erotisme*. See in particular Chapter Five of this
    work, which is entitled 'Transgression'.

26 *Our Lady*, p. 152. 'C'était l'art, la religion, l'amour, qui sont enveloppés
    de sacré [. . . .] car du sacré qu'on appelle, hélas ! le spirituel, on ne rit
    ni ne sourit : il est triste. S'il est ce qui touche à Dieu, Dieu est donc
    triste? Dieu est donc une idée douloureuse? Dieu est donc mal?'
    (*Notre-Dame*, p. 67)

27 *Ibid.*, p. 152. (*Notre-Dame*, p. 67)

28 See, for example, *Our Lady*, p. 183 (*Notre-Dame*, p. 87); *Thief*, p. 88
    (*Journal*, pp. 105-106, 240)

29 *Our Lady*, pp. 253-4. 'Il était à la merci d'une volonté "autre" qui bour-
    rait ses poches d'objets, que dans sa chambre, en les mettant sur la
    table, il ne reconnaissait pas.' (*Notre-Dame*, p. 133)

30 *Ibid.*, p. 228. 'On commence par une petite superstition, puis on tombe
    dans les bras de Dieu.' (*Notre-Dame*, p. 116)

31 *Ibid.*, p. 95. '. . . et la muraille éclate comme un ciel se déchire pour
    montrer l'Homme, pareil à celui que Michel-Ange peignit nu dans
    le Jugement dernier.' (*Notre-Dame*, p. 31)

32 *Ibid.*, p. 111. '. . . des petits couples de mariés voilés de tulle blanc,
    qui s'agenouillent sur un prie-Dieu de tapisserie.' (*Notre-Dame*,
    p. 41)

33 *Ibid.*, p. 294. '. . . sa situation était proche de celle de la mère de Jésus
    parmi les femmes du village galiléen.' (*Notre-Dame*, p. 160)

34 *Ibid.*, p. 100. 'Partez, vous êtes guéri.' (*Notre-Dame*, p. 34)

35 *Rose*, pp. 157-162. (*Miracle*, pp. 300-303)

36 *Pompes Funèbres*, pp. 126-129.

37 *Our Lady*, p. 94. '. . . comme le boirait, s'il buvait, le Saint-Esprit
    en forme de colombe.' (*Notre-Dame*, p. 30)

38 *Rose*, p. 62. 'O ma Solide ! O ma Féroce ! O ma Brûlante ! O mes
    Abeilles, veillez sur nous !' (*Miracle*, p. 230)

39 *Our Lady*, p. 86. '. . . avec la gravité impitoyable des forêts en marche.' (*Notre-Dame*, p. 25)

40 *Q. of B.*, p. 28. (*Querelle*, p. 184): 'determined' in the English translation.

41 *Ibid.*, p. 62. (*Querelle*, p. 205)

42 *Rose*, p. 54. '. . . car envisager sa mort étant un acte grave, il le faisait avec gravité.' (*Miracle*, p. 224)

43 *Our Lady*, p. 240. '. . . un rire strident de fête ou de folie.' (*Notre-Dame*, p. 124)

44 *Ibid.*, p. 89. (*Notre-Dame*, p. 27)

45 *Ibid.*, 184. (*Notre-Dame*, p. 88)

46 *Rose*, p. 112. (*Miracle*, p. 266)

47 *Ibid.*, p. 169. 'Je respectais les superstitions.' (*Miracle*, p. 307)

48 *Ibid.*, pp. 28-29. '. . . des rites d'autant plus importants qu'ils sont obligés, n'étant pas de simples ornements d'une action dont l'essence me demeure encore mystérieuse.' (*Miracle*, p. 206)

49 *Ibid.*, p. 169. (*Miracle*, p. 307)

50 *Pompes Funèbres*, p. 32.

51 *Q. of B.*, p. 70. (*Querelle*, p. 210)

52 *Our Lady*, p. 74. (*Notre-Dame*, p. 18)

53 *Thief*, p. 8. '. . . une longue pariade, chargée, compliquée, d'un lourd cérémonial érotique.' (*Journal*, p. 10)

54 *Our Lady*, p. 80. '. . . roulée dans une guipure blanche.' (*Notre-Dame*, p. 21)

55 See below, pp. 84-88.

56 *Pompes Funèbres*, p. 38.

57 *Rose*, pp. 245-6. (*Miracle*, p. 362)

58 *Thief*, p. 29. (*Journal*, pp. 35-36)

59 *Our Lady*, p. 313. (*Notre-Dame*, p. 172)

60 *Ibid*, p. 289. 'Pour Notre-Dame un geste est un poème et ne peut s'exprimer qu'à l'aide d'un symbole, toujours, toujours le même.' (*Notre-Dame*, p. 156)

61 Sartre, *Saint-G.*, p. 72. 'Le méchant veut le Mal pour le Mal; Genet fait le Mal pour *être méchant*.' (*S. Genet*, p. 75)

62 *Ibid.*, pp. 314-315. 'Il évoque le travail tout en demeurant parfaitement inefficace et gratuit [. . . .] figuration chorégraphique de la transcendance humaine.' (*S. Genet*, pp. 292-293)

63 *Ibid*, pp. 72, 81, 314, 315, 321-2, 324. (*S. Genet*, pp. 75, 82, 292, 293, 298, 300 etc.)

64 Genet's feeling for sculpture is revealed more specifically in his Essay: *L'Atelier d'Alberto Giacometti* (1958)

65 *Our Lady*, p. 82. (*Notre-Dame*, p. 23)

66 *Ibid.*, pp. 142-143. '. . . sort d'un roc taillé en forme d'esclave de Michel-Ange.' (*Notre-Dame*, p. 61)

67 *Ibid.*, p. 143. '. . . comme le Laocoön saisit le monstre et le tordit.' (*Notre-Dame*, p. 61)

68 *Ibid.*, p. 95. '. . . reste solide et immobile comme s'il était, dans la mer, le monstre d'Andromède changé en roc.' (*Notre-Dame*, p. 31)

69 *Ibid.*, p. 176. '. . . dans la pose où nous avons vu que Lou découvrit Alberto, Colosse de Rhodes. . . .' (*Notre-Dame*, p. 82)

70 *Ibid.*, p. 288. (*Notre-Dame*, p. 156)

71 *Ibid.*, p. 289. '. . . creux comme ceux des statues.' (*Notre-Dame*, pp. 156-7)

72 *E.g. Rose*, pp. 21-2, 26, 196, 199. (*Miracle*, pp. 201, 204, 327, 329); *Pompes Funèbres*, p. 20; *Q. of B.*, pp. 72, 89; (*Querelle*, pp. 211, 222); *Thief*, pp. 9, 180; (*Journal*, pp. 12, 214)

73 *Our Lady*, pp. 265-266. 'C'est un moment de bonheur, fait de l'adorable facilité qu'a Mignon d'être ce qui, par sa pose, est cela le plus profondément et que cet essentiel fait revivre là de sa vraie vie.' (*Notre-Dame*, p. 141)

74 *Ibid.*, p. 82. (*Notre-Dame*, p. 23)

75 *Ibid.*, p. 70. (*Notre-Dame*, p. 15)

76 *Ibid.*, p. 172. 'S'il ne touchait plus au sol que par un geste illogique de son cou de pied tendu, ce geste pouvait le faire décoller, quitter la terre et le lancer au milieu des mondes d'où il ne reviendrait jamais, dans l'espace où rien ne pourrait l'arrêter.' (*Notre-Dame*, p. 80)

77 *Our Lady*, p. 282. 'Par la fente adorable comme un sourire ou une erreur, on aperçoit un coin de ciel.' (*Notre-Dame*, p. 152)

78 *Pompes Funèbres*, p. 76.

79 *Rose*, p. 123-124. (*Miracle*, pp. 274-275)

80 *Our Lady*, p. 70. '. . . la pesante réflexion et la décision.' (*Notre-Dame*, p. 15)

81 *Thief*, pp. 100. (*Journal*, pp. 118-9). Cf. also *Q. of B.*, p. 8. (*Querelle*, p. 174)

82 *Our Lady*, p. 146. '. . . enjambait la barre d'appui—geste d'amoureux, de cambrioleur, de danseuse, de somnambule, de baladin—et sautait dans le potager. . . .' (*Notre-Dame*, p. 63)

83 *Rose*, pp. 123-124. 'Avec un léger décalement tous les signes de mon trouble pouvaient devenir les signes d'une colère magnifique. Il suffisait de transposer. Je serrai les dents et je fis bouger mes zygomatiques. Ma gueule dut prendre une expression féroce. Je partis. Mon tremblement devint le tremblement de la colère.' (*Miracle*, p. 274)

84 *Our Lady*, p. 204. (*Notre-Dame*, p. 101)

85 *Ibid.*, p. 204. 'La noblesse est prestigieuse. [. . . .] Les titres sont sacrés. Le sacré nous entoure et nous asservit. Il est la soumission de la chair à la chair.' (*Notre-Dame*, p. 101)

86 *Ibid.*, p. 92. '. . . et Pierrot les garde pour ressembler à Polo-la-Vache et Polo pour ressembler à Tioui et ainsi de suite : une théorie de macs purs, sévèrement irréprochables, aboutit à Mignon-les-Petits-Pieds, faux jeton. . . .' (*Notre-Dame*, p. 29)

87 *Ibid.*, p. 88. '. . . suspendue comme une cage entre ciel et terre.' (*Notre-Dame*, p. 27)

88 *Ibid.*, p. 68. '. . . s'amenuise et s'obscurcit jusqu'à n'être plus, au sommet, qu'une illusion mêlée d'azur.' (*Notre-Dame*, p. 13)

89 *Ibid.*, p. 71. '. . . sur des marches d'air bleu, jusqu'au ciel.' (*Notre-Dame*, p. 15)

90 *Ibid.*, p. 149. '. . . grincent comme des violons qu'on écorche vifs.' (*Notre-Dame*, p. 65)

91 *Q. of B.*, p. 154. (*Querelle*, p. 261)

92 On the deeper significance of the theme of 'levitation' in modern literature, see Durand, G.: *Les Structures anthropologiques de l'Imaginaire*, Paris (P.U.F.) 1963; also Chambers, R.: 'Eugène Ionesco, ou comment s'envoler', in *Studi Francesi* (to appear shortly).

93 *Our Lady*, pp. 212-213. (*Notre-Dame*, p. 106)

94 *Pompes Funèbres*, p. 104.

95 *Thief*, p. 43. '. . . comme pour m'ancrer à votre sol où la solitude et la misère me faisaient non marcher mais voler. . . .' (*Journal*, p. 52)

96 *Our Lady*, p. 193. '. . . les fantômes sournois déchirés par le soleil.' (*Notre-Dame*, p. 94). See also *Our Lady*, pp. 82, 88, 129, 172, 305, 315. (*Notre-Dame*, pp. 22, 26, 53, 80, 167, 172)

97 *Ibid.*, p. 62. '. . . ni esprit ni matière.' (*Notre-Dame*, p. 9)

98 *Ibid.*, p. 109. '. . . et moi, plus doux qu'un mauvais ange.' (*Notre-Dame*, p. 40)

99 *Ibid.*, p. 96. (*Notre-Dame*, p. 32)

100 *Ibid.*, p. 62. (*Notre-Dame*, p. 9)

101 *Rose*, p. 207. (*Miracle*, p. 335)

102 *Ibid.*, p. 147. (*Miracle*, p. 292)

103 *Our Lady*, p. 160. (*Notre-Dame*, p. 72)

104 *Ibid.*, p. 108. '. . . mon horreur serait immense d'être du bout du doigt désigné par Dieu, distingué par lui; je sais très bien que, si malade, j'étais guéri par un miracle, je n'y survivrais pas. Le miracle est immonde. . . .' (*Notre-Dame*, p. 39)

105 *Rose*, p. 7. 'Vision lucide de la chose.' (*Miracle*, p. 191)

106 *Our Lady*, p. 174. 'Quand j'écris que le sens du décor n'était plus le même, je ne veux pas dire que le décor fût jamais pour Culafroy, plus tard pour Divine, autre chose que ce qu'il eût été pour n'importe qui, à savoir : une lessive séchant sur des fils de fer [. . . .] Rien n'avait bougé, et cette indifférence du décor signifiait mieux son hostilité. Chaque chose, chaque objet, était le résultat d'un miracle dont la réalisation l'émerveillait. Et aussi chaque geste. Il ne comprenait pas sa chambre, ni le jardin, ni le village. Il ne comprenait rien, pas même qu'une pierre fût une pierre.' (*Notre-Dame*, pp. 81-82)

107 See the author's 'Le Dieu de Samuel Beckett,' in the *Cahiers de la Compagnie Madeleine Renaud—Jean-Louis Barrault*, No. 44, Oct. 1963.

108 *Our Lady*, p. 236. '. . . une Vierge miraculeuse, qui, afin que le miracle fût total, serait en plâtre colorié.' (*Notre-Dame*, p. 122)

109 *Ibid.*, p. 163. '. . . non [. . . .] parce qu'ils sont terribles . . . mais parce qu'ils sont en plâtre.' (*Notre-Dame*, p. 74)

110 *Ibid.*, p. 302. 'Et rien ne se passa. A quoi bon? Il ne faut pas que le voile du temple se déchire de bas en haut parce qu'un dieu rend l'âme. Cela ne peut que prouver la mauvaise qualité de l'étoffe et sa vétusté. Quoique l'indifférence fût de rigueur, j'accepterais encore qu'un garnement irrévérencieux le troue d'un coup de pied et se sauve en criant au miracle. C'est clinquant et très bon pour servir d'armature à la Légende.' (*Notre-Dame*, p. 165)

111 *Rose*, p. 227. '. . . mon goût profond pour l'imposture.' (*Miracle*, p. 349)

112 Orwell, G.: *Keep the Aspidistra Flying* [1936]: Penguin Books, 1962, p. 217.

113 *Our Lady*, p. 307. '. . . fit ce qu'elle crut bon de faire : des gestes.' (*Notre-Dame*, p. 168)

114 *Ibid.*, p. 304. (*Notre-Dame*, p. 166)

115 *Ibid.*, p. 280. 'J'oserai dire que tous les yeux purent lire, gravés dans l'aura de Notre-Dame des Fleurs, ces mots : "Je suis l'Immaculée Conception".' (*Notre-Dame*, p. 151)

116 *Ibid.*, p. 304. (*Notre-Dame*, p. 166)

117 *Ibid.*, pp. 125-6. 'Sachons déjà que Divine ne vit pas de gaîté de coeur. Elle accepte, ne pouvant pas s'y soustraire, la vie que Dieu lui fait

et qui la conduit vers Lui. Or, Dieu n'est pas doré sur tranches. Devant son trône mystique, inutile de prendre les poses plastiques, douces à l'oeil grec. Divine se carbonise.' (*Notre-Dame*, p. 51)

118 *Ibid.*, p. 307. '. . . ne se fit pas sans mal (douleur) de part et d'autre.' (*Notre-Dame*, p. 168)

119 *Ibid.*, p. 307. 'Nul ne savait ce qui se passait en les tragiques instants de Divine luttant contre Dieu.' (*Notre-Dame*, p. 168)

120 *Rose*, pp. 42-43. '. . . c'est proprement la sainteté, qui est de vivre selon le Ciel, malgré Dieu.' (*Miracle*, p. 216)

121 *Our Lady*, pp. 238-9. '. . . que tout événement de notre vie n'a d'importance que la résonance qu'il trouve en nous, que le degré qu'il nous fait franchir vers l'ascétisme.' (*Notre-Dame*, p. 123)

122 *Ibid.*, p. 72. (*Notre-Dame*, p. 16)

123 *Ibid.*, p. 116. 'Le Jésus dans sa crèche.' (*Notre-Dame*, p. 45)

124 *Rose*, p. 42. (*Miracle*, p. 215)

125 *Our Lady*, p. 310. 'Comme d'autres fois, les jours de grand tralala, jours de débauche mystique : "Si je m'amusais à croire en Dieu?" se disait-elle. Elle le faisait jusqu'au tremblement.' (*Notre-Dame*, p. 170)

126 Sartre, *Saint G.*, pp. 135-146. (*S. Genet*, pp. 131-141)

127 *Thief*, pp. 76-77. (*Journal*, p. 91)

128 Sartre, *Saint-G.*, p. 144. 'Genet joue la croyance'. (*S. Genet*, p. 139)

129 *Pompes Funèbres*, p. 128.

130 *Rose*, p. 207. '. . . se déroulait au Ciel, c'est-à-dire dans la plus haute région de moi-même.' (*Miracle*, p. 335)

131 *Ibid.*, p. 43. 'Libres—disponibles—sans foi, nos aspirations s'échappent de nous, comme la lumière d'un soleil et, comme la lumière, peuvent fuir jusqu'à l'infini, car le ciel physique ou métaphysique n'est pas un plafond. Le ciel des religions est un plafond. Il finit le monde. Il est plafond et écran puisqu'en s'échappant de mon coeur les aspirations ne se perdent pas, elles se révèlent contre le ciel, et moi, croyant m'être perdu, je me retrouve en elles ou dans l'image d'elles projetées au plafond.' (*Miracle*, p. 216)

132 *Thief*, p. 180. 'Rien [. . . .] ne me consolera jamais de ne pas contenir le monde.' (*Journal*, p. 214)

133 *Pompes Funèbres*, p. 157.

134 *Our Lady*, p. 95. (*Notre-Dame*, p. 31)

135 *Ibid.*, p. 162. '. . . comme on avale l'Eucharistie.' (*Notre-Dame*, p. 74)

136 *Ibid.*, p. 129. (*Notre-Dame*, p. 53)

137 *Rose*, p. 271. '. . . qui a le culot en face d'un miracle de le contrarier et de s'opposer à Dieu.' (*Miracle*, pp. 380-381)

138 *Pompes Funèbres*, p. 21

3

TRAPS AND ALLEGORIES
(Miracle of the Rose)

Alles Vergängliche
Ist nur ein Gleichnis. . . . .
Goethe
Symbolism is really quite proper
Edward Gordon Craig

In *Our Lady of the Flowers* Genet performed the extraordinary feat of transmuting the vilest degradations of the Paris underworld of pimps, murderers and male prostitutes into a kind of haunting and macabre poetry. In his second novel, *Miracle of the Rose* (1946), he works a no less singular metamorphosis with equally ungrateful material : the sordid and stultifying brutality of the great prison-fortress of Fontevrault, and the vicious cruelty of the Reform School at Mettray. In neither case is the material, in the usual sense, romanticized. The misery and horror, the nightmare ugliness of the life that he describes, is never glossed over—on the contrary, it is portrayed lingeringly in all its nauseating detail, and the ingenious sadism by which a vengeful society deliberately sets out to reduce its victims—or scapegoats—to a level considerably below that of animals is, if anything, exaggerated. It is hard indeed to imagine a scene more disgustingly subhuman than the martyrdom of Bulkaen at Mettray,[1] or circumstances more degrading than those which accompany the meeting of Genet and Divers in the punishment-

66

block of the Prison.[2] The secret of this transmutation of abject material into patterns of singular, if disquieting, beauty, lies in Genet's use of the *symbol*.

The symbolism of Genet's early poems ('*Le Condamné à Mort,*' '*Marche Funèbre*', '*La Galère*', etc.) is conventional and monotonous; that of his prose is startling and highly original—yet to a large extent, he uses the same actual images in both. The explanation would seem to be that, in the Poems, the recurrent symbols—the Ship, the White Sails, the Sky, the Flowers, the Rose :

> *Le hasard fit sortir—le plus grand des hasards—*
> *Trop souvent de ma plume au coeur de mes poèmes*
> *La rose avec le mot de Mort qu'à leurs brassards*
> *En blanc portent brodé les noirs guerriers que j'aime.*[3]

—remain almost entirely detached from any real experience : they are gratuitous lyric effusions which spring to the surface of Genet's mind without justification and consequently without effect—without reverberations. It is curious to note that (setting aside the subject-matter of the poem as a whole) many of the individual lines from '*Le Condamné à Mort*', taken in isolation, could easily have been written by some adolescent schoolgirl for the Terminal Magazine, under the combined influence of D. G. Rossetti and a passion for the games-mistress :

> *Le ciel peut s'éveiller, les étoiles fleurir,*
> *Ni les fleurs soupirer, et des prés l'herbe noire*
> *Accueillir la rosée où le matin va boire,*
> *Le clocher peut sonner: moi seul je vais mourir.*[4]

Even Jean-Paul Sartre, usually so solemn and so philosophical, is impelled, for almost the only time on record when faced with these effusions, to forget about Husserl and Heidegger, and to remind us that he is also the heir to Voltaire and Chamfort. His analysis of the *Poèmes* is ironic, devastating . . . and extremely funny :

These lines are flat, they stink of plagiarism. This 'poor wee bird' [cf. *Poèmes*, p. 11] has flown straight out of a poem by François Coppée: 'Do birds hide before they die?' No, they do not hide; what happens to Coppée's birds whenever they feel seedy, is that they go away and find a line of Genet to die in.[5]

All in all, the less said about Genet's more conventional poetry, the better. Yet the problem still remains; by what miracle is a brand of symbolic imagery, which is utterly insipid and platitudinous in the context of the *Poèmes*, transformed into a powerful imaginative and artistic force in *Our Lady* or in *Miracle of the Rose*?

There would seem to be several answers, or partial answers. Firstly, because of the violent dynamic contrast between the sordid reality and its conventional poetical symbol. Secondly, because the symbols which, in the *Poèmes*, tend to be gaunt and rather abstract metaphors, are associated in the prose with an extraordinary wealth of visual imagery. Thirdly, because they have a specific function to perform in relation to the actual structure of the works concerned : Genet's novels are all to a greater or lesser extent plotless, but worked out simultaneously on a series of distinct planes in time and space; and it is the symbolism which links these different planes together and thus provides the essential unity of the artist's vision. And finally, because Genet himself, as author, is constantly caught wandering through the garden of his own bright images, explaining them and, by these interventions, linking them to the essential totality of his thought and experience. In other words, the complex symbolic structure of *Our Lady of the Flowers* and of *Miracle of the Rose* is significant, not only because the symbol is a valid technical device in any art, but, more pertinently, because Genet's philosophy of the Mirror—as was suggested in the previous chapter—is at bottom a pure philosophy of symbolism.

We live, without always realizing it, in a world of symbols, from the Crucifix on the wall with its dusty sprig of box-wood tucked away behind it, to the raised and rigid tail-fins of the latest Studebaker, which emphasise—to the profit of some Detroit manufacturer—the subconscious identification between certain forms of precision engineering and the male sexual urge. The everyday symbolist who lies hidden in all of us accepts such identifications, in which a comparatively simple material phenomenon reveals, or incarnates, a broad area of abstract awareness, sometimes of great complexity, as part of normal experience; but the symbolist poet or artist takes this basic acceptance a stage further. For him (as for Genet) there are two worlds : a world of material realities, and an unseen, but more fundamental and more vital world of Platonic essences, absolutes or intangibles. His—the poet's—function is to reveal this essential world, of which he alone has positive intimations; but, since it is of its very nature intangible, he can do so only through symbols—that is, by identifying in material reality the symbolic equivalents that reveal the invisible essence of things. But the problem is now one of choice : for either he must use symbols which are immediately comprehensible as such—the Rose symbolizes eternal beauty; Antigone's defiance of Creon is symbolic of the individual's resistance to the cruel anonymity of the State; etc., etc.—in which case he is threatened by a catastrophic descent into banality; or else he must discover new, untarnished symbols to incarnate his vision, and take the risk (as Mallarmé did) of writing verse which is hermetic and incomprehensible to anyone except himself and his most intimate acquaintance.

. Genet's solution to this dilemma is to use symbols which, on the whole, are childishly elementary, and in consequence immediately comprehensible; but to use them in a context so anomalous as to eliminate the least suspicion of platitudinousness or bathos. As a result, he creates a world which—considered as an assemblage of material phenomena—has realism without reality. Its reality—psychology, cruelty, the thousand-and-one anecdotic but significant commonplaces of eating, loving, being—has evaporated to form a numinous cloud of Essence; whilst the realism—the currently lifeless forms of existence which once served to harbour a significance of their own—now subsists only to provide a violence of contrast with the ideal. If, as Genet believes fundamentally, the meaning of an object can be *detached* from that object and transposed into a different realm of being, from the contingent into the necessary, from the particular into the universal, or from the profane into the sacred, then the symbol is in effect a form of short-cut from one to the other; but a short-cut which can only be taken at the cost of a certain amount of destruction. When *this* rose in *this* surburban flower-bed which I personally have planted, watered and prosaically manured, becomes *the* Rose of 'O Rose thou art sick', it loses its reality as *my* rose in *my* garden; it gains *a* meaning at the expense of *its* meaning. And this precisely is what happens throughout Genet's works—

> The foreshortening proffered by the symbol when borne by what it is meant to signify gives and destroys the signification and the thing signified.[6]

—Harcamone, by becoming THE Murderer, *i.e.* THE Transgressor, the human being who has most irrevocably passed the barrier that separates Profane from Sacred, and who has thus become a Figure of awe and beauty, aura'd in glory like the Saints—Harcamone loses for us (so long as we remain under the spell of Genet's poetry) the brutal and murderous reality that he had for his victims, the girl he strangled or the warder Bois-de-Rose; only just sufficient shell remains of this original reality to startle us when the hallowed but platitudinous abstracts : glory, beauty and halo are applied to a commonplace thug with an I.Q. of about twenty.

A psycho-analyst, were he to suggest a scientific interpretation of Genet's emotional reactions and creative processes, would undoubtedly conclude that this preoccupation with universals is at bottom a standard type of defence-mechanism. Just as Genet finds some consolation for the appalling misery of his early existence in conceiving himself as the unique (and therefore glorious, predes-

tined) object of a Universal Fatality, so there is consolation in transforming one's disagreeable mediocrity as *a* thief into the universal
essence of THE Thief. When the objects that surround one are
verminous, rickety and squalid, there is a possibility of escape from
an otherwise intolerable existence if one can see—and intimately
feel—them as signs of a higher and more interesting meaning :

> [These things] were not commonplace things, the kind you can find any-
> where. They were signs. [. . . .] At Mettray, each object was a sign that
> meant grief.[7]

Escapism of this type is common enough—in fact it is one of the
forms of paranoia. What saves Genet from madness, and at the same
time gives his characters their uniqueness, is that he never ceases
to be aware of it *as* escapism. In this sense also, he always 'dreams
awake'. Thus Genet creates Darling—himself as he might have
been, were it not for this intransigent lucidity. Darling uses his
symbolic identification with an archetype purely as a means of
escape from suffering :

> Darling will never suffer, or will always be able to get out of a tight
> spot by his ease in taking on the gestures of some fellow he admires who
> happens to be in the same situation.[8]

—but Genet himself, whether at Mettray or at Fontevrault, when he
escapes into dreams (the slave-galley, the horseman), and even when
he allows these great symbolic dreams to overflow into his real life,
never loses himself completely. If he has one foot in the world of
the Sacred, he none the less keeps the other firmly planted on the
soil of the Profane—and thus retains his sanity.

As will be clear already, there are two distinct sources of symbolic
transformation : the Object and the Gesture. The transcendental
implications of the Gesture were studied in the previous chapter—
suffice it to add here that not only does the gesture transform an
act into an archetype, but that the individual who performs a gesture
(*i.e.* imitates the *appearance* of an act from another actor) not merely
assumes momentarily the total identity of the person imitated, but is
well on the way to escaping from his own identity into a universal
symbol. Once again, however, a symbolic significance tends to
destroy a real significance, and the gestures which compose the
archetype do not always perform their original functions for the
individual who assumes them—as Culafroy discovers when he tries
to play a home-made violin by performing 'the same gestures as some
pretty youngster in a magazine'.[9] By contrast, what is certain for
Genet's people is that the symbol—belonging as it does to the domain
of transcendental absolutes—has a power, in some cases quite liter-

ally a *magic* power—that the individual object or act can never possess. The power derives from the original creator of the gesture, which accumulates more power from those who subsequently adopt it : thus the Nazi salute, for instance, not merely symbolized power, but actually had the power to terrify or disgust. In the same way art—which is an accumulation of symbols—has power to move and disturb, even though there is no rational source of power, say, in the distribution of colours and lines on a flat surface. The power of a poem, argues Antonin Artaud, lies not in the words themselves (what power has a *word*?), but in a transcendental power which is transmitted from poet to reader, and which the words merely serve to convey and to reveal : 'The poetry *behind* the poetry'.[10] This is also Genet's conception. The symbol *is* power; it can exercise power itself, or transmit power to be exercised by him who identifies himself with the symbol. Thus Querelle's career in the French Navy, for instance, is determined by the symbolic force exercised by a poster representing 'a Marine dressed in white'[11]; but once he has *become* the archetype himself, the power is in him, and acts on others— on Lt Seblon, for instance, who complains :

> Querelle tells his comrades that he is the victim of posters ! I am the victim of posters, and the victim of the victim of posters.[12]

Thus whereas, for Sartre, every act is an assertion of the principle of freedom, for Genet every gesture is a manifestation of determinism. Freedom is only the freedom to submit to the fatal power of Others, transmitted through a universe of symbols.

In the case of Objects, the mechanism of symbolism is rather different. The Gesture is a series of ritual movements which transport their performer from one world into another; but the Object exists simultaneously in both worlds, performs functions in both and exercises the powers of both. The box of matches that Jean Genet carries in his pocket after the funeral of Jean Decarnin is both a 'sacred object'—a symbol of the coffin 'which contained Jean wholly and entirely'—yet at the same time a utilitarian and effective device for lighting cigarettes.[13] But essentially the power of the object-as-symbol lies in the fact that it condenses a whole complex of emotion and experience into a single small part of the totality (the whole of sexual desire, for instance, reduced to the symbolic dimensions of a dagger), and thus, by the same sort of laws as those that govern compression and explosion in the internal-combustion engine (Genet is rather given to this type of quasi-technological analogy), acts with an explosive force proportionate to the degree of condensation. And this explosive force, this sudden release of the imprisoned energy of a vast and panoramic vision imprisoned in the nutshell of a symbol—in a belt-buckle or a sequin—is, in Genet's analysis, the power called poetry.

In an interesting, if slightly diffuse and literary passage in *Querelle of Brest*, this relationship between symbolism and poetry is discussed at some length. Gil Turko, another adolescent delinquent who has murdered a middle-aged stonemason by slashing his throat with a broken bottle, takes refuge in the disused galley-convicts' prison in Brest; as he hides, sounds come to him from the now inaccessible outer world—the sounds of liners and of the dock-yards, the sounds of riveting-tools and cranes—and each of these sounds (that of a chain, for instance) is condensed into a symbol:

> His incarceration enhanced a thousandfold each one of these noises and invested them with far more stirring qualities than ever they had possessed in real life. If the sea is the natural symbol of liberty, then every image that evokes it is charged with symbolic power: indeed, is peculiarly charged with the whole symbolic power of the sea; and the more common-place the image evoked in the mind of a prisoner, the more disturbing the open wound it causes. It would be perfectly natural for a spontaneous glimpse of a steamer in mid-ocean to cause the inner consciousness of a child the deepest sense of despair; but in this case the image of steamer and sea were far less evocative: for Gil, by far the most portentous was the characteristic sound of a chain. (Can it be that the grinding of a chain does release all the attributes of despair, a simple chain with rusted links?) Gil was undergoing—without being in the least aware of it—a painful initiation into the mysteries of poetry. The image of a chain would cut right across a fibre and this incision widen sufficiently to admit the passage of a ship, to let in the sea, the world, till finally it would destroy Gil by taking him out of himself, he who had no other possible existence but in the world which had just administered his death-wound by cutting him off in his prime and obliterating him utterly.[14]

In this passage, and in the long development which precedes it, the Baudelairean theory of 'correspondences' (sound merging into sight, etc.) evolves into the Mallarméan, and thence into the Gene-tian concept of 'symbols'. But what emerges further from this passage is that, in the process of compression, the explosive force is increased a hundred-fold if there is a discrepancy between the nature of the symbol and the material of the container. In the case of Gil Turko, the idea—freedom, escape—is poetic enough, and the images through which it is condensed into the final symbol (the noises of the chain) are almost conventionally romantic: the sea, the ships, the busy docks. The discrepancy comes in Gil himself, who is neither poetic nor romantic, but stupid, brutal, murderous and debased. More often, however, this pattern of discrepancy, although identical in principle, takes on a rather different shape: a startling contrast between symbolic image and original idea or object, in which the one is high-flown and romantic, the other vile and sordid in the

extreme. The Rose—the symbol of symbols—is one of the eternal
platitudes of poetic poetry; but in Genet, instead of signifying beauty,
honesty or pure unsullied maidens, it symbolizes violence, war, betrayal and ignominious debauchery. And it is precisely the violent
compression of the lives, hatreds and emotions of some 2,000 or more
dangerous criminals within the fortress-walls of Fontevrault, and the
further compression of all this dynamic violence within the innocent symbol of a flower, that produces in Genet's mind the explosion
of poetry that he calls *Miracle of the Rose.*

The Central Prison *(La Centrale)* of Fontevrault is an isolated
community cut off from the rest of the world, cruel, intense, superstitious, hierarchical and ascetic—all in all, not very different from
the mediaeval abbey, with its dependent monasteries and convents,
that had originally occupied this same position. The convicts of the
present are simultaneously the monks and lay-brothers of the long-
dead past—an identification which destroys the intervening barrier
of time, thus giving the whole prison a dream-like and sacred
quality which Genet discreetly emphasises by setting the time of
his own arrival there late on Christmas Eve :

> The prison lived like a cathedral at midnight of Christmas eve. We were
> carrying on the tradition of the monks who went about their business
> at night, in silence. We belonged to the Middle Ages.[15]

This is the first introduction to the basic structure of *Miracle of
the Rose,* which consists in eliminating the profane dimension of
time by superimposing different fragments of experience in time
one on top of the other, identifying them and allowing them to
interpenetrate, so that the final reality that survives is timeless and,
in the fullest sense that Genet gives to the word, 'symbolic'.

Much of this technique, this *'décomposition prismatique de mon
amour et de ma douleur',* as Genet terms it elsewhere,[16] is Proustian
in origin. Jean Genet evokes his adolescence at Mettray in much the
same way, and with much the same purpose, as Marcel Proust evoking his own lost childhood at Combray. Proust has his famous
madeleine, and other symbolic or magic objects and experiences
which open the door on the enchanted gardens of involuntary
memory, and give the continuous past a total reality in the instantaneous present; Genet at Fontevrault meets and loves, first Bulkaen,
a young burglar who, earlier in his career, has been at Mettray,
then Divers, in whom he rediscovers an older Mettray-love of his
own generation—and both these take him back in a rush of in-

voluntary memories through the nightmares of his life in the open-prison Reformatory which, in the 'twenties and early 'thirties, had stood in the flowering countryside of Touraine. At times, the Proustian parallel is so exact that one almost suspects parody. The avenue of chestnut-trees at Mettray seems to correspond to the famous hawthorn path in *Swann's Way*; the failure of conscious efforts at memorizing a vanished past puzzle and torment Genet as much as they do Proust—as when Divers reminds him of another delinquent of their generation, one Villeroy, whom Genet remembers all too well :

> . . . but a surprising thing happened : as he went on talking, the image I had retained of my big shot grew dimmer instead of clearer.[17]

—finally, Genet himself describes his experiments with involuntary memory as an attempt 'to redescend to the depths of time', at the end of which 'I regress, with the Divers of old at my side, to a nauseating childhood which is magnified by horror and which I would never have wanted to leave.'[18]

However, if Mettray is to some extent a Combray-through-the-Looking-Glass—and it is understandable that Genet, comparing his own childhood with that of the wealthy, spoilt and hypochondriac young Marcel, must have felt a pretty violent sense of alienation—the parodic element is never dominant. Genet, at this period at any rate, is far too deeply involved in his own experiences, and in his own search for spiritual liberation, to waste much time on the experiences of others, however similar. If *Miracle of the Rose* has a number of affinities with *In Remembrance of Things Past* (including the interventions of the narrator, and perhaps some deliberate elaboration of style), it is also in many significant ways different. (It is characteristic that when, in *Pompes Funèbres*, there is an exact equivalent of the *madeleine* episode—the sudden glimpse by the Narrator of Erik half-hidden in a curtain, evoking a whole panorama of childhood—the childhood evoked is not Genet's own, but Erik's, which Genet 'veut revivre à sa place'.[19]) *Miracle of the Rose* differs from Proust in the fragmentation of its technique, in its total lack of interest in consecutive narrative, but above all in the super-imposing of a *third* plane of experience over and above the Proustian levels of past and present. This is the plane of the *sacred*, of existence which is still technically *in* life, but in fact, outside life, space and time alike—the level of experience which is symbolized by Harcamone. Harcamone, from the mystic solitude of his condemned cell, is already 'beyond life'; he lives 'a dead life',[20] he experiences 'the heartbreaking sweetness of being out of the world before death',[21] and this state is literally, for Genet, 'supra-terres-

trial [. . . .] one of those states which might be called magical [. . . .]
a new mode of being'.[22] Harcamone has, in fact, through his transgression and later through his condemnation, attained that level of
sanctity, isolation and total detachment from profane reality that
Divine aspired to, yet failed to reach—the level at which all miracles
are possible. Genet, Bulkaen and Divers exist simultaneously on
two planes in time and space : Harcamone, on three. Consequently
it is Harcamone who dominates the rest ('he himself soared above
that world'),[23] and not only dominates it but, being himself a symbol,
gives meaning to all the other symbols which compose the worlds
of Fontevrault and of Mettray.

To begin with, if the prison itself is a mystery, a sanctuary,[24] if it
is a daemonic stronghold of 'former powers',[25] and if its prisoners
are giants and heroes that move as in a dream, it is *because of*
Harcamone. Genet has no illusions about the profane reality of his
fellow-inmates : 'Now that the prison is stripped of its sacred orna-
ments, I see it naked, and its nakedness is cruel'[26]—and his rational
lucidity, which never ceases to run concurrently with his visionary
dreams, is merciless in its assessment of their 'unparalleled stupidity'.[27] Yet, just as in the mediaeval monastery, the presence of one
saintly ascetic in his tower could shed an aura of glory over the
whole community, so the presence of one unrepentant murderer in
his condemned cell can lift the prison, and all its convicts, even
its governor and warders, into the dimension of angels and eternity.
The ladder of 'ascension downwards' leads from Mettray to Fontevrault, from Fontevrault to Harcamone. At Mettray, Genet sees
Fontevrault as 'the perfect expression of his truth'[28]; at Fontevrault
he feels the whole building, walls, watch-house, cells and all, ready
to be lifted up bodily and sent to drift away eternally among the
stars. Harcamone, in the solitude of his fourth dimension, can walk
through doors and walls; and in the vision which Genet has of him,
his chains are garlanded with blossom and his heart is the Flower of
Flowers. For Harcamone is not only the symbol that gives meaning
to all the other symbols, but he himself is symbolized by that most
banal, most mysterious and, in the circumstances, most deliberately
inapposite of symbols : the Mystic Rose.

At the head of Genet's long catalogue of particular symbols comes
the flower; and at the head of the list of flowers stands the Rose.
But—and this is essential—not the rose considered *as a rose*, but
the Rose-as-a-symbol. Genet's roses, in other words, are the mirror-
images of roses; they are pure-appearance, they are intellectual or
spiritual artifacts. They appear among his pageantry of symbols
because they have a precise symbolic function to perform; *not* because they are roses. On the whole, Genet would probably be hap-

pier if there were no real flowers in the world at all; in an ideal
existence they would all be artificial. Fashioned of wax or velvet,
and rather crudely botched together at that. If Sartre's report is
reliable, Genet once entrusted him with a secret : he detests flowers.[29]
Animals also, although to a lesser degree. It is striking that, except
for cats[30] and an occasional heraldic lion or brachet, animals have
no part to play in his poetic vision of the world. 'Don't you like
animals?' asked an effusive cat-lover once. 'I don't like people
who like animals,' was Genet's reply.[31] The retort is characteristic.
Genet is anything but a nature lover; he belongs to the town, to the
underworld of the city; and one of the most poetic descriptions in
his writings is 'the excursion down the rue Lepic,' at dawn among
the dustbins of the Butte Montmartre.[32] Not that he *cannot* describe nature—there is an excellent Spanish landscape in *The Thief's
Journal*[33]—but in general he is not interested. His immediate ideal,
in contrast to the harsh severity of his cell, or the foetid poverty
of his life as a down-and-out,[34] is never Rousseau's or Lawrence's
Nature but rather a somewhat childish conception of luxury—the
sort of sumptuous and elephantine opulence that Osbert Lancaster
has characterized as *le style Rothschild*, and which is still to be
found in some of the more expensive brothels in Cairo (it is also
characteristic of 'La Féria' and of *The Balcony*) : '. . . a luxurious
apartment, adorned with gold, the walls hung with garnet-red
velvet, the furniture heavy but toned down with red faille curtains'[35]—a luxury which is fundamentally middle-class and urban.

For Genet, the city—the city of brothels, palaces or prisons—
is something familiar and reassuring : human, at any rate, made *by*
man *for* man. Not so nature. Nature is fundamentally hostile, a
domain of animate, untamable symbols, alive with a life which is
not human but 'magical', and which can only be penetrated by
accepting an alien domination—by surrendering to those heraldic
and uncanny forces. In *The Thief's Journal*, there is a strange and
significant passage in which Genet is hiding in a cornfield, while
attempting to make a clandestine crossing of the Czech-Polish
frontier. At this crisis, the whole of nature—the golden fields, the
fir-trees, the birches—is transmuted into a single heraldic symbol :
Poland, with its two-headed eagles and all its history; and Genet
himself, before he dare penetrate that realm, must himself cease
to be a human individual, and stylize his own reality : 'I would
penetrate less into a country than to the interior of an image'.[36]

More than any other phenomenon in Genet's world, Nature is at
once magical and hostile and two-dimensional. It is legendary rather
than real, like the treasure-islands and cannibal kingdoms of boy-
hood.[37] Even Genet's favourite season, autumn—the 'perpetual

autumn' of Fontevrault,[38] the 'intense and insidious' autumn of Mettray,[39] the damp, dead leaves of the Tiergarten, amidst which Erik meets the Headsman,[40] the constant fogs of Brest or the mists of Antwerp, which give the city 'its sad character and its sordid maritime poetry'[41]—even the autumn seems 'artificial and terrible'.[42] And yet autumn is the season nearest to Genet's own emotions, the most familiar to him, the least oppressive. As a true, if belated, romantic spirit in the vein of Ossian and Senancour, his melancholy, his 'despair', if it finds peace anywhere in the world, finds it among the dripping of dank branches and the mouldering of dead leaves. How infinitely foreign to him, then, are the bright flowers of summer—blossoms that belong to the *bourgeois* world of prosperity, normality and suave summer seasons on the Côte d'Azur!

And yet, the flowers are everywhere : not only roses, but wisteria, dahlias, marigolds, gladioli, monkey-puzzles, catalpas, primroses, geraniums, daisies, lilies, carnations, cherry-blossom, mignonette, peonies, rhododendrons, may-flowers, forget-me-not, camellias, magnolias, thistles, chrysanthemums, holly, pansies, Japanese bamboos, laburnums, daffodils, laurels, edelweiss, iris, mimosa, lilac. . . . A symbol is a sign which leads from one world to another; and flowers, precisely because they exist *in* Genet's world, yet are not *of* Genet's world, are the symbol of symbols. Not that normally they signify anything *exact*[43]; rather, their symbolic power lies in their violent negativity. For the very reason that they are *not* of Bulkaen's world, or Divine's, or Divers', they become capable of *reflecting* that world. They are *not* life—not Genet's life : therefore they become precisely the symbol of all that is not-life. They are transformed into the image of death. They are *not* sordid, therefore they mirror the sordid, they give it reality, but in a new dimension . . . thus when Darling picks his nose, 'from his nostrils he plucks acacia and violet petals'.[44] In the *bourgeois* world, flowers are associated with the Gardens of Paradise; their innocence and beauty are the very image of Heaven : therefore for Genet they become the symbol of Mettray, 'in the blossoming heart of France',[45] and of Hell; they are the 'infernal accessories' that replace the walls of the open-prison, and they are more powerful and more dangerous than the walls, because their power inherits the magic of another world. The young delinquents are only too well aware of the evil aura of this barrier of flowers : 'We were victims of a foliage which was seemingly harmless, but which, in response to the least daring of our gestures, might become electrified.'[46]

Flowers are not obscene, and therefore they become the symbol of obscenity[47]; they are feminine, therefore they signify the male, the 'tough', the criminal, the murderer; they are bright and luminous, and thus they are identified with darkness and with night; they are conventionally beautiful, consequently they become the mirror-images of ugliness, like the flower that is Mario's blackened thumb-nail.[48] For, in the mirror, significances are transmuted, and the most intimate bond between an object and its essential meaning is the bond of opposition. It is the characteristic of the Saint—the adventurer among forbidden and sacred temples—that he is perpetually forced to 'love that which he abhors. . . .'[49] To Genet, flowers are repellent; consequently he is sacred in proportion as his world is made of flowers. Conversely, the power and the beauty of flowers is enhanced and magnified in proportion as they symbolize degradation and brutality—the granitic ugliness of convicts, murderers and traitors :

> *There is a close relationship between flowers and convicts.* The fragility and delicacy of the former are of the same nature as the brutal insensitivity of the latter.[50]

Whether or not we care to label this negative symbolism as cynical or perverse, the fact remains that it lies at the very root of Genet's whole poetic imagination—and that it is effective. The very titles *Our Lady of the Flowers* and *Miracle of the Rose* are powerful and evocative in precise ratio to the failure of these novels to deal with Ste Thérèse de Lisieux or St Francis of Assisi. From a purely literary point of view, we can see some reason for Genet's revolt against the platitudes and the wishy-washy aestheticism of some of the later symbolists—not Mallarmé or Rimbaud, but Joséphin Péladan, perhaps, or François Coppée. There are powerful elements of aestheticism in Genet himself, but—as we shall see—these elements, even if they lead him to some paradoxical conclusions in ethics, are never obsessive enough to cloud his intellect, and he is as deeply concerned as Sartre or Ionesco to understand the meaning of art, and to re-define the traditional concept of beauty in the context of a post-Hiroshima sensibility. In this attempted re-definition, the violent contradiction implicit in Genet's floral symbolism is extremely significant. There are, however, two other factors which contribute to explaining Genet's peculiar obsession with flowers : the first is the accident of his name, the second the accident of his homosexuality.

As a poet, Genet is fascinated by words (it is to be observed that all his flowers have names as resonant to the ear as their petals are resplendant to the eye); and as a mystic, he is intrigued and more than a little awed by the magic of names. In the majority of primitive religions, the Name-of-God has ritualistic significance; it is in itself a symbol, a poem, an incantation endowed with supernatural powers. This mixture of superstition and ritual poetry is passed on by Genet to most of his characters and embodied in their names, or more often in the fabulous and usually beautiful nicknames that traditionally get attached to the more notorious French criminals. These names—the queers, Divine the Gay-time Girl, Mimosa I, Mimosa II, Mimosa the half-IV, First Communion, Angela, Milord, Castagnette, Régine[51] : the convicts, Jeannot-du-Matin (= Genet himself), Lou-Daybreak, Riton-la-Noïe, Bebert the Legionnaire, Black Jim, Laurent, Martinelle, Bako, Dédé from Javel[52]—are like flowers : their mysterious efficacy springs from the dynamic contrast between the poetic enchantments that the words suggest, and the ugly realities which they serve to mask. That such names have a magic-symbolic power, Genet has no doubt; they constitute a sort of electric hedge about their possessor.[53] To betray them to a potential enemy is to increase one's vulnerability, and Adrien Baillon is as hesitant to reveal, even to *Darling Dainty-Foot*, the secret of his marvellous sobriquet, *Our Lady of the Flowers*, as is the superstitious Buganda tribesman to allow himself to be photographed—and for identical reasons.[54] In view of this, it is not surprising that Genet sees manifold significances and symbols in the imagery of his own name : *Genet*, the small but high-spirited horse of the Spanish light cavalry—but also *Genêt*, the flower of the ancient Kings of England, the golden broom.

It is strange that, in *The Thief's Journal*, where Jean Genet discusses his affinity with the golden-flowered *genêt* of the Morvan, the normal relationship between object and symbol is reversed. In the case of Harcamone, the Rose is the symbol of the man; in the case of the broom, Genet is the symbol of the flower : 'I am alone in the world, and I am not sure that I am not the king—perhaps the sprite—of these flowers.'[55] Further on, Genet makes bold to suggest that, through this family relationship, as it were, which he has with one particular species of flower, 'I can regard all flowers without pity; they are members of my family'.[56] I suspect that this is no more than a piece of rather specious whimsicality—certainly its tone is at variance with the less anodyne, if rather more perverse visions of *Miracle of the Rose*. Even so, the phrase 'regard *without pity*' is characteristic; and the probability still holds that part at least of the poet's fascination with flower-symbols is due to the coincidence of his name.

So far, we have been considering some of Genet's most pervasive symbolism in terms of its poetic function in relation to his imagination. But Genet is in addition a self-proclaimed and practising passive homosexual, and the whole of his creative vision is profoundly influenced by this fact. In other words, there are few symbols, religi-

ous or otherwise, in *Miracle of the Rose* or any of the other novels
which are not at the same time fairly precise images of a certain
type of sexual motivation. The majority of these sexual symbols—
and there are dozens of them : hardness, brightness, ice, brittleness,
fragility ('. . . the *porcelain* of which the boy was made . . .'[57]),
gravity (particularly in relation to voices), the burglar's jemmy, the
guitar, the 'java' (a modern dance), jewels, the Renaissance court-
page, the soldier, the sailor, the acrobat, the murderer, the *voyou*,
the cyclist, the archangel, the athlete, the gaucho, the Negro, the
'pimps and apaches with a smoking butt',[58] the dagger, the revolver, the mast of a sailing-ship or galley, the snake, the violin,
the belt and belt-buckle, the statue, the machine, the stone towers
of La Rochelle . . . etc., etc.—all these are straightforward erotic
images evoking the violence, the virility, and the more-or-less
symbolic sadism which the passive homosexual ideally desires to
find in his lovers. But Genet, as the essentially feminine partner in
the union, can experience *himself* as none of these things; nor, on
the other hand, can he sublimate himself and his own desires in
terms of a traditionally feminine symbolism—water, waves, the
mother, the gateway, etc.—since he is not a woman, but only a
man-playing-at-being-a-woman. Of the very few recurrent symbols
that incarnate, not his desire for the triumphant male who is to
subdue him, but rather his own reaction, the most important is that
of the flower—and above all (once again) the Rose. The surge and
pressure of his desire he visualises, not as a knife or sword to penetrate, nor as water to be thrust apart and plunged into, but as
something between the two : as the expansion and unfolding in
colour and richness of the richest and most voluptuous of flowers :
the Mystic Rose. Yet the Rose is by no means only yielding—
'sweeter and more fragrant than the rose petals of Saadi'[59]—but
ever inseparable, in the vision, from its stem : hard, thorn-protected,
as unfeminine as barbed wire or a hempen rope. 'This indifference
like a steely metallic stalk'[60]—the symbol of Genet himself.

So, in the *Miracle*, the central, unifying symbol of the Rose is of
considerable complexity. 'The rose means love, friendship, death . . .
and silence!'[61] Harcamone, the murderer, is the Rose of Death; yet
the warder he kills is known as 'Bois-de-Rose'—the Rose-Wood used
for coffins.[62] The Rose is head and heart and sex—cut off from its
stem, it falls as heavily to the ground as the head beneath the knife
of the guillotine; it is mourning, it is mystery, it is passion; it is
Genet's lovers, and it is Jean Genet himself crushed beneath their
love. It is beauty that symbolizes its mirror-opposite, evil and ugliness, it is the paradox, it blossoms at once in the profane and sacred
worlds. It is the Head of Christ and the Crown of Thorns. It is

Proust's *madeleine*, unlocking memories of Mettray.[63] It is the miracle and the symbol of the miracle; it is profanation, transgression and ultimately—in Genet's special sense—sanctity :

> . . . a door opened by itself and we saw before us a red rose of monstrous size and beauty.
> 'The Mystic Rose' murmured the chaplain.
> The four men were staggered by the splendour. [. . . .] They were in the throes of drunken profanation. With their temples throbbing and their brows beaded with sweat, they reached the heart of the rose. It was a kind of dark well. At the very edge of this pit, which was as murky and deep as an eye, they leaned forward and were seized by a kind of dizziness. All four made the gestures of people losing their balance, and they toppled into that deep gaze.[64]

As is the case with the rose, most of Genet's symbolism is composed of fairly simple, even primitive and childish elements, interwoven to form a complex structural pattern which is far from being as naïve as it might at first appear. Of those rare groups of symbols which retain a certain directness, the most important is the symbolism of colours. For Genet, the 'visionary' colour of the sacred world in any of its manifestations—religious, sexual, poetic—is blue, and *Our Lady of the Flowers*, in particular, is dominated by this colour, which persists to some extent in *Miracle of the Rose*, drops into the background in the later, less mystic novels (note, however, the blue implicit in the Sailor, the Policeman, the French Soldier, and the omnipresent blue-jeans), only to reappear in a sudden outburst in Tableau V of *The Balcony*, the scene where Carmen incarnates the Blessèd Virgin for one of her customers :

> *Carmen:* My blue veil, my blue robe, my blue apron, my blue eyes. . . .
> *Irma:* They're hazel.
> *Carmen:* They were blue on that day.[65]

In *Miracle of the Rose*, the main contrast is between the autumn-colours of Fontevrault—greys, browns and the drab coarseness of the convicts' uniforms—and the summer-colours of Mettray.[66] Black and white usually have the significance of dynamic opposites—particularly, of course, in *The Blacks*, where, however, green is used fairly systematically as the symbol of compromise between the two irreconcilable extremes—or perhaps simply of black trying to be white. Finally, a violent mixture of colours can be the symbol, either of vulgarity—'To achieve harmony in bad taste is the height of elegance'[67]—as in the case of Stilitano's spiv outfit, which contains all the most strident colours on the market with the characteristic exception of blue; or else of physical and mental violence, a symbolic device which first appears in the 'Saints'-Days at Mettray',[68] but which is developed much later into the basic pattern of the décor and costumes of *The Screens*—for instance, in the dresses worn by the *tricoteuses* who attend at the death of Warda[69]—where clashing conflicts of colour appear, either in the dialogue, or else in the stage-directions, in twelve out of the sixteen scenes.

Some symbols are developed into whole dream-sequences, representing yet another dimension in which the action of the novel evolves—a dimension half-way between the profane and the purely mystical. In *Miracle of the Rose*, for example, the convict-galley sequences have this function, interwoven with a wealth of fairly obvious sexual significances. The convict-galley episodes are also related to the autobiographical aspect of the novel, whose theme— if we consider it as an *Entwicklungsroman* in fragmentary form, and as a forerunner of *The Thief's Journal*—is the gradual transformation of Genet from a psychological state of total passivity : 'Note how I speak of that galley on which, though I could have been the master, I accorded myself only the lowliest post, that of cabin-boy'[70]—to one of comparative activity, as the lover (rather than the beloved) of the much younger Bulkaen.

Other symbols have similar dream-extensions, notably that of *le Bagne* (the prison-settlement for transported convicts in French Guiana, and in particular the notorious Devil's-Island); and these broader canvases of symbolism often attract to themselves minor isolated images. For instance, just as the Mast plays an important rôle in the vision of the Convict-Galley, so the Palm-Tree almost invariably accompanies the dream of Devil's-Island. It is interesting to note, however, that in the plays, where there is much less scope for these more extensive panoramas of symbolic unreality, the broad canvases are occasionally broken down into their component elements. Thus, in *The Maids*, 'Monsieur' is threatened with transportation to Guiana, and all three women weave fantasies about the prospect; but the accompanying palm-tree has become detached, only to reappear by itself among the décor and dialogue of *The Screens*.[71] To compensate, as it were, for this defection, the same palm-tree, in *The Thief's Journal*, introduces a sequence which leads, via Palm-Sunday and Christmas to the Nativity—Christ, sanctity, glory, isolation, and so back where we started from : to French Guiana :

> I was about to discover beneath three palm trees the Christmas manger where, as a child, I used to be present at *my nativity* between the ox and the ass. I was the humblest of the world's poor. Wretchedly I walked in the dust and fatigue, at last deserving the palm, ripe for the penal colony, for the straw hats and the palm trees.[72]

However, among these symbols whose subtlety lies neither in themselves, nor in what they signify directly, but rather in the variety of their juxtapositions with other symbols, there are two that deserve special consideration, since they appear to relate to the very essence of Genet's vision of the universe. These are the symbols of the Fissure *(la fêlure)* and of the Veil.

That which moves Genet—that which, provisionally and for want of a better word, we will call beauty—is essentially that which leads his spirit or his senses from one dimension of existence to another: from real to ideal, from profane to sacred, from the shadow to the essence. In a word, the ultimate of experience lies, not in Being, but in Becoming (a concept which has close affinities with the distinction which Goethe draws between *sein* and *werden*, but which, in all probability, is inspired directly or indirectly by Bergson); and this profound conviction breaks through in the most unexpected contexts. Harcamone is the source of wonder in that he is simultaneously dead and not dead: he is the very incarnation of a transition. Similarly, the *jeunes voyous* whom Genet adores are adorable above all in the fact of their adolescence—their passage from child to fully-fledged criminal. With them, as with all other living beings or even things, the ideal, once attained, is just dull; the *adorable voyou* of Genet's imagination falls heavily from grace, for now he is just one more spiv or thug—a perfected, machine-finished and therefore uninteresting article, a mere 'commonplace pimp'.[73]

However, just as a vision compressed into a symbol becomes a source of explosive poetry, so a force of *becoming* compressed within a static perfection is a source of explosive beauty. This is the significance of the symbol of *la fêlure* : the fissure caused by the turbulence of these compressed, dynamic forces of change within, through which the essence of a static perfection begins to escape towards a new dimension. Almost inevitably, the force contained is of a nature diametrically opposed to that of its container. If the perfection of the container lies in its granitic hardness, cruelty, violence, etc., that which emerges through the gash and reveals the presence of another, hidden reality within, will be *la douceur* or some soft strain of gentleness : 'That mournful voice is another flaw through which his deep tenderness escapes from his toughness'[74] —thus writes Genet of the songs that Divers used to sing. If the original material is brutality, the symbol of the other dimension will be cowardice; if beauty, then ugliness; if nobility, then baseness or evil. Divers, Stilitano—both perfected thugs and bullies—become 'touching' because of the 'crack' through which their cowardice escapes :

Anyhow, Divers had that crack, which was intended by the architect, as was the pathetic breach in the Coliseum which causes eternal lightning to flash over its mass.[75]

Perfection lies in the revelation of a potential imperfection, consequently of a transition. Again, it has something in common with Goethe's concept : *'Das Unzulängliche/Hier wird's Ereignis.'* The voices that stir Genet to emotion—and he is extremely conscious of the quality of voices, even though music as such holds little meaning for him—are magical *because* they are cracked.[76] But—and this is important—*both* the forces which compose the dynamic opposition of beauty are an essential and intimate part of the same being; they belong to each other, they are inseparable. It is not 'the Dog beneath the Skin', or the 'Old Adam' concealed within the 'New Adam' : Divers' cowardice is as much a part of Divers—it *is* Divers— as his beauty. The dynamic forces which constitute beauty, and which are symbolized by the fissure, arise from a flagrant contradiction at the very root of existence : the turbulence escapes from its container, the being escapes from the being—yet is still the whole being. Literally : 'we escape from ourselves', and yet 'we are eternally ourselves still'. In the context of Genet's irrationalism, the part *is* the whole; the part which escapes *is* the part which remains—a phenomenon which, in mathematics, is only conceivable when both parts are zero. A positive and a negative zero, as it were. And so beauty also is 'the pursuit of the Impossible Nothingness'.

The second of these two characteristic symbols which seem to spring from the very heart of Genet's vision of the world is that of the Veil. Given the fact that Genet's most fundamental adult relationship with society is that of a paederastic eroticism which, to the vast majority of his readers, is something insurmountably ugly, if not repulsive, the most intriguing problem is to discover by what alchemy he translates this experience into a vision of beauty, valid not only for himself, but even for those others whose primary reaction is one of nausea. To say simply that the experience is transmuted into a tapestry of symbols is not in itself sufficient answer : every artist must possess somewhere, in the depths of his sensibility an innate *awareness* of beauty, in order to give this jumble of symbolic images some form of poetic unity and coherence.

For Genet, this primitive and ultimately irrational awareness of 'the Beautiful' consists in the perception of a solid object—hard, immutable, phallic, with sharp contours of uncompromising rigidity—*veiled* in such a way that its edges are blurred, its outlines made wavering and uncertain, so that there is a space *('un léger décalage')* between the too-immediate reality of the inward object and the too-feminine formlessness of the enshrouding veil—a space for the poetic imagination to dream in. Strangely, Stendhal, over a century earlier, had much the same notion of ideal Beauty, for nothing moved him so much as the sight of a landscape or of a figure gradually receding into the mists, thus allowing his imagination to wander at will between two worlds : for the brutal claims of reality were not so obsessive as to stultify the dream, yet the dream was never gratuitous, being chained always to an awareness, however distant and haze-enshrouded, of reality. Stendhal also uses the term : 'a light veil' [. . . .] 'which is golden in the art of Paul Veronese; in that of Guido Reni, it is as of silver; it is ashen in that of Pesarese'.[77] It is the veil which produces that 'enchantment of distance' which Stendhal discovers in the landscapes of Poussin, and which, to him, symbolizes all the magic and the mystery of immortal art :

> It is this aspect of painting which bewitches the sensitive imagination. [. . . .] It is the means by which painting is related to music, it binds the imagination to complete its pictures. [. . . .] The objects which we recall with the greatest enchantment are those whose details are *half-concealed by the atmosphere*; in our thoughts, they acquire a celestial aura. . . .[78]

With Genet, the veiling of hard outline by soft opaqueness has innumerable connotations and appears in scores if not hundreds of different forms. It is related—obviously—to the delicate balance of masculine and feminine elements which compose Genet's erotic personality; it is related equally to his philosophical or quasi-Sartrian preoccupations, the alternations of appearance and reality, of object and mirror-image, of the I and the Others. In dramatic terms, it announces his fascination with the Mask—with the mask which, as in *The Blacks*, only half-disguises, so that the flour-like mask of the death-white Queen allows the black neck and the black woolly hair of the African actress to appear beneath it. But, in spite of these more-or-less extraneous connotations, Genet's fascination with the Veil appears to have its remotest origins in a fundamental and inexplicable fact of aesthetic sensibility—a sensibility which acts like a powerful emotional generator, sending out currents which affect, to a great or lesser degree, almost every other image and symbol in the poet's vision of the world.

It is the Bride in a black dress beneath a white veil (and thus it links up with the wedding-symbol and the *Veni Creator*); it is the shepherd covered in hoar-frost; it is Our Lady shaving, his pink face 'pink beneath the froth of soap, and hairy'—and it is the fleeting glimpse of the bride or the shepherd that reveals to Culafroy that poetry 'is something other than a melody of curves on sweetness, for the tulle snapped apart into abrupt, clear, rigorous, icy facets'.[79]

It is the dimming veil of distance in time that separates Mettray

from Fontevrault; it is the veil of Divers' voice, and the voice itself
is a veil thrown across, half-concealing and half-revealing the personality behind it.[80] It is the nimbus of the Saint; it is the dusting
of powdered cement or plaster that characterises Harcamone at
Mettray or Gil Turko in the Dockyards; it is the city of Brest, with
its hard, squat, granite houses half-hidden in the mists of autumn;
it is shadow—the shadow of melancholy, of mourning-veils, of 'the
big straw hat on the shaved face of a convict' in Guiana[81]; it is the
Valley of the Shadow of Death. It is the photograph of the murderer Weidmann, obscured by the coarse letterpress reproduction
of the gutter-press; it is primitive violence lightly glossed over by
civilization.[82] It is the adolescent thug bride-veiled by a nickname
redolent of orchids and orange-blossom or the muscle-bound convict, transported to Devil's-Island, asleep under his mosquito-net[83];
it is the web of saliva that Stilitano weaves across his mouth, it is
irony concealing the stark harshness of words or thoughts.[84] It is
the sun-tan of the Légionnaire from the *Bat' d'Af.*; it is snow that
falls across a landscape *'pour adoucir l'arête des choses, l'angle des
gestes'.*[85] It is the veil of affliction. It can be as tenuous and as lovely
as the autumn sun on the façade of a brownstone house[86], or as
grotesque and nauseating as *'une croûte de pain sous les toiles
d'araignée et la poussière'.*[87] It is the tenuous blurring of impre-
cision which Genet, in his writing, throws over the clear-contoured
statements of fact and anecdote : '. . . the fact that this indecision
imparted to the tale a historical tone further embellished it'.[88] It is
the dust-sheet of style flung over the pullulating rubbish-bin of content. 'Glory be to God for veiled things', would seem to be Genet's
echo to Gerard Manley Hopkins—even his burglar's jemmy, as it
lies dormant in the corner of his room, seems veiled in a kind of
'golden mist' of it own vibrations.[89]

This symbol of the Veil not merely dominates Genet's whole conception of art and beauty, but interacts with other symbols that
have an independent existence in their own right. The idea, or
image, of lace, for instance. Lace : the symbol of an inaccessible
femininity, yet at the same time possessing the precision of machinery,
the fragility of glass. The artefact-equivalent of the Flower, as is
evident at the trial of Our Lady, where the spectators 'were shakier
than a bower of wisteria, than the lace curtain of a crib'[90]; the
flower from which springs the rigid stamen of male desire. Black
lace : the emblem at once of mourning and of female sensuality—
among all the whores of the brothel, 'La Féria', Madame Lysiane
alone accords herself the right to wear black lace underwear, 'because black gave an altogether frivolous note to her undies—at
the same time conferring a certain note of gravity'.[91] Darling 'had

lace fingers'[92]; Bulkaen's 'thousand adventures he invented [. . . .] composed a light and fantastic lacework skeleton and organism for him'.[93] The two more monstrous teddy-boys of *The Thief's Journal*, Armand and Stilitano, both betray their fall from idealized masculinity, the one by cutting lace patterns out of paper,[94] the other by perfecting a racket for selling cheap, machine-made lace to credulous country priests as 'genuine hand-made art-work'.[95] Yet lace is also the material of wedding-veils and curtains; lace is the 'veil of gestures' in which Lt Seblon hides himself from the world[96]; lace-like also is the veil of tattooing in which the convicts shroud their bodies—*blue*, in this case, 'the blue lace of tattoos which covered his whole body',[97] with all the esoteric significance attached to the colour blue. Yet, of course, tattooing is itself both an erotic symbol[98] and a sign of primitive magic, as among the Australian aborigines. Tattooing is the latter-day equivalent of those runic and sacred inscriptions which our Nordic ancestors engraved on the blades of their swords.[99] And Genet's own writing in prison?—a tattooing of blue-purple ink or indelible pencil on the rough paper supplied for making bags in the gaols of Fresnes and Fontevrault. And so the symbols intertwine and communicate to each other the wealth and the variety of their significance. For Lt Seblon, the dream is to complete his isolation—Divine would have said his (or 'her') sanctity— by wrapping himself in lace, in curtains, in flags, 'like an Englishman in his rugs'—in those same curtains, perhaps, which are the symbol of death in *Our Lady of the Flowers*,[100] or in those same flags which are the emblem of the enveloping yet masculine thrust of the Nazi armies in *Pompes Funèbres*,[101] or in those same 'long, wide black veils' with which Madame Lysiane takes possession of Querelle.[102] When Le Joyeux laughs, notes Genet, even his laughter is veiled, edged with the same 'blue tattoo-marks' that he carries in the corner of his eyelids.[103]

To realize the full complexity of the symbolism of the Veil, however, there is no need to go beyond one single episode : that of Querelle's descent into the stokehold. Querelle, after the murder of Vic, returns to his ship, and takes on a voluntary fatigue in the stokehold, ostensibly for the extremely practical reason of covering his tracks and giving himself an alibi. But the veil of coal-dust with which he inevitably gets covered has a far more subtle significance than the plain, utilitarian one of misleading any possible witnesses to the crime; it gives him 'the mysterious power of a faun, of an idol, of a volcano, of a Melanesian archipelago ! He was himself, yet he was so no longer.'[104] For Lt Seblon, who catches sight of him thus veiled, his power lies first and foremost in his physical beauty : he seems like a God.[105] But for Querelle himself, who is *inside* the veil, the effect of his quasi-disguise is more Sartrian. 'He was himself, yet he was so no longer.' That which is veiled—like the Image in the Mirror—simultaneously both is and is not what-it-is, and this is its strength. Querelle possesses, as it were, the double power, both of 'being' and of 'nothingness', both of truth and of falsehood; he is endowed with 'the cruel disguise of a mask', yet he is not, strictly speaking, masked; his face is still his own. He is at once a white man and a Negro—'a negro savage, the member of a tribe in which murder ennobled a man', yet a false-negro, 'mysterious, monstrous'. He is the symbol of death—yet only for others; for himself he is life and light : 'a pillar of light to himself, an apparition of darkness to others'. In this episode, we can see Querelle as the ultimate revenge of Jean Genet, who was forced to be in himself a creature corresponding to the external image that others saw of him. Querelle imposes on others an image which does *not* correspond to himself, and yet which *is* himself all the same. And this supreme occasion for revenge is due to nothing more intricate than a prosaic veil of coal-dust.[106]

Thus the symbol of the Veil offers a final link between Genet's mysticism on the one hand, and his existentialist vindicativeness on the other, between the *Veni Creator* of *Our Lady of the Flowers* and (ultimately) the rationalized political violence of *The Blacks* and *The Screens*. None the less, it remains basically an aesthetic concept in origin, and if this analysis of the ramifications of one particular symbol appears to have been rather extensive, it is because it leads us straight on towards the still more fundamental question : what is Beauty within the context of the novels of Jean Genet, and in particular within the context of *Miracle of the Rose*?

It is interesting to note that Genet's theoretical or abstract considerations on the nature of Beauty do not always correspond to those objects or people which he describes in terms which reveal them as beautiful, or which suggest that he himself finds in them some form of aesthetic pleasure. The objects which Genet appears genuinely and deeply to *feel* as beautiful belong almost invariably to that category which I have described by the symbol of the Veil, and they are characterized by the softening or blunting of a hard, sharp contour by the interposition of some other element. The element of conflict or contradiction between the appearance of the veil, and the reality of the object underneath, when it is evoked at all, appears only as a subsequent rationalisation of an involuntary, even of a subconscious form of innate sensibility. By contrast, whenever Genet discusses his *theory* of beauty, he becomes involved immediately in this violence of contrasts between dynamic opposites: and his symbol becomes that of the Fissure—a symbol which, in the first instance, is only rather indirectly associated with the concept of beauty as such. Admittedly, the concepts suggested by these two symbols are by no means irreconcilable; none the less, in the transition from the Veil to the Fissure, there is a significant shift of emphasis, from which we may perhaps infer, in this as in other fields, that Genet's theories tend to be more rigid and more anarchic than his practice.

The initial definition of beauty, for Genet, is that it belongs to those *'puissances qui sont enveloppées du sacré'*; it is taboo, *'car on ne doit pas toucher à la beauté'*.[107] It is endowed with powers that are supernatural, magical and dangerous (particularly in the case of feminine beauty, which Genet places in a category alone : 'a more terrible defensive weapon than barbed wire')[108]; it is an invitation to transgression, an open doorway leading to death, profanation and the unhallowed proximity of the gods.[109] It can possess its beholder, or excite him to the wild desire to possess; yet it is not *in* him. Whatever beauty may be in its ultimate origin, it is, to Genet, clearly not subjective, despite one stray passage in *Miracle of the Rose* which might appear to suggest the contrary : 'That beauty was in me and not in him.'[110] If, for an instant, Bulkaen's beauty appears to be in Genet, it is essentially because it is *not* in Bulkaen. It is independent—detachable, as it were—a force in the universe that penetrates and destroys its beholders, yet is neither in nor at the command of him who wields it.

But the second characteristic of beauty, for Genet, is that it is *movement* : 'ugliness is *beauty in repose*'. It is change, transformation, transmutation. A single *gesture* (which is movement) is already more satisfying than the most *recherché* of objects—even the sculptures of Michelangelo or of Giacometti, except in so far as these give the illusion of movement—and complex gestures are more satisfying still. Gestures such as that of lighting a cigarette, which occur, with variants, a dozen times at least in every novel. It is through the movements of Genet, who lights his cigarette for him, that the prize thug, Armand, discovers the first intimations, if not exactly of beauty, at least of 'elegance' : 'the elegance [. . . .] of the *manifold* play of attitudes'.[111] All things that Genet experiences as beautiful are in motion, the Sailors, the marching companies of ss men, even Mettray, which turns and turns about its own different centres :

> The Colony, including Divers, rotated about that axis: Harcamone. But it, including Harcamone, also rotated about another axis: Divers. And about Villeroy and many others. Its *centre was everywhere.*[112]

It is certainly this that explains Genet's fascination with acrobats and tightrope-walkers—as in the late essay, *The Funambulists*, for instance. Logically, moreover, the faster the movement, the deeper the impact; and in a sense (in spite of the evident paradox) this is true. Like Proust, Genet is bewitched by a beauty glimpsed so rapidly in an instant of time that it is hardly glimpsed at all— such as a boy seen momentarily from the window of an express train,[113] or an expression which flits across a face and is gone for ever, or a tramping figure held for a split second in the headlights of a car. For, as Genet explains elsewhere, the beauty of many acts is revealed only if our eye has the skill to catch them 'in a flash'. 'For the beauty of a living thing can be grasped only fleetingly.'[114]

From this to the notion that beauty is the product of violence is but a step. This is the principle of beauty that Genet discovers at Mettray, or in Bulkaen, who owes his attraction to his ferocity, his 'savage fury, ancient and Greek'.[115] There is something in this of Théophile Gautier's concept, that the supreme beauty can only emerge from the conflict between the will of the artist and the re-sistance of the material :

> Oui, l'oeuvre sort plus belle
> D'une forme au travail
> Rebelle,
> Vers, marbre, onyx, émail. . . .

—and in fact, in the *Atelier d'Alberto Giacometti*, this aspect of the question will to some extent be developed. In the novels, how-ever, Genet's material is neither onyx nor marble, but that of human, or sub-human, nature. His thugs and criminals are the resistant alabaster; his chisel, cruelty : and from the violent conflict of the two—and not from any gentle rationalism or humane psychological detail—there may emerge the glittering jewel of beauty :

> Novels are not humanitarian reports. Indeed, let us be thankful that there remains sufficient cruelty, without which beauty would not be.[116]

But if beauty is violence and conflict, then the chances are, since violence destroys, that beauty is destruction; and once the prin-ciple is admitted, then the supreme beauty must emerge from des-truction taken to its highest point of intensity—which is the destruc-tion of beauty.[117] Of course, this is the point at which Genet's theory and practice seem most evidently to part company : it is hard to imagine the man himself armed with a torch to spark off the barrels of gunpowder which are destined to blow up the Parthenon, or even aiming satanic blows with a hammer to chip off the tail of Giaco-metti's miraculously lugubrious 'Hound'. [118] None the less, the notion corresponds closely enough with Genet's obsession with the problem of absolute evil; and, more immediately, it reflects his struggles with a very real and practical problem, namely, how to transmute into any form of recognizable art the abominable sequence of miseries which has been his own experience of life. And in effect, the dictum: 'Beauty arises from the destruction of beauty' is the ultimate logical consequence of Théophile Gautier's Parnassian belief that beauty is satisfying only when it is the product of a conflict between the artist's vision and the most obdurately resistant of materials.

And by all standards, Genet's materials are obdurate and ungrateful enough : abjection, poverty, degradation, stupidity, cruelty, ugliness. With the difference from Gautier, that the conflict is never one-sided. The Image-in-the-Mirror, when assaulted, even by an artist, hits back. Beauty is not only the conflict of the artist with ugliness; but ugliness, confronted with beauty, or even with the prospect of beauty, deliberately makes itself more ugly.[119] Thus in the conflict between Mario (ugliness) and Querelle (beauty), the dynamic force of the episode, consequently its artistic power, derives from the fact that the two extremes repel each other, and yet are complementary, neither being capable of self-realization except in terms of the other. Ugliness, in other words, even if it is not the direct source of beauty, is the condition without which beauty cannot exist—just as, in sound theology, the existence of evil is explained as the necessary condition, in the absence of which no good is conceivable, good being the product of a free choice which implies the possibility of choosing the contrary. But also—obviously—the existence of beauty emphasises—particularly when the two are in close proximity—the possibility and the violent temptation of its opposite. Lilac and excrement : each luridly highlights the symbolic significance of the other; and Genet is careful to observe that neither is given preference, for then the dynamic intensity of the contrast would be lost, the beauty frittered away.[120]

Ugliness is a function of beauty; and simultaneously, beauty is a function of ugliness. Between them they comprise a totality, negative and positive, neither conceivable without the other, neither having the right to claim that the other is inferior—a sort of aesthetic Manichaeism. 'Beauty is the projection of ugliness',[121] notes Genet, listening again to the cracked voice of Botchako singing hideous pop songs. The principle that beauty was enhanced by ugliness was, of course, admitted by those Court ladies of the eighteenth century, the perfection of whose skin was set off by the funereal black patches that they calculatingly stuck upon their cheeks. On the whole, though, the Pompadours and the Du Barry's probably hoped that something of their beauty at least would survive, even without its contrast. Not so Genet. ' . . . the speck of ugliness [. . . .] the angle that brought the ugliness into view, the line or volume that destroyed the beauty'[122]—these become the essential components of aesthetic awareness, without which beauty cannot be conceived. Vulgarity is the *sine qua non* of good taste.

At bottom, Genet is—or was, at least until he had partly worked the disease out of his system with the novels—an *aesthete*, the direct spiritual descendent of Oscar Wilde and Aubrey Beardsley : but an aesthete in reverse. As with Wilde, he considers ethics as an insignificant by-product of aesthetics, nature as a pale imitation (or mirror-reflection) of art, the choreography of a gesture more significant than its purpose or achievement. 'The beauty of a moral act depends on the beauty of its expression,' he argues in *The Thief's Journal*; 'To say that it is beautiful is to decide that it will be so'[123] : and later, 'the only criterion of an act is its elegance'.[124] Moreover, that this aestheticism is not merely an ephemeral whim, he demonstrates in the *Journal*, where he argues the case in full against one of his own detractors, Bernardini, and concludes

> The good will of moralists cracks up against my dishonesty. Though they may prove to me that an act is detestable because of the harm it does, only I can decide, and that by the song it evokes within me, as to its beauty and elegance; only I can reject or accept it.[125]

But this argument—attractive as it sounds from a Wildean point of view—is entirely specious. To begin with, as we shall see later, Genet *does* propound a coherent, if unusual, system of ethics in their own right, having little or nothing to do with aesthetics. But there is the further objection, that Wilde's aesthetics are totally different from Genet's. Wilde would refuse to condemn an action on the grounds that it was bad, provided that it was beautiful—but this presupposed the implicit Platonic assumption that what was beautiful must, in the last analysis, be good, virtuous and true, and that what was bad, conversely, must therefore be ugly, spurious and false—even if our unnatural and unlovely industrial civilization had so perverted our acts and judgments that the contrary might *appear* to be true. But Genet, who, in a warped sort of way, contrives also to be a Platonist, none the less makes beauty *inseparable* from ugliness, good taste from vulgarity ('Divine [. . . .] is fond of vulgarity. Divine has sure taste, good taste . . .'[126]), and sanctity from transgression. And included in the concepts : ugliness, vulgarity and transgression are many acts and attitudes that the moralist, or even the Wildean Platonist, would call simply evil. Consequently, the assertion that aesthetic criteria are superior to ethical criteria is by no means so innocent as it sounds. It is not merely the condoning of apparent evil in favour of real beauty; it is the positive assertion that evil in combination with beauty—evil, that is to say, as the dynamic principle without which beauty is inconceivable—is superior to the good, so that art and ethics alike are both confounded irretrievably and lost in a satanic maelstrom of gestures. In a word, Genet's symbolic vision transforms the putrescent degradation of reality into a tapestry of beauty, but only at the expense— or rather, joyfully, with conscious and malicious intention—of creating a beauty whose dynamic principle is evil. It is the temptation of Satan. And every honest *bourgeois* reader who finds a shred of beauty in *Miracle of the Rose* is at the same time implicitly acknowledging the power of evil disguised as beauty.

And so is Genet revenged. *Miracle of the Rose* is a trap, but skilfully disguised with allegories, and with flowers. The good people of the world decreed that the child Genet/Culafroy was a thief, and outlawed him, seemingly for ever. But Culafroy became Divine, and Divine grew into Jean-Genet-the-Writer; and page by page, poem by poem, Genet has fought his way back. Now the good people read Genet; but every line they read, without hurling the book into the fire, is proof (for Genet at least) that *his* evil is stronger than *their* good—and that all the ethics in the world are mere hypocrisy, doomed to crumble and evaporate before the sacred forces of poetry and art.

NOTES

1 *Rose*, pp. 266-9. (*Miracle*, pp. 377-8)
2 *Ibid.*, pp. 39-40. (*Miracle*, p. 214)
3 'Marche Funèbre', in *Poèmes*, p. 45. 'Too often, Chance—the greatest of Chances!—conjured out of my pen, to drop it into the heart of my poems, the Rose, together with that word Death, which the dark warriors whom I love wear embroidered on their white armbands.'
4 'Le Condamné à Mort', in *Poèmes*, p. 20. 'The sky may awaken, the stars burst into blossom, the flowers may sigh; and the black grasses of the meadow welcome the dew where the morning comes to drink; the steeple may ring its bells : I alone am due to die.'
5 Sartre, *Saint G.*, p. 437. 'Ces vers sont plats, ils puent la contrefaçon. Ce pauvre oiseau [cf. *Poèmes*, p. 11] s'est envolé des vers de François Coppée : "Est-ce que les oiseaux se cachent pour mourir?" Non, ils ne se cachent pas; mais les oiseaux de Coppée, quand ils ne se sentent pas bien, s'en vont mourir chez Genet.' (*S.-Genet*, p. 405)
   In a more serious vein, however, Sartre does show the precise sources of Genet's 'inspiration' : Mallarmé, Valéry, Cocteau, Verlaine, Hugo, Baudelaire, Coppée, Sully-Prudhomme '. . . et même Monsieur Prudhomme.' (*S. Genet*, p. 410. (*Saint-G.*, pp. 442-3)
6 *Thief*, p. 181. 'Le raccourci que propose le symbole porté par ce qu'il doit signifier donne et détruit la signification et la chose signifiée.' (*Journal*, p. 215)
7 *Rose*, p. 178. '. . . Tout cela n'était pas des choses banales, comme on en peut rencontrer partout. C'étaient des Signes. [. . . .] A Mettray chaque objet était un signe qui voulait dire douleur.' (*Miracle*, p. 314)

8 *Our Lady*, p. 266. 'Mignon ne souffrira jamais, ou saura toujours se tirer d'une mauvaise passe par son aisance à endosser sur soi les gestes d'un type admiré qui se trouve dans cette même situation. . . .' (*Notre-Dame*, p. 141)

9 *Ibid.*, p. 149. '. . . les gestes de je ne sais quel joli gosse d'un magazine.' (*Notre-Dame*, p. 65)

10 Artaud, A. *Le Théâtre et son Double: Oeuvres Complètes*, Paris (Gallimard) 1964, vol. IV, p. 94.

11 Omitted in the English translation. (*Querelle*, p. 263)

12 *Q. of B.*, p. 106. 'Querelle disait à ses camarades qu'il était une victime des affiches! Je suis victime des affiches et victime de la victime des affiches.' (*Querelle*, p. 232)

13 *Pompes Funèbres*, p. 23.

14 *Q. of B.*, pp. 195-196. 'Dans sa prison, chacun de ces bruits déclenchait en lui l'image mille fois plus émouvante de ces choses. Si la mer est naturellement le symbole de la liberté, chaque image l'évoquant se charge de cette puissance symbolique, se charge à soi seule de toute la puissance symbolique de la mer; et dans l'âme du captif, chaque image, en apparaissant, cause une blessure d'autant plus douloureuse que l'image était banale. Il serait naturel qu'à la conscience de l'enfant, l'apparition spontanée d'un paquebot tout entier, voguant en pleine mer, provoquât une crise de désespoir, mais ici le paquebot et la mer prenaient possession de cette conscience avec difficulté : c'était d'abord le bruit caractéristique d'une chaîne (se peut-il que le grincement d'une chaîne déclenche l'appareil du désespoir? Une simple chaîne, dont l'intérieur des maillons est rouillé?). Gil faisait (sans qu'il s'en doutât) l'apprentissage douloureux de la poésie. L'image de la chaîne déchirait une fibre et la déchirure s'aggravait jusqu'à permettre un passage au navire, à la mer, au monde, jusqu'à finalement détruire Gil qui se retrouvait hors de soi-même, et n'ayant plus d'existence possible dans ce monde qui venait de le poignarder, de le traverser, de l'anéantir.' (*Querelle*, p. 284)

15 *Rose*, p. 11. 'La Centrale vivait comme une cathédrale un minuit de Noël. Nous continuions la tradition des moines s'activant la nuit, en silence. Nous appartenions au Moyen Âge.' (*Miracle*, p. 194)

16 *Pompes Funèbres*, p. 15.

17 *Rose*, p. 135. 'Mais il se passait ceci d'étonnant, c'est qu'à mesure qu'il m'en parlait, l'image que je gardais de mon marle, au lieu de se préciser, s'atténuait.' (*Miracle*, p. 283)

18 *Ibid.*, p. 110. 'Une redescente au fond du temps. [. . . .] Je retrouve, auprès de Divers regagné, une enfance nauséeuse et magnifiée par l'horreur, que je n'eusse jamais voulu quitter.' (*Miracle*, p. 264)

19 *Pompes Funèbres*, p. 17.

20 *Rose*, p. 53. '. . . une vie morte.' (*Miracle*, p. 223)

21 *Ibid.*, p. 96. '. . . les douceurs désespérantes d'être hors du monde avant sa mort.' (*Miracle*, p. 254)

22 *Ibid.*, pp. 209-211. '. . . supra-terrestre [. . . .] un état qu'on peut dire féerique [. . . .] une nouvelle manière d'être.' (*Miracle*, pp. 336-8)

23 *Ibid.*, p. 213. 'Il survolait ce monde.' (*Miracle*, p. 339)

24 *Ibid.*, p. 5. (*Miracle*, p. 189)

25 *Ibid.*, p. 34. (*Miracle*, p. 210): 'anciennes puissances'.

26 *Ibid.*, p. 31. 'Dévêtue de ses ornements sacrés, je vois nue la prison, et sa nudité est cruelle.' (*Miracle*, p. 208)

27 *Ibid.*, p. 31. '. . . inégalable bêtise.' (*Miracle*, p. 208)

28 *Ibid.*, p. 92. '. . . l'expression parfaite de ma vérité.' (*Miracle*, p. 252)

29 Sartre, *Saint G.*, p. 393. (*S. Genet*, p. 365)

30 *Pompes Funèbres*, pp. 56-7, 77-8, 103; *Q. of B.*, p. 50. (*Querelle*, p. 197)

31 'Vous n'aimez pas les animaux?' 'Je n'aime pas les gens qui aiment les animaux.' Reported by Simone de Beauvoir, *La Force de l'Âge*, Paris (Gallimard) 1960, pp. 155-156.

32 *Our Lady*, pp. 231-4. 'La randonnée de la rue Lepic.' (*Notre-Dame*, pp. 119-121)

33 *Thief*, pp. 67-70. (*Journal*, pp. 81-3)

34 Even in the *Journal*, Genet rarely makes us conscious of the physical misery of his early life; he is much more concerned with its moral degradation. For comparison, it is interesting to read Orwell's *Down and Out in London and Paris*; or, more especially, Christopher Jackson's *Manuel* (London, Cape, 1965). The parallels between the Chilean adolescent criminal, Manuel Garcès, and Genet as he appears in the *Miracle*, are remarkable. Another writer with first-hand experience of reform-school and prison life is Albertine Sarrazin; however, the various prisons of *La Cavale* (Paris, Pauvert, 1966) appear as havens of comfort compared with those depicted by Genet. For a description of the interior of Fresnes or Fontevrault under the Nazis, see B. Marshall's *The White Rabbit*.

35 *Our Lady*, pp. 74-5. '. . . un appartement somptueux, chargé d'ors, les murs tendus de velours grenat, les meubles de style alourdis, assourdis de faille rouge. . . .' (*Notre-Dame*, p. 18)

36 *Thief*, pp. 42-3. 'Je pénétrais moins dans un pays qu'à l'intérieur d'une image.' (*Journal*, p. 51)

37 *Rose*, p. 101. (*Miracle*, p. 258)

38 *Ibid.*, pp. 56, 126. (*Miracle*, pp. 225-6, 276)

39 *Ibid.*, pp. 126, 157-8. (*Miracle*, pp. 276, 299)

40 *Pompes Funèbres*, pp. 25 *et seq.*

41 *Thief*, pp. 117-8. '. . . caractère de tristesse et de poésie maritime et crapuleuse.' (*Journal*, p, 139)

42 *Rose*, p. 56. (*Miracle*, pp. 225-6)

43 *Pompes Funèbres*, p. 106.

44 *Our Lady*, p. 261. '. . . de ses narines il arracha des pétales d'acacia et des violettes.' (*Notre-Dame*, p. 138)

45 *Rose*, p. 176. (*Miracle*, p. 312)

46 *Ibid.*, p. 115. 'Nous étions victimes d'un feuillage en apparence inoffensif mais qui, en face du moins osé de nos gestes, pouvait devenir un feuillage électrisé.' (*Miracle*, pp. 268-9)

47 *Ibid.*, p. 56. (*Miracle*, p. 226); *Thief*, p. 212. (*Journal*, p. 252)

48 *Q. of B.*, p. 47. (*Querelle*, p. 195)

49 *Our Lady*, p. 170. (*Notre-Dame*, p. 79)

50 *Thief*, p. 7. '*Il existe donc un étroit rapport entre les fleurs et les bagnards. La fragilité, la délicatesse des premières sont de même nature que la brutale insensibilité des autres.*' (*Journal*, p. 9)

51 *Our Lady*, p. 68. (*Notre-Dame*, p. 13); see also pp. 202-3, 228. (pp. 100, 117)

52 *Rose*, p. 104. (*Miracle*, p. 260)

53 *Ibid.*, p. 22. (*Miracle*, p. 201)

54 In Genet's later works, particularly in his plays, his names change character, becoming less mystic-poetic, more intellectual. Thus Diop

(*The Blacks*) suggests the double-vision of Descartes' *La Dioptrique*; Diouf, the combination 'Dieu' + 'Ouf !'

55 *Thief*, p. 38. 'Je suis seul au monde, et je ne suis pas sûr de n'être pas le roi—peut-être la fée—de ces fleurs.' (*Journal*, p. 46)

56 *Ibid.*, p. 39. 'Je peux sans pitié considérer toutes les fleurs, elles sont de ma famille.' (*Journal*, p. 47)

57 *Rose*, p. 136. '. . . le Sèvres dont était fait ce garçon.' (*Miracle*, p. 283)

58 *Our Lady*, p. 65. '. . . macs et apaches avec un mégot qui fume.' (*Notre-Dame*, p. 11)

59 *Q. of B.*, p. 309. '. . . plus douce et embaumée que les pétales de roses de Saadi.' (*Querelle*, p. 344)

60 Omitted in the English version. (*Querelle*, p. 259)

61 *Rose*, p. 209. 'La rose veut dire l'amitié, la mort . . . et le silence !' (*Miracle*, p. 336)

62 *Ibid.*, p. 55. (*Miracle*, p. 225)

63 *Ibid.*, p. 282. (*Miracle*, p. 388)

64 *Ibid.*, p. 285-6. '. . . une porte s'ouvrit d'elle-même, et nous nous trouvâmes en face d'une rose rouge, monstrueuse de taille et de beauté.
—La Rose Mystique, murmura l'aumônier.
Les quatre hommes furent atterrés par la splendeur. [. . . .] L'ivresse de la profanation les tenait. Ils arrivèrent les tempes battantes, la sueur au front, au coeur de la rose : c'était une sorte de puits ténébreux. Tout au bord de ce trou noir et profond comme un oeil, ils se penchèrent et l'on ne sait quel vertige les prit. Ils firent tous les quatre les gestes de gens qui perdent l'équilibre, et ils tombèrent dans ce regard profond.' (*Miracle*, p. 391)

65 *Balcony*, p. 37.
'*Carmen:* . . . Mon voile bleu, ma robe bleue, mon tablier bleu, mon oeil bleu. . . .
Irma: Tabac !
Carmen: Bleu, ce jour-là. . . .' (*Balcon*, pp. 80-1)

66 *Rose*, p. 83. (*Miracle*, p. 246)

67 *Thief*, p. 108. 'Trouver l'accord de ce qui est de mauvais goût, voilà le comble de l'élégance.' (*Journal*, p. 127)

68 *Rose*, pp. 83-84. (*Miracle*, p. 246)

69 *Screens*, p. 144. (*Paravents*, p. 211)

70 *Rose*, pp. 80-1. 'Mais voyez comme je parle de cette galère où, pouvant être le maître, je ne m'accordais que le poste le plus infime : celui du mousse.' (*Miracle*, pp. 243-4)

71 *Screens*, pp. 15, 27, 32, 36, 98, etc. (*Paravents*, pp. 19, 37, 44, 51, 147)

72 *Thief*, p. 69. '. . . j'allais découvrir sous trois palmiers cette crèche de Noël où je venais, enfant, assister à *ma nativité* entre le boeuf et l'âne. J'étais le pauvre du monde le plus humble, misérable je marchais dans la poussière et la fatigue, méritant enfin la palme, mûr pour le bagne, pour les chapeaux de paille et les palmiers'. (*Journal*, p. 82)

73 *Rose*, p. 165. (*Miracle*, p. 305)

74 *Ibid.*, pp. 132-3. 'Cette voix douloureuse, voilà encore une faille par où s'échappe de sa dureté sa tendresse profonde.' (*Miracle*, p. 281)

75 *Ibid.*, p. 85. 'En Divers enfin, il y avait cette fêlure, qui était voulue par l'architecte, comme fut voulue la brèche pathétique du Colisée qui fait qu'un éclair éternal fulgure sur sa masse.' (*Miracle*, p. 247)

76 *Pompes Funèbres*, p. 152.

77 Stendhal, *Histoire de la Peinture en Italie*, ed. Champion, Paris 1924, vol. 1, p. 136. '. . . un voile léger [. . . .] qui est d'or chez Paul Véronèse; chez le Guide il est comme d'argent; il est cendré chez le Pésarèse.'

78 *Ibid.*, p. 152. 'C'est cette partie de la peinture qui attache les imaginations tendres. [. . . .] Par là elle se rapproche de la musique, elle engage l'imagination à finir ses tableaux. [. . . .] C'est des objets dont les détails sont à moitié *cachés par l'air* que nous nous souvenons avec le plus de charme; ils ont pris dans notre pensée une teinte céleste. . . .'

79 *Our Lady*, p. 72. '. . . est autre chose qu'une mélodie de courbes sur des douceurs, car le tulle se cassait en facettes abruptes, nettes, rigoureuses, glaciales.' (*Notre-Dame*, p. 16)

80 *Rose*, pp. 137-8. (*Miracle*, pp. 284-5)

81 *Ibid.*, p. 224. '. . . le grand chapeau de paille sur la gueule rasée des forçats.' (*Miracle*, p. 347)

82 *Ibid.*, 251. (*Miracle*, p. 366)

83 *Thief*, p. 8. (*Journal*, p. 11)

84 *Ibid.*, p. 122. (*Journal*, p. 144)

85 *Pompes Funèbres*, p. 68.

86 *Q. of B.*, p. 9. See also p. 126. (*Querelle*, pp. 174, 245)

87 *Pompes Funèbres*, p. 68.

88 *Thief*, p. 72. '. . . cette indécision faisant au récit rendre un son historique, l'embellissait encore.' (*Journal*, p. 85)

89 *Rose*, p. 62. (*Miracle*, p. 230)

90 *Our Lady*, p. 281. '. . . étaient plus frissonnants qu'une charmille de glycine, que le rideau de dentelle d'un berceau.' (*Notre-Dame*, p. 281)

91 *Q. of B.*, p. 151. '. . . parce que cette couleur rend plus frivoles les dessous—en leur conférant une certaine gravité.' (*Querelle*, p. 287)

92 *Our Lady*, p. 70. '. . . avait des doigts de dentelle.' (*Notre-Dame*, p. 15)

93 *Rose*, p. 45. '. . . mille aventures imaginaires [. . . .] lui conféraient un organisme et un squelette de dentelle.' (*Miracle*, p. 218)

94 *Thief*, pp. 197-8. (*Journal*, pp. 235-6)

95 *Ibid.*, pp. 163-4. (*Journal*, pp. 194-5)

96 *Q. of B.*, pp. 105-6. (*Querelle*, p. 232)

97 *Rose*, p. 235. '. . . la dentelle bleue des tatouages.' (*Miracle*, p. 354)

98 See Bataille, G.: *Eroticism* (tr. Dalwood), photo facing p. 256.

99 *Our Lady*, pp. 223-4. (*Notre-Dame*, pp. 113-4)

100 *Ibid.*, p. 77. (*Notre-Dame*, p. 19)

101 *Pompes Funèbres*, p. 127.

102 *Q. of B.*, p. 240. '. . . longs et larges voiles noirs'. (*Querelle*, pp. 311-2)

103 *Pompes Funèbres*, p. 15.

104 *Q. of B.*, p. 100. '. . . la puissance mystérieuse d'un faune, d'une idole, d'un volcan, d'un archipel mélanésien. Il était lui-même et il ne l'était plus.' (*Querelle*, p. 228)

105 *Ibid.*, p. 101. (*Querelle*, p. 229)

106 *Ibid.*, p. 102. (*Querelle*, p. 230)

107 *Pompes Funèbres*, p. 54.

108 *Q. of B.*, p. 202. '. . . un rempart plus terrible que les barbelés.' (*Querelle*, p. 288)

109 *Pompes Funèbres*, p. 85.

110 *Rose*, p. 157. 'Cette beauté était en moi, et non en lui.' (*Miracle*, p. 299)

111 *Thief*, p. 198. '. . . l'élégance [. . . .] du jeu *nombreux* des attitudes.'
   (*Journal*, p. 236)
112 *Rose*, p. 166. 'La Colonie, dont Divers, tournait autour de cet axe:
   Harcamone. Mais elle, dont Harcamone, tournait autour de cet axe:
   Divers. Puis autour de Villeroy et de beaucoup d'autres. Son *centre*
   était partout.' (*Miracle*, p. 305)
113 *Pompes Funèbres*, pp. 66-67. *Cf.* Proust and the girl glimpsed from the
   train on the way to Balbec.
114 *Rose*, pp. 10-11. 'Car la beauté de la chose vivante ne peut être saisie
   que lors d'un instant très bref.' (*Miracle*, p. 193)
115 *Ibid.*, p. 82. '. . . sa fureur sauvage, antique et grecque.' (*Miracle*,
   p. 244)
116 *Ibid.*, p. 208. 'Les romans ne sont pas des rapports humanitaires.
   Félicitons-nous, au contraire, qu'il reste assez de cruauté, sans quoi
   la beauté ne serait pas.' (*Miracle*, p. 336)
117 *Ibid.*, p. 106. (*Miracle*, p. 262)
118 See *Giacometti*, p. 55 (bottom plate).
119 *Q. of B.*, p. 220. '. . . afin de ne pas être obligé de se mépriser.' (*Querelle*,
   p. 299)
120 *Our Lady*, p. 96. (*Notre-Dame*, pp. 31-2)
121 *Rose*, p. 21. 'La beauté est la projection de la laideur.' (*Miracle*, p. 200)
122 *Ibid.*, p. 201. 'Le point de laideur, l'angle suffisant pour indiquer la
   laideur, la ligne ou le volume détruisant la beauté.' (*Miracle*, p. 330)
123 *Thief*, p. 18. 'De la beauté de son expression dépend la beauté d'un
   acte moral. [. . . .] Dire qu'il est beau décide déjà qu'il le sera.'
   (*Journal*, p. 23)
124 *Ibid.*, p. 216. 'L'élégance est le seul critère d'un acte.' (*Journal*, p. 257)
125 *Ibid.*, p. 172. 'La bonne volonté des moralistes se brise contre ce qu'ils
   appellent ma mauvaise foi. S'ils peuvent me prouver qu'un acte est
   détestable par le mal qu'il fait, moi seul puis décider, par le chant
   qu'il soulève en moi, de sa beauté, de son élégance: moi seul puis
   le refuser ou l'accepter.' (*Journal*, p. 204)
126 *Our Lady*, p. 84. 'Divine [. . . .] aime la vulgarité. Divine a le goût sûr,
   goût bon. . . .' (*Notre-Dame*, p. 24). See also, *Rose*, p. 109. (*Miracle*,
   p. 264); *Q. of B.*, p. 32; (*Querelle*, p. 186); *Thief*, p. 61. (*Journal*,
   p. 73); etc.

4

THE GOLDEN LEGEND OF A PROFESSIONAL
BURGLAR

(The Thief's Journal)

Both *Our Lady of the Flowers* and *Miracle of the Rose* are to some
degree autobiographical; they represent an intrinsic stage in Genet's
own personal struggle with himself. Seeing himself as the scapegoat
and victim of the massed forces of a whole society, feeling the hand
of an ineluctable fatality against him from the instant of his conception, Genet had no strength of will or purpose in him to enable
him to rise above the circumstances and conquer them. Many great
men have suffered from the disadvantage of an illegitimate birth—
Erasmus, Leonardo da Vinci, D'Alembert, Alexander Herzen, to
name the first that spring to mind—and have triumphed in the end.
So also has Genet : but by a method directly opposed to that which
rises above difficulties and surmounts them. Genet chose rather a
total acceptance, a complete passivity, resigning himself without a
struggle to the worst that Destiny could offer, and identifying himself consciously with the uttermost limits of degradation. Morally
reprehensible, of course, from the Baden-Powell point of view; yet
paradoxically having some affinities with those Cornelian heroes—
Don Rodrigue, Polyeucte—who, finding themselves in an intolerable
situation as the direct consequence of the working of God's purpose,
achieve their resolution by *willing* to accept their own destruction—
that is, by identifying themselves with the Purpose that has decreed

their own annihilation. The condition, however, for redemption achieved in this way is that the final acceptance should be rational and above all lucid. Don Rodrigue *knows* that, by challenging and killing Don Gomès, Chimène's father, he is destroying all that he holds dear; yet he accepts his duty in the full light of this awareness, and makes the higher Will his own without an instant of self-deception.

How far Genet's downward course into crime and degradation was the product of a similar lucidity, it is impossible to decide. Writing many years after the fatal turning-point had been reached and the direction chosen, Genet himself maintains that the choice was calculated and deliberate :

> The mechanism was somewhat as follows (I have used it since): to every charge brought against me, unjust though it be, from the bottom of my heart I shall answer yes. Hardly had I uttered the word—or the phrase signifying it—than I felt within me the need to become what I had been accused of being.[1]

—and Sartre, in search of a living example to illustrate his philosophy of *authentic* freedom and responsibility, accepts Genet's claim without over-much hesitation. But if, as seems probable, this crisis arrived when Genet was scarcely fifteen or sixteen, and perhaps even a few years earlier, such an extraordinary gift of existentialist lucidity seems a bit improbable. Rather we may suppose that Genet's decision not to resist his own innate tendencies, but rather to follow them as fast and as far as possible, was the result of some scarcely-formulable but violent emotional revolt in the child's mind; and that the lucidity which was essential to give significance to events and to transform a very commonplace criminal into a hero-martyr of metaphysical Destiny, came considerably later. In fact, the precise function of *Our Lady of the Flowers* and of *Miracle of the Rose* seems to have been to realise this lucidity : to enable Genet, by writing about himself directly (as 'I') and at the same time indirectly (as Divine, or Culafroy, or Bulkaen) to identify himself consciously with his own existence, yet together with this to detach himself from it, to look at it objectively from the outside, and thus to establish his own individuality as something independent of, and greater than, that which Destiny had made him.

After 1944, however, the intense subjectivity which marks the poems and the first two novels begins gradually to disappear. *Pompes Funèbres* is still written in the first person; yet the 'I' is no longer the central figure, and its role is largely confined to that of stage-manager, with occasional comments in the manner of a Greek chorus; while in *Querelle of Brest* this same 'I' had disappeared almost completely, so that the road is open for a new, and now almost purely objective form of art in the dramas. In about 1947, however, just before this final, triumphant attainment of objectivity, Genet seems to have halted for one last glance at his own past, in *The Thief's Journal*; and so it is perhaps desirable to consider this fragmentary autobiography here, even if it disrupts the chronological order, so as to have an overall picture of Genet's life as it appeared to him in the lucidity of retrospect, and to try and establish some sort of relationship between his experience and the art which resulted from it. For if *Our Lady* covers the essential period of his childhood, and *Miracle of the Rose* his adolescence, the *Journal* fills in the gap of his early manhood, that is, the period which runs approximately from 1932 to 1939.

The difficulty is, of course, that Genet's retrospective lucidity, whose function is to discover a transcendental purpose in a heterogeneous collection of gratuitous and largely discreditable actions, tends to adjust the facts to suit the general picture, much as Bossuet treated universal history in order to make it illustrate an *a priori* thesis. To reorganise personal experience is the poet's undeniable right, and Genet can certainly never be accused of making himself out to have been better than he was; but this poetic licence undoubtedly makes things very difficult for the biographer. Mettray no longer exists; prison authorities are understandably reluctant to allow literary critics to pry into their more recent records; and burglars tend to leave regrettably few historical traces of their sojourn upon earth. Largely, therefore, we are forced to accept what Genet has written about himself—and we have ample warning that this *may* in many cases be pure invention. To take one small, unimportant, but very revealing instance. In *Miracle of the Rose*, Genet describes how he came to write his first poem at the instance of Bulkaen : 'He asked me to write a few lines of verse about a subject which he gave me . . .'[2] and the description of the scene, which takes place at Fontevrault, is followed immediately by a reference to '*Le Condamné à Mort*'. But in conversation with Sartre, Genet also described how he came to write his first poem, now specifically designated as '*Le Condamné à Mort*'—in totally different circumstances :

> I was pushed into a cell where there were already a number of prisoners in civvies (so long as one is only on detention, one is allowed to hang on to one's two-piece suit). As far as I was concerned, although I had put up an appeal, I had been required, by mistake, to put on convict uniform. This unexpected garb seemed an evil omen; I was treated with contempt; and later I had a hard job to get back into the swim. Now, among them, there was a prisoner who used to write poems to his sister— idiotic, whining things that everybody admired immensely. Finally, in exasperation, I declared that *I* could write stuff like that as well. They

challenged me to prove it, and so I wrote *Le Condamné à Mort*; I read it to them one day, and their contempt for me only increased; I finished the reading in a storm of jeers and insults, and one of the prisoners said to me: 'Poems like that, I toss one off every morning'. When I was released, I made a particular point of finishing off this poem, which was the more dear to me as it had been the more insulted.[3]

It is not *absolutely* clear that the two episodes refer to the same first poem, but at least there is a very strong element of confusion. The difficulty is that *both* versions of the event fit admirably with the pattern of significance that is Genet's life as he sees it in retrospect: both, in fact, constitute admirably dramatic settings—the sort of settings in which a first poem which is the beginning of a long road to redemption *should* have been written. So there is no more guarantee of accuracy in the version given verbally to Sartre than there is in the episode written down in *Miracle of the Rose*. This caution must be borne in mind whenever we come across what looks at first sight like a clue to the sources of Genet's creative imagination. In *Querelle of Brest*, for instance, Gil Turko murders Théo in a café in the rue du Sac. In *The Thief's Journal*, Genet notes that, in Antwerp, 'I lived on the Rue du Sac, near the Docks.'[4] Is one version more factual, or less fictitious, than the other? There is no reason why it should be. *The Thief's Journal* is a superb novel; it may also be an accurate autobiography, but it may just as well be the autobiography of a dream. We can only say that Genet *seems* to have told us something of the story of his life.

Born on 19th December 1910, in a public maternity ward, 22 rue d'Assas, Paris VIe. Promptly abandoned by his mother, a prostitute. Adopted by the State *(L'Assistance Publique)* and sent to foster-parents in the country. Early memories of farm and village life in the Morvan, of woods and fields: *'Le "champ d'honneur" est un long et large terrain vague, derrière l'habitation de mes parents adoptifs.'*[5] Intense insecurity born of a feeling of being unwanted and of not belonging, leading to childish outbreaks of thieving. Crisis: the child Genet caught red-handed and branded a thief by the whole village. The crude psychology behind this attempt to shame the child out of his bad habits misfires: Genet continues thieving, but more systematically now, becomes a hardened delinquent, is sent to the open-prison reform-school at Mettray, probably at about the age of fifteen or sixteen. Stays there some while, escapes, wanders about France, living by begging and petty larceny. (At some point, either immediately before, or immediately after Mettray, he appears to have been adopted by a popular *chansonnier*, who gave him his first notions of writing verse; but after a few weeks he robbed his host and disappeared again.[6]) Volunteers for a five-year term in

the army, deserts after a few days, 'taking with me some valises belonging to negro officers'.[7] As a deserter, finds France distinctly uncomfortable, crosses the border into Spain, joins the throng of
destitute riff-raff in the Barrio Chino district of Barcelona. Lives for
a while by theft, but finds that prostitution 'was better suited to
my indolence'.[8] Then begins a sort of parody of the eighteenth-
century gentleman's Grand Tour of Europe : not from palazzo to
palazzo, but from prison to prison. Cadiz. Huelva, Xerès, Alicante.
'All Andalusia'—in the summer of 1934, if the dating is to be trusted.
Gibraltar. Italy (arrested). Rome, Naples and Brindisi. Albania
(cattle-stealing?). Santi-Quaranta. Corfù. Serbia, Austria, Czecho-
slovakia (expelled by police). Poland, ('where I tried to circulate
counterfeit zlotys'), Brno, Slovenia. Hitler's Germany, where,
characteristically, he felt so out of place and ashamed among an
entire nation with the same anti-social leanings as himself that he
left in a fit of disgusted embarrassment, to finish up in Antwerp,
which seems to have been his centre of operations during much of
the period shortly before the war. But he records also spells of prison
in Palermo and Souchak, and he claims to have been at Saint-
Brieuc in 1939, when Maurice Pilorge was guillotined.

The many occasions when he was arrested abroad were essentially without consequence. Genet had no love for France; yet his
poet's fascination with his own native language[9] drew him back
there constantly, at great risk to himself. Arrest in France was a
different matter altogether, not only emotionally,[10] but also legally.
French law decrees that an offender convicted more than a certain
number of times for the same felony may be incarcerated for life
by way of preventive detention : the system referred to in *Miracle
of the Rose* as *la Relègue*. Exactly where and on what occasions
Genet was arrested is not known; but, by 1943, he was already
threatened with *la Relègue*.

From 1942 onwards, however, he had begun to write, originally
on paper supplied for making bags in the prison-workshops. (On one
occasion, a warder discovered hidden in his cell the entire manu-
script of *Our Lady*, confiscated it and burnt it; Genet simply began
all over again.) Gradually his talent began to be noticed—originally,
perhaps, by Olga Barbezat, who used to do prison-visiting. Olga
Barbezat's husband ran a small press, and from time to time brought
out numbers of an esoteric literary review, *L'Arbalète*—which,
incidentally, was also to publish the original version of Sartre's *No
Exit (Huis Clos)*, under the title *Les Autres* (1944)—and in it he
published Genet's first poems, and the opening sections of *Our Lady*.
Cocteau became enthusiastic, and began to refer to Genet as 'the
greatest writer of our time'; and it was through Cocteau that his

name first came to the ears of Sartre and Simone de Beauvoir.[11] In July 1943, Genet was up before the Courts again, and Cocteau wrote directly to the *Président* of the *19e Chambre Correctionnelle,* in an attempt to stave off the dreaded sentence of preventive detention—apparently successfully, for we find Genet out of prison again in 1944, and breaking rather abruptly in on a gathering that included Sartre, Camus and Simone de Beauvoir at the Café de Flore. During the hectic days of the Liberation of Paris (there are traces of them in *Pompes Funèbres*) Genet was still at liberty, and we hear of him dining with Sartre, Simone de Beauvoir and Michel Leiris while a stray German plane returned to drop nuisance-bombs on the streets of Paris[12]; but soon, despite the publication *in toto* of *Our Lady of the Flowers, Miracle of the Rose* and *Pompes Funèbres* and his rapidly-growing reputation among men of letters, the call of his old trade proved too strong; particularly as by now he had made some interesting and wealthy acquaintances among the bourgeois intelligentsia, whose flats might well be worth a clandestine visit. This time there was no escape : *la condamnation à la Relègue perpétuelle* was pronounced, and Jean Genet was in prison for life. At this point there occurred an event of the type which causes some to shudder at France as the eternal hotbed of Jacobinism and anarchy, others to revere her as the mother of the arts. In 1947, a group of famous writers, led by Sartre himself, Cocteau, Mauriac and Mondor, addressed an appeal to Monsieur Vincent Auriol, then President of the Republic, that Genet should be pardoned on account of his outstanding talents. Monsieur Auriol listened, was persuaded, signed the free pardon—and invited Genet to dinner at the Palais des Champs-Elysées.[13]

From that moment onwards, although with some waverings of purpose, Genet appears to have 'gone straight'. Certainly his growing fame, and the income that began to go with it, must have helped, as did also, apparently, the influence of a new lover, whom he refers to as Lucien Sénémaud—*Le Pêcheur du Suquet*—and who, for once, was not from the criminal underworld.[14] Even so, the change was not made without some regret :

> The more I love Lucien, the more I lose my taste for theft and thieves [....] but a great sadness crushes me [....] it is regret for my Legend [....] How much more intoxicating to the point of dizziness, falling and vomiting, would be the love I bear him, if Lucien were a thief and a traitor.[15]

In any case, it is with Lucien that *The Thief's Journal* comes to an end; and, whether or not it is due to the influence of the young fisherman, Genet's subsequent career belongs to the calm records of literary biography, and not to the black and fabulous pages of the State Penitentiaries.

'Regret for my Legend. . . .' Jean Genet's 'legend' is created essentially for himself, only incidentally for others. It is a stylised version of his life, in which the substructure of fact is deeply and perhaps irretrievably buried beneath a garishly-coloured surface of symbolism and interpretation.[16] So there can be no question, as yet, of a biography of Jean Genet; he has given us the legend, and it is with this that we are necessarily concerned, since the legend is his vision of himself.

The essence of the Legend—and it is this belief which makes it possible for him to stand apart and look at his own life with something like detachment—is that he is already dead : or better, perhaps, in Beckett's phrase, 'never been properly born'.[17] His reminiscences of a vanished world are, in a much more precise sense than Chateaubriand's, a kind of *Mémoires d'Outre-Tombe*. He was never properly born because his mother never wanted him; and from the image of this woman who rejected him and thus robbed him of life springs his vision of all women as nauseating, filthy, evil-smelling creatures, almost the only element in Divine's degraded life that 'she' finds unspeakably repulsive :

> She would have been mortified at seeing herself mistaken for those horrible titty females. 'Oh! those women,' she would say, 'those wicked, wicked things, those sailors' tarts, those tramps, those dirty nasties. Oh! those women, how I hate them!'[18]

Alternatively, if women are not simply the symbol of a grotesque and stinking impurity, they are portrayed as unfeeling, false and and egotistical (Madame of *Pompes Funèbres*, or of *The Maids*), or else as hags, or fools—at all events, as vermin to be exterminated. In Antwerp, Genet observes with pleasure how Stilitano maltreats his mistress Sylvie : 'I still respect him, for [. . . .] he was never gentle with his girl.'[19] In the later novels and in the plays, beginning perhaps with the almost touching portrait of 'the little skivvy' in *Pompes Funèbres*, Genet's merciless condemnation relaxes slightly, and he discovers in the character of the Prostitute—in *The Balcony*, for instance, or in *The Screens*, or in the *Atelier d'Alberto Giacometti*—a prototype of woman who, because she is sterile—'*mes grandes, mes longues stériles*', says Madame Irma of her 'girls'[20]—is debarred from motherhood and cannot therefore betray life as Genet had had his life betrayed. But in the *Journal*, the only form in which

Genet can bear to imagine his mother is as a creature even more decrepit and degraded than himself.[21]

The real moment of death, however, comes for Genet when, in the eyes and words of others, he becomes a thief. At that instant, the being that he had been, the child, unconscious of its individuality, yet the more alive and individual by the very fact of this unconsciousness, died and was replaced by an artificial being, 'made of others' words' : aware of itself, yet aware that it can *only* know itself as others see it, never as it is. For in fact, it is-not; it is dead. So Genet's life-story is in fact a death-story; every movement he makes or remembers making is—once again—a gesture; it is the flourish of a galvanized corpse. The dead who live in his memory and mind are more alive than he himself who remembers them.[22] The wretched 'Carolines' of Barcelona—the prototypes of Divine and Mimosa II—are dead even as Divine herself is dead : nothing but shadows : 'They were all dead. What we saw walking in the street were Shades cut off from the world.'[23] Harcamone in his condemned cell lives out his dead life to infinity[24]; but imprisonment for life—the dreaded *Relègue*—is no less a state of being dead-alive—and this state, Genet has known, has heard the words actually spoken to him by the President of the Tribunal. Yet for Genet, it was not a first, but already a third death-sentence; and when the words came at last, they seemed to have been there from time immemorial, from the beginning; they existed already, waiting for him, while he lay still in his unknown mother's womb.

The heart of the Legend, then, is that Genet is dead : killed by a traumatic experience in childhood, just as the original Marcel Proust was killed by his mother, the night that she refused him her customary kiss, and replaced by another being, identical in appearance, yet soul-less, devoid of essence, a mere mirror-reflection of himself. On the other hand, though, '*la mort est sacrée. Tout ce qu'elle a touché, fût-ce du bout de l'aile, est tabou*'[25]; and so Genet is hedged about with all the defences of the walking corpse—untouchable, ghostly-transparent, miraculous, stalking blindly through a nightmare towards defilement and sanctity. But firstly through defilement. And so it is the catalogue of Genet's humiliations and degradations that forms the bulk of the *Journal*, even more than of *Our Lady* or of *Miracle of the Rose*—for these are the raw materials of which the Legend will be woven.

In the Legend, if not in life, the essential characteristic of Genet's plunge into abjection is that it is deliberate : to be effective as a means of salvation, degradation must be absolute, and it must be willed. It would be wrong to think of Genet merging naturally with the background of the underworld : to begin with, he was far too intelligent to be acceptable to the average thug or pimp, who immediately felt suspicious of a being apparently part and parcel of his world, yet at every turn revealing a critical mental liveliness that passed his understanding. On top of which, Genet's homosexuality cut him off from a large part even of that criminal world which he had chosen; on his lips, the rough, self-consciously virile *argot* of the bars of the boulevard de Clichy or the rue Godot de Mauroy not only sounded strange, but was actively offensive to the monarchs and tyrants of that society. Typically when Mimosa, in a courageous moment of would-be masculinity, risks the phrase 'his screwy stories', she is rudely interrupted and called to order, for 'The queens on high had their own special language. Slang was for men. It was the male tongue.'[26]

In a sense, Genet was as much an outsider, an *hors-la-loi*, in the company of Armand or Seck Gorgui as among the right-thinking bourgeoisie who had exiled him in the first place. But this very solitude—like that of the unwashed and thoroughly unhygienic hermit in his 'azure desert'—is one of the primary elements of sanctity. To perfect it, Genet must be at once different from his companions, and *more* abject, *more* degraded than they. Normally, if they are destitute, it is against their will, and they are ashamed of it; only with the extremest forms of degradation does the shame begin to disappear. The Absolute begins only on the other side of despair—of that unspeakable despair which is exemplified by the beggars of Barcelona.[27]

Only the ultimate forms of degradation, in fact, have any real significance for Genet. His ascetic temperament violently rejects any possible compromise with well-being. 'I lacked taste for earthly happiness',[28] he comments in a revealing aside in the *Journal*; what tempted and fascinated him was to search out, by a supreme effort of will, those occasions for shame and humiliation against which his very body instinctively revolted. It was the classic combat for the mastery of spirit over matter, but in a reversed context. Genet *forced* his body, and even his higher senses, to accept what was repugnant to them: 'Indeed, though my mind endured, even desired, humility, my violent young body rejected it.'[29] In the full awareness of his artistic gifts, he chose vulgarity, bad taste, ugliness; desperately proud, he invited humiliation; sensitive to luxury and cleanliness, he welcomed a meal begged in an old bully-beef tin from the pig-bucket of an army-camp[30]; intelligently and lucidly he insulted his own intelligence by reading penny-dreadfuls, by listening to the most moronic of pop-songs and by exalting above the dialogues of Plato or Wilde the illiterate and vulgar platitudes exchanged between criminals and convicts. In the same way, and with identical intentions, Gide's intellectual ascetic, Alissa, deliberately rejects the whole world of culture and letters and reads nothing but the more inane devotional pamphlets put out by the Church for village Sunday-schools and pious old women. For Divine, and even for Darling, the conquest of instinctive resistances against horror are a necessary prelude to salvation. Divine shaves off her own eye-brows 'to be even more repulsive', in much the same spirit as Cula-froy had forced himself to handle Alberto's snakes. 'Culafroy and Divine, with their delicate tastes, will always be forced to love what they loathe', comments Genet; and of Darling, even more emphati-cally, he remarks 'The only way to avoid the horror of horror is to give in to it.'[31]

The comparison—however paradoxical—with the traditional saint, or with Alissa, is perhaps in one respect misleading. For St Theresa of Avila, as for St Catherine of Siena, humiliations are a means to an end—salvation, sanctity—and end and means are always quite distinct. On the one hand, an intoler-able present; on the other, a blissful future into which that present will eventually be transmuted. But Genet's belief in an after-life is certainly hazy, if not non-existent. The sacred world which constitutes his sanctity is present here and now, it is the obverse face of that which exists and is experienced at this moment, and the sacredness of humiliation lies in the actual experi-ence of humiliation, which is therefore not so much a means to an end, as an end in itself—or at least it is inseparable from, and simultaneous with that end :

> This idea of humiliation detached itself from what conditioned it [. . . .] and it remained alone, by itself alone a reason for being, itself its only necessity and itself its only end.[32]

The significance of the experience, in fact, lies precisely in the *awareness* of that experience, just as for the Greeks, the conscious-ness of virtue was in itself both the spur to, and the reward of, virtuous acts. What matters is 'the *knowledge* that my soul was rotten'[33] : simply to *be* a kind of vermin is not enough—'I was thus a louse,' writes Genet of his first adventures as a beggar, '*and con-scious of being one*'.[34] And to increase the consciousness of this abjection, Genet paints it verbally to himself, finds symbols that condense the dispersed episodes of reality into a very quintessence of horror and humiliation—in fact, he develops his extraordinary native talent for brilliant and arresting images ('. . . those words, coming from him, were like the black velvet seaweed that a diver brings up round his ankles'[35]; 'The moon struck ten'[36]; etc.) into a kind of nightmare of surrealistic horrors. His visions are those of a Lautréamont who has looked too long at Hieronymus Bosch and at Dali. He sees a corpse 'lying in a glass of champagne in the middle of a Greek landscape with truncated ringed columns,'[37] or else he catches sight of himself, in an instant of 'marvellous horror' as 'a corpse being pursued by the corpse that I am', as a 'smiling alligator', as a mouth turned inside out and swallowing its own head, or as a refuge of birds and insects, bees, snakes and 'tobacco-coloured velvet caterpillars'.[38]

The moral of *The Thief's Journal*—as of the two early novels— is that an innate passivity, pushed to its logical conclusion of total acceptance, will eventually be transformed into a generating principle of force, and a germ of spiritual activity. Sartre, by a lucid effort of will, contrived after many years to overcome his obsessions (the hallucination of crabs and crayfish which, even so, reappear somewhat unconvincingly among the mouldings of the ceiling in *Altona*); Genet, by contrast, cultivates his obsessions, revels among them—if necessary, invents them. When he was committed to Mettray, it was, in all probability, for theft. But this rather commonplace downfall is insufficiently dramatic; how much more convincing if, like Villeroy, he had murdered his father; or, like Harcamone, strangled a child. Or stabbed another boy in the eye with a pen-knife . . . the latter becomes his dream, his obsession. Alberto, the snake-catcher from Culafroy's village, dies of a pen-knife wound in the eye given by another boy[39]; Querelle's first murder occurs when he drives a pen-knife into the eye of a young Russian in Shanghai[40]; and in *Miracle of the Rose*, Genet attributes a similar 'execrable gesture' to himself.[41] That there is any more truth in this than in Sartre's belief that he was constantly being pursued by lobsters down the main streets of Rouen is highly improbable; but the difference in the subsequent use made of the hallucination is typical. Sartre relegates his crustaceans among the dreams of his less desirable characters; Genet attributes them as a reality to himself, as part of his total passivity in the pursuit of absolute rejection. Unable to be, in real life, either sufficiently evil, sufficiently abject or sufficiently passive to satisfy his thirst for the Absolute, Genet makes up for these deficiencies in his dreams, and then artistically blurs the boundary between life and imagination.

The search for absolute passivity, then, is the main theme of the Legend of Genet's life. In spite of this, however, there is a secondary theme, a current moving, as it were, in precisely the opposite direction. Half-hidden beneath the would-be Saint in everlasting pursuit of ultimate humiliation there are traces of the would-be male, the hero, absorbed in a desperate effort to overcome his innate passivity and to replace it by that conventionally active state of mind which is summed up in the term, virility.

Even Divine, without much success, at one point makes a gallant attempt at virilization; on meeting Our Lady, 'Something different, a kind of feeling of power, sprang up (in the vegetable, germinative sense) in Divine. She thought she had been virilified.'[42] Divine's reactions, partly tragic and partly grotesque, to the arrival of Our Lady, are certainly an intimate and brilliantly imaginative portrayal of some of Genet's own fundamental dilemmas. It is an inescapable part of the torture of the ageing homosexual, that the normal relationship between active and passive in a heterosexual partnership is reversed, producing a state of psychological uncertainty which is incapable of direct resolution. The young homosexual, sensing himself to be feminine and passive, will tend—as would a woman—to look for an older and more dominating partner; but the older partner will himself tend towards passivity, and so may himself desire to be dominated. As he grows older, the homosexual will inevitably develop some rudimentary paternal instincts, and so look for partners younger than himself (just as Genet turns towards Bulkaen in *Miracle of the Rose*)—yet he cannot but hope that it is they who will exercise the masculine domination sexually, while in all other respects it is he who will be the senior partner in the relationship. The younger man who is prepared to accept—or, more often, to *pretend* to accept—the older man's prestige and authority (and income), while himself offering the active element in the sexual partnership, is himself a contradiction in terms—a fundamentally abnormal and often anti-social contradiction, simultaneously exploiting and pretending to be exploited : and it is this which accounts for the fact that, both in real life and in fiction, a homosexual relationship between an older man and a younger partner so often degenerates into a tale of scandal, blackmail and misery[43]. Invariably it is the older man who is the 'sucker'.

That the ageing homosexual should dread the future is not surprising. Jean Genet's way of mastering this dread was, firstly, to exteriorise it—to try and portray its problems and its terrors in the life of the ageing Divine, and, by confronting them without self-deception, to try and overcome them in himself. His second method is that which we have been discussing, namely, to steep himself so utterly in degradation, to familiarise himself beforehand with such depths of misery and humiliation (and when real life failed to produce enough horror, then continuing the journey in imagination), so that, when the dreaded moment came, it could not be worse than that which had already happened. And his final method was to try and virilize himself by some other activity, so that, as he grew older, he might escape the desperate contradiction of being passively dependent on a younger man. It is the awareness of this contradiction—undermining the ageing homosexual's life, and filling with pathos an existence which the rest of society sees only as absurd or disgusting—which is the source of that all-pervading sense of despair that characterises the novels; and for Genet himself, the virilizing activity by which alone the despair might be conquered revealed itself as the positive, dangerous and 'manly' vocation of the professional burglar.

This revelation, however, was only gradual. Before the solution could be so much as guessed at, Genet was obliged to pass through infinite gradations of impotence and anguish. The despair which colours almost every instant in the lives of his people has many apparent causes (imprisonment, *la Relègue*, the fear of death, the shock of arrest, etc.) but only one real one : the inner spiritual contradiction of the homosexual whose very existence is the embodiment of an impossible ideal. By the force of his desire (and in Genet, sexual desire, for all the emphasis which is laid on it as something purely physical, is never more than the outward sign of a spiritual longing) he strives towards that which, if it were granted, would annihilate him—or rather, would give to the hopeless Void of his own individuality a new and mystical dimension. The ultimate, or ideal, experience of love involves the destruction of the Self. It is the miraculous quality of the sexual act that it produces a sensation of total union outside time with another being; both separate beings are dissolved into a single, boundless, de-personalized awareness outside themselves, through which each escapes from the hopelessness of finite imprisonment within a single, limited existence. This is the wonder of the sexual act; its degradation occurs when this possibility of escape from the profane into the sacred, from the humdrum into the transcendental, is not even envisaged at the outset (prostitution, or a failed marriage); the despair and the anguish come when this escape *is* envisaged, hoped for, longed for—and never realized. For the older homosexual, the void of despair is all but inevitable; but it is Genet's genius, particularly in *Our Lady of the Flowers*, to describe the despair itself in such a way that it becomes symbolic of *all* sexual-mystic relations which have failed, and not only of an abnormal relationship. The quality of the despair reduces the particular characteristics of the act almost to insignificance : the sexual ambiguity of Divine, as it were, de-personalizes 'her', transforms her into an abstraction, an allegory of the contradictions in man, with one foot in one world and one in another, unable to be wholly brute or wholly angel.

If Divine and all her companions, Mimosa the Great, Duckbill, Queen Oriane, Queen of Rumania . . . are not merely grotesque and repulsive, but also tragic, it is because of this intimate despair which envelops them like a cloud of incense, yet which none of them can trace to its source. They only know that there is no escape from it. It is their invisible glory. At the funeral of Divine,

> . . . within themselves, secretly, Milord, the Mimosas, Castagnette, in short, all the queens [. . . .] came noiselessly together again, though emitting a slight scent of hopelessness which no one divulged.[44]

Despair is the force which drives Our Lady to confess his murder; it pierces him 'like an arrow'[45] and produces that fissure which is the symbol of his transcendence : 'Hopelessness draws you out of yourself'.[46] It is the impotence of the lover to unite wholly with his beloved which furnishes an intimation of the impotence and the absurdity of all human effort in the eventual context of death; and the awareness of death drives the wretched victim—literally 'in desperation'—back once more to the evanescent promises of love.[47]

Yet, as with all negative and passive elements in Genet, despair, by its very intensity, *can* become a source of strength—irrational, admittedly, but powerful enough all the same. While there still remains hope, then the wretched human creature is still committed to *this* world, to *this* society, its deceptive promises and its inevitable and bitter disappointments. Once there is *no* hope left, once the despair is absolute, then he is outside this world, he is free, he has escaped—and perhaps he can set up another world, his own, a mirror-world, in opposition. 'It was on the basis of the monster that new principles were ordained, principles constantly combatted by the forces of the world'[48] comments Genet in telling of the despair of the woman who was delivered of a 'monster'—an idiot child; and later he begins to glimpse the realization of despair as an absolute condition of existence, the unique possibility of something that might be happiness :

> I wish for a moment to focus attention on the reality of supreme happiness in despair : when one is suddenly alone, confronting one's sudden ruin, when one witnesses the irremediable destruction of one's work and self.[49]

Obviously, the temptation simply to accept the despair originating from his own sexual and psychological contradictions, to universalize it and to see it as a general characteristic of the human condition, was very strong in Genet, particularly in *Our Lady of the Flowers*; and perhaps, even now, it is a temptation which has never been completely overcome. None the less, as he grew older, the very fear of the practical, as opposed to the transcendental, consequences of a total acceptance of degradation, drove him to fight against this inner *angoisse,* and to look anew at his own contradictions with a faint, dawning hope that, somehow, it might be possible to resolve

them. And if, as we have argued, the roots of despair lay in the
intolerable conflict of masculine and feminine elements in Genet's
own physical and psychological constitution, then the one hope of
resolution and of eventual escape from the resulting spiritual
impasse lay in attempting to shape the remainder of his life in a
more male and dominating mould. If he could succeed in this,
then perhaps the sexual urge to feminine passivity would pass away,
and the destructive, paralysing psychological contradictions vanish
with it. For Genet, the symbol of his own passivity was Divine, the
male prostitute; the symbol of activity is Bulkaen, the professional
burglar; and one of the main themes of the Legend, as told in
Miracle of the Rose and in *The Thief's Journal*, is Genet's own
transition from one to the other.[50]

The difficulty about being a burglar, for Genet, is that the benefits accruing from the trade for one in quest of virility may be
countered and nullified by the temptation to burgle, not for profit,
but for aesthetic pleasure. Genet himself observes—not without
some pride—that he tended to be more interested in *objets d'art*
than in cash : 'Perhaps I was the first crasher ever to leave without
bothering about cash . . .'[51]—and, at the beginning at least, he was
more concerned with being THE Thief—that is, with modelling each
gesture choreographically upon some ideal-archetypal ballet—than
with obtaining results. 'I love the act of stealing because I find it
elegant in itself',[52] he writes in *Miracle of the Rose*; the temptation
to consider the whole process as something stylistically satisfactory
(as an art, or specifically as a *poem*, a series of symbols) was obviously
very strong. 'What I have sought most of all has been to be the
consciousness of the theft whose poem I am writing.'[53] Whether an
aesthetic burglar makes an efficient burglar is open to doubt. Jean
Genet—in retrospect—is comparatively proud of his style. 'I was
a clever thief. Never have I been caught red-handed, in "flagrante
delicto" '[54]; yet, in spite of this mild outburst of self-praise, the facts
seem to contradict Genet's optimism. By 1943, he is alleged to have
been convicted nine times for theft in France alone, which hardly
argues 'a clever thief'; moreover, any burglar who considers burglary as 'a succession of cramped though blazing gestures'[55] is liable,
sooner or later, to find himself designing similar aerial arabesques
with the aid of handcuffs—which, incidentally, constitute yet another of Genet's innumerable symbols of virility.

Thus, gradually, we find Genet concerned to reduce burglary
from an art to a science. In this, one of the first milestones was his
meeting with Armand, who, in spite of being 'double-crossing, evil-
minded, sly, crooked and brutal'—or because of it—contrived to
teach Genet the rudiments of a realistic attitude, and so for the first

time shattered the rigid carapace of his aestheticism. 'What I need is dough,' begins Armand's homily, which Genet records in *The Thief's Journal*: 'A job is good when you pull it off.'[56]

It is this first impressive dose of realism—consequently, of virilization—that accounts for the high esteem in which Genet holds the abominable Armand during much of his life in the late 'thirties—at any rate, from then on, he begins to take his burgling and his other criminal activities much more seriously: still not for what they may yield in themselves, but at least for the sense of virility which they give him. In theory, if not in practice, his preference shifts from the delicate skills of the cracksman (Guy), shoplifter (Darling: 'It was bold, but more beautiful'[57]) and pickpocket (Stilitano) to the less subtle, more brutal tactics of robbery with violence and stick-ups. In spite of this, however, he himself seems to have remained chiefly a house-breaker *(un cambrioleur)*; and around the furtive acts of breaking and entering, there collects a whole body of symbols, ecstasies, semi-mystic experiences, psychological analyses[58] and moral sentiments. As a crasher *(un casseur)*, Genet, who died in childhood when he was branded a thief by others, now finally regains his authenticity: he is-what-he-is. 'I wanted to be myself, and I was myself when I became a crasher'[59]; as a crasher, he finds among others of the confraternity an élite society to which he can at last belong; finally, as a crasher, he discovers in himself the beginnings of physical and moral courage, and thus he begins his liberation from passivity.

It is perhaps unfair to argue that much of this sounds very unconvincing. The fact remains that, for Genet as he weaves the Legend of his life, his conversion to burglary has all the significance of a drive for freedom. 'I went to theft as to a liberation, to the light,'[60] he comments; and at this stage he clearly equates liberty with virility—in fact, with sexual normality. It is interesting to see how Genet's concept of liberty evolves. In the earliest writings, the *Poèmes* and *Our Lady of the Flowers*, the word rarely occurs—Genet seldom experiences even the normal prisoner's longing for freedom, or for 'that little tent of blue which prisoners call the sky'. On the contrary—and the psychology of this is revealing—he seems to feel fundamentally more at home in prison than outside. Cells, discipline, punishment—all these things fulfil some obscure need in himself. 'I recognize that [prisons] have their foundations within myself; they are the signs of the most violent of my extreme tendencies.'[61] But the last part of this assertion is probably a misinterpretation—at all events, we can find much more probable explanations in other passages. At the root of Genet's attitudes, as he reveals them in his autobiographical writings, we find an unmistakable inferiority-complex—understandable enough, given the circumstances of his childhood and adolescence—betraying itself as an overwhelming need for security. Even at the height of its violence, his revolt against civilization is the revolt of the small child against the discipline of the nursery; he must oppose a rule of order, destroy it, deny it, annihilate it—but always *within the framework of that order*. Just as the child who is naughty is not merely restored to order by punishment, but in many cases actually calmed by it, so that, if the expected punishment is not forthcoming, the result can be an uncontrollable emotional disturbance, since the whole secure order of the universe is thereby dissolved and reduced to chaos. Genet's revolt against society presupposes the existence of an order in that society formidable in its power and capable in the end of forcing him into submission. In fact, by violating the order of society, Genet not only satisfies his instincts of rebelliousness, his anarchic individualism, 'the most violent of' his 'extreme tendencies', but at the same time he provokes from those forces of law, order and discipline the reaction which he so desperately needs in order to give him that missing sense of security without which he cannot live. To such a child—or man—*total* freedom (that of the permissive method, that of a genuinely anarchic community) is intolerable. The truth of this in relation to Genet is strikingly illustrated in his reactions to life in Nazi Germany. Here was a whole people living *outside* the social-moral law, 'an entire people that has been placed on the index'; to break the law within a society of outlaws, Genet felt, was not only useless—since there was no sense of transgression, no satisfaction in opposing an established hierarchy and discipline—but, more serious still, the revolt would fail to produce the calculated reaction. In Hitler's Germany, Genet felt suddenly free—and so he ran away as fast as possible :

> If I steal here, I perform no singular deed that might fulfil me. I obey the customary order; I do not destroy it. I am not committing evil. I am not upsetting anything. The outrageous is impossible. I'm stealing in the void.[62]

'I know no hoodlums who are not children,'[63] remarks Genet perspicaciously, commenting on the character of Stilitano. He himself, in this respect, is an admirable illustration of the dictum. Nearly all his dreams are dreams of security; much of his later philosophy— especially in *Querelle of Brest*—is the intellectual rationalisation of a deep emotional need to exist within the unshakable framework of an established order. His sexual passivity, in all likelihood, has similar origins. 'No doubt, to reassure myself, to bolster my insecurity,' (the observation comes towards the end of the *Journal*) 'I had to assume that my lovers were wrought of tough matter.'[64]

Symbol of security : the Monarch who dwells in his great stone palace, surrounded by guards, ritual and luxury : 'what security in the carpets, in the mirrors!'[65]—both *The Balcony* and *The Blacks* show the transmutation of one of the characters into 'a Queen'. But on the whole the prospect of Genet himself becoming a sovereign ruler and living in a palace is fairly remote; and so the dream of security finds its realization nearer at hand : in La Santé, in Fresnes, in Fontevrault. Mettray, for all its dream-qualities, was unsatisfactory in one respect : it had no walls, only flowers, which were terrifying, the very image of Hell, because they offered only the appearance, never the reality, of an encircling rampart. But the *real* prison is different :

> Prison offers the same sense of security to the convict as does a royal palace to a king's guest. [. . . .] The prison surrounds me with a perfect guarantee. [. . . .] Nothing will demolish it, not blasts of wind, nor storms, nor bankruptcies. The prison remains sure of itself, and you in the midst of it sure of yourself.[66]

At bottom, therefore, liberty means very little to Genet. Later, under the probable influence of Sartre, it becomes an abstract and metaphysical concept (especially in *Querelle of Brest*); later still, in *The Screens*, a political ideal, albeit an exceedingly hazy one; but in Genet's own experience, it means nothing more than the realization of himself as himself—the establishment of his authenticity—and to a lesser extent, a liberation from some of the more unbearably shameful aspects of his dependence upon the virility of others. It was probably not in Genet's power, even had he proved a more successful burglar than was in fact the case, to take this 'march towards maleness'[67] to its final conclusion; but at least it helped him to bridge the gap between dreams and reality, to see himself objectively as a distinct personality instead of as the reflection of an ideal or as the shadow of an archetype, and finally to realize his own limitations : 'It is not my destiny to be a great bandit. [. . . .] The poetry of the great birds of prey eludes me.'[68]

Undoubtedly, the progress from catamite to burglar was significant, but perhaps its importance was not precisely that which Genet himself accords to it. It was a stage of self-realization, a transitional step in the long process of developing his powers of lucidity, an introduction to the final liberation, which occurred when both catamite and burglar eventually gave way to the poet.

No less than the flowers, cigarette-butts, blue-jeans and angels, the figures who dance ceremoniously through the pages of Genet's novels are symbols and allegories rather than living beings. Occasionally—particularly in *Querelle of Brest*—there are glimpses of a more traditional psychology, based on character and observation—Robert, for instance, making love to Madame Lysiane[69]— but in general, Genet is as disinterested in, and as mistrustful of, a conventionally psychological literature as are Brecht and Ionesco. His people move and act in accordance with laws and motives which are either above or below those of normal, everyday humanity— they are driven, either by a blind and brutal sexuality (which has little or nothing to do with *sensuality*), or else by a transcendental and poetic awareness of the essential patterns of existence. In other words, Genet's characters—like those of Racine or Corneille—are created *a priori* : their essence exists elsewhere (in Genet's mind, or among God's angels); they are merely the shadow or the reflection of an idea. '*Tous les personnages de mes livres se ressemblent*',[70] observes Genet in *Pompes Funèbres*—necessarily so, since they are all footnote-illustrations to a thesis, and usually the same thesis.

That the characters in Genet's novels should thus be reducible to abstractions, mere emanations of the mind of their creator, is not surprising, since Genet—at least if we are to believe the Legend— employs a similar process of de-personalization in real life. It is Stendhal's method of crystallization taken to extremes. Stendhal at least started with a real being, then wove about her a fantasy of dreams and ideals, until finally it was his own creation that he fell in love with—an artefact bearing little if any relation to the original Giulia or Méthilde or 'Madame Azur', now deeply hidden underneath. But Genet starts with the ideal already in his mind—his essence, or archetype—and then selects, seemingly more or less at random, a living being to whom it can be attached. Thus even in real life he *creates* characters to people his existence : as was once done to him, when his own individual reality was destroyed and supplanted by a different image of reality devised by others, so he now does to those whom he encounters. He has an idea or an ideal of The Police—and so, when he meets Bernardini, he creates him deliberately in terms of that image :

> Little by little I came to understand his beauty. I even think that I created it, deciding that it would be precisely that face and body, on the basis of the idea of the police which they were to signify.[71]

—and this, of course, is power; for where he has created, there also he can destroy. Bernardini's reality-as-a-policeman, (the only reality which concerns him), or Stilitano's reality-as-a-pimp, are dependent upon his goodwill and imagination; he has only to lose interest for an instant, and Stilitano's beauty, glory and immortality are no more, and Stilitano himself merely one more forgotten,

anonymous petty gangster who once haunted the brothels of Barcelona and the dockside bars of Antwerp.[72]

Other people, in fact, have no significant existence of their own;
they are merely pretexts for the flowering of an ideal, hat-pegs on
which to hang a dream. This is true, even of those whom Genet has
loved most deeply, even of Lucien Sénémaud[73]; but if it reduces
the whole of his world to an abstraction, at the same time it gives
him a broad and extraordinary tolerance. It is only in the later
plays that we begin to encounter elements of satire and criticism.
In the novels, Genet is uncritical in his admiration even of the most
brutish and the most unlovely—a Riton, a Stilitano—and logically
so; for if he has created them as they are, because he wanted them
that way, what is the sense of saying that they should have been
different? He has only to un-peg the dream, and they are gone for
ever.

We must keep this in mind when we come to consider how far
the novels are subjective—that is, based on fragments of real experience. Because Genet creates imaginatively those whom he lives
with—including himself, the 'I' of the Legend—their transposition
into the framework of a novel is at once extremely easy to perform,
and very difficult to analyse. Divine and Darling, Bulkaen and
Divers are clearly based on life; but life itself is already transfigured,
if not half-created, by imagination. There is no clear line of demarc-
ation between the fiction of *Miracle of the Rose* and the autobiography *The Thief's Journal*. *All* reality, for Genet, is an allegory,
whether lived or dreamed. *All* his characters are reflections of himself, in that it is *he* who perceives them and (in most immediate
phenomenological tradition), by perceiving them, *creates what he
perceives*. With the best will in the world, he cannot describe
Bulkaen as-he-is, but only as-he-is-perceived—that is, as he is in the
mind of Jean Genet. 'I realized it was a mistake to attribute to
Bulkaen the sweetness [which his beauty] instilled in me [. . . .]
for that beauty was in me and not in him.'[74] And since all per-
ceptions—but most particularly those which conjure up an emotional reaction—are essentially the product of the mind of the perceiver, it follows that, whatever Genet describes, he is necessarily
describing himself. 'It is absolutely essential that I come back to
myself',[75] he advises the reader in *Our Lady of the Flowers*; and in
the *Journal*:

> I shall not make use of words the better to depict an event or its hero,
> but so that they may tell you something about myself.[76]

Fundamentally, then, all Genet's characters—including his 'I'—
are composites : he himself is in part made up of others, and these

others, conversely, are partly or largely fashioned out of himself. Perceiver and perceived are inextricably interwoven. This composite character of subjectivity is reflected in the fragmented structure of the novels themselves : a patchwork of detached, sometimes incompleted episodes, where dream fuses with reality, and whence Genet's own voice is never long absent, commenting on his characters, or commenting on one character through the voice of another, identifying himself, dissociating himself, becoming a tone of voice or a fragment of a diary, loving the Headsman in the place of Erik, living Divine's childhood through the sensibility of Culafroy, loving Darling as Divine :

> It is Darling whom I cherish most, for you realize that, in the final analysis, it is my own destiny, be it true or false, that I am draping (at times a rag, at times a court robe) on Divine's shoulders.[77]

—transposing in time, 'retracing the course of my life',[78] transposing in tone,[79] interpreting, but always weaving his life into its Legend, and then transferring fragments of the Legend back into his life :

> Through writing I have attained what I was seeking. What will guide me, as something learned, is not what I have lived, but the tone in which I tell of it. Not the anecdotes, but the work of art. Not my life, but the interpretation of it. It is what language offers me to evoke it, to talk about it, render it. To achieve my legend. I know what I want.[80]

Concerning the composite origins of his characters, Genet is often naïvely confiding. He takes the reader into his confidence, tells how he used the real Negro murderer, Clément Village, as a model for Seck Gorgui . . . and then, rather less naïvely, proceeds to introduce this same Clément Village into the novel as a character in his own right.[81] Genet himself is (or was) Culafroy; and Culafroy reconstitutes Alberto out of the gestures, together with the various colours of the trousers, of all the other men in the village[82]; Genet is (or was) Divine, and Divine invents, or reconstitutes, Marchetti out of her treasured stock-in-trade, her 'stock of thighs, arms, torsoes, faces, hair, teeth, necks, and knees . . .'[83]; Genet in person composes the figure of the Galley-Captain out of the real memories of 'a handsome German soldier'[84] . . . the only two characters who are shown as utterly *un*related, as two quite distinct and discontinuous beings having nothing at all in common with each other, are Divine and Culafroy, who are in fact identical. The technique, in fact, is perhaps not *quite* so naïve as Genet would like to make us think.

Moreover, having diffused his subjectivity over the whole range of his characters, and intermingled their identities both with each others' and with his own (and with that of an ambiguous Jean who is both himself and the Other), he then introduces a new character who is likewise both perceiver and perceived : the Reader. Long

before Robbe-Grillet and Robert Pinget, before Butor and even before Nathalie Sarraute, Genet was puzzling away at the fundamental
question of the *nouveau roman*, in so far as this form of the novel
is directly related to phenomenology. If Jean Genet, perceiving
Clément Village, gives meaning—*his* meaning—to Village, and
then chooses to call this composite, Village-plus-significance-of-
Village, Seck Gorgui, then the reader likewise, having perceived
Seck Gorgui, will give to Seck Gorgui a new meaning of his own.
If the writer creates the characters, it is only so that the reader may
recreate them in his own fashion. The classical novel, in which the
writer manipulated clear-cut, objective characters for the benefit
of a passively-observing reader is, in a phenomenological context,
a patent absurdity. Writer, reader and heroes form an indissoluble
unity, all composed of elements of each other, all shuffling
and re-shuffling their identities and their experiences in a
single kaleidoscopic vision—the vision which is art. Why should
Genet do all the imagining and creating, when the reader will intervene anyway, and refashion the same material in his own image?
First involve the reader as an *object*—involve him in the mists and
fogs of Brest, for instance, together with '. . . a drunken sailor reel-
ing home on a heavy pair of legs', and other figures of similar substance : 'a docker stooping over his girl, a lurking tough armed,
perhaps, with a swiftsure knife; me, you, all of us, our hearts pound-
ing.'[85]—and then let him get to work as *subject*. 'I leave you free to
imagine any dialogue',[86] writes the Genet-Divine in *Our Lady of the
Flowers*, while the Genet-Seblon of *Querelle of Brest* goes further :

> We should like these reflections and observations, which cannot fully round
> out and delineate the characters in this book, to encourage you to become,
> not so much onlookers, as the very characters themselves. These creations
> would then, little by little, detach themselves from your own specific
> actions.[87]

and later Genet describes still more precisely the self-effacement of
the writer in favour of the creative effort on the part of the reader :

> However, in order not to irritate the Reader too greatly, and being certain
> that he, by the workings of his own discomfiture, will complete the con-
> tradictory, the twisted progress of the notion of murder in ourselves, we
> have denied ourselves much.[88]

To return to Genet and his characters, however. What emerges
is an extremely complex relationship between reality and imagination : for not only does the writer, by the act of perceiving characters in reality, create them both in fact and in fiction; but further,
by the specific act of creating them in writing, he destroys them in
reality. His imagination appears (to himself at least) to have a
vampire-like power to suck the reality out of sleeping victims, and

to make it nourish his own life. He possesses them in dreams; and dreams, we must remember, belong to the sacred world of transcendence, and therefore have more power—more magic—than rational science will normally allow them. In reality (to return to Plato's image) the meeting of two beings is but a ghost of communication between shadows; but in dream, the shadows yield up the place they have usurped to the ultimate reality which is Essence. And so the dream of Divine makes love to the dream of Darling, and possesses and is possessed in a way that no possession is possible by waking daylight.

Thus Genet kills his models to fashion his dreams, his characters. Which is only a highly melodramatic way of expressing what invariably happens in art, when the artist models his vision on reality. What, to us now, is Antoine Berthet, if not the very dead and dried-up carapace of a once-living being, whose whole essence has been sucked out of him to fill with life a dream in Stendhal's mind : a dream which the artist then called Julien Sorel? 'The work flames and its model dies',[89] notes Genet of the Bulkaen-reality as he is translated into the Bulkaen-dream of *Miracle of the Rose* :

> The more I write about Bulkaen, the less attractive I find him. [. . . .] And now I feel only infinite pity for the poor birdie that can no longer fly because I have plucked all its feathers.[90]

Once the dream-Bulkaen had come into being, the real-Bulkaen not only died for future generations, but died on the spot for Genet himself. Compared with his own dream-incarnation, he became dull, insipid and crude—and Genet ceased to love him. In other words, not only does the reality of Genet's experience reflect directly in the vision which is his novels, but, conversely, the fact of writing down the vision has repercussions in his life.[91] Writing, in fact, is an *act*— no different from other acts in an existential vision of the universe : a free choice (*'Ecrire, c'est choisir'*[92]) for whose repercussions from now until the end of time he who acts has absolute responsibility. *But*—and at this point we take up once more the tale of Genet's evolution—for this mirror-image of a man, whose every would-be act had hitherto resolved itself into a *gesture* (i.e. the appearance of an act, having no repercussions and involving no responsibilities), the act of writing is the first act-in-reality that he had achieved. This, and not his balletic burglary, was the real beginning of his liberation. By abstracting the reality of some unknown convict, by absorbing it into himself and then translating it (image to word to ink to paper to printing-press) into the being we know as Bulkaen, Genet has changed (albeit in an imperceptible way) the course of fate. The convict is changed, for he will die (who knows, is already dead?)

yet will live on as Bulkaen; the reader is changed, for now Bulkaen is in him, in his life, whereas before he was not; and Genet—most important of all—is changed, in that, by his act, he has conquered his own emotions instead of being conquered by them. His fatal passivity has for the first time become active; he has taken charge of his own destiny.

This discovery that, through writing, he has the power to influence destiny, exercises an irresistible fascination over Genet. At first he is content to *feel* himself as destiny, controlling the lives of his characters without their realizing it, condescendingly 'allowing' Darling and Divine the luxury of an electric radiator (stolen!) in their little flat, so that they may have 'a short respite, even a bit of happiness',[93] permitting Ernestine to think herself free when she is in fact determined by her creator's quite arbitrary will ('She is serving a text she knows nothing about'[94]) or filling Our Lady's heart with anguish at the thought of those alternative possibilities which his life might have offered—allowing him to torment himself 'by what it might also have been but will not be, *because of me.*'[95]

In *Our Lady of the Flowers*, in fact, Genet simply amuses himself by playing at being God, or fate, or nemesis. But the more he contemplates this new-found power, the more complex its implications grow. If those characters, for whom he is God, are modelled on real, living beings—particularly on beings who, in the past, determined *his* fate—then does he now retrospectively control theirs? Seemingly, yes. For all significance is ultimately retrospective. And by the time he has absorbed their reality into his imagination, their original existences (as with Bulkaen's) grow void and meaningless, and even if, in the novel, he allows them to act as in fact they acted in reality, their actions now serve a lucid and coherent purpose—*his* purpose—even though at the time they had no notion of it. *He* knows what they were doing, and why, or what they were, better than they knew themselves; and even if he distorts them, this very distortion 'is therefore what they also are, though unaware of being it.'[96] If they—in this case, the staff at Mettray—thought that they were controlling Genet's destiny, they were right—but only because, in the pattern of the book, Genet himself shows that it was necessary that they should do so. 'They were writing my story.' But at the same time, and without their knowing it, Genet was *creating* their significance. 'They were my characters. They understood nothing about Mettray. They were idiots.'[97]

At this point, however, Genet stops dead; for his outburst of joy at the discovery that he could play at being God, not only in the present with imaginary destinies, but retrospectively with real ones, yields before the realization that he is cornering himself in an absurd and untenable position—which, incidentally, must also be the logical predicament of God, if God exists, and is logical. For if—to take an example—Lt Seblon *is* Genet, then any other character who judges, or misjudges, Lt Seblon (Querelle, for instance) is judging, or misjudging, his own creator, his own destiny. Querelle is therefore *free*. Jean Genet, like God, has created man in his own image, and given him his freedom. But if God, who is also destiny, then gives a preview of what *will* happen to Querelle, there now arises an impossible conflict of two freedoms. For either God is free—in which case he can alter this destiny whenever he wishes to; or else Querelle is free, in which case *he* can determine his fate in spite of God. In the latter instance, any statement made by God/ Genet about the future of man/Querelle is a potential lie. Or alternatively, if God/Genet can determine the destiny of man/Querelle, then, as soon as he makes a statement about man/Querelle, and if that statement is true, man/Querelle *must* follow it—in spite of any subsequent afterthoughts on the part of God/Genet. That is, once the prophecy is made, Genet is as much determined by Querelle as Querelle is by Genet :

> In our desire to give the fullest possible explanation of the psychological ambience of our hero, we cannot help but lay bare our own soul. Please be liberal in your judgement of the attitude we choose to adopt—in view, or rather *prevision* of any desired end—in that it may lead us to discover the given psychological world which upholds the liberty of choice; but, if it become necessary, in the course of deepening the intrigue, for one of our heroes to voice his real opinion, please reflect that we should at once be faced with the dilemma—arbitrary, no doubt—that this character might escape the clutches of his author. He would thereby single himself out. In that case we should have to admit that one component factor would be revealed—after the event—by the author.[98]

The problem, for anyone so metaphysically punctilious as Genet, is tricky, and the author (like God?) only gets round it by a subterfuge, and a pretty unconvincing one at that. If, as the last passage quoted suggests, the pre-vision of the future is to be regarded only as a statement concerning the psychological dispositions of Querelle *in the present*, yet which can be altered by the discovery, in the future, of hitherto unsuspected psychological factors, then God's omnipotence, not to speak of his omniscience, is pretty inadequate. In the complex relationships between Querelle, fate and Lt Seblon, Genet's adventures in the role of God come to a sudden standstill. God, in fact, shows up better as a dramatist, where the characters are not so well situated to argue back. None the less, and in spite of this set-back on the plane of metaphysics, the final evolution of Genet towards virility—his 'march towards maleness'—is completed.

The word becomes the Act. The pseudo-poet of the *Poèmes*, still half-entangled with the catamite, has been transformed into the genuine, creative poet of *Querelle of Brest*, *The Maids* and *The Blacks*.

Genet's conception of the nature and functions of poetry, and of the role of the poet in the universe, is extremely romantic and at the same time very complex. In conversation, according to Simone de Beauvoir, his 'poet's arrogance' may simply appear affected and grotesque[99]; none the less, the same ideas reappear frequently in his novels and essays—in particular in *The Funambulists* (1958)— and together make up a coherent pattern of semi-mystic concepts which would certainly not have seemed unfamiliar to Baudelaire or to Rimbaud, and which probably owe something to both.

To begin with, poetry, for Genet, is a *force*; it is not produced, or created, by the poet; it exists already in the universe, independently of any individual, and the poet's function is first to discover it, and then to transmit it to others. The poet plays the part of medium at a spiritualist séance; like the Voice in *The Screens* which transmits the spirit of the dead Si Slimane, he must first totally abandon his own will and life and personality, in order that the unseen powers of the occult may gather in him and clothe their transparent essence in visible images formed with words. The poet must die before he can hope to be transmuted into that vehicle for a reality infinitely greater than himself. 'The author of a beautiful poem is always dead',[100] asserts Genet in *Miracle of the Rose*—and this, of course, fits in well with the Legend. Genet's own childhood— or rather, the child that he once was—exists only beyond the grave : 'Since my childhood is dead, in speaking of it, I shall be speaking of something dead',[101] but it is only *because* both child and childhood are dead that they are now able to form the substance of poetry.

This theme is developed in detail in *The Funambulists*. The essence of all art resides in the *object*, or at best in the living being considered as an object—as pure appearance, as mirror-image, as gesture, as movement. Art is the expression, or the realization, of the soul of the cosmos. It is secreted in what we normally call the inanimate, but of course, for Genet, there is no such thing as the inanimate in the literal sense of the word, for the *anima* is precisely the attribute of the object considered as *Ding-an-sich*, whereas the subject, the observer, man with his spirit and his intellect, is that being who can perceive, but never give rise to, poetry. In Sartrian terms, poetry is an attribute of the *en-soi*; the negative *pour-soi* can perceive poetry, while at the same time recognizing that it is itself of a different essence altogether. All Genet's ideal lovers—and each one of his lovers is a poem, a work of art—are in the strictest sense objects; they are invariably described as inhuman or soul-less or unfeeling or indifferent—as they must be, if he is to feel them as the material of poetry. The enemy, the destroyer of poetry, is intellect—which again explains why every one of Genet's mythical heroes—a Harcamone, a Bulkaen, a Riton, a Stilitano, an Armand—is, intellectually speaking, a monument of moronic imbecility. An Armand who showed the first glimpse of intelligence would forthwith cease to be a pure object, and on the spot, all the poetry in him, and consequently all Genet's devotion, would vanish into air. Art is the awareness of the occult significance of objects—their magic, their symbolic otherness, their supernatural reality, their alternative, or sur-real existence on the plane of the sacred. Thus Genet's art is fundamentally surrealist, in a most specific and literal sense of that abused word. It seeks beyond appearance for traces of an irrational and imperceptible reality which, none the less, is contained *in* the appearance as an explosive force, seeking to break through its physical container by the first available fissure. It is a search, at once for the-face-behind-the-face (which is identical, perhaps, with the mirror-image of the visible face); or, to revert to Antonin Artaud's phrase, for 'the poetry *behind* the poetry'.

The poetry of an object, then, is *in* the object; it is not in the poet. The statue is contained from all eternity within the uncut block of stone, the dancer's gestures, the acrobat's leaps and darts, are *in* the dancer and the acrobat from all time; the artist realizes what is already there :

> Your leaps and bounds and stunts were within you but were unaware of it. Thanks to your charms, they know that they are and that they are yourself, illustrating you.[102]

The poet, it follows, is he who co-operates with objects to per-perfection, in order that they may reveal in and to themselves their own essential reality. Poetry *may* coincide with beauty, but not necessarily so. Beauty, as we have seen, is the product of a violent, even a destructive, opposition between contradictory forces, between the will to shape a material and the resistance of that material to all attempts to shape it. Art—or poetry—is the gentle releasing of the qualities in the material by the artist. This is an important distinction, whose significance was already apparent to Genet in *Our Lady of the Flowers* : 'For a long time I thought that the poetic work posed conflicts : it cancels them.'[103] Poetry is independent of beauty, certainly in any conventional sense. Beauty arises out of the artist's

conflict with his material; poetry is released from the material by
his love for it, or even reverence. Giacometti loves his clay, the funambulist loves his high-wire, Genet loves his thugs and murderers
and convicts. His love brings his material to life in the form of art,
for a spectator into whom this higher, mystic life will flow.

But since art is co-operation with the inanimate, the artist, in
order to co-operate, must himself be inanimate—that is, once again,
dead. It is through his own inanimateness that he will transmit the
animate poetry of things to others. 'Death—the Death of which I
speak', Genet addresses his tightrope-walker, 'is not the death that
will follow your fall, but the one which precedes your appearance
on the wire.'[104] But the artist is also alive, because, as he creates—
and all creation is an act of solitude—he is, provisionally at least,
his own spectator; as the statue emerges from the clay, *he* is the
first to see it, to judge of its perfection. He is thus (yet again!) both
himself and his own double, the Figure and its own Reflection, the
one alive, the other dead :

> But nothing—and above all not applause or laughter—will keep you
> from dancing for your image [. . . .] So dance alone. Pale, livid, anxious
> to please or displease your image : but, it is your image that will dance
> for you.[105]

Moreover, the very concept of perfection belongs not to the province of the profane, the living, but only to that of the Absolute, the
sacred—*i.e.* the dead. 'The person who will dance will be dead—
intent upon and capable of all beauties.'[106] This theme—the relationship between poetry and death—is one which is developed at
length throughout *The Funambulists*, which is an essential docu-
ment if we are to grapple with Genet's whole conception of poetry,
and with that identification of the poetic with the macabre which is
such a remarkable feature of the novels, in particular *Pompes
Funèbres*.

To return, however, to the opposition between poetry and
beauty—or at least, conventional beauty. Poetry, for Genet, is the
intensely emotional experience of a transcendental reality perceived
in, or through, the inanimate (which again suggests the reason why
most of his best writing consists of a series of vivid *visual* images
or symbols); poetry *may* also be beauty when there is a violent contrast between the inanimate object (usually sordid, ugly, evil, mis-
shapen) and the symbol of its transcendental reality—the flower,
the rose, the iridescent wings of angels. Hence the extraordinary
and very disturbing contrast in Genet between form and content.
The symbols are not just intended to be beautiful in themselves;
they are quite deliberately made *too* beautiful, and consequently

the beauty-poetry for which Genet is seeking—'to which my nerv-
ousness was going to make me pervious'[107]—is created by contrast—
the contrast between 'the most wretched of lives' and 'words that
are too beautiful'.[108]

The roses and the angels' wings, in fact, are more than just misleading. They are a cunning and elaborate piece of camouflage. They
are the false appearance of beauty, the *lie*, which disguises the
reality, the truth, which is poetry. Genet is as emphatic as Sartre
about the 'treacherous untruth' that is conventional beauty,
although not quite for the same reasons. Sartre—who hates nothing
so much in the world as an aesthete—finds beauty unbearable, not
only for metaphysical reasons, but also in so far as it hides the
hunger, poverty, cruelty and misery of the vast majority of the
world's inhabitants : 'The world can get by very well without literature'. For Genet, beauty is also an appearance which hides a
reality—but in his case, the reality is the sacred force of poetry, and
not the intolerable shame of social injustice. In the majority of
cases, poetry is reached by the *rejection* of beauty. Of Andalusia he
writes :

> I dared not even notice the beauty of that part of the world—unless it
> were to look for the secret of that beauty, the imposture behind it, of
> which one will be a victim if one trusts it. By rejecting it, I discovered
> poetry.[109]

The importance of this passage lies in the fact that Genet, in his
role as a poet, is driven to reject *even* the particular beauty of Spain.
For Spain—with its solitude, its aridity, its blueness, its asceticism,
its 'shameful and humiliated poverty'[110]—is the very image of that
'desert of the self' which Genet equates with sanctity : and the poet
and the saint are only obverse faces of the same being. Spain, for
him, is *'my* Spain',[111] and significantly, Genet concludes *The Thief's
Journal* with the memorable phrase : 'that region of myself which
I have called Spain'.[112] Yet even in Spain, which appeals more than
any other land to his thirst for the Absolute, and which he calls
elsewhere 'the only possible road' towards his goal of sanctity—
even in Spain, beauty is suspect. Poetry is that which remains when
the *appearance of beauty* is recognized for what it is : a lie.

But this brings us back to the problem of Genet's subjectivism and
to the relationship between his life as lived, and its Legend as he
tells it. The life was a series of impressions, facts, events, realities;
the Legend is pure poetry :

> . . . for I refuse to live for any other end than the very one which I found
> to contain the first misfortune : that my life must be a legend, in other
> words, legible, and the reading of it must give birth to a certain new
> emotion which I call poetry.[113]

But if poetry is the truth which emerges when the facts—the appearances—are perceived, and in the very instant of their perception, are recognized as being lies, then what of the facts that Genet tells us go to make up the retrospective poem of his life? True or false? Logically, if we take Genet's definition of poetry at its face value, then every apparent truth (and especially every truth that has the least semblance of anything other than the most squalid ugliness) will be a lie, and *known to be a lie* to Genet in that same instant when he sets it down as a truth. In any case, in the present state of our knowledge of the details of Genet's career, the question is purely academic :

> Was what I wrote true? False? Only this book of love will be real. What of the facts which served as its pretext? I must be their repository. It is not they that I am restoring.[114]

Life or Legend? Truth or lies, or lies deliberately failing—like the White Queen in *The Blacks*—to pass for truth beneath the gestures of a purely ritual masquerade? A Golden Legend is not the same thing as history—and if we choose to confuse the two, it is not for the lack of warning on the part of Genet.

NOTES

1 *Thief*, p. 156. 'Le mécanisme en était à peu près celui-ci (depuis lors je l'utiliserai) : à chaque accusation portée contre moi, fût-elle injuste, du fond du coeur je répondrai oui. A peine avais-je prononcé ce mot—ou la phrase qui le signifiait—en moi-même je sentais le besoin de devenir ce qu'on m'avait accusé d'être.' (*Journal*, pp. 185-186)

2 *Rose*, p. 108. 'Il me demandait d'écrire quelques vers sur un sujet qu'il me donnait.' (*Miracle*, p. 263)

3 Sartre, *Saint G.*, p. 427. 'On me poussa dans une cellule où se trouvaient déjà plusieurs détenus en vêtements 'de ville'. (On garde son complet veston tant qu'on ne fait que de la préventive.) Pour moi, bien que j'eusse fait appel, on m'avait obligé, par erreur, à endosser le costume des condamnés. Cet accoutrement insolite semble de mauvais augure; on me méprisa; par la suite j'eus les plus grandes peines à remonter le courant. Or, il y avait parmi eux un détenu qui faisait des poèmes à sa soeur; poèmes idiots et pleurnichards qu'ils admiraient beaucoup. A la fin, agacé, je déclarai que je serai capable d'en faire autant. Ils me mirent au défi et j'écrivis le *Condamné à Mort*; je le leur lus un jour et ils ne firent que me mépriser davantage; je terminai la lecture au milieu des insultes et des railleries, un détenu me dit : 'Des vers comme ça, j'en fais tous les matins.' A ma sortie de prison, je m'attachais tout particulièrement à terminer ce poème qui m'était d'autant plus cher qu'il avait été méprisé davantage.' (*S. Genet*, pp. 396-7)

4 *Thief*, p. 71. 'J'habitais rue du Sac, près des Docks.' (*Journal*, p. 85)

5 *Pompes Funèbres*, p. 63.

6 Sartre, *Saint G.*, p. 426. (*S. Genet*, pp. 395-6)

7 *Thief*, p. 39. '. . . en emportant des valises appartenant à des officiers noirs.' (*Journal*, p. 48)

8 *Ibid.*, pp. 39-40. '. . . plaisait davantage à ma nonchalance.' (*Journal*, p. 48)

9 *Ibid.*, pp. 27, 64. (*Journal*, pp. 33, 76)

10 *Ibid.*, p. 129. (*Journal*, p. 152)

11 Simone de Beauvoir, *Lo Force de l'Âge*, pp. 594-5.

12 *Ibid.*, p. 612.

13 Cf. the case of Caryl Chesman in the U.S.A.

14 *Haute Surveillance* and *Un Chant d'Amour*, as well as *Le Pêcheur du Suquet*, are dedicated to Lucien Sénémaud. The *Journal du Voleur*, incidentally, is dedicated to Sartre and to Simone de Beauvoir ('*le Castor*').

15 *Thief*, pp. 209-10. 'Plus j'aime Lucien et plus de moi s'éloigne mon goût du vol et des voleurs [. . . .] mais une grande tristesse m'écrase [. . . .] c'est le regret de ma Légende [. . . .] Combien plus grisant, jusqu'au vertige, la chute et le vomissement, serait l'amour que je lui voue, si Lucien était un voleur et un traître.' (*Journal*, pp. 248-250)

Of Genet's life after 1947, we have practically no detailed knowledge. One of the very few reliable sources of information, however, is the third volume of Simone de Beauvoir's memoirs, *La Force des Choses* (Paris, Gallimard, 1963, translated as *The Force of Circumstance*, London, Weidenfeld & Nicholson). This contains no coherent account of Genet's career, and strangely, makes not a single reference to Sartre's writing of *Saint-Genet*, but the following details and episodes are mentioned in passing: Genet's attitude—basically hostile— to the German Occupation troops (p. 14); his friendship for the novelist Violette Leduc (p. 30); his ideas on the theatre (p. 63); the publication of the *Poèmes* (p. 83); his request to be allowed to visit certain 'centres de redressement' (p. 86); his ideas on the use of argot (pp. 87-88); his relations with Sartre to whom he gives the MS of *Miracle de la Rose* (p. 89); his relations with Lucien Sénémaud, and the writing of *Pompes Funèbres* (p. 90); his quarrels with M. Gallimard, whom he accuses at one point of losing the MS of *Pompes Funèbres* (p. 90); his visits to Simone de Beauvoir (p. 91); the continuation of his quarrel with Gallimard (p. 92); his reaction to the tapestry, *La Dame à la Licorne* (p. 108); his criticism of· Simone de Beauvoir's manner of dressing (p. 135); Jouvet's production of *Les Bonnes* (p. 144); Sartre's successful efforts to secure the award of the *Prix de la Pléiade* for *Haute Surveillance (Death-watch)* and *Les Bonnes (The Maids)* (p. 147); the publication of *Pompes Funèbres* (p. 195); Genet gives Simone de Beauvoir advice on buying a car (p. 270); Genet as the only surviving friend of Sartre and Simone de Beauvoir from the old, heroic days of Existentialism (p. 273); Genet's motivations as a writer (p. 338 note); his article on Rembrandt (p. 460); and finally and unexpectedly, his presence at a lecture given by Mendès-France (p. 465). Fragmentary as are most of these indications, they are likely to prove vital for some future biographer. There is, incidentally, a further glimpse of Genet at the official reception given for Jean Cocteau after his election to the Académie

Française. It was Cocteau himself who insisted on introducing Genet to Queen Elizabeth of the Belgians.

16 One aspect at least of the Legend *does* appear to be pure invention: that part where, both in *Pompes Funèbres* and in the *Journal*, for the better illustration of his argument, Genet suggests that, during the War, he collaborated with the Nazis. Even had he wished, in practice, to join the notorious *Milice* (and there is no evidence that he did: cf. *La Force des Choses*, p. 14), he would first have had to contrive to remain out of prison for long enough to make his collaboration effective.

By contrast, what is hidden in the Legend, yet which clearly played a large part in Genet's life in reality, is the wide reading that, at *some* time (when? in prison? in between burglaries?) he must have done. Reform Schools are not generous with culture in their educational programmes: yet obviously Genet knows Proust and Jouhandeau and Dostoievsky and Apollinaire—the *dépouilles opimes* of *Notre-Dame* (p. 86) must surely come straight from *Alcools*—and the symbolists and the surrealists and the classical dramatists, and Michelangelo and Giacometti and Rembrandt, and Plutarch and the abbé Prévost, and Dickens and the Père de Foucauld . . . in fact, most of those artists and writers who would normally be known to the highly-educated Frenchman, such as Sartre, who had spent the larger part of his youth uninterruptedly acquiring culture.

17 Beckett, S. *Watt*, Paris (Olympia Press), 2nd. ed., 1958, p. 274 (Addenda)

18 *Our Lady*, pp. 240-1. '. . . Elle eût été contrite de se voir confondue avec l'une de ces horribles femelles à tétons. "Oh! ces femmes, les mauvaises, les mauvaises, les abjectes, les filles à matelots, les gueuses, les pas-propres. Oh! ces femmes, que je les hais!" disait-elle'. (*Notre-Dame*, p. 125)

19 *Thief*, p. 112. 'Je le respecte encore car [. . . .] à sa femme il refusa toujours la tendresse.' (*Journal*, p. 133)

20 Text omitted in the English version. (*Balcon*, pp. 65-6)

21 *Thief*, p. 17. (*Journal*, pp. 21-22). In the view (privately communicated) of Genet's translator, Bernard Frechtman, Genet's resentment of his mother, and his attempt to find substitutes (Mettray, Fontevrault, etc.) is a necessary starting-point for any psychological study of the author or his work.

22 *Pompes Funèbres*, p. 113.

23 *Thief*, pp. 89-90. 'Toutes étaient mortes. Ce que nous en voyions se promener dans la rue, étaient des Ombres retranchées du monde.' (*Journal*, p. 107)

24 *Rose*, p. 53. (*Miracle*, p. 223)

25 *Pompes Funèbres*, p. 120.

26 *Our Lady*, p. 100. 'Ses histoires à la flan [. . . .]. Les tantes, là-haut, avaient leur langage à part. L'argot servait aux hommes. C'était la langue mâle.' (*Notre-Dame*, p. 34)

27 *Thief*, p. 147. (*Journal*, p. 175)

28 *Ibid.*, p. 151. 'Il me manquait le goût du bonheur terrestre.' (*Journal*, p. 179)

29 *Ibid.*, p. 26-7. 'En effet, si mon esprit supportait, désirait même, l'humilité, jeune et violent mon corps refusait l'humiliation.' (*Journal*, p. 33)

30 *Ibid.*, pp. 70-71. (*Journal*, p. 84)

31 *Our Lady*, pp. 304, 170, 94. '. . . pour se rendre plus répugnante' [. . . .] 'Culafroy et Divine aux goûts délicats seront toujours contraints d'aimer ce qu'ils abhorrent.' [. . . .] 'Le seul moyen d'éviter l'horreur de l'horreur est de s'abandonner à elle.' (*Notre-Dame*, pp. 166, 79, 30)

32 *Thief*, p. 79. 'Cette idée d'humiliation se détacha de ce qui la conditionnait [. . . .] et elle demeura seule, de soi-même seule raison d'être, seule nécessité d'elle-même et seul but de soi.' (*Journal*, pp. 94-5)

33 *Ibid.*, p. 64. '. . . de me savoir l'intérieur de l'âme pourri.' (*Journal*, p. 76)

34 *Ibid.*, p. 14. 'Je fus donc un pou avec la conscience de l'être.' (*Journal*, p. 18)

35 *Rose*, p. 87. 'Ces paroles étaient dans sa bouche comme l'algue de velours noir qu'un plongeur ramène autour de sa cheville.' (*Miracle*, p. 248)

36 *Our Lady*, p. 173. 'La lune sonna dix heures.' (*Notre-Dame*, p. 81)

37 *Ibid.*, p. 107. '. . . couché dans une coupe de champagne au milieu d'un paysage grec de colonnes annelées.' (*Notre-Dame*, p. 39)

38 *Ibid.*, p. 202. (*Notre-Dame*, p. 99)

39 *Ibid.*, p. 282-4. Also pp. 73, 167-175. (*Notre-Dame*, pp. 152-3; also pp. 17, 77-82)

40 *Q. of B.*, p. 200. (*Querelle*, pp. 286-7)

41 *Rose*, p. 216. (*Miracle*, p. 341). Since the time when I developed the argument which I have based on this passage, it has been confirmed by Genet himself that his original sentence to Mettray was *both* for theft *and* for stabbing another boy in the eye with a pen-knife. However, I have decided to let my original version stand, since the principle which it illustrates—the interweaving of fact and legend—is still valid, even though, in this particular instance, there appears to be a solider basis of fact than I at first believed to be the case.

42 *Our Lady*, p. 142. 'Quelque chose de nouveau, comme une sorte de sentiment de puissance, leva (sens végétal, germinatif) en Divine. Elle se crut virilisée.' (*Notre-Dame*, p. 61)

43 *Cf.* the novels of Angus Wilson, for instance.

44 *Our Lady*, p. 71 '. . . en elles-mêmes, secrètement, Monseigneur, les Mimosas, Castagnette, toutes enfin, les tantes [. . . .] se rejoignirent sans bruit mais en dégageant un léger parfum de désespoir que personne ne décela.' (*Notre-Dame*, p. 15)

45 *Ibid.*, p. 301. (*Notre-Dame*, p. 164)

46 *Rose*, p. 190. 'Le désespoir vous fait sortir de vous-même.' (*Miracle*, p. 323)

47 *Ibid.*, p. 94. (*Miracle*, p. 253)

48 *Thief*, p. 24. 'C'est à partir de lui que s'ordonnèrent de nouveaux principes, sans cesse combattus par les forces du monde.' (*Journal*, pp. 29-30)

49 *Ibid.*, p. 186. 'Je désire un instant porter une attention aigüe sur la réalité du suprême bonheur dans le désespoir : quand on est seul, soudain, en face de sa perte soudaine, lorsqu'on assiste à l'irrémédiable destruction de son oeuvre et de soi-même.' (*Journal*, p. 221)

50 One suspects, incidentally, that the psychological benefits of burglary were largely imaginary, and that in any case they were probably small compared with those which must result from the intellectual domination of an international audience. Merely in terms of cash, a new play by Jean Genet is guaranteed to extract more money from

the pockets of the prosperous bourgeoisie than a hundred burglaries. Which probably goes to prove Cocteau's point, although perhaps not exactly in the way that Cocteau meant it: 'Un de ces jours, on se rendra compte que c'est un moraliste'.

51 *Rose*, p. 29. 'Premier peut-être d'entre les casseurs, je sortis sans m'être préoccupé du liquide.' (*Miracle*, p. 207)

52 *Ibid.*, p. 220. 'J'aime l'acte de dérober parce que je le vois, en lui-même, élégant.' (*Miracle*, p. 344)

53 *Thief*, p. 84. 'Ce que j'ai recherché surtout, c'est d'être la conscience du vol dont j'écris le poème.' (*Journal*, p. 100)

54 *Ibid.*, p. 84. 'Je fus un voleur habile. Jamais on ne me prit sur le fait, en "flagrant délit".' (*Journal*, p. 100)

55 *Ibid.*, p. 195. '. . . . une succession de gestes étriqués, mais brûlants.' (*Journal*, p. 232)

56 *Ibid.*, p. 167. 'Ce qu'il me faut, c'est le fric. Le beau boulot, c'est de réussir.' (*Journal*, p. 198)

57 *Ibid.*, p. 255. Mignon: 'c'était audacieux, mais plus *beau*.' (*Notre-Dame*, p. 134)

58 *Thief*, pp. 138-40. (*Journal*, pp. 163-5)

59 *Rose*, p. 26. 'Je voulus être moi-même, et je fus moi-même quand je me révélai casseur.' (*Miracle*, p. 205)

60 *Ibid.*, p. 112. 'Je suis allé vers le vol comme vers une libération, vers la lumière.' (*Miracle*, p. 266)

61 *Thief*, p. 79. 'Je reconnais qu'elles [les prisons] ont leurs assises en moi-même, elles sont les signes de mes tendances extrêmes les plus violentes.' (*Journal*, p. 94)

62 *Ibid.*, pp. 110-111. 'Si je vole ici je n'accomplis aucune action singulière et qui puisse me réaliser mieux: j'obéis à l'ordre habituel. Je ne le détruis pas. Je ne commets pas le mal, je ne dérange rien. Le scandale est impossible. Je vole à vide.' (*Journal*, pp. 130-1)

63 *Ibid.*, p, 112. 'Je ne connais pas de voyous qui ne soient des enfants.' (*Journal*, p. 132)

64 *Ibid.*, p. 198. 'Pour me rassurer, sans doute, pour étayer mon inconsistance, j'avais besoin de supposer mes amants taillés dans la plus dure des matières.' (*Journal*, p. 236)

65 *Ibid.*, p. 78. '. . . dans ces tapis, quelle sécurité, dans ces miroirs. . . .' (*Journal*, p. 93)

66 *Ibid.*, pp. 78-9. 'Au détenu la prison offre le même sentiment de sécurité qu'un palais royal offre à l'invité d'un roi [. . . .] La prison m'entoure d'une garantie parfaite. [. . . .] Rien ne la démolira. Coups de vent, tempêtes, faillites n'y peuvent. La prison reste sûre de soi et vous au milieu d'elle sûrs de vous.' (*Journal*, 93-94)

67 *Rose*, p. 26. '. . . cette marche vers l'homme.' (*Miracle*, p. 204)

68 *Ibid.*, pp. 173-4. 'Il n'est pas dans mon destin d'être un grand bandit [. . . .] La poésie des grands oiseaux de proie m'échappe.' (*Miracle*, pp. 310-11)

69 *Q. of B.*, p. 203. (*Querelle*, p. 289)

70 *Pompes Funèbres*, p. 63.

71 *Thief*, p. 169. 'Peu à peu je comprenais sa beauté. Je crois même que je la créais, décidant qu'elle serait ce visage et ce corps, à partir de l'idée de police qu'ils devraient signifier.' (*Journal*, p. 201)

72 *Ibid.*, p. 115. (*Journal*, p. 136)

73 *Ibid.*, p. 216. (*Journal*, p. 256)

74 *Rose*, p. 157. 'Je compris que j'avais tort de donner à Bulkaen cette douceur que [sa beauté] mettait en moi [. . . .] cette beauté était en moi et non en lui.' (*Miracle*, p. 299)

75 *Our Lady*, p. 198. 'Il faut qu'à tout prix, je revienne à moi.' (*Notre-Dame*, p. 97)

76 *Thief*, p. 13. '. . . j'utiliserai les mots non afin qu'ils dépeignent mieux un événement ou son héros mais qu'ils vous instruisent sur moi-même.' (*Journal*, p. 17)

77 *Our Lady*, p. 109. 'Mignon surtout je le chéris, car vous ne doutez pas qu'en fin de compte, c'est mon destin, vrai ou faux, que je mets, tantôt haillon, tantôt manteau de cour, sur les épaules de Divine.' (*Notre-Dame*, p. 40)

78 *Ibid.*, p. 80. '. . . remontant le cours de ma vie.' (*Notre-Dame*, p. 21)

79 *Thief*, pp. 239-240. (*Journal*, pp. 284-5)

80 *Ibid.*, p. 183. 'Par l'écriture j'ai obtenu ce que je cherchais. Ce qui, m'étant un enseignement, me guidera, ce n'est pas ce que j'ai vécu mais le ton sur lequel je le rapporte. Non les anecdotes mais l'oeuvre d'art. Non ma vie mais son interprétation. C'est ce que m'offre le langage pour l'évoquer, pour parler d'elle, la traduire. Réussir ma légende. Je sais ce que je veux. . . .' (*Journal*, pp. 217-8)

81 *Our Lady*, pp. 177-190. (*Notre-Dame*, pp. 83-91)

82 *Ibid.*, p. 73. (*Notre-Dame*, p. 16)

83 *Ibid.*, p. 144. '. . . réserve de cuisses, de bras, de torses, de visages, de cheveux, de dents, de mains, de genoux.' (*Notre-Dame*, p. 62)

84 *Rose*, p. 79. '. . . un beau soldat allemand.' (*Miracle*, p. 242)

85 *Q. of B.*, p. 26. 'Un marin saoul chancelant sur des jambes épaisses, [. . . .] un docker courbé sur une fille, un voyou peut-être armé d'un couteau, nous-mêmes, vous, au coeur palpitant.' (*Querelle*, p. 182)

86 *Our Lady*, p. 134. 'Je vous laisse libre d'imaginer le dialogue.' (*Notre-Dame*, p. 56)

87 *Q. of B.*, p. 28. 'Nous aimerions que ces réflexions, ces observations que ne peuvent accomplir ni formuler les personnages du livre, permissent de vous poser non en observateurs mais en créateurs de ces person-nages qui, peu à peu, se dégageront de vos propres mouvements.' (*Querelle*, p. 184)

88 Omitted in the English translation of *Q. of B.* 'Toutefois, afin de ne pas trop agacer le lecteur, et certain qu'il complétera, par son propre malaise, le contradictoire, le retors cheminement de l'idée de meurtre en nous-mêmes, nous nous sommes refusé beaucoup.' (*Querelle*, p. 215)

89 *Rose*, p. 207. 'L'oeuvre flambe et son modèle meurt.' (*Miracle*, p. 335)

90 *Ibid.*, p. 206-7. 'Au fur et à mesure que j'écris de lui, je débarrasse Bulkaen de tout l'attrait que je lui voyais. [. . . .] Et je n'ai plus qu'une infinie pitié pour ce pauvre piaf qui ne peut plus voler parce que je l'ai dépouillé de toutes ses plumes.' (*Miracle*, pp. 334-5)

91 This two-way interaction of life and art is one of the main themes developed by another contemporary novelist, Michel Butor, especi-ally in *Degrés*.

92 *Pompes Funèbres*, p. 10.

93 *Our Lady*, p. 103. 'Un peu de répit, de bonheur même.' (*Notre-Dame*, p. 36)

94 *Ibid.*, p. 75. 'Elle sert un texte qu'elle ignore.' (*Notre-Dame*, p. 18)

95 *Ibid.*, pp. 136-7. '. . . par ce qu'il aurait pu être encore, et qu'il ne sera pas *grâce à moi*.' (*Notre-Dame*, p. 58)

96 *Rose*, p. 226. '. . . est ce qu'ils sont *aussi*, eux-mêmes ignorant de l'être.' (*Miracle*, p. 349)

97 *Ibid.*, p. 109. 'Ils écrivaient mon histoire. Ils étaient mes personnages. Ils ne comprenaient rien à Mettray. Ils étaient idiots.' (*Miracle*, p. 264)

98 *Q. of B.*, pp. 293-4. 'En voulant préciser le mouvement psychologique de nos héros, nous voulons mettre au jour notre âme. Noter librement l'attitude que nous choisirions—en vue peut-être ou plutôt en *prévision* d'une fin convoitée—nous conduit à la découverte de ce monde psychologique donné sur quoi s'appuie la liberté du choix mais, s'il le faut, pour le déroulement de l'intrigue, que l'un des héros prononce un jugement, réfléchisse, nous nous trouvons tout à coup en face de l'arbitraire : le personnage échappe à son auteur. Il se singularise. Nous devrons donc admettre qu'un facteur le composant sera—après coup—décelé par l'auteur.' (*Querelle*, p. 334)

99 Simone de Beauvoir, *La Force de l'Âge*, p. 595.

100 *Rose*, p. 162. 'L'auteur d'un beau poème est toujours mort.' (*Miracle*, p. 303)

101 *Ibid.*, p. 30. 'Mon enfance étant morte, en parlant d'elle je parlerai d'une morte.' (*Miracle*, p. 207)

102 *Funambulists* in *E.R.*, p. 49. 'Tes sauts, tes tours, tes bonds étaient en toi et ils n'en savaient rien. Grâce à tes charmes, ils savent qu'ils sont et qu'ils sont toi-même t'illustrant.' (*Le Funambule*, p. 204)

103 *Our Lady*, p. 262. 'J'ai longtemps cru que l'oeuvre poétique proposait des conflits; elle les annule.' (*Notre-Dame*, p. 139)

104 *Funambulists* in *E.R.*, p. 46. 'La Mort—la Mort dont je te parle, n'est pas celle qui suivra ta chute, mais celle qui précède ton apparition sur le fil.' (*Le Funambule*, p. 180)

105 *Ibid.*, p. 46. 'Mais rien—ni surtout les applaudissements ou les rires—n'empêchera que tu ne danses pour ton image. [. . . .] Danse donc seul. Pâle, livide, anxieux de plaire ou de déplaire à ton image : or, c'est ton image qui va danser pour toi.' (*Le Funambule*, pp. 179-80)

106 *Ibid.*, p. 46. 'Celui qui dansera sera mort—décidé à toutes les beautés, capable de toutes.' (*Le Funambule*, p. 180)

107 *Thief*, p. 47. '. . . à laquelle ma nervosité m'allait rendre perméable.' (*Journal*, p. 56)

108 *Rose*, pp. 275-6. (*Miracle*, p. 384)

109 *Thief*, p. 67. 'De la beauté même de cet endroit du monde je n'osais m'apercevoir. A moins que ce ne fût pour rechercher le secret de cette beauté, derrière elle l'imposture dont on sera victime si l'on s'y fie. En la refusant je découvris la poésie.' (*Journal*, p. 79)

110 *Ibid.*, p. 230. '. . . pauvreté honteuse et humiliée.' (*Journal*, p. 273)

111 *Ibid.*, pp. 143 and 80. (*Journal*, pp. 169 and 95-6)

112 *Ibid.*, p. 240. '. . . cette contrée de moi que j'ai nommée l'Espagne.' (*Journal*, p. 286)

113 *Ibid.*, pp. 106-7. '. . . car je refuse de vivre pour une autre fin que celle même que je trouvais contenir le premier malheur : que ma vie doit être légende, c'est-à-dire lisible, et sa lecture donner naissance à quelque émotion nouvelle que je nomme poésie.' (*Journal*, p. 126)

114 *Ibid.*, p. 89 note. 'Ce que j'écris fut-il vrai? Faux? Seul ce livre d'amour sera réel. Les faits qui lui servirent de prétexte? Je dois en être le dépositaire. Ce n'est pas eux que je restitue.' (*Journal*, p. 107 note)

5

LOVE THINE ENEMY

(Pompes Funèbres)

Hatred of God may bring the soul to God.
W. B. Yeats

Un tué, ça m'émeut. Quinze mille tués,
c'est de la statistique.
Philippe Berthelot

Genet's third novel, *Pompes Funèbres* (1947), marks the beginning
of the transition, discussed in the previous chapter, from an essentially autobiographical form of writing to something rather more
objective. In this way, it is a landmark on Genet's road to liberation—which does not, however, mean that it is necessarily an outstanding achievement in its own right. Rather the contrary. It is
certainly the weakest of the four novels and, with the exception of
the *Poèmes*, perhaps the poorest work that he has so far published.

To begin with, its technique is uncertain. Its opening pages hark
back to a far more conventional form of structure than had been
the case either with *Our Lady of the Flowers* or with *Miracle of the
Rose*, and its narrative framework is at once more rigid and more
intrusive than in the earlier works. Consequently, the insistent and
by now rather monotonous technique of fragmentation tends to become irritating (there is no really convincing reason why the *petite
bonne* episodes should be scattered a page here and a page there
across the book, since—unlike the convict-galley episodes in *Miracle*

of the Rose—they form a coherent sequence, and further—unlike the Lt Seblon episodes in *Querelle of Brest*—this sequence is strictly chronological). Some of the episodes—the Hitler-Paulo sequence, for instance—are developed to a length which bears no proportion to their significance. Worse still, the dialogue, if only because, in a large part of the book, Genet avoids using the *argot* which fascinates him and of which he is the master, is dull, the symbolism is repetitive and uninspired, the thought occasionally collapses into banality; and if any single one of Genet's writings deserves the epithet pornographic, in its plainest sense, it is certainly *Pompes Funèbres*. The ultimate indictment of pure pornography, as every educated reader of *Justine* or of *Histoire d'O* eventually finds out to his disappointment, is that it is phenomenally dull : the verbal variations which can be attained to describe purely *physically* a physical act are miserably few.

It seems fairly clear that one of the reasons for the unsatisfactory nature of much of *Pompes Funèbres* lies in the impact of Jean-Paul Sartre. Sartre, as we have seen, was one of the first to recognize Genet's extraordinary talent, one of the first to help him and to foster his literary reputation. But on a purely intellectual level, it is unquestionable that part of the sympathy that Sartre felt for Genet sprang from the fact that the philosopher saw in the authentic criminal a superb living illustration of the truth of certain of his own convictions; and without fail, an illustration as quick-witted as Genet would tend, having once grasped the ideas, either to identify himself with them, or else consciously to refute them. Yet Genet's mysticism is at bottom about as far removed as possible from the intransigent rationalism of *Being and Nothingness*, and his attempts to absorb, or even to understand, Sartre, are not always successful. Not only are there passages in *Pompes Funèbres* which appear to be direct reminiscences of Sartre—in particular, Riton's attempts to murder the cat echo Daniel's attempts to do the same thing in *The Age of Reason*, while the Last Supper of the Nazi detachment on the roofs of Paris reads almost like a parody of the final meal which Mathieu shares with the French *chasseurs* on the church-tower in *Death in the Soul*—but, more seriously, certain purely abstract concepts appear to have been adopted from *Being and Nothingness*, developed or refuted, without any complete understanding of their implications. To take an isolated but characteristic example : in *Being and Nothingness*, in discussing the problem of sincerity in relation to the emotions, Sartre argues that a sorrow *(une tristesse)* which *knows itself* to be a sorrow is already conscious of its appearance-as-sorrow, and consequently can never be absolute : 'The being-in-itself of sorrow perpetually haunts my consciousness of being sorrowful [. . . .] as a value which I can never realise'.[1] Genet, in terms borrowed from a slightly more flexible vocabulary, takes up an identical theme in *Pompes Funèbres*:

> *Est-il bien sûr que le chagrin est plus grand si l'on en a davantage con-science? On a conscience de son chagrin quand on garde l'esprit braqué sur lui, quand on l'examine dans une tension qui ne fléchit pas: il vous dessèche alors comme un soleil regardé en face, son feu vous dévore à tel point que j'éprouvai longtemps une brûlure à mes paupières. Mais il arrive aussi que le chagrin désagrège les facultés, disperse l'esprit. [. . . .] Nous souffrons de ne pouvoir fixer notre chagrin; nos actes s'enveloppent d'une aura de lassitude et de regret qui fait paraître les actes faux—faux de très peu, vrais en gros, mais faux puisqu'ils ne nous comblent pas. Un malaise les accompagne tous.*[2]

The result is a much-weakened Sartrian argument which, to make matters worse, is not even good Genet, since the premises are not essentially his own, whereas the startling power of Genet's para-doxes comes from the fact that, when he is at his best, he never puts forward a case unless he *feels* it—either as something absolutely true in itself, or else as something so diametrically opposed to the conventional attitudes that it alone is capable of expressing the depths of his inner violence and his otherness. In *Pompes Funèbres* and in all Genet's later works, the influence of Sartre is considerable; but its value is problematic. For if, on the one hand, Sartre seems to have taught Genet to argue out his paradoxes more systematically than before—as in *Querelle of Brest*—on the other hand, he has given Genet's quest for objectivity, in its later stages, a slant towards socialist commitment—as in *The Blacks* and *The Screens*—which is perhaps directly at variance with Genet's inherent tendencies and convictions, and which leads to a form of literary expression which is undoubtedly far more positive and moral than *Our Lady*, but in the end, maybe, less convincing. In a sense, Sartre has encouraged, if not actually inspired, Genet's conversion to literature. Genet him-self in the early novels, and again in the *Journal*, makes a clear distinction between poetry and literature, and invariably speaks of the latter with contempt. Poetry is his awareness of the trans-cendental, it expresses what he *is*, what he feels, urgently and directly; literature involves making patterns with words in a calm spirit of objectivity. Sometimes he seems to hope that the two can be recon-ciled, as in *Pompes Funèbres*[3]; but more often, Genet feels that words, and the whole art or trade of writing, are inferior substitutes for a good burglary, and that all the books in the world might be consigned to the flames if thereby a single beautiful *gesture* might be preserved. But after 1948-9 this attitude becomes less and less prevalent, and with *The Balcony*, it seems that Genet's conversion

to the pleasures of abstract argument—or even to pure showmanship and delight in virtuoso techniques—is complete. Perhaps it is
unfair to blame Sartre for this change; perhaps it would have come
in any case. And *possibly* it is all for the best. None the less, there
is an intensity which is felt whenever Genet is arguing, however
fantastically, along his own lines, which is lost when he argues,
however literally and soberly, along those of Sartre; and here and
there (particularly in *The Balcony*) we find some disquietingly
muddled thinking as Genet struggles to reconcile what he really
feels with what Sartre tells him a genuinely authentic social outcast *ought* to feel.

The story of *Pompes Funèbres*, although coherent, is still rudimentary. Jean Genet's friend and lover, Jean Decarnin[4] (the interchangeability of Christian names here is a gimmick which becomes irritating in the long run, as does the equally artificial and
tricky alternation of pronouns from 'he' to 'I') has been killed by a
sniper—either a German or a Vichy-Government militiaman—
during the street-fighting which accompanied the liberation of Paris
in 1944. Jean Decarnin, it seems, was a communist *maquisard* (here,
disquietingly, for the first time we find Genet tending to ally himself
with the acceptable side); Jean's brother, Paulo, probably a collabor-
ator. At the funeral and afterwards, Genet meets Jean Decarnin's
mother and her lover, whom she has hidden from the vengeance of
the mob: a Nazi officer named Erik Seiler.[5] Genet visits the spot
where his friend was killed and indulges in some macabre meditations; later he goes to the cinema and watches on a newsreel the
vengeance of the crowds on a militiaman whom they have managed
to capture after the fighting among the rooftops. Gradually, as the
film proceeds, the despair and tragic love which Jean Genet had
borne towards Jean Decarnin are transferred to this unknown traitor
and enemy, whom he decides to call 'Riton'; and piece by piece he
puts together a phantasmagoria of episodes, some recent, some
going back into the past, which finally bring together Erik and
Riton in a potlatch of love and death among the chimney-stacks
at the hour when Jean Decarnin was killed. Interwoven with this
main narrative are two other themes: the first involving Paulo in
a drearily detailed relationship (perhaps titillating for homosexual
readers, although I doubt it) with a hopelessly unimaginative
symbolic figure whom Genet calls 'Hitler'; the other, of incom-
parably greater power and inventiveness, involving the little kitchen-
maid who had been Jean Decarnin's mistress, and who must now
trudge towards the cemetery under the summer sun to bury her
dead child. *La petite bonne* is the first female character who is
sympathetically portrayed in Genet's work; and the portrayal is full

of implications, both social and artistic, which will be developed later.

The ostensible main theme of the book—the macabre rituals of death and sex—are in fact not the most essential, certainly not the most original aspect of the novel. It is only when Genet watches the reactions of the audience in the cinema at the end of the newsreel that the tale suddenly begins to emerge from mediocrity, for at this point a genuinely new idea—and a most typically Genetian paradox at that—has come into being : the mirror-identity of love and hate.

In order to appreciate the significance of this notion, it is perhaps necessary, first of all, to look in some detail at the idea, or ideal, of *love*, as it emerges from Genet's novels. The first problem, of course, is to try and disentangle Genet's notion of love from the complex impulses of sexuality which, at first reading, appear to dominate all his own, and his characters' reactions, from the most violent to the most intimate and obscure.

Let us take, first, the concept of sexuality as such. Sexually, all Genet's characters—most typically Divine—are symbols of a excessively passive homosexuality. One and all feel themselves as objects, as having more in common with the world of Things than with the world of Beings, until they are given life by the Other, who comes to them from outside equipped with all the supra-natural powers of virility, and who, by destroying their identity-as-object, bestows on them a new kind of identity—a reality which is experienced as life, yet which, since it belongs essentially to the Other, not to the Self, cannot be conceived clearly as constituting an individuality. The effect on Divine—or on Lt Seblon, or apparently on Jean Genet himself—of this submission to the life-force of the Other is three-fold. At the outset, it is experienced as a destruction, accompanied by pain and violence, of the original, comfortable identity of the Self-as-object : Darling, observes Divine (or Genet?), '[entered] in me until there was no room left for myself'[6]—that is to say, the experience includes a considerable dosage of pure masochism[7] which, as is quite usual in this type of psychology, evokes in dream-form a sublimating compensation that adopts the guise, either of sadistic actions, or else of objects suggesting a violent sadistic impulse—the spikes, for instance, that guard the main door of La Féria, which are 'a symbol of the cruelties that attend the rites of love.'[8]

The second effect of the impact of the Other is that the former object is almost literally brought to life—but with a life and an identity which are felt as something *stolen* from the male being who originally appears as possessor and conqueror, so that the conqueror is in fact the conquered, the possessor is the possessed, and the male warrior is secretly and cannibalistically consumed by his own would-be victim. Thus is the passive creature revenged of its own passivity; its very weakness is in the long run more deadly than the glistening muscles of the stokers or the SS men—a theme which is specifically developed in the Hitler-episodes of *Pompes Funèbres*.[9]

In the third and final stage, however, the once-passive being, having sucked the life out of its conquerors (as Divine sucks the life-blood of Darling and of Our Lady) and ultimately destroyed them, comes to realize that all the same, its new identity, its 'life', even if conquered, is still *borrowed*, and therefore is and will remain tormentingly alien to itself and indefinable. It is no longer the passive, yet clear-cut identity of the Self-as-object; it is an active identity—but which or what? It is neither the Self nor the Other, but something in between. Or rather, almost *anything* in between. As Divine notes after her dispossession by Darling, '. . . now I am one with gangsters, burglars and pimps, and the police arrest me by mistake.'[10]

Here we have the origins of those problems of elusive identity which form the theme of so much of Genet's later writings, in particular *The Maids* and *The Balcony*. And in this sense, much of the structure of Genet's thought is determined in the first instance by this basic, and very personal, pattern of sexual reactions. Similarly the dreams of violence, the consciousness of an intimate relationship with objects, the mystic concept of possession ('Nothing [. . . .] will ever console me for not containing the world'), the innate tendency to *la méchanceté* which is the characteristic of the passive homosexual, and which is essentially an awareness of the hidden powers of revenge which lie in his very weakness—all have their origins, directly or remotely, in the accidental phenomenon of Genet's passive homosexuality. None the less, this underlying sexual structure is not in itself entirely constant. The purely passive element, whose psychology predominates and sets the whole tone of the first two novels, is much less exclusive in *Pompes Funèbres*, where the *moi*-narrator comes to be identified with the primarily active and virile Erik; while in *Querelle of Brest*, the structures of passivity are, broadly speaking, confined to the character of Lt Seblon, and even he—a competent naval officer, self-assured in the armour of his authority, his habit of command, his uniform, even his hair-cut— is so much more successful than Divine in transforming himself into a male that his femininity is never more than intermittent, and he himself is aware of it only from time to time, 'invading his whole body and filling it with milk'.[11]

All in all, the psychological substructure of *Querelle of Brest*, while still remaining characteristically homosexual, is essentially that of the active possessor rather than that of the passive possessed. Whether this evolution—which continues and is in fact developed still further in the later plays—originates in a genuine 'progress towards virilization' in Genet himself, or whether it represents a positive, imaginative achievement by an author who was by now sufficiently assured of his talent to risk exploring the problems of a type of personality which is fundamentally alien to him, it is hard to decide. Probably something of each is involved. In any case, the change is one of the most notable features in the evolution of Genet as an artist.

However—and while making all due allowance for the influences, conscious or subconscious, of a particular form of sexuality on the structure, and even on the philosophy, of the novels—it would be completely wrong to attribute *all* the emotional characteristics to this special origin. The most striking feature of Genet's vision of the world is that each of its major components, although it may ultimately have its remoter origins in a limited and primitive sexual reaction, none the less, by its subsequent developments, transcends these origins so completely, that we should normally forget about the particular sexual act which constitutes their beginning, were it not for the fact that, every now and then, Genet deliberately gives us a reminder. And it is precisely the shock of contrast between the ineffably abstract and the brutally physical which gives the novels their power; above all, because the traditional opposition between Hedonism and Platonism, between profane and sacred, is here shown to be false. For Dostoievsky, grappling with similar ideas, the significance of the *Brothers Karamazov* was that Dmitri (brutality) and Alyosha (idealism) were sons of the same father. Genet goes a step further : the Saint and the Criminal, the Satyr and the Angel, are complementary aspects of a single indivisible identity.

There is no clearer instance of the manner in which Genet builds up a complex metaphysical argument upon the foundations of a primitive sexual reaction, than in his theory of animism. This theory is so important (we have already seen its contribution to Genet's theory of the nature of poetry) that it is worth examination in some detail. At the root of all lies the fact that the passive homosexual feels himself treated as an object by his more active partner. To feel oneself an object is to have experiences in common with the world of objects, and yet still to know oneself a man; it is to live a borderline existence between the domains of animate and inanimate creation. And gradually, as Genet's thought and sensibility develop under their own impetus, he begins to feel that, between these two symbolic opposites, there is no really clear dividing-line. If anything, as an outcast of animate society, he feels himself more in tune with objects than with men. He talks to them—Saïd, in *The Screens*, talks to the stones and the palm-trees, while Leïla goes a step further and holds a conversation with Saïd's trousers.[12] And in return, they talk to him—not with the language that men have tried to give them, but with the voices of their own singularity, their own existence as absolute objects. The normal language of an object—in particular, of a man-made object—is its meaning. A hammer, for instance, says to the carpenter : 'I exist for the purpose of driving nails into wood'. If it did not say this, it would not be a hammer. But this type of language is a *social* function. The hammer-maker had certain assumptions and preconceptions in common with the hammer-user; and the voice of the hammer is in fact the voice of these communal preconceptions concerning the function of the object.

But Genet, at odds with all society, rejects this type of language, or rather, simply refuses to listen to it. Instead, confronted with objects, he listens to the voice of their identity-as-objects; he sees them *as themselves*, and not as functions of society. He addresses them with grave politeness, and they, often enough, return the compliment. Harcamone is aware of the politeness that objects show towards him; Green Eyes, in *Deathwatch*, is even terrified by their *douceur*. For Genet, man is not so much the master of objects, as their partner in the common enterprise of life—and above all this is true of the artist. Stilitano, an artist in his own way, thinks of the process of shoplifting a pair of wire-cutting pliers as a delicately combined operation between himself and the tool that he desires :

> So well did he know the nature of steel, and the nature of that particular fragment of polished steel called pliers, that it remained, to the point of fatigue, docile, loving, clinging to his shirt. . . .[13]

If this is true even of a not-too-competent house-breaker, how much more so of the higher forms of art? 'Talent,' writes Genet, 'is courtesy with respect to matter; it consists in giving song to what was dumb[14]—and this song is poetry : the poetry, as we have seen, of the Funambulist, or of Alberto Giacometti. In the case of the latter, the relationship is so intimate that the gestures of the living being are continued directly into the metal, the gestures of the metal prolonged into those of the man—and if the sculptor loves his material, the material, in return, loves the sculptor :

> I understand what binds the sculptor to his clay, the painter to his paints, each workman to the matter he works with, and the docility and acquiescence of the matter to the movements of one who animates it.[15]

However, relations between man and object are not always so idyllic. In *Pompes Funèbres*, we find Genet grumbling at *'l'imbécillité d'une planche de sapin'*,[16] and even the light-fingered Stilitano is not always successful as a tamer of the refractory nature of Things. A single clumsy gesture is enough, and the object takes offence : 'At times, however, these objects, which are irritated by a clumsy movement, would hurt him. Stilitano used to cut himself.'[17]

This is the beginning of another development. If objects on the whole are well-disposed towards Genet himself, or towards the artist who understands them, they are relentlessly hostile to Man in general—above all, to Social Man, who, like some brutal circus-trainer, imposes *his* will and meaning on them, and arrogantly ignores their own. And then the objects take their revenge. It is the furniture which turns informer in *The Maids*[18]; while Culafroy feels the hostility of the whole inanimate world at once,[19] and Clément Village, after the murder of Sonia, for the first time becomes aware of the fundamental attribute of sunlight : 'malevolence'.[20] The gentle Leïla treats the needles that prick her as a mother treats her over-boisterous children, with tenderness and tolerance :

> *Mother:* Has it pricked you again?
> *Leïla:* Don't be angry with it, it's only playing.[21]

But in other circumstances, the revenge of objects can be very much more serious. Men have designated objects by their function, and thus believe that they have mastered them, reduced their own voices to servitude and given them a new, more docile voice, dictated by society. But the living object beneath this dead and stylised function can still re-assert itself and subtly turn the tables on its masters. Man took metal and fashioned it in the image of a social function, and called it a revolver. Which implies that *he* will use the revolver, as and when he wants. But suppose the revolver should subvert that meaning for its own purposes? Suppose that it should say to its self-styled master: 'Here I am, I *am* my function, use me and use me *now* !'—then, by the assertiveness of its very existence, the revolver has turned the man into a murderer. It has 'dictated his attitude'.[22] In the conflict between animate and inanimate, the metal has conquered, the tool has destroyed its master by the very fact of its existence, just as the hydrogen bomb will inevitably do; just as (in a gentler context) the bronze has won its victories over Giacometti.[23] In so far as the universe, in Genet's vision, is governed by a tragic and ineluctable fatality, this fatality works through the inanimate. Objects are the strong right arm of God.

And there is still a further consequence, for it is Genet's concept of the independent voice of objects which forms his direct link with Camus, Ionesco and the 'Pataphysicians, and plunges him headlong among the paradoxes of the Absurd. Genet seems to have developed

his irrationalist philosophy almost unaided, by a logical development of specific first principles that originated in his own experience.
There are hardly any traces of specifically absurdist influences in the
novels, nor, even in the dramas, so much as a hint of Ionesco until
The Screens.[24] There is nothing superficial about Genet's *chosisme*;
it is inherent in his vision of the world and of society. For if the
meaning of an object is the voice which is given it in terms of its
social function, and if Genet rejects lock, stock and barrel the key
concept of the society which gave it that voice, then the meaning
of every object becomes utterly arbitrary, dictated only by itself and
the bare fact of its existence. There are no categories of objects :
there are no clothes-pegs, since the concept-category 'clothes-peg'
implies a function, consequently a system of communication, consequently a society within which to communicate. There is merely
that object, hanging on a wire. Everything becomes autonomous;
every moment in time an absolute and independent instantaneity
without past or future : it becomes impossible to count (relevantly)
up to ten, because a sequence of numbers implies a sociological
relationship which now, for Genet, is no longer a reality. There *is*
only one number : the number *one*. Consequently, as in Ionesco,
there are no surprises. Since every event is autonomous and unique,
the fact of its existence is merely the fact of its existence : nothing
more. Surprise at this fact implies a comparison, and therefore a
relationship, with other facts—but this relationship has evaporated
into air. 'I saw clearly,' asserts Genet in the *Journal*, 'and *anything
could have happened*.'[25]

It would seem incontrovertible that any such 'pataphysical awareness of the total arbitrariness of phenomena must have held certain
inconveniences for the professional burglar, and Genet's repeated
convictions are hardly to be wondered at. Yet in the end, it is not
as the burglar that he will be remembered, but as the philosopher;
and the pages of the *Journal* which develop this vision of the autonomy of objects are among the classic documents in any history of
the Absurd. Genet is in Antwerp, when suddenly the whole world
of phenomena begins to disintegrate, dissolving into Negation, just
as it did a few years later for Ionesco, when the tritely lapidary
sentences of his *Handbook of Conversational English* dissolved into
the nightmare of *The Bald Prima-Donna* :

> I felt I was perceiving things with blinding lucidity. Even the most trivial
> of them had lost their usual meaning, and I reached the point of wonder-
> ing whether it was true that one drank from a glass or put on a shoe.
> [. . . .] I had the revelation of an absolute perception as I considered, in
> the state of luxurious detachment of which I have been speaking, a clothes-
> pin left behind on a line. [. . . .] I felt lost and absurdly light.[26]

Many years later, this characteristic awareness of the arbitrary autonomy of objects will dictate his final attitudes towards the essential problems of politics, socialism and commitment; for Genet's awareness of the world becomes increasingly one which acknowledges an equal right of love (or hate) and solitude for every individual being and object. Every being, every object, argues Sartre in *Being and Nothingness,* is-what-it-is. Every being, every object, counters Genet in *Giacometti,* not only is what it is, but *has a right* to be what it is, and to continue to be what it was. But what it *will be* depends on itself : no mere human being has a right to decide the future for anyone or for anything else . . . not even for a clothes-peg. And the autonomous reality of the clothes-peg is a far more real phenomenon than the utilitarian definition which Social Man has imposed upon it. If Socialism claims to dictate *our* future and *our* social functions, then not only men, but even clothes-pegs will revolt—and take their revenge. But this is leading us straight into the problems of *The Balcony,* and *The Screens.*

To return to *Pompes Funèbres.* The purpose of the preceding digression has been to demonstrate the type of abstract, philosophical developments which in Genet's novels, may originate from a simple accident of sexual experience. These developments may take us into the realms of politics, metaphysics, art or religion, yet the sexual starting-point is never forgotten, and Genet returns to it again and again with a crude assault of violence whose effect is magnified by contrast. This is the secret of Genet's technique, and thus, ultimately, the purpose of his resolute pornography. And among the many abstract concepts which fill the novels, there is also an ideal of love, which is at the same time rooted in, and yet completely distinct from, sexual experience.

In *Pompes Funèbres,* the relationship between Erik and Riton follows a specific, conventional, homosexual pattern. None the less, the notion of the meaning and the nature of love which emerges from this relationship transcends its own origins so completely that, at times at least, Genet's vision applies just as aptly to a normal as to an abnormal love-affair. Its beginnings lie in the idiosyncratic and the particular; its conclusions reach out towards the universal.

To begin with, love is an *extreme* form of emotional experience, and, like all Absolutes in Genet, has more in common with other Absolutes, even when these are at first sight diametrically opposed to it in nature, than with similar emotions of lesser intensity. 'I have never known what friendship could actually be',[27] he confesses in *Our Lady of the Flowers*—and in fact friendship holds no more interest for his characters than it does for those of Racine. Friendship is relative and provisional; love is mystic, sacred, and, in the strictly Platonic sense, essential—that is, it introduces him who experiences it into the domain of essences, which, like beauty, etc., have an eternal and immutable reality in their own right, regardless of their identification with any individual. Love is *light*—the inconceivable brilliance of light, that is the Light of God[28]; yet love is darkness, 'the shadow of the shadow',[29] which fills the universe with a night of darkness darker than itself. (Here again, incidentally, opposing-Absolutes merge into identity—a not uncommon experience with mystic visionaries who, like Blake, or even Stephen Spender, apprehend light as the darkness which is in effect the shadow cast by the light-of-light which is God.) 'Thou art a sun unto my night,' exclaims Genet/Divine, 'My night is a sun unto thine!'[30] Love is the mystic purification that makes chaste the most degrading of sexual catacylsms.[31] Love is a fatal, implacable, destructive force, a thunderbolt hurled at random by the gods, 'against whom I butt and crumble',[32] as Des Grieux is broken and torn by his blind, inexplicable love for Manon Lescaut—who, characteristically, is one of Genet's favourite heroines, the ideal symbol of eroticism and violence, combining in herself 'that Eternal Couple : the Saint and the Criminal'. Love is the solitude that leads to sanctity, love is suffering and suffering is the exaltation of love.[33] Love is the immanence of God, the immediate awareness of eternity : it is communion, the solemn ceremony of the Mass,[34] while separation from the beloved is despair and the death of the soul. By contrast, *'renoué, c'était la paix avec le monde, le calme, la sécurité'*.[35] Yet the lover—as is the case with Proust's narrator in *In Remembrance of Things Past*—is never loved in return. For Genet, the ideal Other, the beloved, is the mirror-image of himself. The Others have called him a Thief—that is, they have substituted *their* opinion of him for his own knowledge of himself. Therefore he can only know himself through a reflection of himself in the Other, and only *love* that same reflection in an idealized form. In so far as the mirror reflects the Image, so there may be the illusion of a love returned[36]; but in so far as the Other *is* the Mirror, then this mirror, like all other mirrors, is in itself indifferent. It reflects indifferently whatever is shown to it. If it were otherwise, if the mirror showed partiality for one object rather than another, then its reflection would be distorted, consequently no longer idealized, no longer lovable. 'You're not my sweetheart, you're myself,'[37] cries out Divine to the soldier Archangel; yet Archangel, like Darling, like Our

Lady, is a very monument of granitic indifference : 'He sang with
his body; he did not love [. . . .] he went his melody'[38]; and this
essential quality of indifference is found in all those who evoke the
most powerful emotions of love : in Stilitano or in Armand[39], in
Bulkaen, in Botchako, in Erik and in Querelle. For an emotion is
only absolute when it has *itself* as an object—or, to be more precise,
its own reflection—for then it generates, within the narrow circle
of its own limits, the sort of energy that electrons generate moving
within the eternal yet infinitely small circles about their own fixed
centre. In fact, Image and Reflection together make up a self-
sufficient yet dynamic totality—in love as in all other phenomena
in human experience : 'What love is : the knowledge and understanding of separation from one particular being, of what it means
to be divided, and knowing that we are able to look at ourselves
through our own eyes'.[40] Once the forces of love escape from the
circle, that is, once the lover fixes his affections on an Other who
is *not* his own reflection (and no woman, of course, can be the
mirror-image of a man, as Madame Lysiane discovers to her despair), then the vital energy is lost, and in its place all manner of
secondary and irrelevant forces—tenderness, sentimentality, friendship, *douceur*—are generated, which only serve further to detract
from the violence and the crystal hardness, '*comme un couteau de
verre*', of love conceived as an absolute.

If these are the intransigent metaphysics of absolute love, there is
of course some compromise on the practical plane. Even though
the ideal beloved should be beautiful, indifferent, evil (since he must
reflect Genet's evil) and in addition inconceivably stupid (a mirror
requires no intelligence!)—yet he will inevitably have *some* individual characteristics, if only moral ones; and here it is the lover's
concern to adapt himself to the same level, whether upwards (as in
the case of Lucien Sénémaud) or downwards, as in the case of most
of the fictional *beaux voyous* of the novels. If the beloved is a
coward and a traitor, then the lover likewise must make himself a
coward and a traitor, otherwise the equality that subsists between
Figure and Image is destroyed[41] : 'For people can love each other
only on the same moral level'.[42]

On the other hand, since the absolute of love lies essentially in the
recognition of the lover's own double in the beloved, and thus operates in a rigidly closed circle of subjectivism, at least one of the more
devastating miseries of normal love—jealousy—is absent. Since the
beloved is by definition indifferent to the lover, the loss of his
emotions to some other attraction is fundamentally irrelevant. Jealousy, in Genet, is never more than a passing pin-prick suffered by
vanity. Divine feels jealous on one fleeting occasion of Our Lady[43];

and at one point Genet himself, somewhat inconsequently, remarks : *'la seule différence entre l'amour et l'amitié, c'est que cette dernière ne connaît pas la jalousie'*[44]; but these isolated instances have no lasting significance. On the contrary, in *The Thief's Journal*, Genet himself comments on his own lack of jealousy[45]; and among the fictional characters, intricate emotional relationships involving three or more protagonists are not uncommon—in *Our Lady of the Flowers*, for instance, the interwoven loves of Divine, Darling, Our Lady and Seck Gorgui at times become extremely complex. In the last analysis, this is quite logical : for if the beloved is first and foremost a mirror reflecting the image of the lover, then the mirror can reflect, and be reflected, in further mirrors *ad infinitum* without in any way affecting the intensity or clarity of the original image. If A and C both love B, this can only mean that A and C both find their own images in B, and therefore *may* find their own images in each other. The immediate consequence is that A finds yet another reflection of himself, either in C directly or, more intensely still, in C refracted through B. This is the new intensity of emotion that Genet discovers as he seeks for the reflection of another lover— Rocky—in the eyes of his own beloved Bulkaen; yet Bulkaen is looking for yet a further reflection—that of Hersir—in the eyes of Rocky.[46] Thus, through love, a chain of reflections is stretched to infinity across the world, in space, but also in time, 'from the long dead to the far unborn', in Samuel Beckett's words; and the windowless monad of a single love, without destroying the intensity of its own closed circle, is at the same time capable of an extension embracing the whole of life.

If jealousy plays so small a role in *Pompes Funèbres*, it is because for Genet, as distinct from Proust, jealousy is not an Absolute. The Absolute which corresponds to love, and which is, so to speak, its double, is hatred.[47] And since hatred is one of the most powerful emotions, a hatred shared between two persons for a third will give them that common identity, each reflecting the other's image, which is the first condition of love. *'Une haine commune peut seule donner une pareille force à l'amitié,'*[48] remarks Genet (without a hint of political irony) in *Pompes Funèbres*. But an initial hatred at the origin of a common love is essentially not that which interests Genet in his third novel. His concern is to try and grasp intellectually the process by which a sensation or emotion can merge into its opposite when pushed to an absolute extreme. This is the principal subject of *Pompes Funèbres*, and, as developed by Genet in the form of one of his most unlikely paradoxes, it forms a powerful weapon in his shock-attack upon preconceived ideas and ethical-emotional values.

To argue in the abstract that hate and love may be conceived as

identical, or at least as strangely similar emotions, is almost a platitude (a love-hate relationship, etc.). But as soon as Genet develops
the practical implications of the platitude, it turns out to be profoundly disturbing. If love can induce hate, and hate, love, then
you may find love where you expect hate, and hate where all the
evidence suggests love. A father who loves his son may, 'sous les
yeux consternés et scandalisés du public',[49] react with love towards
his son's murderer. Jean Genet loved Jean Decarnin; Jean Decarnin
has been murdered by the militiaman Riton; now the combined
effect of a previous love and the tragic despair of death drive the
present emotion to the point where it becomes an Absolute. Its corresponding opposite-Absolute is hatred for the murderer, Riton.
But at this point of white-heat, the two emotions become interchangeable, and Genet finds himself not hating but loving Riton,
as his form of revenge : 'Ma haine pour le milicien était si forte,
si belle, qu'elle équivalait au plus solide amour'.[50]

The point to grasp is that it is a revenge—and not only in Christ's
sense, that to love one's enemy is to heap coals of fire on his head.
Riton and Jean Decarnin were anonymous soldiers fighting a street-
battle; therefore that one should kill the other is the result of
destiny—i.e. of the unseen, deterministic working-out of material
laws of cause-and-effect, a materialistic fatalism which is the final
denial of human freedom. By the operation of the same laws, it is
'scientifically' predictable that Jean Decarnin's lover will hate his
murderer. Thus, by loving Riton—and by willing to love Riton—
Genet is compelling (in the field of the emotions at least) a cause
to produce the diametrical opposite of its logical effect; he is dis-
rupting the whole sequence of determinism in the universe, and
thereby asserting his own liberty, while at the same time he plunges
Riton into the domain of the gratuitous and the absurd. So, when
Christ said 'Love thine enemies', he became—if we take the commandment at all literally—the instigator of Genet's paradox, and
at the same time the ancestor of Jarry and Beckett and Ionesco,
and the First Prophet of the Absurd.

As if this were not paradoxical enough, Genet takes the argument
further. The identity of dynamic opposites is a complete, or active,
reality, only when one of them is applied to a negative : in mathematical terms, $+ 1 = - 1$ only when the $- 1$ refers to a negative
quantity, so that the equation becomes : $+ 1 = - (- 1)$. In
emotional terms, the (negative) hatred that Genet feels for Riton
can only become the equivalent of the (positive) love he feels for
Jean Decarnin, if Jean Decarnin and Riton are themselves in some
ways opposites—that is, if Riton is the negative of Jean Decarnin.
And this is in fact the case in the novel :

Sa beauté et ses gestes étaient le contraire de la beauté de Jean et de ses gestes. Je fus aussitôt illuminé, d'une lumière intérieure. Un peu d'amour passa sur Riton. [. . . .] Tous les gestes de Riton tuaient ceux de Jean. . . .[51]

Given the same intensity of love for each *('Sur Riton se déversaient les mêmes fleuves d'amour dont pas une goutte n'était retirée à Jean. . . .'*[52]), the gestures and the beauty of each carry equal weight— and thus cancel each other out. *'Je l'ai tué, tu vois'*,[53] says Riton, of Jean—but it is equally true that Jean has annihilated Riton, For Jean, being now dead (having been killed already by Riton with his rifle), is now immune to this secondary, metaphysical assassination . . . whereas Riton, still alive, is not. So now the advantage lies with Jean, who can exterminate Riton in Genet's mind by negating his value—his beauty and his gestures. So once more, by loving Riton, Jean Genet enables Jean Decarnin to wreak his vengeance, in a way perhaps more effective than any other. 'Love thine enemies that thou mayest the better annihilate them.'

This extraordinary piece of irrationalist dialectic is characteristic of the later Genet, and, in spite of its difficulty and its deliberate shifts of premiss from concrete to abstract, is about the most impressive argument in *Pompes Funèbres*. It foreshadows clearly the sort of themes which will be treated in *The Blacks* and in *The Balcony*, in which the purely emotional revolt of the first two novels is transformed into the vitriolic subversiveness of paradox. In *Our Lady of the Flowers*, Genet was still seeking to realize in his vision— perhaps also to incarnate in his own person—a slightly adolescent ideal of absolute evil; the identity-of-opposites argument of *Pompes Funèbres* is the first step in an evolutionary process which leads eventually to a far more practical and effective kind of protest against the iniquities of our society: a half-Nietzschean, half-Socratic dialectic of destruction.

Jean-Paul Sartre, in one of the most illuminating pieces of argument in *Saint Genet*,[54] has demonstrated that to seek by an act of will to identify oneself with absolute evil involves a logical impossibility. 'To be Evil', and at the same time 'to be a consciousness *within* evil' exceeds the range of human limitations; absolute evil is conceivable only in the context of a being whose essence is not confined within the boundaries of logic or rationality—in God, or in the negative equivalent of God, whom we call Satan. Absolute evil is as much the gift of Divine Grace as is absolute good—a fact that Genet later comes to realize clearly, since this black Grace, its operation and its failure to operate, form the central theme of *Deathwatch*.

To take only three of Sartre's many arguments : (i) to *desire* total evil, and subsequently to *achieve* total evil is to realize one's desire; but a desire fulfilled is a good for him who desires, therefore the evil is no longer total. (ii) Evil is a negative concept in itself, it is the opposite of the Good. It implies fundamentally the destruction of that which exists, and an absolute evil is that which destroys absolutely. But whatever is to be destroyed must first exist, therefore good precedes evil, and evil is relative to the good. Thus an absolute evil must at one and the same time be both absolute and relative, which is impossible. (iii) That which is absolute is perfect. But imperfection is less good (the word used now in a transcendental-aesthetic or Cartesian sense) than that which is perfect. Therefore an evil which fails to be perfect is more un-good than one which succeeds. Thus absolute evil is only absolute if it is not absolute—which (again) is impossible. And so on. To some extent, these arguments depend on what we mean in various contexts by the words good and evil, and it is the weakness of Sartre that he rarely asks himself such questions. However, neither does Genet; and all in all Genet's actual experience seems pretty well to confirm the conclusions of Sartre's abstract arguments. That he *desired* at one point to incarnate an absolute evil is unquestionable, whatever the motives : childish revolt, anarchism, social protest, rebellion against God, or the more complex awareness of himself as a negative, *un néant*, a non-existent mirror-opposite of all that was positive, real and other-than-himself. As a child and as an adolescent, he tried to identify himself with that monster of evil, Gilles de Rais (note how the name 'Gil' recurs in *Querelle of Brest*), the ruins of whose castle still stood in that same countryside where Genet was brought up, among fields filled with *'fleurs de genêt'*.[55]

At the outset, Genet's fascination with evil is abstract and aesthetic. As an artist, nothing short of perfection holds the slightest attraction for him; and having been disqualified—in his own imagination at any rate—by the circumstances of his birth from any hopes of attaining to an absolute good, 'absolute evil' remains the only form of moral perfection that lies within his grasp. Its fundamental appeal lies, not in the fact that it is evil, but that it is absolute, and thus belongs to the transcendental domain of beauty, sanctity, purity, etc., to which Genet is ever aspiring. Querelle, for instance, is evil *because* he is pure and beautiful—these attributes go together in exactly the same manner as, for Plato, Truth, Beauty and Goodness are but alternative facets of an identical reality[56]—

or such, at least, is the view of Lt Seblon. Constantly, epithets suggesting brightness rather than darkness are associated with evil :
lucide; *candide*; *bleu*; *gloire*; *auréolé*; etc. The fascination of Mettray lies in the way in which a felt presence of absolute evil is reflected in the flowers, the bright colours, and the lithe young bodies
of the adolescent defaulters : 'The scents remained scents, and the
pure air just as pure, but the evil was in them.'[57]

But if this search for the Absolute considered as a form of
aesthetic perfection is probably the principal motive underlying
Genet's *'hantise du mal'*—and it is perhaps this concern with an
aesthetic ideal which explains why it is that, after *Our Lady of the
Flowers*, there are very few traces of the sort of woolly-minded,
neo-romantic satanism that we meet with, say, in Baudelaire—there
are of course many other forces at work simultaneously. 'A taste
for singularity, together with the fascination of the forbidden, combine to deliver me up to Evil', notes Genet at this time; and if the
concept of the forbidden harks back to Divine, the notion of *la
singularité* is a later development, and one of the *leitmotifs* of
Querelle of Brest, and particularly of *Pompes Funèbres*.

If Divine is aware of her 'solitude', and Genet himself, in *Miracle
of the Rose*, of his isolation, Erik and Querelle are more conscious
of their *singularité*. The difference again lies in the gradual change
from pure passivity to a more active experience of life and art. Divine
essentially *submits* to the evil of her destiny, and sanctifies it by
willing it to be what it is, *i.e.* by using a mental attitude to transform a contingent accident into a necessary Absolute. Divine's will
changes the significance of events without changing the events themselves. But Erik and Querelle use their will-power actually to fashion
their own destiny, to fashion it in the image of an absolute evil that
exists already in their minds. Erik deliberately shoots a child playing with a dog in order to force a victory over his own instinctive
humanity; Querelle murders as much as an exercise in stoical self-
discipline as for any other reason; and even Riton joins the Vichy
Milice with a full and premeditated awareness of what he is doing.
Ultimately, the object of *la singularité* is the same as that of Divine's
solitude; but its intensity is increased by a feeling of purpose, of
pride, of exceptionality. Like Divine, Erik and Querelle known themselves to be aristocrats—not of misfortune, however, but of evil.
The mediocrity of virtue, like that of happiness, is for the common
run of mortals, the bourgeoisie; the heroic soul in quest of the
Absolute, must take the more austere road of transgression. He must
become a monster, a Dracula, an object of fear and detestation for
others, an object of repulsion to himself, like Kafka's human cockroach :

> Querelle has not yet accustomed himself to the idea, never properly formulated, of being a monster. [. . . .] He was afraid lest some light, emanating from the innermost depths of his soul, might not be illuminating him, might not be in some way from inside his scaly carapace be giving off a reflection of his true being and rendering it visible to those who would be constrained to give him chase.[58]

Querelle's solitude-in-evil—his monstrousness, his alligator-form with its *'mâchoire énorme'* is secret, known only to himself. That of Riton, by contrast, is open and visible to all; it is as though he bore on his forehead the mark of Cain, 'the sacred sign of the monster'.[59] By joining the abominated *Milice*, by acting as a spy and hired gunman against his own people, his own family and friends, on behalf of the Nazi occupiers, Riton succeeded in cutting himself off far more completely than any other being—far more than Divine, with her mere tincture of degradation—from the society of men. His German masters despised him as a coward, intolerable to their own militaristic ideal; he combines the isolation of the murderer (*Cf.* Clément Village who, after the murder of Sonia, 'was the only living thing'[60]) with the loneliness of the thief; and on top of all this he knows himself to be a homosexual. Nor is any contact, any communication possible even between himself and others who have done like him—his fellow-troopers in the *Milice*; for, since one and all are traitors, each will gladly betray the other at the slightest opportunity. It is hard to imagine a greater moral solitude—a solitude compared with which Divine's degradation is almost convivial. Riton is, in every significant sense, *'hors de ce monde'*, no less than Harcamone. He exists in *'une solitude inconcevable'*. By a single act of will, he has attained the Absolute: for he, and all his kind *'ne furent pas seulement haïs, mais vomis'*.[61]

Others among Genet's acquaintance follow Riton's footsteps into the *Milice* : Lucien Sénémaud, the 'Pêcheur du Suquet', or Armand, that monster of brute inhumanity in the *Journal*[62]—or at least, Genet likes to *imagine* them as members of that infamous organization. No other society of men offers so perfect an opportunity for reaching the Absolute through the isolation that results from the practice of deliberate evil—for the Waffen SS, to which Erik belongs, are heroes at least in their own country and among their own people. *Pompes Funèbres* is full of such symbols of solitude and *singularité*. The Monarchs of the World, who come forth in procession to meet the Little Skivvy on her road to the cemetery, are the very embodiment of the loneliness of power reinforced by the loneliness of ritual : *'Chacun dans ce cortège était seul, capturé dans un bloc de solitude'*[63]; but lonelier even than they is that inconceivable solitude of total evil which men called Hitler—the Hitler of Berchtesgaden, surrounded by a limitless void *'hérissé des plus hautes cimes du monde. . . .'*[64]

If the novel, after its very hesitant beginning, captures our interest for the first time when Genet introduces the paradox of love and hate, it comes to life with the character of Riton; and its climax is reached, not so much in the final scenes among the rooftops, but in the episodes following the repression of a rebellion among civil prisoners in a *Centrale*, when the militiamen execute the insurgents who have attempted to overthrow the guards. This is one of the most sadistic and horrifying scenes that Genet has ever described; and, because its horror is moral rather than physical, it is of unforgettable power. But it is also fascinating as a critical stage in the dialectic of absolute evil. The problem as formulated by Genet is as follows : if—as by common consent is admitted—murder is the most serious of crimes, then a young man who, for no reason other than gratuitous hatred of the human race, murders, not in passion, but in an icy parody of inhuman justice, some seven-and-twenty of his fellow-countrymen, and enjoys the experience (riding off to town afterwards to celebrate)—such a man has surely ventured as far along the road to the Absolute as our limited human imagination can conceive. He has, in fact, transcended his own humanity; he has done more than the Prince of Evil himself, for the latter, not being human, has fewer resistances to conquer.

The results of this imaginative experiment with evil, all in all, are disappointing :

> *Tuer un homme est le symbole du Mal. Tuer sans que rien ne compense cette perte de vie, c'est le Mal, Mal absolu. Rarement j'emploie ce dernier mot, car il m'effraie, mais ici il me paraît s'imposer. Or, et les métaphysiciens le diront, les absolus ne s'ajoutent pas. Atteint une fois grâce au meurtre—qui en est le symbole—le Mal rend moralement inutiles tous les autres actes mauvais. Mille cadavres ou un seul, c'est pareil. C'est l'état de péché mortel dont on ne se sauvera plus. On peut aligner les corps si l'on a les nerfs assez forts, mais la répétition les calmera. C'est alors que l'on peut dire que la sensibilité s'émousse comme chaque fois qu'un acte se répète, sauf dans l'acte de créer.*[65]

Three elements, apparently, enter into this essential failure of the crucial experiment : the fact that an isolated *act* of absolute evil is limited in time—it cannot produce a permanent *state* of evil, yet at the same time, because in the moment of its realization it did attain to a maximum intensity of evil, all subsequent acts of lesser intensity are, so to speak, valueless. Nor, secondly, can a permanency of evil be established by repeating the same act, since repetition merely dulls the sensibility, and the essence of absolute evil is 'consciousness *within* Evil'. Nor, finally, is it at all clear to Genet himself—in spite of a general consensus of opinion to this effect—that murder *is* in fact the supreme manifestation of evil. Murder can be, sometimes is, glorious, heroic, even praiseworthy. Brutus, Charlotte Corday, Hamlet, Lorenzaccio—these, to say the least of it, are ambiguous cases. And the Soldier, whom Genet idealizes, is not only trained to murder, but *expects* to receive glory for his achievement. Not only the soldier, moreover. Any murderer, by the fact that he has violated the supreme taboo and consciously risked the supreme penalty himself, is a creature apart, an exceptional being above the common herd, who deserves not only the abhorrence, but also the respect of the crowd—just as Our Lady observes the respect of those who come to attend his trial. To assume then, without further discussion, that murder is the symbol of absolute evil is unconvincing—at least, it is to Riton. Querelle later will take the argument a good deal further. We are back at our original starting-point. An act of absolute evil is a work of art, perfected and unique; and that which is unique and perfect cannot be *absolutely* bad—its perfection and its uniqueness are its flaws, they put it on the side of the angels.

Moreover, for Genet, the problem is also practical. His quest for the Absolute is not merely an idle literary exercise. Literature comes later in his life : his first preoccupation is to *live* through the experience of evil and, by his acts and his way of life, to incarnate his opposition to the order of the world. Now, there is no evidence or suggestion that Jean Genet ever tried his hand at assassination; perhaps he is simply not inclined that way; but in any case, a murder would mean that, in his search for the Absolute, he would be staking everything on a single throw—if his experiment were unsuccessful, it is unlikely that he would have much chance to make a second.

Or, on a different level again, if the commandment : 'Thou shalt not kill' does in fact emanate from a Divine Authority (and is not merely the simplified formulation of a standard social imperative), then consciously to defy the supreme law of God is the act at least of a Prometheus, if not of a martyr. It is the revolt of human dignity and human liberty—a tragic, hopeless and doomed revolt, but none the less a valid protest for all that—against the degrading servitude imposed by a superior will or a transcendental determinism. It is in this light—momentarily at any rate—that Erik considers his murder of the child : *'Le doigt sur la détente. Le plus haut moment de liberté était atteint Tirer sur Dieu, le blesser et en faire un ennemi mortel. Je tirai. Je tirai trois coups.'*[66]

If this sounds at first like a bit of paradoxical bravado, we must remember that Genet is not alone in being puzzled at the implications of the idea. Sartre works out some of them in *Erostrate*, Gide some others in *Les Caves du Vatican*; and Dostoievsky's Raskol'nikov and Svidrigaïlov, who both argue along the same lines, are neither of them villains in the normal sense of the term. To defy God may be as unprofitable as Don Quixote's defiance of the Windmills, or as vainglorious as King Canute's defiance of the waves, or as miraculous as David's challenge to Goliath : but none of these figures is the embodiment of absolute evil.

So Genet's problem is to find a form of evil which (considered as a Fine Art) is less perfect, and therefore more absolute than murder. A crime which holds no element of glory or grandeur or uniqueness about it, yet whose very pettiness and meanness cause it to weigh heavier in the scale of misdeeds. A crime, preferably, which will cause its perpetrator to live in a clinging, enveloping atmosphere of evil, rather than a crime which is soon over and done with—and avenged. A crime for which there may be no official punishment, for life in prison is after all life in a community, whereas what is sought is the utter solitude of the social and moral outcast. A crime which admits of no heroic exceptions, which is condemned alike by all right-thinking people and by the common criminals themselves. A crime which is too stupid and vile to be profitable, yet at the same time not absolutely profitless, lest there should adhere to it some faint suspicion of disinterestedness. An abject crime, finally : a crime which needs no special tools, no special strength or skill or ingenuity or courage—a crime that Genet can imagine for his heroes, and at the same time be guilty of himself.

This ideal crime is *treachery*—not international treason on a grand scale, with all the issues of peace and war at stake, although Genet did at one time (at least according to the Legend) consider this as a possibility and a temptation,[67] rejecting it finally on the grounds that most European states were so ashamed of the trade that 'they ennoble it for its being shameful'—but rather the drab and abject day-to-day betrayals of the paid informer, the concierge, the stool-pigeon and the nark. 'It is not the more dazzling crimes [. . . .] that I would like to know about,' he remarks in *The Thief's Journal*, 'but rather the more dismal, those which are called sordid and whose heroes are gloomy.'[68] Not that Genet appears to boast of any patriotic sentiments to deflect him from the grand-scale betrayals of espionage. It is not so much that he hates his own country (he refers at one point to 'my disgust with, rather than my hatred of France'[69]), but he has no particular reason to love it either. Above all, though, it is the fact that patriotic sentiment, in France perhaps more than in any other country in Europe, is the prerogative and banner of the right-thinking bourgeoisie,[70] that forces Genet to adopt an anti-patriotic standpoint. No small part of the shock-value of *Pompes Funèbres* when it first appeared was due to its exaltation of the pro-Vichy *Milice*, its glorification of the Nazi officer, Erik, and to passages such as that in which France is compared to a cringing *tapette*, and Germany to a rampaging and brutal *mac*[71] :

> *Il me plaît que la France ait choisi ce travesti charmant d'une effroyable putain religieuse afin, comme Lorenzaccio sans doute, de mieux tuer son marlou.*[72]

Curiously enough, so violent and obscene are some of Genet's diatribes against his native land that occasionally one suspects a bit of sheer *panache* and perversity, and that Genet is at bottom rather more patriotic than he would willingly allow anyone to believe.[73] This suspicion is reinforced by the heavy stress that Genet lays on cowardice as the ideal supporting vice to the perfect crime of treachery. If an aggressive and chauvinistic patriotism is one of the less tolerable features of the French bourgeoisie, it is equally true that few nations are so obsessed by the problem of physical courage—even Sartre, whose ideas are anything but those of the conventional Monsieur Prudhomme, seems to suggest in his plays and novels that physical bravery is the one quality without which all the rest are valueless. Perhaps, at heart, Genet is still sufficient of a Frenchman to agree, and perhaps it is because he agrees that he turns the proposition inside-out with such ferocity. All Genet's major characters are indescribable cowards—Lt Seblon, and Gil Turko are cowards; Riton and Bulkaen are 'cowardly, as males are'[74]; 'Stilitano, Pilorge, Michaelis were cowards. And Java too'.[75] And Darling. And Our Lady. And, above all, Alberto.[76] For Alberto-the-Snakecatcher—and therefore for Genet—cowardice is the one vice without which all the others are ineffective : the essential starting-point in any serious attempt to scale the formidable heights of absolute evil.

In so far, then, as Riton makes a conscious bid for the Absolute, it is not as a murderer, but as a coward who is at the same time an informer, a traitor, a spy. For Genet himself, this concept is so fundamental that his analyses—not only in *Pompes Funèbres*, but in almost everything that he has written—of the psychology, sociology and metaphysics of betrayal are among the profoundest and the most original that have been attempted. All four novels (not to mention the *Journal*) have treachery as the basis of their plots : Darling betrays Divine for Mimosa II, and on top of that, 'sells his friends to the cops'[77]; Divers betrays Harcamone[78]; Riton betrays his country to the Germans, Pierrot betrays prisoners to the *Milice*; Querelle betrays Gil Turko to Mario, the Chief of Police. In the strange introduction to *Our Lady of the Flowers*, after invoking the murderers Pilorge, Angel-Sun and Weidmann, Genet summons up the ghost of Marc Aubert :

A young ensign, still a child, committed treason for treason's sake: he was shot. And it is in honour of their crimes that I am writing my book.[79]

—the same Marc Aubert who reappears later, in *The Thief's Journal,* among those of whom the poet writes : 'They depart from your rules. They are not faithful.'[80]

Many complex motives contribute to Genet's fascination with the notion of betrayal. The ideal form of betrayal is that of one petty criminal by another to the police for cash; for not only is this a plunge into the very depths of the sordid and the abject, but it re-solves, or promises to resolve, the basic paradox which suggests that absolute evil is impossible, because the perfection of the Absolute is a defect in the evil. By the act of betrayal, a will to evil in one malefactor exploits an act of evil to bring about the *failure* (= imperfection) of evil in another, and thus the perfection of the whole entity includes a partial, but necessary, imperfection—the fissure (to return to a symbol discussed earlier) through which the mystic forces of beauty escape and become visible. In this way, Genet argues, treachery *is* beauty :

> Betrayal may be a handsome, elegant gesture, compounded of nervous force and grace. I definitely reject the notion of a nobility which favours a harmonious form and ignores a more hidden, almost invisible beauty, a beauty which would have to be revealed elsewhere than in objection-able acts and things. No one will misunderstand me if I write : 'Betrayal is beautiful.' [. . . .] Indispensable for achieving beauty : love. And cruelty shattering that love.[81]

The last sentence of this quotation, however, brings us to the second main element that goes to make up the fascination of be-trayal. Not only is betrayal a form of sacrilege (and this is the par-ticular significance of Riton and Pierrot in *Pompes Funèbres*) in that it violates the sacred laws of the community; but in addition, it destroys that most binding and most tenacious of relationships which holds the Saint in bondage to the world and keeps him from the perfection of his solitude : Love. For Racine, murder was only truly tragic—that is, transcending the limited and relative laws of ethics, and thus confronting the eternal and essential reality of the Universe—if it took place in a context of love : Hermione ordering the death of Pyrrhus, Phèdre contriving the destruction of Hippolyte. In an identical fashion for Genet, the act of betrayal is insignificant unless it involves the betrayal of the beloved, and the catastrophic shattering of love. It is at once sacrilege (the breaking of one of the strongest of taboos); self-conquest and self-discipline; the attain-ment of solitude; and finally, a form of partial suicide, for if the beloved is the mirror-image of the lover who, by the miracle of love, contemplates himself through the eyes of the Other, and in this

Other has his essential being, the destruction of the Other is simultaneously a destruction and a liberation of the Self. What is left to the Self *after* the destruction of the Other is problematic; but it is at least conceivable that, in the moment of paroxysm which shatters the one half of the double-image which is human reality, the Self may, for the first and only time, know itself as having a unique and authentic existance—that it may, if only for one instant in all eternity, succeed in being-what-it-is.

Thus it is at the height of his love for Erik that Riton destroys him, just as (reversing the process) Lt Seblon destroys himself and his career at the height of his love for Querelle. In *Pompes Funèbres* there is an admirable existential-psychological analysis of the mechanics of betrayal[82] which stresses the authentic realization of the Self through the mystery of a ritual act of transgression; and there is a further passage which dissects in detail the act of treachery in a context of absolute evil[83]; but the most complete statement of this theme, which dominates the whole internal structure of the novel, and which reveals the hidden and at first sight inconceivable link between Genet's ascetic immoralism and the Jansenistic amoralism of Racinian tragedy, is to be found in *The Thief's Journal*. Here, as Genet himself prepares to betray his lover and mentor, Armand, all the metaphysical and emotional threads are gathered together in one essential paragraph, which concludes :

> The idea of betraying Armand set me aglow. I feared and loved him too much not to want to deceive and betray and rob him. I sensed the anxious pleasure that goes with sacrilege. If he were God (he had known pity), and had he been well pleased with me, it were sweet to deny him. And better still was the fact that Stilitano, who did not love me and whom I would never have betrayed, should be helping me.[84]

The suggested relationship between the betrayal of love and the defiance of God, which is found at the end of this passage, is particularly significant, as is also the idea of fear, which is in itself an important component of Genet's concept of transgression, and recurs in innumerable different contexts—as a fundamental trait in the character of Divine,[85] of Gil and of Mario[86]; as an element in the ideal of cowardice; and as an obsessive feature in Genet's remorseless self-analysis of his own existence and his own abjection :

> . . . *je connaissais la présence aigüe et incandescente de Jean Genet, fou de peur. Mais peut-être n'eussé-je jamais autant conscience de moi-même qu'en de tels instants.*[87]

Fear is an instrument, a means of lucidity; it is also intimately involved in that feeling of evanescence (the 'sickening lightness of cork', etc.) which forms part of Genet's irrational poetic consciousness of the world; but essentially, of course, fear is the beacon which guides the Saint along his dark and degrading path to sanctity, for evil would not be evil if the good did not fear it, nor would the·acts of the evil-doer be anything but air unless he feared the vengeance of the good.

In the universe of Jean Genet—this universe of appearances and symbols which we explored in Chapter 3—there is a perpetual conflict between male and female, active and passive, rigid and yielding, glass and veils, brittleness and flexibility, *la dureté* on the one hand, and on the other, *la douceur* or *la tendresse*. This same symbolic confrontation of opposites is clearly evident in Genet's vision of evil. The supreme evil of betrayal is essentially passive, feminine : it is Genet's own road to salvation, the road that leads through flowers and dreams to ultimate degradation; and most of the imagery associated with it is passive also.[88] By contrast, the active form of absolute evil— the dream-evil that Genet sees in the Other, the master, the male, is murder, with its characteristically rigid symbolism : the knife, the revolver, the glass stiletto, etc. Our Lady murders, Divine betrays. In *Pompes Funèbres*, this division into active and passive manifestations of evil is even more clearly marked, with Riton and Pierrot, the betrayers, involved in a tapestry of passive symbolism, while Erik, the Headsman, and above all Paulo stand for the evil which is murder. Significantly also, betrayal is conceived above all as a *feeling*, emanating from within the being who betrays; murder is visualized as an *appearance*, it is external, it defines the features and the contours of the murderer; and its symbolic characteristic is malevolence—*la méchanceté*.[89]

The power of Genet's obsession with the concept of evil lies in the fact that pure rationalistic analysis, revolt, mysticism and erotic symbolism are combined in about equal proportions, and that each has its own contribution to make to the general picture. The erotic appeal of certain categories of evil has been recognized from time immemorial; the *divin marquis*, de Sade, invented nothing, he merely gave his name to a particular manifestation of a fairly general experience. But the specific form of evil which is associated with homosexual psychology is that of malevolence rather than sadism proper—that is, the appearance, or the dream, of a certain type of cruelty, rather than its actual practice. Genet's murderers, from Our Lady to Querelle, are a walking catalogue of these dream-qualities, almost as they might appear in a handbook of abnormal psychology. As opposed to the betrayer, who is flexible, mobile, almost protean and all-too-human, the Headsman—or Erik—is expressionless, wooden in his *rôle de justicier impassible*,[90] immobile, inhuman. Darling deliberately chooses the part of inhumanity, and Genet—provisionally identifying himself with his dream-burglar— approves. 'Dehumanizing myself is my own most fundamental tendency.'[91] The *miliciens* of *Pompes Funèbres* have '*le corps et le regard sévères*'[92]; but their appearance and attitude is no more than a reflection of those rigid little men, the young delinquents of Mettray.[93]

The list of instances of this type of imagery that can be found in *Pompes Funèbres* is too vast to be analysed in detail : it includes the concepts of *dureté, rigueur,*[94] *rigidité, sévérité, inflexibilité,*[95] *cruauté* (Riton : '*J' voudrais êtr' celui qui fait pleurer les mères*'),[96] purity, inviolability, fragility,[97] sobriety, asceticism, indifference, machine precision, elegance, etc., etc. . . . and again and again, malevolence.[98] '*De tous les petits mecs que j'aime fourrer dans mes livres, c'est le plus méchant*',[99] notes Genet of Paulo; and, in the case of Jean Decarnin, the imagery is further complicated by a twist which even allows Genet's characteristic flower-symbolism to be employed to the same purpose : for the symbol of Jean Decarnin is the holly, and the leaves of the holly, '*rigides, vernies, ont la couleur de la méchanceté*'.[100]

That Genet should choose to idealise criminals and murderers; that he should sing the praises of the Nazi armoured divisions with their swastika banners[101]; finally, that among all personages, real or imaginary, of our time, he should elect Hitler to be the symbolic incarnation of his own identity[102]—these facts seem to constitute about as clear a statement as could be made concerning his attitude towards the rest of the world. 'Drunk with violence and despair', he describes himself defiantly in *Pompes Funèbres*[103]; if the real world is the positive, the good, then Genet has chosen the image-in-the-mirror, the negative, the evil, the forbidden. In other words, in spite of his quest for solitude and singularity, he is prepared at least to dream of an organized community which shall be the diametrical opposite of the society which has cast him out, branded him an untouchable and used him as a scapegoat. If he has the courage to defy God, he can also find the strength to deny the virtues of bourgeois society. In the company of other outcasts like himself, he is prepared to accept a Herculean task : that of organizing 'a forbidden universe'.[104] The task, however, is not just Herculean. It is impossible, and he knows it. Organized bands of criminals (he returns to the subject again and again) are a figment of the imagination; the community of outlaws belongs to the domain of the *roman-feuilleton*. There is only one place where, with all the will in the world, those who defy the positive virtues of society can constitute an anti-society of their own, and that is in prison—which is why the more intellectual criminal may feel more at home in prison than at liberty : prison is the realization of an unformulable ideal, that of the forbidden universe. For Genet, nothing *less* than absolute evil, absolute denial, will suffice; to defy society, the outcast must reject *all* the virtues of society. But one of the essential virtues of society is its constitution, the respect of law, order and the liberty of others that makes it possible in the first place. He who rejects society must reject its principle; but then, logically, he cannot constitute another society in opposition. He is condemned to solitude, to isolation, whether he wishes it or not.

Essentially, therefore, Genet's attitude towards society is one of complete negation. Theoretically at least he is alone against the rest of the world. Every other living human being is his enemy. But in practice, of course, this is not so. The world that he opposes is that of *bourgeois* society, its hierarchies, its laws, its conventions and its values. It is the world of *you* who have the money, the education and the perversity to buy and read books such as *Our Lady of the Flowers* and *Pompes Funèbres*. 'In the evening as *you* open your window to the street. . . .'[105] '*You* are concerned for your honour, your reputation, *you* devise ways and means of saving them.'[106] Genet's hatred for the bourgeoisie is deep-rooted, bitter and apparently ineradicable—as is the case with so many modern French writers, from Flaubert, through Proust, to Sartre and Ionesco. It is significant that the typical French intellectual, in his attitude to the bourgeoisie, is so much more bitter, so much more consciously hostile and destructive, than his equivalents in other countries—significant, and perhaps, in the field of world-politics, vitally important, since the marxist-communist view of the bourgeois is essentially French in its intellectual and emotional origins. In England, hostility such as that of D. H. Lawrence in his poem 'How beastly the bourgeois is!', or of Siegfried Sassoon's war poems, is exceptional. Even in Germany, Herr Biedermeier has moments of generosity : he is never so petty, mean, cruel or vicious as Monsieur Prudhomme. Probably the political history of France, beginning with the repression of the working-class movement in 1849-50, but especially since the massacres of the Commune in 1871, has much to do with the almost unspeakable contempt and hatred that we find incarnated, say, in the little scene when Antoine Roquentin, in Sartre's *Nausea*, visits the Municipal Museum at Bouville. Yet Sartre himself, of course, is a typical product of the bourgeois intelligentsia.

The point is, then, that Genet is anything but isolated in his violent opposition to the middle-classes—indeed (and this is the most evident explanation of a fact that has puzzled a number of his critics and, one almost suspects, has rather perturbed Genet himself) he could have done nothing better calculated to make himself acceptable to a bourgeois *avant-garde* than to attack the social background of his readers. This was the one certain way (had he desired it) to disguise his origins and to make himself indistinguishable from any other brilliant young product of the *Lycée* and the *Ecole Normale Supérieure*. It is not Genet's hostility to the middle-classes which is original : it is his intimate knowledge of the various worlds-in-opposition that he sets up to defy and eventually to destroy the bourgeoisie.

Sartre, for instance, has an intimate knowledge of the class that he would like to eradicate, but only the vaguest acquaintance with the proletariat that he would like to see perform the act of eradication. Montherlant has rather a better knowledge of his idealized aristocracy, but very much less chance of realizing his dream of revolution-from-above. But Genet has seen with his own eyes the destruction of society by the Nazi armies and the Gestapo; he *knows* the outlaws—the convicts, the criminals and all the rest of the submerged tenth, the Negroes, the domestic servants, the waiters, the prostitutes, the Algerians, the political refugees, the informers, the delinquents, the down-and-outs, the homosexuals, the under-nourished, the underprivileged and the under-educated who compose this world outside the world; and by combining in imagination the destructive organization of Nazism with his inborn understanding of the outcast, he conjures up a picture of hostility to the Establishment which is nightmarish in quality. It is a logical impossibility, of course, because it combines anarchy with organization—yet it *could* happen. It did happen. It happened when the market-women marched on Versailles demanding bread and returned with the King a prisoner; it happened when half the vicious and depraved delinquents of France—like Riton or Pierrot—enrolled in the *Milice*. Genet envies them, for they were able to commit the crimes that he dared not undertake himself.[107]

None the less, in this vision of the two worlds in opposition, there are unresolved problems. As an outcast from the greater world, Genet *belongs* to 'a smaller, enclosed and isolated world'.[108] He knows and cherishes, almost as talismans, all the signs that signify exclusion from the society of right-thinking people, and where possible he deliberately cultivates these signs himself, to emphasise his deliberate rejection of that other universe. He wears his hair, still today, as close-cropped as that of the convicts who inhabit Fresnes or La Santé. His sweetest music, his poetry, is the *argot* of the underworld—an *argot* so impenetrable when used by Our Lady

that M. le Président of the Assize Court has to have it translated
for him into standard French before he can grasp what the pro-
ceedings are about. He observes affectionately that the trousers of the
Mettray-delinquents have only one pocket : 'This is something else
that isolate them from the world'.[109] He cherishes the grotesque
tattooing of the modern criminal almost as much as the *fleur-de-
lys* brand-mark on the shoulder of the old-time galley-slave—in fact,
he looks on the tattooing as a sort of self-branding, by which the
excluded deliberately signify their acceptance of their exclusion, and
thereby dominate their own fatality.[110] But all this—his awareness
of his deep emotional and poetic attachment to the little world of the
oppressed and the humiliated—only serves to deepen the fundamental contradiction. For Riton, as a member of the abominated
Milice, is a symbolic illustration of Genet's ideal in two ways which
exclude each other. On the one hand, he is a member of an organized
opposition to society, which, *because* it is organized, can hope to
annihilate that society; yet the ultimate significance of his actions
depends on their leading him to the solitude and sanctity of absolute
evil, which goal can only be achieved through the unanimous re-
probation of his fellow-*miliciens* (thus destroying the organization)
and of the bourgeois order which he is destined to destroy. '*J'ai*
besoin *de la condamnation de ma race*' notes Genet of himself;
Riton is yet another illustration, this time in political terms, of the
logical impossibility of absolute evil : for evil only *knows* itself to
be evil by comparison with the good; yet to *be* evil, it must destroy
the good—and then, how shall it know itself to be evil ?

It is this inherent contradiction that accounts for Genet's extremely
ambiguous and fluctuating attitude towards social problems.
Emotionally he belongs to the society of the oppressed and the under-
privileged; so logically, his opposition to the bourgeoisie should be
counterbalanced by action in favour of the victims. Indeed, when
there is a sufficiently scandalous paradox involved, as in *L'Enfant
Criminel*, where he could undertake a carefully-argued defence of
adolescent murderers against the Authorities and the Establishment,
he will do so with glee. But in more acceptable cases, he hesitates.
For, precisely because the Cause is not wholly unacceptable, he will
no longer stand alone. Solidarity is purchased only at the price of
singularity, and this is a price which, before *The Blacks*, Genet is
not prepared to pay. Yet there are episodes in *Pompes Funèbres*
which suggest that, eventually, he may be prepared at least to try
and make the sacrifice of his isolation, and to exchange—or rather
part-exchange—solitude for socialism. A peculiar brand of socialism,
but of that more in the later chapters. In *Pompes Funèbres*, it is the
pathetic and very moving figure of the Little Skivvy who, tenta-

tively and in the almost wordless solitude of a dream-world, begins
to emerge as a positive symbol, in opposition to the viciously satirical
portrait of Madame, the Parisian bourgeoise at her most detestable:
domineering, stupid and arrogant, selfish, hypocritical and sly. Yet
'the Little Skivvy' is an anomaly for all that; for, as a figure of isolation and abjection, she corresponds to Divine, or to Genet himself
in his search for sanctity through the absolute *negation* of common
values; yet if she is negative, then Madame is positive—a case which
might be argued metaphysically, yet which makes arrant nonsense
in the eyes of anyone with a socialistic, or even a social, conscience.
And it is all too evident that Genet has an emotional social con-
conscience, if not an intellectual one. At any rate, in *Pompes
Funèbres*, the Little Skivvy is left to live out her nightmare all alone;
for her tragedy, like that of Claire and Solange, is not of the sort that
inspires, or could be solved by, honest social indignation. In a sense,
all Genet's writings are a plea for the oppressed; yet once the
oppressed are successfully integrated into a socialist Utopia—and
Genet after them—then his road simultaneously to sanctity and
damnation will be closed. Saints are not encouraged in the Welfare
State.

In point of fact, of course, Genet has already been caught in the
trap. For him, the two worlds are now one world, save only in his
imagination. The bourgeois world has taken him back into itself.
Already in 1947 he foresaw the dilemma, and conceived his reintegra-
tion into society as an exile.[111] His search for the Absolute, in fact,
has failed—as perhaps it must necessarily fail. Absolute evil, for
the human being, exists only in vision; and the vision, to have
existence, must be realized as art. But its realization as art destroys
its absoluteness as evil—and incidentally transfers its creator bodily
from the world-in-opposition to the world of right-thinking people.
Whatever *Pompes Funèbres* achieves—and there are some striking
passages—it certainly fails to solve the problem, either of the Absolute, or of Evil. Henceforward, Genet will be forced to deal with
the question in new and radically different ways, beginning with the
labyrinthine intellectual algebra of *Querelle of Brest*.

NOTES

1 Sartre, *Being and Nothingness*, p. 61. 'L'être-en-soi de la tristesse hante
perpétuellement ma conscience d'être triste [. . . .] comme une valeur
que je ne puis réaliser.' (*L'Être et le Néant*, p. 101)
2 *Pompes Funèbres*, p. 73.
3 *Ibid.*, p. 114.
4 The name Decarnin, omitted in the text, is mentioned in the dedication.

5 There are hints of the original model of Erik in *The Thief's Journal*, p. 95. (*Journal*, p. 112)

6 *Our Lady*, p. 70. '. . . entrait en moi jusqu'à n'y plus laisser de place pour moi-même.' (*Notre-Dame*, p. 15)

7 *E.g. Rose*, pp. 151-2, 267. (*Miracle*, pp. 295, 378); *Thief*, p. 46. (*Journal*, pp. 55-6), etc.

8 *Q. of B.*, p. 34. '. . . le signe de la cruauté accompagnant les rites de l'amour.' (*Querelle*, p. 187)

9 *Pompes Funèbres*, p. 85.

10 *Our Lady*, p. 70. '. . . je me confonds maintenant avec gangsters, cambrioleurs, macs, et la police, s'y trompant, m'arrête.' (*Notre-Dame*, p. 15)

11 *Q. of B.*, p. 32. '. . . débordant pour s'épandre dans tout son corps qu'elle remplissait de lait.' (*Querelle*, p. 186)

12 *Screens*, pp. 15 and 22-23. (*Paravents*, pp. 19 and 30-31)

13 *Thief*, p. 49. 'Il connaissait si bien la nature de l'acier et la nature de ce particulier fragment d'acier bruni qu'on nomme une pince qu'elle restait, jusqu'à la fatigue, docile, amoureuse, accrochée à sa chemise.' (*Journal*, p. 59)

14 *Ibid.*, p. 99. 'Le talent, c'est la politesse à l'égard de la matière, il consiste à donner un chant à ce qui était muet.' (*Journal*, p. 117)

15 *Ibid.*, pp. 141-2. 'Je comprends ce qui lie le sculpteur à sa terre, le peintre à ses couleurs, chaque ouvrier à la matière qu'il travaille, et la docilité, l'acquiescement de la matière aux gestes de celui qui l'anime. . . .' (*Journal*, pp. 167-8)

16 *Pompes Funèbres*, p. 19.

17 *Thief*, p. 49. 'Il arrivait pourtant que le blessassent ces objets qu'un geste maladroit irrite. Stilitano se coupait.' (*Journal*, p. 59)

18 *Bonnes*, pp. 45-6. This passage is cut in *The Maids*.

19 *Our Lady*, p. 174. (*Notre-Dame*, p. 81)

20 *Ibid.*, p. 186. (*Notre-Dame*, p. 89)

21 Text cut in *The Screens*.
'*La Mère:* Elle t'a encore piquée?
Leïla: Ne la blâmez pas, elle joue.'
(*Paravents*, p. 32)

22 *Our Lady*, p. 74. (*Notre-Dame*, p. 17)

23 *Giacometti*, p. 17.

24 In *The Screens*, however, *cf.* the absurd developments of language as pure sound, almost certainly derived from plays such as *The Bald Prima-Donna*. *Screens*, pp. 57, 58, 59-60. (*Paravents*, pp. 84, 86, 88-9)

25 *Thief*, p. 118. 'Je voyais clair et *tout* pouvait arriver.' (*Journal*, p. 139)

26 *Ibid.*, pp. 116-7. 'Je crus percevoir les choses avec une éclatante lucidité. Ayant, même la plus banale, perdu sa signification usuelle, j'en vins à me demander s'il était vrai qu'on buvait dans un verre ou qu'on chaussait un soulier [. . . .] J'eus la révélation d'une connaissance absolue en considérant, selon le détachement luxueux dont je parle, une épingle à linge abandonnée sur un fil de fer [. . . .] Je me sentais perdu et absurdement léger.' (*Journal*, pp. 137-8)

27 *Our Lady*, p. 113. 'Je n'ai jamais su ce que pouvait être au juste l'amitié.' (*Notre-Dame*, p. 43)
The term *amitié* (friendship) can be confusing as Genet sometimes uses it to describe an intense emotional relationship between two

males, as opposed to *amour* between male and female. *Cf. Miracle*, pp. 215-216; *Pompes Funèbres*, pp. 22, 44, 48, etc. In the passage here quoted, Genet makes it clear that he means the lesser emotion by referring to it shortly after as *amitié fraternelle*.

28 *Rose*, p. 102. (*Miracle*, p. 259)

29 *Thief*, p. 178. (*Journal*, p. 211)

30 *Our Lady*, p. 98. 'Tu es un soleil apporté dans ma nuit. Ma nuit est un soleil apporté dans la tienne.' (*Notre-Dame*, p. 33)

31 *Rose*, p. 252. (*Miracle*, p. 367)

32 *Our Lady*, p. 127. '. . . se bute et se pulvérise.' (*Notre-Dame*, p. 51)

33 *Pompes Funèbres*, p. 50

34 *Rose*, p. 64. (*Miracle*, pp. 231-2)

35 *Pompes Funèbres*, p. 122.

36 *Rose*, pp. 48-9. (*Miracle*, p. 220)

37 *Our Lady*, p. 158. 'Tu n'es pas mon ami, tu es moi-même.' (*Notre-Dame*, p. 71)

38 *Ibid.*, p. 155. 'Il chantait son corps, il n'aimait pas [. . . .] il allait sa mélodie.' (*Notre-Dame*, p. 69)

39 *Thief*, p. 120. (*Journal*, p. 142)

40 *Q. of B.*, p. 87. 'L'Amour: conscience de la séparation d'un seul, conscience d'être divisé, et que votre vous-même vous contemple.' (*Querelle*, pp. 220-221)

41 Yet again Corneille springs irresistibly to mind. What is Genet's ideal, if not a reversed image of the Cornelian *amour-mérite*?

42 *Rose*, p. 37. 'Car on ne peut s'aimer que sur un même plan moral.' (*Miracle*, p. 212 and see also p. 240)

43 *Our Lady*, p. 227. (*Notre-Dame*, p. 116)

44 *Pompes Funèbres*, p. 22.

45 *Thief*, p. 239. (*Journal*, p. 284)

46 *Rose*, p. 150, 197, 245-6, 275. (*Miracle*, pp. 294, 328, 362, 383-4)

47 Again, similarities with Proust. Many of the functions of *la haine* in Genet are identical with those ascribed to *la jalousie* in *A la Recherche*, including that of inspiring intellectual curiosity, and thus, eventually, intelligence: 'La haine, soudain, à Robert, donna un début d'intelligence'. *Q. of B.*, p. 208. (*Querelle*, p. 292)

48 *Pompes Funèbres*, p. 132.

49 *Ibid.*, p. 44.

50 *Ibid.*, p. 36.

51 *Ibid.*, pp. 37-8.

52 *Ibid.*, p. 38.

53 *Ibid.*, p. 39.

54 Sartre, *Saint G.*, pp. 150-171. (*S. Genet*, pp. 145-164)

55 *Thief*, p. 39. (*Journal*, p. 47)

56 *Q. of B.*, pp. 306-7. (*Querelle*, p. 342)

57 *Rose*, p. 266. 'Les parfums restèrent parfums, et l'air aussi pur, mais le mal y était.' (*Miracle*, p. 377)

58 *Q. of B.*, p. 21. 'Querelle ne s'habituait pas à l'idée, jamais formulée, d'être un monstre [. . . .] Il redoutait qu'une lueur quelconque venue de l'intérieur de son corps ou de sa propre conscience ne l'illuminât, n'accrochât dans sa carapace écailleuse le reflet d'une forme et le rendit visible aux hommes. . . .' (*Querelle*, pp. 179-180)

59 *Our Lady*, p. 65. '. . le signe sacré des monstres.' (*Notre-Dame*, p. 11)

60 *Ibid.*, p. 186. (*Notre-Dame*, p. 89)

61 *Pompes Funèbres*, pp. 50-51.

62 *Thief*, p. 136, also pp. 133-5. (*Journal*, p. 162; also pp. 157-160)

63 *Pompes Funèbres*, p. 140.

64 *Ibid.*, p. 113.

65 *Ibid.*, pp. 141-2.

66 *Ibid.*, p. 69.

67 *Thief*, pp. 43-4. (*Journal*, pp. 52-3)

68 *Ibid.*, p. 176. 'Ce n'est pas [les crimes] les plus éclatants que je voudrais connaître, mais les plus sombres, ceux dont on dit qu'ils sont sordides et dont les héros sont ternes.' (*Journal*, p. 209)

69 *Ibid.*, p. 27. '. . . mon dégoût—non ma haine—de la France.' (*Journal*, p. 33). The Frechtman translation gives this passage a different sense, by changing the punctuation.

70 *Cf. Screens*, scene xii, pp. 84-85. (*Paravents*, pp. 123-7). This scene is heavily cut in the English translation.

71 For a typical reaction, see Robert Poulet in *La Lanterne Magique*.

72 *Pompes Funèbres*, p. 113.

73 Simone de Beauvoir notes the same thing, and observes a considerable discrepancy between Genet's *conduites* and his *propositions abstraites* (*Force de l'Âge*, p. 595)

74 *Rose*, p. 76. '. . . lâches comme le sont les mâles.' (*Miracle*, p. 240)

75 *Thief*, p. 11. 'Stilitano, Pilorge, Michaelis étaient lâches. Et Java.' (*Journal*, p. 14)

76 *Our Lady*, p. 283. (*Notre-Dame*, pp. 152-3)

77 *Ibid.*, p. 91. '. . . vend ses amis aux flics.' (*Notre-Dame*, p. 28)

78 *Rose*, pp. 104-5. (*Miracle*, p. 261)

79 *Our Lady*, p. 61. 'Un enseigne de vaisseau, encore enfant, trahissait pour trahir: on le fusilla. Et c'est en l'honneur de leurs crimes que j'écris mon livre.' (*Notre-Dame*, p. 9)

80 *Thief*, p. 75. 'Ils s'écartent de vos règles. Ils ne sont pas fidèles.' (*Journal*, p. 89)

81 *Ibid.*, pp. 216-7. 'Trahir peut être un geste beau, élégant, composé de force nerveuse et de grâce. J'abandonne décidément l'idée de noblesse qui distrait au profit d'une forme harmonieuse, une beauté plus cachée, presque invisible, qu'il faudrait déceler ailleurs que dans les actes et les objets réprouvés. Personne ne se méprendra si j'écris: "La trahison est belle" [. . . .] Indispensable pour obtenir la beauté: L'amour. Et la cruauté le brisant.' (*Journal*, pp. 257-8)

82 *Pompes Funèbres*, pp. 116-126. Possibly based on, or inspired by, the curiously similar analysis of the sensation of vertigo in Sartre, *Being and Nothingness*, pp. 30-35. (*L'Être et le Néant*, pp. 67-71)

83 *Ibid.*, pp. 52-3.

84 *Thief*, p. 234. 'L'idée de trahir Armand m'illuminait. Je le craignais et l'aimais trop pour ne pas désirer le tromper, le trahir, le voler. Je pressentais la volupté inquiète qui accompagne le sacrilège. S'il était Dieu (il avait connu la pitié) et qu'en moi il eût mis sa complaisance, il m'était doux de le nier. Et mieux, que m'y aidât Stilitano qui ne m'aimait pas et que je n'eusse pu trahir.' (*Journal*, p. 278)

85 *Our Lady*, pp. 145-6. (*Notre-Dame*, pp. 62-3)

86 *Q. of B.*, pp. 63, 130, 257. (*Querelle*, pp. 205-6, 247, 320, etc.)

87 *Pompes Funèbres*, p. 143.

88 *Ibid.*, p. 116.

89 *Ibid.*, p. 115.

90 *Ibid.*, p. 76.
91 *Our Lady*, p. 92. 'M'inhumaniser est ma tendance profonde.' (*Notre-Dame*, p. 29)
92 *Pompes Funèbres*, p. 142.
93 *Rose*, p. 241. (*Miracle*, p. 359)
94 *Pompes Funèbres*, p. 34 (Paulo)
95 *Ibid.*, p. 17 (Jean Decarnin)
96 *Ibid.*, p. 59.
97 *Ibid.*, p. 71.
98 *Ibid.*, pp. 18, 20, 34, 35, 53, 138, etc.
99 *Ibid.*, p. 35.
100 *Ibid.*, p. 138.
101 *Ibid.*, p. 88.
102 *Ibid.*, p. 50.
103 *Ibid.*, p. 108.
104 *Thief*, p. 7. (*Journal*, p. 10)
105 *Our Lady*, p. 64. 'Le soir quand vous ouvrez votre fenêtre sur la rue.' (*Notre-Dame*, p. 11)
106 *Rose*, p. 27. 'Vous avez le souci de votre honneur, de votre réputation, vous calculez pour les sauver.' (*Miracle*, p. 205)
107 *Pompes Funèbres*, p. 51.
108 *Rose*, pp. 57-8. (*Miracle*, p. 227)
109 *Our Lady*, p. 224. 'Voilà encore ce qui les isole du monde.' (*Notre-Dame*, p. 114)
110 *Rose*, p. 151. (*Miracle*, p. 294)
111 *Thief*, p. 229. (*Journal*, p. 272)

6

MURDER AND METAPHYSICS

(Querelle of Brest)

> *L'homme n'est qu'un effet commun, le monstre qu'un effet rare; tous les deux également naturels, également nécessaires, également dans l'ordre universel et général.*
>
> Diderot

It is characteristic of Jean Genet that he composes his novels very quickly indeed, writing almost continuously day and night, only to flag from exhaustion before reaching the end. 'I have written too much, I am weary,' he complains in the *Journal*. 'It has been so hard for me to achieve so inadequately what my heroes do so quickly.'[1] All his novels show some signs of this weakening towards the end; but only in one was the tailing-off so serious that Genet himself felt compelled to remedy it. *Querelle of Brest* was originally written in the autumn of 1946, and was in fact left unfinished. 'A sudden weariness made us abandon *Querelle*, which was already beginning to get frayed.'[2] In this incomplete form it was published in November 1947, accompanied however by a promise from Genet that he proposed to rewrite and complete it, and to give this new version to his readers in 1948 under the title *Capable du Fait*. In fact, it was not until 1953 that the revised text saw the light of day; but during the period of nearly ten years which separates the writing of *Pompes Funèbres* (1944) from the publication of the final version of *Querelle of Brest,* Genet's mastery of the genre had improved out of all recognition. Technically, *Querelle of Brest* is Genet's highest achievement in the novel : it is less lyrical, less subjective, less 'poetic', and perhaps less haunting than *Our Lady of the Flowers*; but on the other hand it has a far more substantial structure, it develops its themes with a persistence in logic (or anti-logic) which was missing from the earlier works; it creates a whole new range of characters, symbols and images to replace the purely personal obsessions of *Our Lady,* which, by dint of repetition, threatened to become monotonous; and finally, in the character of Madame Lysiane, for the first time it introduces a woman who plays an essential part in the development of the plot, yet who is neither a hag, a mother-symbol, a slavey so downtrodden and ugly that she has lost all semblance of femininity, or simply *une saleté.*

There is no more striking evidence of Genet's success in his gradual conquest of objectivity than the manner in which, step by step, his writings overcome his fundamental distaste—a distaste which seems literally to amount to nausea—for women. Beginning with Juliette, the Little Skivvy of *Pompes Funèbres,* one can trace this development in its steady progress, first to Madame Lysiane, then to Claire and Solange of *The Maids* (although it is possible to argue that the relationship between the two sisters is merely an analysis, in feminine guise, of the sort of relationship that could easily develop between two passive homosexuals[3]); then come the prostitutes of *The Balcony*—a particular aspect of femininity which will be discussed again in *The Screens* and in the *Atelier d'Alberto Giacometti*—until the final point is reached with the creation of Vertu *(The Blacks),* who is the first, and so far the only woman to whom Genet has given life, and who is young, beautiful, normal and completely sympathetic.

In this line of development, Madame Lysiane represents a clearly-defined stage. In order to be able to understand her, and to portray her with at least a suggestion of sympathy, Genet first of all finds himself obliged to modify her femininity, and to change her reality-as-a-woman into something else. This he achieves by transforming her, both in his own eyes, and in those of his characters, into an *object,* possessing the semi-magical status of the inanimate. She is essentially an *article de luxe*—an *objet d'art et de vertu* in the same category as Genet's other symbols of luxury : the carpets, the curtains, the Second-Empire mirrors, the crystal chandeliers. She is never described as 'beautiful'; invariably as 'rich', 'opulent', 'gorgeous', 'generous', etc. She is '. . . an oriental pearl hidden inside the nacreous casket of an oyster, able to open, and close, its valve at will.'[4] She is 'sumptuousness incarnate'.

Not only do Querelle and his brother Robert, her lover, her *mac*, think of her in this way, but she herself feels that she belongs rather to the domain of soft-furnishings than to the living world of men and women :

> She felt herself to be an integral part of the luxuriously illuminated rooms, dazzling lights and sounds of dance tunes, and at the same time to be evolving this very sumptuosity at every outlet of her breath, the warm breath emanating from the depths of the breast of a remarkably opulent woman.[5]

On the other hand, Madame Lysiane has none of the passive characteristics of Genet's earlier hero-heroines. She is neither abject nor humiliated, nor (in the context of the novel) a prostitute—she is in fact the Madame of the brothel, La Féria, and her relationship with Robert involves a profound emotional experience—nor does she embody the ideal of betrayal which was symbolic of Divine or Riton, or, in *The Thief's Journal*, of Genet himself. She is, as far as Genet can realize the concept at this stage, a genuine and positive feminine being. In the same way, Georges Querelle is essentially male : he incarnates Genet's basic masculine symbol, that of THE Murderer—but more significantly, he is able to absorb into himself the feminine symbol of the 'betrayer' in such a way as to dominate it completely, instead of allowing himself to be dominated or determined by it. Betrayal, for Querelle, is a means to an end, a carefully-calculated, rationally-argued end : it is a subsidiary component of his primary identity as THE Murderer, and if Querelle himself uses some strangely distorted metaphysics to justify his treacheries, in every case the actual act of betrayal is the outcome of an argument, never of an emotion. By contrast with *Our Lady of the Flowers*, the dramatic conflict of *Querelle of Brest* is not one between active and passive responses to a situation, with passivity as the central figure, gradually absorbing and destroying the active; rather it arises from a complex inter-relationship of *active* sexual awarenesses—both male and female—among themselves, and these complexities are merely *observed* from outside by a *passive* witness— Lt Seblon, who has only a marginal role to play in the story itself, and whose commentary takes the form of paragraphs and pages from a secret diary.

At the same time, all these characters are much more subtle— that is, less rigorously stylized—than their predecessors, and consequently they are much more credible as portraits of reality. Even Querelle, who comes nearest to being a pure symbol—not only is he THE Murderer, but he is also THE Sailor[6]—is more complex than the sadist Erik or the thugs Botchako, Seck Gorgui and Armand. To begin with, he is aware of himself as a *monstre*—which is not, in his case, the same thing as a Saint. Also he is far more intelligent than Our Lady or Harcamone—with the result that he is the only one of Genet's gallery of murderers who does not finish up on the guillotine. He still has the typical gravity of Genet's idealized heroes; yet it is not 'malevolence' that characterises his expression, but rather his strange and impenetrable smile : his 'sad',[7] his 'slanting' smile, his smile that appears 'in the corners of his lips'[8] : 'Already, at the age of fifteen, Querelle had smiled with the vivid smile that was to single him out for the rest of his life.'[9]

The explanation is that Querelle possesses a quality which none of Genet's earlier characters had enjoyed, with the half-exception of Stilitano[10] : irony. The Devil is said to have a pleasing smile. Querelle is sufficiently master of himself—and aware of his own mastery—to contemplate the perfection of absolute evil for its own sake; he is no longer emotionally involved (as Gil is) in a revolt against the established order of things. Armand charges like a maddened bull against the law, and if this violence and this destructiveness prove his own strength, they also prove 'the power of the rules over him.'[11] Querelle is infinitely superior to these somewhat crude and childish attitudes; for him, evil is an art to be practised for its own sake. It is as though, in this last novel, Genet had given up trying to solve the dilemma of absolute evil, and—being an artist—had decided that a perfect evil was justified on aesthetic grounds, even if the perfection of an act detracted from its efficacy considered as evil.

The increased complexity of Querelle is balanced by that of Lt Seblon; for Seblon is as real, and as moving, a portrait as can be found anywhere of a man whose secret tendency to passive homosexuality is in constant, tragic conflict with the outward circumstances of his life. Divine could realize her passive tendencies through the femininity of her dress, her gestures, even her language; Lt Seblon is forced—and indeed forces himself—to an appearance of arrogant masculinity, yet realizes that every barked order, every swagger of the épaulettes, is a profound and heart-breaking contradiction within himself. The relationship between Divine and Our Lady is disastrous, but at least it *is* a relationship; that between Querelle and Lt Seblon is tragic precisely because it is *not* a relationship. Between every human instinct of the Lieutenant, and himself as he is forced to appear to Querelle, stands the insurmountable barrier of his own uniform. Lt Seblon, in fact, can only show himself to the world as his own double; and the Double, in all its intricate complexities of significance, is in effect the central theme of *Querelle of Brest*.

The double-murder, to start with. In the everlasting fogs of

Brest—mists veiling granite—Querelle murders Vic, his messmate, who had been his accomplice in smuggling opium past the watchful eyes of the customs[12]; and, perhaps in the same instant, Gil Turko, a young stone-mason employed on construction-work in the dock-yards, goaded beyond endurance by the taunting contempt of Théo, a middle-aged workmate, fills himself with brandy to fire his cour-age, and slashes his enemy's throat with the butt-end of a broken bottle. From this moment onwards, the two alien destinies begin to coincide—with this difference, that whereas Gil, terrified and hiding from the police in the disused *bagne* of Brest, is the victim, Querelle is the master of his fate, or at least as near master as any mere mortal can ever hope to be. Querelle sees in Gil his own reflection, his imitator, his young apprentice who might perhaps, one day, grow up to be the equivalent of himself. He takes care of Gil, feeds him, argues with him, encourages him, secretly exploits him—and finally, for good measure, betrays him to the police. But the relationship Querelle-Gil Turko is only the most central of a whole series of mirror-reflections and doubles; for Querelle himself has another double—a real one this time, not a mere potential—in his identical twin-brother Robert; and Madame Lysiane loves Robert, but she also loves Querelle, being at most times unable to distinguish be-tween them. Mario, the Chief of Police in Brest, has his double in Norbert, known as 'Nono', the proprietor of the brothel La Féria and the husband of Madame Lysiane. And, in the absence of any other living being, there are always mirrors, the great wall-mirrors of La Féria, against which a man—Mario—can lean and prop himself up against his own reflection, so that he 'appears to be prop-ping himself up against himself'.[13]

The outstanding achievement of *Querelle of Brest* as a novel lies in the way in which structure, plot, ideas and symbols are integrated, forming an imaginative pattern in which every element serves to reinforce the other. The symbol of Querelle's dangerous virility is the granitic, the vertical; but Querelle himself is flexible and smiling, his symbol is transferred *outside* himself, it is the ramparts of Brest where he murders Vic, it is the dock-yard wall over which the packet of opium must be passed, it is the walls of La Rochelle in Querelle's childhood memories.[14] Querelle is THE Murderer, but THE Wall is Querelle. Gil and Théo are both masons—wall-builders. The law is a wall to be scaled or penetrated[15]; Querelle's stolen jewels are a 'sacred wall' that protects him and promises him inviolability.[16] The wall holds the mirror and the mirror holds the double; but even without the mirror, Querelle, when he leans up against the wall of the *bistrot* on the occasion of his first encounter with Gil Turko, finds in its immutable resistance an essential awareness of his own existence; from the first he is '. . . subtly aware of the opposition between his living, bodily weight, the cascading tumult of his dorsal muscles, and the shadowy but indestructable mass of the wall behind him.'[17]

In place of the roses and the angels, Genet now uses a much more abstract, sophisticated and in the end more powerful type of symbol : the right-angled triangle, the triangle formed by a man propped up against a wall, the triangle which is visible, like the mark of Cain, in Querelle's actual face, where the crookedly-raised eyebrow forms a right-angle with the crookedly-slanted smile.[18] There is a geometrical precision in *Querelle of Brest* which contrasts significantly with the comparative formlessness, the viscosity, of *Our Lady of the Flowers* or *Miracle of the Rose*.

Querelle of Brest, however, is not merely rigorously conceived in its structure and its symbolism; its ethical paradoxes are worked out 'rigorously' as with 'a mathematical problem',[19] and Genet moves inexorably from a *défense et illustration* of prostitution and burglary to one of the most elaborate apologias for murder since de Sade. It is at this point that we should perhaps once again stop and consider the writer's motives, although these are in fact so complex, that it is difficult to state at any given moment that one predominates to the exclusion of all the rest. However, it may be possible to divide these motives into three broad categories : the mystic-sexual; the social-paradoxical; and the profoundly philosophical. The first tends to glorify crime and violence for its own sake, with as much passionate eroticism, yet perhaps as little desire for realization, as in any other form of erotic dream or vision—the soldier in barracks gloats over his pin-up, yet, faced with Miss Vera Lynn in person, would probably turn scarlet with tongue-tied embarassment and scuttle for safety and consolation to the nearest NAAFI. The second has more immediate implications, since it can be elaborated into a theory, and a theory can become the inspiration of a Party, and a Party can turn murder into assassination—yet in Genet's case, his anarchism, his solitude, his search for the Absolute and for sanctity are in violent contradiction to the demands for discipline and the need for half-truths which are the hallmark of politics. The third is a pure abstraction, posing the sort of problem which has tormented innumerable thinkers for generations, without there being the breath of suspicion that these careful analysts of the human condition, having seen that some degree of evil was inevitable, would therefore wish to encourage it. On the contrary, to perform a lucid

analysis of a process of thought, and to show that this process must
inevitably lead to catastrophe, is sometimes the best, if not the only
means of defence against the impending danger. There are few more
lucid assessments of the extent of evil in the world than Voltaire's
Candide—yet Voltaire is one of the great progressive humanitarians
of all time. Bertrand Russell can hardly be accused of desiring to
provoke a nuclear war, however horrifyingly his arguments show its
inevitability. Or—if it seems exaggerated and slightly absurd to
compare Genet with these figures who deliberately use horror as a
warning—there are innumerable writers and scholars who see modern
man as a creature faced with an ethical dilemma to which there is
no obvious or immediate solution. To take—more or less at random—
the concluding paragraph of a new and brilliant study of the
eighteenth-century moralist, Helvétius, who, in the year 1758, published a treatise entitled *De l'Esprit* :

> Helvétius had in fact taken ethics to such extreme limits that the
> *philosophes* could no longer take a middle path in their desperate search
> to find a secure basis for ethical values. After *De l'esprit* moralists were
> faced with the unwelcome choice of either proceeding from Helvétius'
> eulogy of self-interest to a justification of crime, or of rejecting his whole
> theory and returning to authoritarianism. In other words, the eighteenth
> century was left with the moral nihilism of de Sade on the one hand or
> on the other the ethical rigorism of Kant or Catholicism. The choice was
> between the absurd and the dogmatic, between the violent and the sacred—
> both equally distasteful to the *philosophes*. Helvétius made the eighteenth
> century face this fundamental dilemma : the twentieth century is still
> searching for its solution.[20]

If Dr David Smith, who wrote this passage, had wanted an
example of a twentieth-century writer at grips with the Helvétian
dilemma, he could scarcely have found a more impressive case than
Genet. Rejecting the dogmatic out of hand, Genet argues his way
headlong into the absurd—and then leaves the unhappy reader to
get out of the difficulty as best he may.

Yet it is also because Genet is simultaneously a mystic, an anarchist and a philosopher-moralist—and because these three elements
are often in flagrant contradiction with each other—that it is so
hard to reach specific conclusions about Genet's evil intentions.
Paradox by itself is an uncertain weapon to handle. Coupled with
satire—as in the case of Orwell—its purpose is usually clear enough;
coupled instead with emotional mysticism, it is at logger-heads with
itself, and its purpose is ambiguous. Yet this very ambiguity is the
more disturbing and, ultimately, the more thought-provoking. To
applaud Hitler in satirical paradox is little better than a banality;
to make out a paradoxical argument in favour of Nazism, and then
to support it with an intense emotional *plaidoyer*, is both scandalous

and disquieting. And it is precisely this balance between emotion and paradox which forms the unique originality of Jean Genet. A purely emotional plea for, say, a return to the philosophy and practice of Auschwitz and Dachau could—in the context of present-day Western Europe at any rate—be the work only of a crank, a mad sadist or a dangerous political reactionary. Genet makes precisely such a plea, and then apparently adds insult to injury by supporting it with rational arguments. But the effect of the two in conjunction is to reverse the direction of our attention. Instead of the arguments leading us forward step by step until we are convinced that their ultimate goal—the concentration-camp—is the right one, the abominable nature of the end sends us back over the arguments, and starts us enquiring whether their initial premises can conceivably be correct, if such is their logical conclusion. Yet these initial premises are—in the majority of cases—the basic tenets of our ethics and of our religion : the concepts of sacrifice, of sanctity, of the Absolute, of the value of suffering, of humiliation . . . etc., etc. Heydrich was a Roman Catholic, after all.

In this sense, it is more important that Genet should convince us of his faith in his arguments than that he should persuade us that he himself believes in their unacceptable conclusions; and this is in fact the development that we find in the novels from *Our Lady of the Flowers* to *Querelle of Brest*. In *Our Lady*, what is important is that we should share Genet's vision of the glory of Adrien Baillon, or of the sanctity of Divine—and such is the power of his poetical imagination that he all but succeeds. In this later period, however, he is much more hesitant about ultimate values, and not afraid even to contradict himself if necessary. 'I do not deny this most monstrous of my sons',[21] he asserts in *The Thief's Journal*, 'I want to fill the world with its loathsome progeny'. But, in *Pompes Funèbres* he takes the opposite point of view :

> J'ai tué, pillé, volé, trahi. Quelle gloire atteinte! Mais que n'importe quel assassin, voleur ou traître n'ose aller se prévaloir de mes raisons. J'ai eu trop de mal à les conquérir. Elles ne valent que pour moi. N'importe qui ne saurait bénéficier de cette justification. Je n'aime pas les gens sans conscience.[22]

In *Querelle of Brest*, the shift is complete. That Querelle is a murderer is relatively unimportant compared with the arguments used to justify this vocation; the conclusion is subservient, in fact, to the methods by which it is arrived at. And so we find Genet deliberately contriving a rationalistic ethic whose main *raison d'être* is to progress, by irrefutable steps, towards an unacceptable conclusion. If, in addition, he can make this conclusion correspond to an ideal born of his own erotic fantasies; and if he can besides en-shroud the whole process, from first premiss to final conclusion, in his own brand of transcendental mysticism, and then make it seem that this mysticism has its roots equally distributed between the *Little Flowers of St Francis*, the *Golden Legend*, the *Imitation of Christ*, the *Gospel according to St John* and the *Brothers Karamazov*, then everyone is perfectly happy. Except, of course, the reader.

It may seem slightly grotesque to talk about a code of ethics in relation to Genet; none the less, his characters, without exception, know themselves to be following a set of rules; and they are aware also that it is no easier to behave in exact accordance with their own categorical imperatives than it is to be a Saint according to the precepts of the Church or the Sunday-School. To live perpetually in 'a world which is the mirror-opposite of the normal world' is no easier than to perform all the commonplace acts of daily existence in reverse. We have already seen how hard it is for the Saint to detach himself from the world, and how he can only finally destroy the bonds of love and friendship that frustrate his desire for anchoritic solitude by resorting to betrayal, theft and murder. But even harder than to reject the bonds of social and emotional affinities ('. . . he that hath left house, or brethren, or sisters, or father, or mother, or wife, for my sake . . .'), is to reject, or even criticise, the traditional concepts of Good and Evil in themselves. If the ultimate aim is the sanctity of total isolation, then all acts which contribute to this end are good, all which hinder progress towards it are bad. Assuming (as Genet and most moralists since Hobbes do assume) that good and evil are relative concepts—relative to the human sensations of pleasure and pain, relative to man-in-society— then eventually the Saint, who has conquered his body's desire for pleasure, and who has rejected society, who lives in a domain of transcendental Absolutes beyond the accidents and affections of life, will likewise be 'beyond good and evil'. This is the state towards which Divine is moving, even though, as Genet carefully points out, she is not yet there : 'Divine is not beyond good and evil, there where the saint must live.'[23] Meanwhile, there is an intermediate stage, in which the concepts good and evil still have a role to play, but where they are relative to sanctity rather than to society, to death (or better, to eternity) rather than to that temporary state which is what we normally call life. In a sense, this is at bottom sound theology : 'He that findeth his life shall lose it; and he that loseth his life for my sake shall find it'. If life, in its variety of senses, is to be equated with the good, then there are, implicit in Christ's admonition, two contradictory concepts of the good : the good which is eternal life, to which the means is death; and the good which is temporal life, and which must be rejected. Christ's absolute good, in fact, and Hobbes' relative good, are irreconcilable opposites : in strict logic, one or the other must be considered as bad. Yet our society is based on an ethic which claims simultaneously to uphold *both* concepts, recommending on the one hand conventionally moral acts which assume that human life and happiness represent a value to be cherished, and on the other a set of eschatological doctrines and ascetic aspirations which assume that this same human life and happiness are valueless and should be sacrificed in favour of a higher ideal. This is the paradox which lies at the root of all Genet's ethics :

Si le mal suscite une telle passion, c'est qu'il est lui-même un bien puisque l'on ne peut aimer que ce qui est bien, c'est-à-dire vivant.[24]

It is this dichotomy between two contradictory concepts of the good, the absolute and the relative, which has bedevilled European thought since the eighteenth century, and which was brought to the surface by thinkers such as Mandeville and Bayle, Hobbes, Helvétius and Voltaire. The great modern humanists—of whom Sartre is an outstanding example—make their choice by rejecting the concept of an Absolute-eternal good in favour of a temporal or material good : in which case, logically, the goodness of the Saint or the ascetic is a form of social evil, heartily to be discouraged.[25] Genet, as an orthodox Catholic who is not at all a humanist, takes the opposite point of view, and follows it to its conclusion even more logically than Sartre. If—for the Saint—the good things of the world are in fact evil, then what the world in the abstract calls good is also evil, and perhaps then what the world calls evil is good.[26]

For the down-and-out whom Genet has been, the act of detachment from the material goods of this world offers little difficulty : it is already accomplished. The main problem, then, is mental : to shake one's mind out of the humanistic (and ultimately materialistic) rut, and to shuffle off the clinging conventions of goodness as a social ideal—and this is extremely difficult : '. . . as we know, it was very hard for Divine to be immoral'.[27] It is difficult, partly because the convention is so deep-rooted; partly because to act logically as though one believed *exclusively* in eternal values brings one into conflict with all right-thinking people; partly because man seems to have been created a social animal, and therefore is endowed with certain basic social instincts, including *la bonté* (Rousseau called it 'pity') which are difficult to eradicate. *La bonté* is in fact one of the recurrent problems for Genet's characters. '*Madame est si bonne*', Claire and Solange—themselves both *des bonnes*—repeat to each other as they consider this evil-minded and egotistical *bour-*

geoise who is their mistress; and Genet himself only succeeds in praising with some semblance of enthusiasm *la bonté* of the unspeakable Armand because Armand is more brute than human being, and because Genet discovers eventually that the only way to eradicate this social instinct is literally to dehumanize both himself and his fellow-beings, and to consider them as objects : 'My relations with men were beginning to be those which usually exist between men and things.'[28]

When Divine decides to induce her neighbour's child to fall off the balcony, it is a deliberate attempt to 'kill her goodness'; and when the child dies, 'she was superhuman', comments Genet, 'her goodness was dead.'[29] Later, in *Querelle of Brest*, a human being who has reached this state of detachment, at once superhuman and inhuman, is described as *affranchi*, [literally, a 'freed-man', a being freed from the slavery of moral scruples] and both Querelle and Lt Seblon are far more *affranchis* than Divine. Querelle is so detached that he can murder with a smile; but, strangely, in Genet's view, Seblon is still more detached than Querelle, in that he alone, of all Genet's characters, envisages self-destruction intelligently and lucidly as the supreme act of dehumanization, instead of as the indirect consequence of the destruction of others. 'The Lieutenant proved more unscrupulous [*affranchi*] than all the Querelles of the Fleet put together : there was not a man among them to touch him.'[30]

It is in this context of a transcendental ethical logic that we must look at Genet's ideology of assassination. In all cases it is the mind, or the soul, of the murderer that interests him, never those of the victim. Even Théo, the most carefully-delineated of all Genet's victims, is little more than a shadowy personage in the background; while Vic is merely a lay-figure in naval uniform. Murder fascinates Genet, not so much for its own sake, as on account of its rank in the scale of evil *'selon le monde'*.[31]

In other words, in every act of murder, we are concerned not with one symbol, but with two, and it is important to distinguish between them, since Genet himself deliberately confuses the issue. On the one hand there is the murderer, a symbol of active virility, hardness, malevolence, etc.—a typical homosexual erotic object; on the other, there is the act itself, as a symbol of evil, with all its implications. The interest of *Querelle of Brest* lies in the way in which Genet develops the second aspect of his problem, to the comparative neglect of the first.

To begin with, the act of murder is seen as an act of liberation— in every sense. Liberation from conventions, liberation from society, liberation both from oneself and from God. It is the supreme act that destroys the *status quo*, whatever that may be. It is not so much—as Gide considered it, in *Les Caves du Vatican*—the culminating *acte gratuit* that liberates man from the determinism of the material universe, as the point at which—irremediably—man opts for his own freedom. *'J'allais faire le premier geste décisif pour ma liberté'*,[32] reflects Erik on the outbreak of war in 1939, war being the tacit permission to experience the metaphysical consequences of murder without the normal interference by society. The act of murder is the absolute dividing-line between the material and the transcendental, the profane and the sacred. Once crossed, the past no longer has any relevant existence, time ceases; the future is an open choice, and the necessity for choice has itself been freely chosen. The Old Adam has been annihilated, the New Adam has replaced him, there has been a substitution. But it is a substitution of spirit in place of matter. The material body, the Old Adam, is doomed in any case, is to all intents and purposes dead already, as Harcamone has realized. And since the body is already annihilated and buried in quicklime, the spirit is free with a freedom that otherwise is inconceivable.

Inconceivable—but also terrifying, anguishing, as is all *absolute* freedom in an existentialist universe—as is the freedom of Sartre's Oreste in *The Flies*:

> I am neither the master nor the slave, Jupiter. I *am* my liberty. [. . . .]
> There is nothing in heaven, neither right nor wrong, nor anyone to
> give me orders.[33]

—but, as with Electre, Oreste's sister, the weight of total liberty can easily prove overpowering. Rather than bear the burden of absolute freedom, Electre repents, returns to the fold of morality and the bosom of Jupiter. Genet's murderers, on the whole, are made of stronger existentialist material. They are curious to know the temptation of repentence,[34] but only as an intellectual curiosity. It is not only that they are not prepared to repent—for one and all *accept* their act—but even if they wished to, they could not. The act is irremediable. In killing their victim, they have simultaneously killed themselves, and God.

It is difficult, without knowing the exact extent of Genet's reading, both in prison and outside, to assess the influence of Dostoievsky on his thought. All the internal evidence suggests that it is considerable, from allusions to *Crime and Punishment* in *The Thief's Journal* ('I wanted to be the young prostitute who accompanies her lover to Siberia'[35]), to the whole structure of Genet's ethics. 'If there is no God,' argues Dostoievsky, 'then *everything* is permitted'— and where everything is permitted, the entire mechanism of the universe is gratuitous, absurd, with that monstrous and frightening absurdity which is explored later by Camus in *The Myth of*

Sisyphus and by Ionesco in *Exit the King*. Where God exists, man is enclosed, safely and snugly, within the laws that God has ordained. Where God exists no longer, then man, who can conceive God, *is* God, and all his compressed energies explode into the vacuity, the Nothingness of the infinite, so that, in the end, these energies, meeting no resistance, return along those paths traced by the curvature of empty space and, returning, destroy their own source and creator. So Svidrigaïlov is destroyed, and Ordinov, and Stavrogin, the hero of the *Possessed*. By contrast, Raskol'nikov, realizing the threat of an utterly absurd annihilation in a universe where he has destroyed God, yet not possessing the moral courage to take his place, with all the absolute responsibility that this implies, confesses his crime, and so restores the framework of law, order and metaphysical security.[36]

Querelle of Brest is permeated through and through with Dostoievskian philosophy—or rather, with its critique. D. H. Lawrence once summed up Dostoievsky's mysticism, based on the image of the humiliated Christ, in three devastating lines :

> . . . And the Dostoievsky lot :
> 'Let me sin my way to Jesus'
> —So they sinned themselves off the face of the earth.

So it is with Querelle and Riton and Lt Seblon—save that they, perhaps, are more lucidly aware of what they are doing. Lt Seblon, for instance, takes Dostoievsky's mystic faith in the humiliated Christ just one step further than Dostoievsky himself was prepared to take it, and so runs straight into D. H. Lawrence—and accepts the verdict : he *will* (if this is the way to Christ and sanctity) 'sin himself off the face of the earth' :

> It is thanks to Jesus that we can extol humility, since He made it a hallmark of divinity. Divinity deep within one—for what reason is there to deny the powers of this world?—opposed to those powers, and strong enough to triumph over them. And humility is born only of humiliation. Otherwise it must be regarded as false vanity.[37]

But Seblon is not a murderer. Seblon is only following in the footsteps of Alyosha Karamazov—it is Querelle who is successor to Raskol'nikov; and Raskol'nikov, when he kills the old woman, discovers that he also has killed both God and himself. Himself first of all, then God-in-himself, since God is his own mirror-image. 'After committing the first murder, Querelle had experienced the feeling of being dead'[38]—but Riton, as a *milicien* executing *maquisards* during the Occupation, had already passed through the same experience : '*Il était déjà mort à la douleur et mort tout simplement puisqu'il venait de tuer sa propre image*'.[39]

But the murderer, having killed God, *is* God. 'He has set himself up as a god, on an altar, whether of shaky boards or azure air.'[40] Like Christ, he is dead, and yet still alive. Like God, he has stopped the passage of time; like God, he can make the dead rise up and speak—for it is his victim, not he, who will call miraculously into being the Judge and the crowds and the executioner and all the ritual of the Assizes. 'The murderer makes blood speak. He argues with it, tries to compound with the miracle.'[41] Like God, he has destroyed one order, only to give himself the freedom to create a new world and a new order, in which he himself is the controlling will, the deity—as happens again with Clément Village, when he has killed Sonia, his Polish mistress: 'he sublimated himself.'[42] Where there *was* God, there *is* nothing. And where there *was* Village, or Our Lady, or Harcamone, or Riton, or Querelle, there is again nothing. A non-existent (self-murdered) Self, destined to shoulder the entire moral responsibility of the universe. The prospect is terrifying, overwhelming. Yet this is the responsibility that Genet's murderers assume. They place—like Sartre—the whole weight of *l'être* upon the anguished elusiveness of *le néant* :

> No longer was any particle of Querelle remaining in his own body. His body was an empty shell. Facing Vic was no one; the murderer was about to attain his perfection.[43]

—this is their *gloire*. They are the very prophets of Existentialism.

The conviction—whether rationally argued, as in Sartre or Beckett, or merely *felt*, irrationally apprehended, as with Genet or Ionesco—that the principle of cognition, the centre of awareness, in a word, the essential Self, is *negative*, a Void, a dimensionless element of Nothingness in contrast with the Totality, the Plenum of all that exists as an object of consciousness—this is one of the dominating themes of contemporary French philosophy. Nor does Genet in any way differ from the conclusions of his less scandalously controversial fellow-writers. Only his vocabulary sets him slightly apart. He still, albeit with precaution, uses such words as *âme*, where Sartre will talk about *le pour-soi* or the 'pre-reflexive cogito'. Moreover, being a mystic, he can allow his Querelle to take refuge, to enfold himself carefully and deliberately, in the *néant* of his own being, whereas the more rationalistic Beckett takes his *Unnamable* through some two hundred pages of searchings for the undiscoverable and non-existent Self, and in the end leaves him in an anguish of despair at having failed to locate what he *knows* must be there all the time, yet which he understands, with all the tragic lucidity of a mathematician faced with the problem of resolving π into a rational number, he can never grasp, nor conceptually define, nor even *name*, until zero shall have become a positive number . . . that is, until time shall have stopped, and the three common dimensions of our familiar universe shall have given place to the foreign and inconceivable dimensions of a world without space and without duration.

For Genet, there is a soul and there is a body. But the soul, with all its qualities and its defects, can only be made manifest through the body. What we *see* of the Other *is* the soul of the Other, which appears in all the acts and movements of the body. Admittedly, these movements reveal (or seem to reveal) the impulses of a hidden, inner Self; but this Self is a void, a Nothing; and therefore the visual manifestations, since they are *inspired by nothing*,[44] are in themselves the essential reality of the soul. Appearance *is* reality, argues Genet in echo of Sartre : therefore the body, which contains the appearance of the soul, *is* the soul, whose invisibility is no more mysterious than that of the inner organs—the kidneys, say, or the appendix.[45] Assuredly there *is* a more essential element of the Self, hidden away behind the visible phenomena of soul and body; but (like *le pour-soi* in its relations with *l'en-soi*), it owes its essentiality to its non-existence. To take an image : a field-gun is known by its phenomena—the visible and tangible, solid gun-metal of which it is composed, the features which constitute its definition and its danger and which inform us of its purpose; but the essential reality of the gun is the hole in the centre of the barrel, through which the shell must pass . . . and this centre is a Void, itself formless, unnamable and indefinable, in relation to which the metal covering, which gives the Void name, form and definition, is basically an alien and irrelevant disguise :

> On dit l'âme d'un canon, qui est la paroi, moins que la paroi même, intérieure du canon. C'est cette chose qui n'existe plus, c'est le vide brillant, acéré et glacial qui limite la colonne d'air et le tube d'acier, le vide et le métal—pire: le vide et le froid du métal.[46]

This concept of the Void at the centre of Self is as essential to Genet as it is to Beckett or to Ionesco, although it is rather less in evidence in the novels before *Querelle of Brest*. It is because the inner reality is a Void that, when Darling imitates the gestures— the external appearance—of Divine, he actually *becomes* Divine : appearance (gesture) = body + soul, in so far as the soul can be conceived as something positive at all. Appearance is a positive form imposed on a negative essence : the essence remains an independent substance, but can only be known through the form which it receives; and in this sense it *is* the form which it has.

In the case of the murderer—of Querelle—the act of killing destroys the appearance, the visible form, of the victim; it cannot destroy the essence, since this, like the hole in the barrel of the gun, being negative, is indestructable. On the other hand—and here the analogy with the field-gun breaks down—the Void which is the essence of Self is not merely that-which-is-not : it is dynamic, in that it *is* the Self. Although negative in essence, it is nevertheless the active principle of individual life. There is, as it were, a dynamic essence at large in the world, seeking a form. In principle, it can take *any* form, transmute itself into *any* appearance of reality. Thus the dead Jean Decarnin of *Pompes Funèbres* '. . . *peut avoir existé momentanément sous n'importe quelle forme*'—an old beggar-woman or, for that matter, a dustbin[47]—while Genet, whose symbol for his essential Self is repeatedly the glass transparency of some pellucid object, experiences the sensation that his poetry is simply his Self transmuted into a new form—the form of words and images.[48]

The living being can be aware of his own essential Self, his life-principle, in innumerable different forms—Querelle at one point actually *becomes* the bit of broken rampart in which he is hiding his jewels[49]; but the murderer, as we have seen, uses his act of murder as a supreme move in the process of dehumanization. Fundamentally then, the murderer, in the same instant that he kills the appearance of his victim, kills the life-element in himself . . . and then, in Genet's peculiar and mystic vision of the world beyond reality, the obvious thing happens. The negative life-essence of the victim takes possession of the murderer; and in every significant sense, the slayer becomes the person he has slain. After the murder of Vic, Querelle becomes Vic, just as, after each of his previous murders, his own personality has been usurped by the personality of his victim.

The details of this singular argument, with its suggestions of primitive magic, superstition and occultism—however fascinating they are—should not blind us to its real significance, which is not so much that of the possession of the soul of the murderer by the victim, as the much more characteristic assertion that the act of murder destroys the original identity of the murderer and, by leaving him alive, yet without an identity which he can continue to recognize as himself—therefore without a past—leaves him at the threshold of a totally unbearable liberty. He has chosen, and his choice was to destroy all previous choices, and thus to destroy his Self which was the only possible guide that could have aided him in future choices. Yet, since he has also, in the same act, by destroying the law of God, destroyed the God who made it, his is now the responsibility that once was God's. He is alone, a Void, dead though apparently still alive, a legislator without a code or even a memory, who is responsible for the Totality of the universe, and perhaps even for God himself. With less than half these responsibilities, Raskol'nikov preferred confession and the 'Dead House' in Siberia.

Nor are Genet's people any better equipped to play the part of
God than Dostoievsky's. It is not remorse which drives them to confession, but liberty. For the intolerable burden of total liberty that
descends on the criminal once he has successfully defied the Absolute,
there is only one remedy : expiation. For Monsieur le Président of
the Assizes, punishment appears as society's revenge on the criminal;
for Our Lady, for Harcamone and, in a strange and visionary manner, for Querelle, punishment is the criminal's only refuge against
the non-existence of God.

Thus, step by step, as first we disentangle, and then bring together
again the various elements that constitute Genet's picture of the ideal
murderer, we discover a being far more complex than the rather
blatant symbol of erotic violence that he appeared to be at first
sight. He is a being who, in the beginning, aspires to sanctity through
the rejection of the world and its values; who, in the process of
rejecting these values, as embodied in the categorical imperatives of
society, finds that, instead of attaining sanctity, he has accidentally
or knowingly annihilated both God and himself, and conquered
an intolerable liberty; and who finally finds himself faced with the
problem of reconciling his ambition with his achievement through
some form of expiation. With the exception of Querelle, all Genet's
murderers reach their apotheosis in the forty days which French
law allows between sentence and execution; Querelle alone—by in-
flicting his own obscene punishment on himself—discovers the way
to prolong his apotheosis (albeit in diluted form) beyond the allotted
forty days, and thus prepares the road for Genet's later characters,
who turn their unabated instinct for violence to rather less self-
frustrating—or less egotistical—ends.

The relationship between crime and punishment is extremely close :
both concepts are, as it were, two inseparable halves of the *same*
act. The ideal criminal does not hope to escape justice; his crime
includes, as an intrinsic part of its reality, the inevitability of its
punishment—its expiation—which negates its existence, and thus,
out of the conflict of negative and positive, creates that dynamic
void which is the condition of transcendental or superhuman experience. In so far as the criminal envisages the attainment of this
transcendental state as his ultimate aim, it can be argued that
Genet's murderers commit their crimes *in order that* they may be
negated by expiation—that is, that the first object of crime is its
related punishment : 'Querelle must be regarded as a joyous moral
suicide.'[50]

How far this self-annihilating duality : crime/punishment, can coldly and rationally be planned in advance as a means of penetrating the domain of the Absolute is a different matter, and one that Genet will argue out in detail in his first play, *Deathwatch*. Setting this problem aside for the moment, however, the fact remains that all Genet's murderers (and even his lesser criminals, his bruisers and burglars), having once committed their crime, live in an intolerable state of suspense until they are condemned. 'Incapable, in fact, of knowing whether or not he will be arrested,' observes Genet, 'the criminal lives in a state of uncertainty, of which he can rid himself only by denying his act, that is to say, by expiation.'[51] Clément Village requires every atom of strength that he possesses, after the murder of Sonia, not to rush off to the nearest police-station and 'burst into tears'[52]; while, when Our Lady himself finally confesses to the murder of the old man, after he has been arrested on the much less serious charge of trafficking in cocaine, Genet suggests that, fundamentally, the reason for this confession was that he was *afraid* of a lesser punishment and therefore of an incomplete expiation. For the metaphysical presupposition which underlies Genet's famous duality : 'the eternal couple of the Saint and the Criminal' is that the punishment must *exactly* fit the crime : positive and negative must cancel each other out absolutely, otherwise the result is not Zero—the Void—but something less or more than Zero; and all that is less or more than Zero is profane, not of the sacred world. 'If I love their crime,' writes Genet of his ideal criminals, 'it is for the punishment it involves'.[53] Any failure in this exact and mathematically precise cancellation of positive by negative, therefore, is envisaged by Genet with horror; anything which upsets the balance— whether it be the punishing of the innocent or more emphatically the pardoning of the guilty—threatens the whole delicate structure of transcendence; it is Genet's private nightmare, through which 'The horror entered me. I chewed it, I was full of it.'[54]

This, however, brings us face to face with another problem, and one which is central in Genet's strange vision of the significance of life. Genet's saints, we must remember, if they are essentially pagan, are never entirely de-Christianised, nor would they wish to be. Moreover, real saints also make their appearance here and there in the novels : St Stephen, St Theresa, St Catherine and all the cohorts of the *Golden Legend*. And St Vincent de Paul.

St Vincent de Paul is one of the more problematic figures in Genet's hagiological hierarchy. In a sense—though not exactly in Genet's sense—the doctrine of the expiation of sins is fundamentally Christian : with this difference, that Christ himself, as Divine realizes,[55] being incapable of sin, took on himself the sins of others;

and in a lesser way, St Vincent de Paul, in a celebrated episode when he freely exchanged places with a condemned criminal in the galleys, and took his terrible seat at the oar, imitated the Redeemer in that he, who was without sin, accepted the consequences of the sins of another. '*Agnus Dei qui tollis peccata mundi. . . .*'

Genet's religiosity (to avoid for the moment the word 'religion') is one of the profoundest aspects of his nature; and in view of his own direct experience of crime and punishment, it is not surprising that no part of the Christian doctrine should haunt his imagination more persistently than the image of a Christ who takes upon himself the sins of the world, or than the figure of St Vincent de Paul chained to the oar of his galley. Instinctively he is tempted to involve this concept of the redemption of others with his own ideal of sanctity; but rationally he cannot do so, for it is in flagrant contradiction with the rest of his metaphysic. The chastisement of an innocent, as we have seen, destroys the whole concept of transcendence. So Genet's admiration of St Vincent de Paul is none the less tempered with very serious criticism : in order, from the heart of his Charity, to assume the *sins* of his fellow-mortals, he should first have assumed their crimes. Merely to accept their punishment is an inspiring, but basically a gratuitous, a wasted, a hopelessly superficial act of mercy. For in fact—in the Absolute sense—the Saint achieved nothing that was relevant to the situation; he merely destroyed its significance. The punishment has significance only in terms of the crime; to demand the first without the second is to split the two halves of an inseparable duality and to make nonsense out of both.

Implicitly, this criticism of St Vincent de Paul is also a criticism of Christ—or, for that matter, of God. If Christ has not sinned, then he cannot redeem. Only a God who has proved himself capable of sin—of evil—can redeem the sins, or alleviate the punishment, of his creatures. The grotesque, the ludicrous *curé* of *Pompes Funèbres*, after his vision in the latrines, seems to be following up the same line of argument : '*Il fallait à Dieu cet admirable péché*'.[56] If Genet himself—who, as a writer, occupies the same position as God in relation to his characters, his Creation—is prepared to take on their punishment, it is only because he is first prepared to participate in their crimes. This also is the attitude of Lt Seblon towards Querelle :

> By denying his generosity, he [the Lieutenant] destroyed it at its source, leaving in its place a feeling of indulgence towards the criminal, and, further still, a sense of moral participation in the crime.[57]

—and in this, Seblon is a more effective Redeemer than St Vincent. If this is one of the central themes of *Querelle of Brest*, it is also an intrinsic part of Genet's idea of his own mission as a poet and a novelist. It is his justification—more than this, it explains his *need*—for creating a world of evil and sordid creatures, and for participating emotionally and imaginatively in their crimes. Is it even conceivable that God, having similarly created a world abounding with evil, should then stand by like some pious Sainte-Nitouche, and merely wrinkle up his nose in disgust at what he himself has created?

> Creating is not a somewhat frivolous game. The creator has committed himself to the fearful adventure of taking upon himself, to the very end, the perils risked by his creatures [. . . .] Every creator must thus shoulder— the expression seems feeble—must make his own, to the point of knowing it to be his substance, circulating in his arteries, the evil given by him, which his heroes choose freely.[58]

It is the virtue of Genet's symbolism to discover significance in all things; it is perhaps his intellectual triumph as a writer that, having despaired of avoiding or annihilating evil, he has instead discovered a metaphysically positive meaning in that which is normally considered to be very negation of significance, much as Albert Camus at about the same time was discovering the positive significance of the Absurd.

Another reason that explains Genet's fascination with the ideal murderer is that murder, of all crimes, of all human actions, is the most *irremediable*; and the very word irremediable plunges us straight into the heart of another major theme of *Querelle of Brest* : the problem of time.

Time, for Jean Genet, is one of the greatest mysteries, in that, simultaneously, it both is and is not a reality. It is both a necessity and an impossibility—as is illustrated by the basic structure of *Querelle of Brest*, which, in the manner of its presentation, destroys the normal sequences of time,[59] yet nevertheless presents a coherent story, with a logical or anecdotic sequence of causes and effects which illustrates the fact that, in spite of the apparent breakdown, time continues to flow on regardless, and in a habitual manner. Genet—or Man—finds himself, as it were, caught between two irreconcilable forces : that of the instantaneous present, his *être*, his consciousness; and that of sequence, which takes acts or words more or less at random out of the present and situates them in an unattainable past, whence they can continue to dominate the present, yet themselves lie for ever out of reach.

In other words, there seems to be a radical difference in quality

between the act and the being who performs the act. The being *is*;
the act *was*. For one inconceivable instant the two coincide, but
thereafter they belong to different worlds. Yet, fatally, the past
which is the act has the power to destroy the present which is the
being; on the other hand, by no effort in the world can the being
destroy the act. It follows, then, that the being is outside time, and
that, contained within the being (and therefore similarly outside
time) is the reason for the act; but the act itself is *in* time and therefore has no clear and distinct relationship with him who performed
it. But the most disturbing feature is that the human intelligence,
which resides *within* the being, for whom all sensations are in the
instantaneous present, is incapable of understanding anything which
is outside the present, any more than (in normal circumstances) the
animate can conceive what it is to be inanimate : instead, Genet's
people are constantly engaged in contemplating every act-in-time,
breaking it down into a series of components, each one of which
represents an instantaneous present, and thereby *proving* the act
has no real existence in the past. In spite of which proof, the act
persists in keeping its own inviolable reality, and, in revenge against
the being who has sought to destroy its continuity by dissolving
it into contiguity, it rises up against its enemy and destroys
him.

The inner world, then, the consciousness of man, is timeless, just
as the sacred world of the Absolute is timeless and eternal. There is
no future separate from the present, since the consequences of the
act are contained *in the act now*; they may only appear in a distant
future, but they *are* already in the present, and have been in essential or potential existence from all time. The murderer's death-
sentence comes into being in the same instant as he kills his victim;
yet he does not *become* a murderer by his act. For Genet, the murderer exists by virtue of a transcendental act of Grace, determined
for all eternity by forces outside time (as Querelle is determined
by his stars) : consequently the being (the murderer), the act (the
murder) and its consequences (the sentence) have all an absolute
and simultaneous existence, to which time is essentially irrelevant.
A prophecy of the future is nothing more than a revelation of
the present. 'In a year, a man will throw himself from the rock,'
prophesies Solange to Culafroy, looking at the Roc du Crotto; and
from that moment the precipice becomes as sacred as though the
event had already happened. Culafroy and Solange are filled with
'piety for one of the future dead', and Solange, having dredged the
tragedy up out of time-to-come, becomes responsible for it in the
present : the future suicide-leap becomes 'the tragedy of which
she's the author'.[60]

In point of fact (at least in an existentialist context) there is nothing absurd or far-fetched about this. There is no past or future in nature, only an immediate present. It requires a human awareness, equipped with memory, with imagination, above all with language, to transmute a present reality into a sequence in time; without words, there is no past, and words again are always in the present. They *are*. Thus when Genet compares Clément Village's anguish *now* with that of Our Lady in the future, he writes deliberately : 'He refused to see the gulf [. . . .] *a hundred pages later*, Our Lady of the Flowers did not resist'[61]—a hundred *pages*, and not 'a hundred days'. For as we read these words on page 188 of *Our Lady of the Flowers*, page 275 (Our Lady's confession) is already written; there is no question that it *will be*; it *is*. Hence that anomalous and sinister past tense : 'Our Lady *did not resist*'.

Time, then, is a monstrous conundrum for Genet's characters, and, like Beckett's Vladimir and Estragon, they propose various solutions to try and solve it, for it is a patent unreality that can exercise the power and all the dangerous influence of a reality. The prisoners of Fontevrault construct calendars showing the entire duration of their sentence—yet every day so marked must be visible simultaneously, for to put them in a book means that, to look through the book, time must be used, minutes, or perhaps only seconds—yet those few seconds suffice to restore duration, and the hard-won timeless instantaneity disintegrates into twenty endless years of torture and hard-labour.[62] The Little Skivvy, on the other hand, deliberately dissolves her awareness into the inanimate objects that surround her, just as Querelle dissolves himself into the ramparts of Brest, for the inanimate is outside time, and for the living being who identifies himself with the inanimate, time will come to a stop : '*Chaque objet conservait en soi un temps immobile d'où le sommeil était banni.*'[63]

At Mettray, 'time was multiplied by time'[64]; but when, in a mixture of vision, dream and memory, the past of Mettray is superimposed on the present of Fontevrault, time disappears, and Mettray and Fontevrault co-exist in an eternal-instantaneous present—as 'a finished state, monstrously immobilized'.[65] Querelle, who thinks of himself as a 'monster'—an alligator—conceives the past as his own tail, which he can see, and the present as his head which, to him, is invisible—yet with every movement, head and tail proceed together, for they are both equally himself.[66] His past is a projection backwards through time of his present reality, just as Mettray 'carries on, continues in time' into the future/present of Fontevrault.[67] Harcamone, whose second murder threatens to repeat the gestures of the first, becomes aware that all time is cyclical[68]; but

then every gesture, being an archetype rather than an act, having
its significance in the past while its appearance is in the present,
similarly destroys the reality of time, suggesting, instead of continuity, an 'eternal series of cycles like infinite reflections in a mirror.'

> 'You are the reflection in time of a past act, like the reflection in space
> seen in a mirror. [. . . .] We are a book of familiar and living history in
> which the poet can decipher the signs of Eternal Recurrence.'[69]

Here, then, is the enigma. Time is an unreality, and man, a being
essentially outside time (the more so if his soul, his inner Self, is a
Void), can, by a simple twist of will or dream, defy the apparent
laws of time, just as Harcamone defies the related laws of space
and walks straight through the doors of his condemned cell. And
yet the *act*, which originates in the will of a timeless being, drops
like a stone straight into the category time, and from the moment
of its completion is irremediable. For the purposes of Genet's investi-
gation, murder is the perfect symbol and example of the 'irremediable act'. Not only in Gil Turko's tormented self-questionings, but in
every one of the novels we find traces of Genet's anguish when confronted by the total, inexplicable impotence of man faced with
certain utterly simple phenomena which, logically, it should be
possible for him to master, precisely because they *are* so simple. The
barriers are so fragile, like the wall of flowers at Mettray which was
'more fragile than the past and equally impassable'[70]; nor need the
act itself be violent or extraordinary or difficult—it suffices to drop
a little gardenal into Madame's evening cup of lime-tea, and the
irremediable exists. For 'a *trifle*', observes Genet in *Our Lady of the
Flowers*,[71] the whole destiny of a man may be changed; and elsewhere :

> The slightest carelessness—sometimes even less than a gesture, an un-
> finished gesture, one you would like to take back, to undo by reversing
> time, a gesture so mild and close, still in the present moment, that you
> think you can efface it—Impossible!—can lead, for example, to the
> guillotine.[72]

In consequence, all Genet's characters, with varying degrees of
success, are struggling to achieve that tiny victory over time which
looks so easy and is in fact so difficult : 'retracing their steps into the
past.' Divine is the first to try, and her method is so simple that it
almost works. She reduces herself to a state of total immobility—
in fact, like the Little Skivvy after her, she *becomes* an object; and
the object being timeless, time flows on into the future while she
remains behind, lost and dreaming somewhere in the wake of her
own past. Or at least, so it seems, for she never completes the experiment. By remaining stationary, and thus in effect moving back-

wards into the past, for long enough, Divine realises with sudden consternation that she will eventually come face to face with the First Cause of all, and, her religious sensibility being what it is, she can no more face the prospect of this than the Christian Saint can contemplate the prospect of suddenly finding himself face to face with God; consequently she takes fright and 'released a gesture that very quickly set her heart beating again'.[73]

Gil, on the other hand, attempts to reduce his act to timelessness—and thus to render it accessible, consequently reversible—by decomposing it into a series of gestures, and then each gesture into a series of static poses, inanimate and motionless as the hands of statues, contiguous with each other, as are the innumerable still frames that compose the film of a motion-picture, and, like these, having no inherent continuity in themselves, but only by dint of an illusion when passed through a special mechanism. In this case, Gil believes, the mechanism—the projector—is his own mind : reduced to a series of gestures—the same sort of gratuitous, timeless gestures that Querelle also cultivates, as when he lights his cigarettes[74]—Gil hopes that he can simply cut them out of his past, just as, with scissors, one can cut out a sequence from a film. Or alternatively, even if this should prove too difficult, he further believes that, by removing the element of continuity, he can at least dissolve the *significance* of the act into a series of gestures, or poses, each one of which, in itself, is insignificant; for the hand of a statue holding a knife is not in itself significant, or at least not significant in the same way as it is when the hand moves, the knife flashes and the victim falls. The essence of the act is movement, the essence of movement, time :

> Gil [. . . .] tried to nullify his act by breaking it down into a series of actions, each one perfectly harmless in itself. 'What if I did open a door? One has a perfect right to open a door; what if I took hold of a bottle?—one has every right to take hold of a bottle; if I broke a bottle? nobody has a right to stop that; if I put the jagged edges against the skin of the neck? there's nothing so very terrible in that, one has the right to do it. To exert a little pressure and then to press them home a little further?—that's not so terrible either. If I let a little blood flow? One can do it, one has the right to do it. To let a little more blood, and then a little more still?'
>
> Thus it was possible for the crime to be reduced to next to nothing, to be reduced to such an infinitely small scale of measurement that it is impossible to determine the point of balance at which what is lawful emerges—and yet still adheres to what is lawfully permitted and remains inseparable from it—into what is illegal and results in actual crime. Gil did his utmost to reduce his crime to this level, to scale it down to vanishing point.[75]

What defeats Gil in his intentions is that his murder—he realizes it too late—was 'an error' : a typically Genetian development, which links up indirectly with his search for authenticity and his Cornelian belief that the only way effectively to master one's destiny is to accept it. This is the difference between Querelle and Gil. Gil gets no profit whatsoever from his crime, and it is this which causes him to regret it and to think of it as a mistake. Not that he would simply bring Théo back to life, but rather he would re-murder him, but this time in rather more profitable circumstances. All the same, to regret an act is to fail to accept responsibility for it : it is the same, in effect, as having not willed the act in the first place. And so, when Gil comes to the problem of dissecting his total act into its component non-significant gestures, the point at which innocence turns into crime turns out to be a Void. Where there should have been a positive act of will, there is only a failure, an absence; con-sequently the essential element is negative and cannot be grasped. Gil finds that he *can* go back over his acts, *can* dissolve them into contiguity and thus eliminate the terrible sequences of time; but that which is not there cannot be immobilized. The fatal significance of the murder of Théo lies in the fact that it was all a mistake.[76]

To make matters worse, and so finally to complete his downfall, Gil uses the very process which, had he used it in a context of authenticity, might have procured his metaphysical salvation, yet which, as it is, serves only to deny his responsibility still further. Working backwards in time, Gil invents a determinism for himself, thus proving to his own satisfaction, and ultimate damnation, that he was completely irresponsible for the act which is attributed to him :

> As for Gil, having done the deed, he wished to justify it by proving it to have been inevitable, and to this end he *stepped back again* into his past life. He went about it in the following way : 'Supposing I'd never met Roger. . . . Supposing I'd never come to Brest. . . . Supposing . . . etc.; etc.', until he reached the conclusion that the crime, even though it had run in the blood of his body and down the veins of his arms, none the less must have its source somewhere outside him.[77]

By contrast, Querelle, using the same technique as Gil, but starting from a point of view of total acceptance, succeeds where his younger apprentice fails. Step by step, Querelle decomposes his act into 'rustling and luminous gestures'; and at each point he stops and tests the authenticity of every move, to make sure that it rings true, 'disentangling the skein', as it were, of the whole episode, and pre-senting it objectively 'to God, or some other judge and jury'.[78] It is, moreover, in order to establish still more solidly his position of authenticity, or total responsibility, that Querelle rejects Gide's concept of the *acte gratuit*. It was precisely the gratuitousness of

Gil's murder—its purposelessness—that enabled Gil to deny, or at any rate to begin to doubt, his responsibility. In theory, admittedly, a gratuitous murder corresponds more closely to the ideal of Absolute Evil than a crime committed for profit. Lafcadio's murder of an unknown stranger in a train[79] has about it an aura of metaphysical and aesthetic perfection which is lacking from Querelle's murders—crimes which are committed, directly or indirectly, for gain. But we have already seen the logical objections to any scheme for attaining to the perfection of Absolute Evil; and Querelle calculates that he is nearer to the Absolute if he can know without an instant of doubt that every gesture of his total act was the deliberate reflection of his conscious will, than if he merely recognizes the aesthetic pleasures of gratuitousness. This explains the rather strange symbolic role played by jewels in *Querelle of Brest*. Querelle always tries to take his profit in the form of jewellery, which, being more or less indestructible, will continue throughout time to guarantee the authenticity of his act : and, to increase the efficacy of this guarantee, with a curious throw-back to the rituals of primitive or black magic, Querelle sanctifies his jewels, and at the same time makes them an inseparable part of his own being, by some form of blood-sacrifice—usually by the murder of that individual who had been his accomplice in procuring the booty. In ideal circumstances, this accomplice is also his closest friend, perhaps also his lover. Thus to the concept of a ritualistic sacrifice is added that of the tragic betrayal of the beloved : the murder of Vic, therefore, is simultaneously part of the manœuvre to obtain the jewels, the betrayal of an intimate friend, the blood-sacrifice which binds the jewels indissolubly to Querelle himself, and the guarantee of the eternal authenticity of the act : 'Querelle transmogrified his friends into bracelets, necklaces, gold watches, and earrings.'[80]

To make doubly sure, moreover, Querelle has the fantastic ingenuity always to allow one small slip in every crime he commits—in the case of Vic, he leaves a cigarette-lighter under the body—and this slip, the *'petit fait faux'*, is his lifeline, his ultimate safeguard. For, as he goes back into the past, reconsidering his gestures one by one, he discovers—just as Gil discovered—that his act included a mistake; but unlike Gil, he knows that his error is the hall-mark and final guarantee that the whole sequence was deliberate. Not that the slip itself was deliberate at the time of its commission; but it becomes deliberate retrospectively as a result of its discovery : Querelle allows himself to make *a* slip; when he discovers *the* slip, he identifies it with the one that he had allowed for. Subsequently, this error becomes his talisman, the symbol of his absolute authenticity, so that he invariably keeps about him some traces of his victim which, if ever he were suspected, would suffice to condemn him out of hand. Moreover, these deliberately-welcomed errors serve another purpose—again the opposite of Gil's. If the crime were *perfect*, it would comprise a perfect alibi, a perfect guarantee of immunity for its perpetrator, and consequently a diminished sense of responsibility. Since the basis of Querelle's character—in more ways than one he is the ideal Existentialist—is to take total responsibility for every single act that composes his existence, the deliberate imperfection of the crime destroys his alibi, makes him potentially vulnerable, and so forces him constantly to accept, and to continue to accept until the moment of expiation, the responsibility for what he has done.[81]

Not, of course, that Querelle has actually solved the mystery of time, except in the way in which Genet solves all the mysteries of God's purpose in relation to man : by accepting them, by appropriating them, as it were, and by making them *his* mysteries, to dispose of as he will, rather than God's. Gil desperately desires to change his past, but cannot do so; Querelle (we have at least this impression) is sufficiently master of himself and of time to be able to 'retrace his steps' into the past and to reshape his destiny, his acts, exactly as he wishes. Only he doesn't wish. By the controlled effort of an inhuman will, he desires that everything shall be exactly as it was. And is. If the irremediable act is willed to be as it is in all its significance until the end of time, then there is no longer any meaning in the concept 'irremediable'. Querelle has eliminated the dichotomy between act and essence, between *was* and *is* by making them coincide in the absoluteness of his own authenticity. He is the authentic murderer for all time.

As we saw in Chapter One, however, authenticity is anything but a simple concept for Genet. The total being is invariably the Figure taken together with his own Image, possibly with a third element also, to observe and to be conscious of this duality. Consequently Querelle, who is ethically the most authentic of Genet's creations, cannot expect to be complete, or in the metaphysical sense authentic while he remains in isolation as himself. Like the Sailor in *'Adame Miroir*, he is incomplete without his Image. And this brings us to the second major theme of *Querelle of Brest* : the symbolism of the Double.

There is nothing radically original, of course, in the concept of the Double as such. It was a favourite device among the Romantics : Jean-Paul Richter uses it, and Chamisso, and Gérard de Nerval, and E. T. A. Hoffmann, and Dostoievsky, and R. L. Stevenson.[82] But none of these develops the idea so completely, or gives it such profound significance, as Genet. Or rather, whereas most writers start from an assumption of unicity, both in themselves and in their characters, with the consequence that the appearance of the Double is always mysterious, frightening and at bottom miraculous, Genet takes the duality of the human consciousness as his initial premiss, with the result that this duality invades every aspect of reality, and is accepted as a normal manifestation of the universe, both material and metaphysical. It is because duality is the very principle of existence that the saint—or the poet—in search of transcendence has to make such inconceivable efforts to wrench himself free from his own image in the mirror, in order to achieve his isolation, his *singularité*. Duality is the very stuff of poetry : a single object is-what-it-is; two identical objects in proximity, for Genet, sing aloud the glory of God :

> *Des choses qui, inanimées quand elles sont solitaires, chantent—et ne chantent que l'amour—dès qu'elles rencontrent l'amie.*[83]

There is no need at this stage to recapitulate in any detail the sort of arguments that Genet uses to explain his obsession with duality : his awareness of himself as a reality existing only in the consciousness of the Other; his homosexuality which makes him see his lover as the mirror-image of himself, and which develops later as an objective concept, so that duality in itself becomes a sex-symbol, as it is for Madame Lysiane, or for Dédé as he contemplates Mario and his colleague in the police[84]; his existentialist dialectic which posits a fundamental dichotomy between observer and object observed, so that the observer who observes himself is already, in a quite literal sense, a double . . .[85] suffice it here to recall once more that this notion of duality—sometimes, but only occasionally, proliferating into symbols of the Trinity, and thence, like a hall of mirrors, into infinite multiplicity—lies at the very root of Genet's vision of the universe. And if there were any doubts as to its significance, the extent to which this symbol itself permeates every aspect of Genet's fourth and final novel would be sufficient to dispel them.

To return once more, for instance, to the double-murder which forms the plot of *Querelle of Brest*. Here what is so characteristic is that Gil, who, at the outset, had denied responsibility even for his *own* murder—the killing of Théo—eventually comes to accept the fact that he has willed, not only the murder of Théo, but also the murder of Vic, and to accept responsibility for both—the two crimes, in fact, having merged mysteriously into one in the adolescent's mind. Lt Seblon, on a more abstract level, is compounded of innumerable dualities—mirror-opposites in his case : male and female, body and soul, positive and negative, a worldly ethic and a transcendental ethic[86] . . . etc. Querelle, veiled in coal-dust, is the double of the real Querelle underneath. Gil is both himself, Gil Turko, and the alien 'murderer who was called Gil Turko' whom he reads about in the papers. Querelle is both Querelle and 'un enculé'—a being so totally different as to be unrecognizable, yet at the same time identical : himself. Every name is the double of the person who possesses it, having an independent life and purpose of its own. 'His name exposed him, exposed him stark naked [. . . .] Gil had never altogether accustomed himself to his own name.'[87] In contrast, two separate beings—Jean Genet and Jean Decarnin— with identical names become indistinguishable. Jean Genet literally *absorbs* Jean Decarnin. In the same way, he who takes upon himself the sins of others, who takes responsibility for their being, *becomes* those others, absorbs them into himself. Christ *becomes* the world that he has redeemed; Mario envelops, absorbs and purifies Dédé[88]; Jean Genet is the double of his heroes, who in turn are the double of himself. He does not create Querelle; he merely recognizes him, for he is there all the time, in himself, he *is* himself :

> Step by step we should have come to realize that Querelle—already flesh of our flesh and bone of our bone—was beginning to grow, to develop his personality within our deeper conscience and derive sustenance from the best in us, above all from our despair at not being in any sense part of him, yet having so much of him in ourselves.[89]

Beneath all these specific instances lies the one general assumption which, as we have seen, penetrates and colours the whole of Genet's poetic imagination : that our existence in all its aspects belongs simultaneously to the Sacred and the Profane, that these two worlds are identical in *appearance*, yet incompatible and utterly alien in significance : the profane rose which is a flower genus *rosaceae*, and the Mystic Rose which is the Heart of Christ or of Harcamone are the identical object; but the meaning of that single object is double. The Symbol, in other words, is the transcendental Double : it is both itself and the object symbolized. This is the essential mystery of Genet's world; and in this sense (but not in the sense that it is something rare, or exceptional, or that it breaks the natural laws of existence) the Symbol is *miraculous*. And because the Symbol is, in the last instance, a miracle—an instantaneous means of translation into a sacred world which, at the same time, leaves one irremediably in the profane—and further, because the Symbol is the epitome of the mystery of the Double, then any phenomenon which is a Double partakes of the mysterious and miraculous qualities of the Symbol.

Even in the most banal of circumstances : two wrist-watches side by side, two maidservants, two brothers, two palm-trees, two murderers. Is Robert a murderer too, wonders Querelle? He 'hoped so, because it would be so wonderful if such a miracle could take place and exist in the world.'[90]

Duality, then, is itself symbolic : in a curious way, one might argue that, for Genet, it symbolizes the very principle of symbolism, or perhaps that it is the symbol of itself. And this is the mystery which *Querelle of Brest* sets out to explore, roughly under three headings : the being who, like Lt Seblon, is two-in-one; the beings who, like Querelle and Robert, are one-in-two; and the interdependence of mirror-opposites, symbolized in the mutually antagonistic roles (or functions) of Mario and Nono.

Of Lt Seblon, there is no need to say more than has been said already; and the mysteries of interrelated functions will be discussed later, in the context of *The Balcony*, where they constitute the main theme of the play. By contrast, the concept of the Double, considered as one individual split into a dual identity, reaches its climax in *Querelle of Brest*, although it had already made its appearance in *Miracle of the Rose*, in the passages where Genet comments on his extraordinary physical resemblance to Divers. In the earlier novel, however, the central problem is the projection of a single identity over an intervening interval of time; just as Fontevrault is the projection-in-time of Mettray, so Jean Genet is the projection-in-time of himself, previously incarnated as Divers, performing the identical gestures with the identical intentions, but annihilating the reality of time in the process. 'I was continuing him. I was being projected by the same ray, but I had to focus myself on the screen, had to make myself visible, two years after him.'[91]

In *Querelle of Brest*, however, the resemblance of Querelle and Robert is simultaneous in time, and therefore the essential problem is different. Here, it is not time which is annihilated, but the ultimate reality of the Self. If the centre of perception, and consequently of identity, is a Void, then there is no reason why the positive superstructure which is built around this negative principle should have one particular form of identity rather than another, or one rather than any number. To return to Genet's own image : around the identical Void which forms the essential element of the cannon, any number of guns, from revolver to howitzer, may be constructed. So it is with Querelle and with Robert. As *positive* personalities, they are hostile, incompatible—symbolically, they fight in the street whenever they happen to run into each other[92]; yet, as negative essences, they are indistinguishable; their common Self is the unity from which their apparent duality proceeds. And

Querelle, having through his murders learnt the secret of retreating into the Void of his inner Self, there discovers himself to be 'at one' (literally) with Robert. They meet 'so deep down in the subconscious that they could distinguish nothing.'[93] :

> [Querelle] closed his eyes. His mind slipped back into the dim and distant recesses of the past where he became at one with his brother. As he identified himself with Robert, there emerged from this confusion first certain words and then, thanks to an over-simplified thought-process perhaps, clearer and more living ideas. These rose to the surface of his mind as he began to disentangle himself from his brother.[94]

Given the fact, then, that their essence is a unity, the problem remains that of the relationship between their dual existences. Here, of course, they are the victims of a logical impossibility : for, as two material phenomena attempting to occupy the same area in space at the same instant, they are doomed to irreconcilable hostility; yet as a single essential identity, they cannot tolerate their own separation. In *Querelle of Brest*, this logical impossibility becomes an allegory on the nature of Love, continually trying to escape from itself into the Other, continually forced into the realization that the Other, by the very fact of his or her Otherness, inevitably and eternally excludes the Self. At the same time, it is an allegory of that identity of hate and love which we have already studied in *Pompes Funèbres*; while, in different terms, it shows the Sartrian *pour-soi* seeking its liberation from the *en-soi*, which is at once Not-Itself, and yet the only aspect of itself that it can ever know, or remember, or conceptually define, and which, therefore, constitutes its personality. Like Querelle and Robert, the basic human entity of perceiver/perceived is at once unity and duality, yet can never become absolutely one or the other. 'It was at the instant when he made up his mind to strike his brother that Robert knew the purest split-second of liberty,' observes Genet, as Robert makes a desperate bid for separation in duality; yet the direct result of this bid is that the two brothers, '. . . rather than attempting to destroy one another, appeared to want to become united, to melt into a unity which would create, from the two characters in question, a very rare animal indeed.'[95]

Querelle and Robert, then, constitute in symbolic form the duality of perceiver/perceived, or Figure/Reflection, that lies at the basis of human identity. But, as we have seen, they can only constitute a unity in the darkness and the Void of their essential Selves—that is, in a realm beyond awareness; precisely in that domain which Sartre would name the 'pre-reflexive cogito'. To perceive themselves, to have consciousness of themselves, not as two hostile singularities, but as a composite unity, yet another point of observation is needed, a third state of consciousness outside the one and equally outside the other; and this is the role which, symbolically, is attributed to Madame Lysiane. In ontological terms, Madame Lysiane, Querelle and Robert are all aspects of an identical consciousness in its vain and desperate struggle to know itself. Madame Lysiane begins the story as the mistress of Robert : Robert who, in real life, is a competent *mac*, the typical successor of Armand or Stilitano; but who, in metaphysical life, is the *en-soi*, the external, visible manifestation of an identity. Later, however, Madame Lysiane meets Georges Querelle, and, tentatively at first, begins to love him—as is inevitable, since Querelle is the *Pour-soi*, the indefinable, negative, nameless essence of Robert's positive Self. As she knows both more intimately, she begins to love both equally—yet here her torture begins, for she can neither understand the relationship between them (the relationship between *en-soi* and *pour-soi*), nor see how she can play any part in it. Her first reaction is to lose her temper with Robert; her second, to hurl rebukes at God for having created a universe where the simplest forms of human relationship, once enquired into, turn out to be a maze of logical impossibilities. 'I'm sick of it,' she protests, to which simplified *cri de coeur*, Genet specifically adds : 'She addressed this reproach to God, and beyond, higher than that, to life itself.'[96]

Eventually, however, having tried and failed to detach Robert from Querelle ('You see, my love, I only want you to be absolutely your own self. If I'm unhappy, it's because I see you as two'[97]), she begins to discover the truth. If *en-soi* and *pour-soi* require an outside source of perception to *know* themselves as a single unity, they do not require that knowledge in order to *complete* that unity. The observer must be—in Sartre's terms—a consciousness-without-a-subject, in other words, another negative, another *pour-soi*, but in this case a *pour-soi* without the corresponding *en-soi* which constitutes its apparent identity. Madame Lysiane can be an identity in relation to Querelle, or again in relation to Robert; but in relation to the two-in-one, her only role is that of the Void-of-perception, the *Néant*, which, by being Not-Them, constitutes their identity. She is the Other *(l'autre)* who can reduce me, my eternal individual consciousness, to the status of an object; but (and here Genet is replying to Sartre in precise philosophical terms) if I realize myself as an authentic and conscious totality, if I accept myself as an indissoluble unity of positive and negative, then I, as this unity, can defeat the petrifying dynamism of the Other, and reduce *him* to the status of a *Néant*. The Other can still define me, but is eternally excluded from having any part in, or any power over, that which he defines. 'There's no place for me,' laments Madame

Lysiane, 'For me to come in between the two of you would be to make myself a sight too small'[98] :

> 'You only think of things as concerning yourself. I no longer exist. I no longer exist in any way. What am I? How am I going to be able to get in between the two of you?'

—and more significantly still :

> 'It's draining me, draining me, draining me, this likeness between the two of you.'[99]

In the end, the unity of the two brothers proves indissoluble, and it is Madame Lysiane who is destroyed. But she is not alone. Dédé is fascinated by this dual identity, and so is Mario. But Mario is of stronger moral fibre, and, much as the problem haunts and hypnotises him, in the end he rejects the temptation, and so finally saves his own identity.[100]

This, admittedly, is only one aspect of the extremely complex philosophical and metaphysical symbolism of the innumerable images of duality in Genet's novels; it is enough to show, however, that, beneath its violence, its sexual obsessions and its all-pervading mysticism, *Querelle of Brest* is at least as closely argued as, say, Simone de Beauvoir's *L'Invitée*, and considerably more adept in the handling of some very abstruse philosophical material than are many of Sartre's novels after *Nausea*. Furthermore, out of this same duality between Querelle and his brother there emerges yet another essential consideration : what, for Genet, is the nature of Truth?

In studying the Legend of Genet's life, we were left with the unsatisfactory conclusion that poetry for Genet emerged from the contradiction of a lie, which knew itself to be a lie, asserting itself as though it were a truth.[101] We are now perhaps in a position to clarify this paradoxical belief. For Genet, the essence of truth lies in ambiguity. Truth is simultaneously both sacred and profane, and therefore any statement which relates *exclusively* to one or other of these aspects is at best a half-truth, probably a falsehood. The truth of Querelle lies in his relationship with Robert, and vice-versa; the Legend of Genet's life becomes a truth when it is taken in conjunction with the facts, even if it contradicts them. The facts by themselves are absurd and meaningless; the Legend by itself may be a lie; the Legend and the facts together constitute a truth. In the same way, the rose becomes a truth when it is the symbol of the Sacred Heart : the Sacred Heart by itself is an inaccessible and vain piece of religiosity, the flower by itself, merely a gratuitous specimen of vegetation : one of 'those coloured things', as Max Beerbohm says, 'flowers, I think they are called, that you can buy at Solomon's.' Somewhere between the two extremes—and including them both simultaneously—is the area where the Truth lies : it is not the Mask which is real, nor yet the face beneath the Mask, but the two taken together, in all the richness of their ambiguity and mutual hostility. That the Mask is a lie, that appearance is no more than a deception, excludes neither from having an essential part to play in the communication of the truth which is Genet's vision of the world.

Nor can we ever say that Genet himself is unaware of the lies that he tells about reality. He shows us his murderers as demi-gods—yet he knows better than most of us how sordid, miserable and sub-human are most of the thieves and bullies, prostitutes and down-and-outs of our society. On the contrary, it is *because* he knows the factual truth—and from time to time tells it—that his visions of a different reality have the dynamic truth of symbols. This, per-haps, is what Georges Bataille, for all his perspicacity, fails to real-ize when he accuses Genet of making a fool of the reader, and re-proaches Sartre for having let himself be taken in.[102] Whether we find Genet's vision acceptable or not is beside the point : what seems clear beyond doubt is that there is no question of Genet's sincerity. A paradoxical sincerity, admittedly, which insists that there is more truth in ambiguity—and even in treachery—than in any plain state-ment of fact. 'I wrapped myself up in it in order to return to the hotel,' reminisces Genet, recalling the occasion when he stole a carabinieri's cape in Barcelona,

> and I knew the happiness of the equivocal, not yet the joy of betrayal, though the insidious confusion which would make me deny fundamental oppositions was already forming.[103]

—but then Genet is not the only writer of our time to insist that there may be more *fundamental* truth in dreams or visions, in dynamic contradictions or evident impossibilities, than in many a compendium of commonplace evidences; more philosophical relevance in Zeno than in Pythagoras. And was it not his friend and mentor, Cocteau, who argued that *'pour être vrai, il faut mentir'*?

Thus, in Genet, there is no significant difference between the symbol—which has for centuries been widely accepted as a means for incarnating a truth which is difficult to crystallize otherwise in conceptual terms—and all other forms of ambiguity : puns, masks, disguises, equivocal situations, improbabilities, fake miracles and so on. Which is the true Querelle : Georges or Robert? As Madame Lysiane discovers, neither one nor the other, but both. The truth is Figure *plus* Image, genuine *plus* fake, rose-flower *plus* rose-symbol. The *meaning* (the only ultimate truth which is of any value) emerges from a confrontation of reality with its opposite. Admittedly, this may not be the *only* concept of truth : but, argues Genet, echoing

Michel de Montaigne, it is *his* truth, and therefore valid at least for him : 'The explanations I am giving occur to me spontaneously. They seem valid for my case. They are to be accepted for mine alone.'[104]

We have plenty of scholars and encyclopedists to give us facts; we have very few poets to give us visions. And in any final assessment of *Querelle of Brest*—in fact, of Genet's whole output as a novelist—we must keep this in mind. To distort the facts, to embroider upon reality, even to write pornography, is no evidence in itself of insincerity; and there is probably at least as much truth in the relationships between Querelle and Lt Seblon, Robert and Madame Lysiane, Mario and Nono and Dédé, as there is in *The Naked and the Dead* or in *Weekend in Dinlock*. And rather more than in most of the columns of the daily press.

[My concern is] to be sincere, less in the exactness of the given facts than in my obedience to those somewhat raucous accents which alone could express my emotion, my truth, the emotion and the truth of my friends.[105]

NOTES

1 *Thief*, p. 100. 'J'ai trop écrit, je suis las. J'ai tant de mal pour réussir si mal ce que font si vite mes héros.' (*Journal*, p. 118)
2 Omitted in English translation of *Q. of B.* 'Une brusque lassitude nous a fait abandonner *Querelle*, qui déjà s'effilochait.' (*Querelle*, original edition, n.p., 1947, p. 7)
3 There is some evidence of a similar process of sexual transposition in Proust.
4 *Q. of B.*, p. 35. '. . . une perle océanienne parmi les nacres d'une huître qui peut ouvrir sa valve quand elle veut, et la refermer aussi.' (*Querelle*, p. 188—Gallimard edition)
5 *Ibid.*, p. 130. 'Elle se sentait issue du luxe des glaces, des lumières et des airs de java, en même temps que cette somptuosité était sa propre exhalaison, son haleine chaude élaborée dans son sein profond de femme véritablement opulente.' (*Querelle*, p. 247)
6 *Ibid.*, p. 8. (*Querelle*, p. 173)
7 *Ibid.*, p. 97. '. . . sourire triste.' (*Querelle*, p. 226)
8 *Ibid.*, p. 19. '. . . sourire en coin . . . sourire en biais.' (*Querelle*, p. 179)
9 *Ibid.*, p. 17. 'A quinze ans, Querelle souriait déjà de ce sourire qui le signalera toute sa vie.' (*Querelle*, p. 178; see also p. 216)
10 See *Thief*, p. 234. (*Journal*, p. 278)
11 *Ibid.*, '. . . la force de ces règles sur lui.' (*Journal*, p. 278)
12 Even in the final (French) version of *Querelle*, there are still occasional slips and inconsistencies which betray Genet's disdain for formal narrative structure—for the 'anecdote'. For instance, the quantity of opium to be smuggled by Querelle and Vic is described variously as 2 kgs (p. 181), 5 kgs (p. 189) and 10 kgs (p. 194). While on the subject of inaccuracies, this is perhaps the place to deplore the unforgivable number of misprints in the Gallimard text.

13 *Q. of B.*, p. 39. (*Querelle*, p. 190)

14 *Ibid.*, p. 49. (*Querelle*, p. 197)

15 *Ibid.*, p. 69. (*Querelle*, p. 209)

16 *Ibid.*, p. 156. (*Querelle*, p. 262)

17 *Ibid.*, p. 20. '. . . pour se sentir opposer sa masse vivante, la musculature tumultueuse de son dos, à la masse indestructible et noire de la muraille.' (*Querelle*, p. 179)

18 *Ibid.*

19 *Thief*, p. 191. '. . . avec la rigueur d'un problème mathématique.' (*Journal*, p. 227)

20 Smith, D. W., *Helvétius: A Study in Persecution*. O.U.P., 1965, p. 223

21 *Thief*, p. 73. 'Je ne renie pas ce plus monstrueux de mes fils. Je veux couvrir le monde de sa progéniture abominable.' (*Journal*, p. 87)

22 *Pompes Funèbres*, p. 100.

23 *Our Lady*, p. 109. 'Divine n'est pas par-delà le bien et le mal, là où le Saint doit vivre.' (*Notre-Dame*, p. 40)

24 *Pompes Funèbres*, p. 136.

25 Sartre, *Saint G.*, pp. 195-204. (*S. Genet*, pp. 185-190, etc.)

26 Oscar Wilde develops the same paradox in *Salome*: 'It may be that the things which we call evil are good, and that the things which we call good are evil. There is no knowledge of any thing. . . .'

27 *Our Lady*, pp. 162-3. 'Divine, on le sait, avait beaucoup de mal à être immorale.' (*Notre-Dame*, p. 74)

28 *Thief*, p. 70 'Mes rapports avec les hommes commençaient d'être ceux des hommes habituellement avec les choses.' (*Journal*, p. 83)

29 *Our Lady*, p. 308. 'Sa bonté fut morte.' (*Notre-Dame*, p. 169)

30 *Q. of B.*, pp. 233-234. 'Le lieutenant était plus affranchi que tous les Querelles de la Flotte, il était le pur des purs.' (*Querelle*, p. 307)

31 *Pompes Funèbres*, p. 67.

32 *Ibid.*, p. 68.

33 Sartre, *The Flies*, pp. 309-310. 'Je ne suis ni le maître, ni l'esclave, Jupiter. Je *suis* ma liberté, [. . . .] Il n'y a plus rien eu au ciel, ni Bien, ni Mal, ni personne pour me donner des ordres.' (*Les Mouches*, Paris, Gallimard, 1947, pp. 100-101)

34 See *Pompes Funèbres*, pp. 67-8.

35 *Thief*, p. 77. 'Je voulais être la jeune prostituée qui accompagne en Sibérie son amant.' (*Journal*, p. 92)

36 Any careful study of Dostoievsky's ideas (in particular as they are expounded in *Notes from Underground*) reveals such a striking similarity with those of Genet, that the temptation to conclude in favour of a direct influence is overwhelming. As a detail, it is interesting to compare Dostoievsky's attitude towards the convict-murderer Orlov (in *Notes from the House of the Dead*) with Genet's admiration for, say, Botchako.

37 *Q. of B.*, p. 308. 'C'est grâce à Jésus que nous pouvons magnifier l'humilité, puisqu'il fit d'elle le signe même de la divinité. Divinité à l'intérieur de soi—car pourquoi se refuser les puissances terrestres—s'opposant à ces puissances il faut que cette divinité soit forte pour triompher d'elles. Et l'humilité ne peut naître que de l'humiliation. Sinon elle est fausse vanité.' (*Querelle*, p. 343)

38 *Q. of B.*, p. 78. 'Querelle, après son premier meurtre, connut le sentiment d'être mort.' (*Querelle*, p. 215)

39 *Pompes Funèbres*, p. 140.

40 *Our Lady*, p. 131. 'Il s'érige en Dieu, soudain, sur un autel, qu'il soit de planches basculantes ou d'air azuré.' (*Notre-Dame*, p. 54)

41 *Rose*, p. 99. 'L'assassin fait parler le sang. Il discute avec lui, veut transiger avec le miracle.' (*Miracle*, p. 257)

42 *Our Lady*, p. 186. (*Notre-Dame*, p. 89)

43 *Q. of B.*, p. 69. 'Plus rien de Querelle n'était présent dans son propre corps. Il était vide. En face de Vic il n'y avait plus personne : le meurtrier venait de toucher à sa perfection.' (*Querelle*, p. 209)

44 In this sense, Genet is rather closer to Beckett's source, Malebranche, than is Beckett himself. *Cf.* Malebranche : 'Ne rien voir, c'est ne point voir : penser à rien, c'est ne point penser. . . .' (*Recherche de la Vérité*, IV—ix—para 3). *Cf.* A. J. Ayer's criticism of Sartre's ontology (M. Cranston, *Sartre*, 1962, pp. 47-48).

45 *Pompes Funèbres*, p. 41.

46 *Ibid.*, p. 20.

47 *Ibid.*, pp. 49-50.

48 *Thief*, p. 192. (*Journal*, p. 229)

49 *Q. of B.*, p. 147. (*Querelle*, p. 257)

50 *Ibid.*, p. 72. 'Nous appellerons Querelle un joyeux suicidé moral.' (*Querelle*, pp. 211-12)

51 *Ibid.*, pp. 72-73. 'Incapable en effet de savoir s'il sera ou non arrêté, le criminel vit dans une inquiétude qu'il ne peut abolir que par la négation de son acte, c'est-à-dire son expiation.' (*Querelle*, p. 212)

52 *Our Lady*, p. 188. (*Notre-Dame*, p. 90)

53 *Thief*, p. 10. 'Si j'aime leur crime, c'est pour ce qu'il contient de châtiment.' (*Journal*, p. 13)

54 *Our Lady*, p. 107. 'L'horreur entrait en moi. Je la mâchais. J'en étais plein.' (*Notre-Dame*, p. 39)

55 *Ibid.*, p. 305. (*Notre-Dame*, p. 167)

56 *Pompes Funèbres*, p. 129.

57 *Q. of B.*, p. 235. 'Niant sa générosité, le lieutenant la détruisait en soi-même et ne laissait subsister qu'une indulgence à l'égard du criminel, et davantage encore une participation morale au crime.' (*Querelle*, p. 308)

58 *Thief*, pp. 185-6. 'Créer n'est pas un jeu quelque peu frivole. Le créateur s'est engagé dans une aventure effrayante qui est d'assumer soi-même jusqu'au bout les périls risqués par ses créatures [. . . .] Tout créateur doit ainsi endosser—le mot serait faible—faire sien au point de le savoir être sa substance, circuler dans ses artères—le mal donné par lui, que librement choisissent ses héros.' (*Journal*, pp. 220-221)

59 See esp. *Q. of B.*, p. 233. (*Querelle*, p. 307) (Mistranslated in English text)

60 *Our Lady*, pp. 237-8. 'La tragédie dont elle est l'auteur.' (*Notre-Dame*, p. 123)

61 *Ibid.*, p. 188. 'Il refusa de voir le gouffre [. . . .] *cent pages plus tard* Notre-Dame ne résista pas.' (*Notre-Dame*, p. 90)

62 *Rose*, pp. 52-3. (*Miracle*, p. 223)

63 *Pompes Funèbres*, p. 80.

64 *Rose*, p. 72. 'Le temps [se] multipliait par lui-même.' (*Miracle*, p. 238)

65 *Ibid.*, p. 56. '. . . un état fini, monstrueusement immobilisé.' (*Miracle*, p. 226)

66 *Q. of B.*, p. 21. (*Querelle*, p. 180). There is no need to stress the Bergsonian element in the whole of this argument.

67 *Rose*, p. 39. '[Mettray] se continue, se prolonge dans le temps.' (*Miracle*, pp. 213, 251)

68 *Ibid.*, p. 55. (*Miracle*, p. 225)

69 *Ibid.*, pp. 223-4. 'Vous êtes le reflet dans le temps d'un acte passé comme sur un miroir le reflet dans l'espace. [....] Nous sommes un livre d'histoire familière et vivante où le poète sait déchiffrer les signes de l'Eternel Retour.' (*Miracle*, pp. 346-7)
   The style, as well as the theme of this passage, is full of Proustian reminiscences.

70 *Ibid.*, p. 42. '. . . plus fragile que le passé et aussi infranchissable que lui.' (*Miracle*, p. 216)

71 *Our Lady*, p. 290. (*Notre-Dame*, p. 157). *Cf.*, of course, Pascal's 'nez de Cléopâtre'.

72 *Ibid.*, pp. 104-5. 'La plus légère imprudence—quelquefois même moins qu'un geste, un geste pas achevé, qu'on voudrait reprendre, défaire en remontant le temps, si bénin et si proche, encore dans le moment, qu'on dirait pouvoir l'effacer—Impossible!—peut conduire jusqu'à, par exemple, la guillotine.' (*Notre-Dame*, p. 37)

73 *Ibid.*, p. 117. '[Elle] déclenchait un geste qui bien vite refaisait battre son coeur.' (*Notre-Dame*, p. 45)

74 *Q. of B.*, p. 163. (*Querelle*, p. 265)

75 *Ibid.*, pp. 173-4. 'Gil [. . . .] essaya de détruire son acte en le décomposant en gestes dont chacun était inoffensif : "Ouvrir une porte! On a le droit d'ouvrir une porte. Prendre une bouteille? On a le droit. Casser une bouteille? On a le droit. Poser les parties coupantes contre la peau du cou? Ce n'est pas terrible, on en a le droit. Appuyer? appuyer encore? Ce n'est pas terrible. Faire sortir un peu de sang? On le peut. On en a le droit. Un peu plus de sang, encore un peu plus? . . ." Le crime pouvait donc se réduire à très peu de chose, se réduire à cette insaisissable mesure qui va du permis jusqu'à cela qui fait—mais touche le permis et ne peut s'en détacher—que le meurtre est commis. Gil s'acharna à réduire le crime, à le rendre aussi tenu que possible. Il obligea son esprit à fixer ce point qui sépare le "permis" du "trop tard".' (*Querelle*, p. 271)
   The theme of the 'elusive dividing line' was developed by Gide in *Les Faux-Monnayeurs*, from which source Genet probably derives his inspiration.

76 *Ibid.*

77 *Ibid.*, p. 176. 'Partant de son acte, afin de le justifier, le voulant rendre inévitable, il *remontait* sa vie. Procédant ainsi : "Si je n'avais pas trouvé Roger . . . si je n'étais pas venu à Brest . . . si . . . etc." il en arrivait à conclure que le crime, s'il avait coulé dans son bras, son corps et le cours de sa vie, sa source était hors de lui.' (*Querelle*, p. 273)

78 *Ibid.*, p. 154. '. . . gestes bruissants et lumineux [. . . .] comme si cet acte détricoté s'adressait à Dieu, ou à quelque autre témoin et juge.' (*Querelle*, p. 261)

79 *Cf.* Gide, *Les Caves du Vatican*, Livre de Poche, pp. 198-9.

80 *Q. of B.*, pp. 283-4. 'Querelle transforme ses amis en bracelets, en colliers, en montres d'or, en boucles d'oreilles.' (*Querelle*, p. 328)

81 *Ibid.*, p. 79. (*Querelle*, p. 215)

82 For a full study of the literary origins of this theme, see Tymms, R.: *Doubles in Literary Psychology*, Cambridge (Bowes and Bowes) 1949.

83 *Pompes Funèbres*, p. 33.

84 *Q. of B.*, p. 176. (*Querelle*, p. 272)

85 This theme is developed in two important passages: see *Pompes Funèbres*, p. 54; and *Q. of B.*, p. 233 (*Querelle*, p. 307)

86 See *Q. of B.*, pp. 235-6. (*Querelle*, p. 309)

87 *Ibid.*, p. 248. 'Son nom l'exposait, et l'exposait tout nu. [. . . .] Gil ne s'habitua jamais tout à fait à son nom.' (*Querelle*, p. 315)

88 *Ibid.*, p. 57. (*Querelle*, p. 202)

89 *Ibid.*, p. 25. 'Peu à peu, nous reconnûmes Querelle—à l'intérieur déjà de notre chair—grandir, se développer dans notre âme, se nourrir du meilleur de nous, et d'abord de notre désespoir de n'être pas nous-même en lui mais de l'avoir en nous.' (*Querelle*, p. 182)

90 *Ibid.*, p. 185. 'Il l'espérait, car il serait beau qu'un tel miracle fût réussi, existât dans le monde.' (*Querelle*, p. 278)

91 *Rose*, pp. 262-3. 'Je le continuais. J'étais projeté par le même rayon, mais je devais me préciser sur l'écran, me rendre visible, deux ans après lui.' (*Miracle*, p. 374)

92 *Q. of B.*, pp. 134-40. (*Querelle*, pp. 250-3)

93 *Ibid.*, pp. 16-17. (see also p. 155) '. . . à une telle profondeur qu'ils n'y pouvaient rien voir.' (*Querelle*, p. 178; see also pp. 261-2)

94 *Ibid.*, p. 24. 'Querelle [. . . .] ferma les yeux. Il regagnait cette région de lui-même où il se retrouverait avec son frère. Il s'enfonçait au sein d'une confusion avec Robert mais d'où il tirait, d'abord les mots, ensuite et grâce à un mécanisme pourtant élémentaire, une pensée claire, peu à peu, vivante, et qui, à mesure qu'elle s'éloignait de ces profondeurs, le différenciait de son frère.' (*Querelle*, p. 181)

95 *Ibid*, p. 138. 'C'est en décidant de frapper son frère que Robert connut le plus pur instant de liberté [. . . .] Plutôt que de se détruire, ils paraissaient vouloir se joindre, se confondre dans une unité qui, de ces deux exemplaires, obtiendrait un animal beaucoup plus rare.' (*Querelle*, pp. 250-1)

96 *Ibid.*, p. 207. ' "J'en ai marre, moi." Elle adressait ce reproche à Dieu, et plus loin, plus haut que lui, à la vie même.' (*Querelle*, p. 291)

97 *Ibid.*, p. 209. 'Mais, mon chou, je voudrais que tu soye tout seul. Si je suis malheureuse, c'est parce que je vous vois deux.' (*Querelle*, p. 293)

98 *Ibid.*, p. 208. 'Il n'y a pas de place pour moi. Moi, pour passer entre vous deux, faut pas trop que j'y compte.' (*Querelle*, p. 292)
   The image of the 'outsider' excluded from the intimacy of two other beings because there is 'no space between them' is a characteristically homosexual reaction. *Cf.* Gide, *passim*.

99 *Ibid.*, p. 206. 'Vous ne faites plus que vous regarder. Moi, j'existe plus. Qu'est-ce que je suis? Où que je vais passer, entre vous deux?' [. . . .] 'Ça me vide, ça me vide, ça me vide, vos ressemblances.' (*Querelle*, p. 290)

100 *Ibid.*, pp. 285-6. (*Querelle*, p. 329)

101 See above, pp. 124-8.

102 Bataille, G., *La Littérature et le Mal*, p. 207.

103 *Thief*, pp. 27-8. 'Je m'en enveloppai pour revenir à l'hôtel [. . . .] et je connus le bonheur de l'équivoque, non encore la joie de la trahison, mais déjà la confusion s'établissait, insidieuse, qui me ferait nier les oppositions fondamentales.' (*Journal*, p. 34)

104 *Ibid.*, p. 43. 'Les explications que je donne se présentent spontanément
   à mon esprit, elles paraissent valables pour mon cas. On les accep-
   tera pour le mien seul.' (*Journal*, p. 52)
105 *Enfant Criminel*, p. 151. '[Mon souci est] d'être sincère moins par
   l'exactitude des faits que par l'obéissance aux accents un peu rauques
   qui seuls pouvaient dire mon émotion, ma vérité, l'émotion et la
   vérité de mes amis '

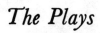

The Plays

7

THE SMALL BOY WHO WAS NIGHT

(*Deathwatch* and *The Maids*)

> *Il faut croire que le drame essentiel,*
> *celui qui était à la base de tous les*
> *Grands Mystères, épouse le second*
> *temps de la Création, celui de la*
> *difficulté et du Double, celui de la*
> *matière et de l'épaississement de*
> *l'idée.*
>
> Antonin Artaud

In turning from the novel to the drama, Genet simply realized his symbolism in a new dimension. It is usual to classify plays such as *The Maids*, or *The Blacks* among the landmarks of the Theatre of the Absurd, and, in so far as they use techniques common to the circus and the music-hall, to Ionesco and Arrabal and to the rest of the *avant-garde*, the label of absurdism is quite useful. Yet essentially it involves a contradiction. Far from denying the significance of human experience, Genet is constantly concerned to discover new dimensions of meaning. Admittedly the profane world, taken in isolation, tends to reveal itself as gratuitous, while the domain of mystic or sacred experience is inhuman, unfathomable, and all in all beyond the range of our mortal faculties to comprehend. But it is precisely at the point where the two meet that poetry is created— the point at which dream is simultaneously reality, where the invisible coincides with the visible, where the object is both itself and the revelation of something not-itself, where the meaninglessness of the unique act in time is identical with the timeless, archetypal gesture. It is not—and this cannot be stressed too often—that Genet has a Blake-like vision of a profounder reality beyond, and detached from, apparent reality: it is the revelation of two co-existent and insep-arable realities, each simultaneously made manifest in the other, of meaning discovered in un-meaning at the same time, and in the same instant of perception, that un-meaning is apprehended in meaning, that holds him fascinated. In other words, the essence of his imagination lies, not in the symbol conceived as the key, the open-sesame, to a transcendental reality, but in the dualistic nature of the symbol itself.

Thus Genet's drama is not—in the Maeterlinckian sense—a theatre of symbols (although there are plenty of them: in fact most of the individual symbols that we have examined in the novels— the flowers, the lace, the mirrors, the veils, the palm-trees, the colours, the *bagne*, and so on—are destined to reappear again and again); rather, the drama is in itself *the* symbolic act. The drama is both true and not true simultaneously—it commands, or should command, absolute belief, but only in a context of absolute unbelief; and the absolute belief (or suspension of disbelief) is only valid if it knows itself to exist in a context of unrealities—that is, if it is unceasingly aware of itself as an illusion. Thus there are (in Genet's sense) two opposing categories of non-drama: a drama which creates no trans-cendental illusion whatsoever, which is simply 'the description of everyday gestures seen from the outside'[1]; and a drama which creates a perfect illusion, and which thus loses all contact with the profane reality on which it is based. The first is the world of the Absurd, the gratuitous, where no miracles are possible; the second is the world of the *true* miracle, the province of angels, perhaps, but not of poets. And in between the two, narrowly sandwiched, lies the domain of the fake miracle, of which Genet writes in *Comment jouer Les Bonnes*:

'It is necessary, simultaneously, to believe in it and to refuse to believe in it; but in order that we may be able to believe in it, it is necessary that the actresses should refrain from acting in a realistic style.'[2]

The best summary of this very precise demand for a total belief in an illusion which is perceived *as* an illusion and which therefore splits the spectator into a duality—one half believing, the other half knowing that the belief is based on an illusion—comes at the end of the remarkable *Lettre à Pauvert sur les Bonnes*, in the form of a little parable, 'the small boy who was Night':

A young writer told me how, in a Public Garden, he once watched five or six small boys playing at soldiers. Divided into two camps, they were getting ready to attack. Night, so they said, was coming on. But, up there in the sky, it was noon. So they decided that one of their number should be Night. The youngest and the weakest of them, having been transformed into an elemental force, now became the Lord of Battles. 'He' was the Hour, the Instant, the Ineluctable. From far away, it seems, he approached, calmly as the cycle of the seasons, but weighed down with the sadness and the solemnity of twilight. As he drew nearer, the others, mere mortal Men, became edgy, anxious. . . . But, as they saw it, the child was arriving too early. He was fast by his own clock; unanimously, soldiers and captains decided to eliminate Night, who promptly reverted to the rank of private in one of the camps. . . . This, and this only, is the formula upon which drama must be based, if it is to thrill me.[3]

The extraordinary originality of Genet's drama—which only in the later plays will begin to show its affinities with Brecht—lies in this concept of the nature of Symbolism when translated into dramatic terms. The small boy is both the Symbol of the Night, and, as such, is aura'd with magic and majesty like a god descending among the faithful, yet at the same time is merely a small boy playing soldiers, and can be divested of his cloak of divinity at any moment. It follows that the true drama is an illusion which simultaneously succeeds and destroys its own success: whereas the two extremes of non-drama are both (in purely theatrical terms) illusions which succeed too well—in fact, they represent the two extremes of drama in the realistic tradition, against which the whole of the present-day *avant-garde* is in revolt. Of these, the first, the 'description of everyday gestures seen from the outside', produces the illusion that there is no illusion to produce, that we are just watching ordinary people doing ordinary things in the back-kitchens and bed-sitters of our most ordinary industrial England—or France, or Germany or for that matter Moscow or Djakarta, given the appropriate audience: the result is the same—

> The dreary dullness of a drama which too accurately reflects the visible world, the actions of men, not Gods.[4]

The second produces the illusion that our real world is merely illusory, and that we have been translated into another dimension altogether—to Verona or Mantua, to Thebes or Aulis, to seventeenth-century Port-Royal where the Jansenists are arguing about Grace, or to Renaissance Spain where Doña Prouhèze has left her satin slipper in the arms of the Virgin Mary.

For Genet, then, realism, in so far as it is the aim of realism to produce a total illusion, is to be discarded; but so also is total non-realism. Significantly, Genet has no theory of realism or anti-realism as such; he does not claim, as for instance does Ionesco, that the imaginary is more real than reality, or that total reality must necessarily include the dream and the nightmare as an integral part of human experience. Rather he claims that *poetry* (which may or may not be equated with reality) emerges from the dynamic conflict of the real with the transcendental. In dramatic terms, this means the simultaneous presence on the stage of real and unreal objects, the alternation of player and character, of realistic act and symbolic-significant gesture. In *The Screens*, where the *décor* is drawn on screens by the characters themselves as required,[5] Genet notes specifically :

> Near the screen there must always be at least one real object (wheel-barrow, bucket, bicycle, etc.) the function of which is to establish a contrast between its own reality and the objects that are drawn.[6]

and in *The Maids* the same principle of conflict is already laid down in Genet's introduction :

> If possible, the flowers will be real flowers, the bed a real bed. The producer must understand, for after all I can't explain everything, why the bedroom must be the more or less faithful reproduction of a feminine bedroom, and the flowers, real flowers, whereas the costumes must be monstrous, and the style of acting, for the actresses, slightly lurching.[7]

At the back of this specifically dramatic concept, however, lies a more fundamental idea, which can be traced in every stage of Genet's writing, long before he conceived the notion of writing for the theatre. For if the drama is destined to be exactly *half* real-life, it is because real-life is already half drama. If the inner Self, the soul or identity of man is a Void, then *appearance* is the basic constituent of human reality : the human being simultaneously is-what-he-is and is-what-he-appears. Divine *becomes* the ideal boxer whose movements she imitates, just as Darling involuntarily catches—and is betrayed by—Divine's mannerisms, for then he becomes Divine going through the motions of being Darling-the-shoplifter . . . and even store-detectives are sharp-eyed enough to spot the discrepancy. Thus there is no clear dividing-line between acting and being. 'Perhaps you were playing at coming',[8] muses Genet, without the least rancour, of one of his dream-lovers; and why should there be rancour, since the ultimate reality of man is his potential ability to act—and therefore to *be*—a hundred different parts, from the Queen of Rumania to a dustbin.

Behind all these, is there another reality? Possibly, but it is a negative, an Absolute, and therefore cannot be defined in terms of language, nor even wordlessly experienced, save in terms of other Absolutes, which similarly lie outside the range of conceptual definition. Only in the experience of an absolute despair—as is the case with Ernestine or with Harcamone—may there arise the first faint intimations of a Self distinct from the parts it plays, or may be capable of playing. Thus the death of Divine gives Ernestine the chance

> to free herself, by an external despair, by a visible mourning consisting of tears, flowers and crape, from the hundred great roles which possessed her.[9]

Yet even here, characteristically, it is only by *acting* the role of despair (just as Madame, in *The Maids*, immediately conceives her emotion at the arrest of her lover in terms of its appearance : 'my black dresses for my visits to the gaol'[10]), that Ernestine can realize her essential identity in terms other than those of acting : an insoluble conflict and contradiction, from which there is literally no escape. In real life, as on the stage, reality can be conceived only in terms of appearance; yet appearance has significance only in terms of a non-conceptual reality.

But this is only the beginning of Genet's vision of the 'Great Mystery', as Artaud calls the drama. Just as, for Sartre, the unnamable ideal is a state where *en-soi* and *pour-soi* merge into a single identity, and perceiver forms an indissoluble unity with perceived, so also for Genet, the most intriguing aspect of the duality : reality/appearance is when both correspond so closely as to produce an identical phenomenon, yet without the distinction between them ceasing to be—the beggar who, to excite compassion, devises with supreme cunning a fake sore which serves to cover up a precisely identical *real* sore hidden underneath[11]; or the gangster who, like Stilitano, pretends to be . . . a gangster.[12]

Here you have the perfect twist in dialectic which delights Genet, which makes the world 'turn turtle' into unreality, and which is the source of all beauty, poetry, philosophy—and drama. It is the obsession with disguise, with imposture, that has always exercised a haunting fascination on his imagination, but at the same time adapted to the belief that to assume a gesture is to be possessed by the archetypal reality implicit in that gesture. Tartuffe, for instance, means nothing to Genet; he would argue that, essentially, by acting the man-of-God, Tartuffe *becomes* the man-of-God (and indeed there are perhaps passages in Molière's text which seem to support the beginnings of this idea); if he does *not* become what he pretends to be, then his pretence is technically incompetent. By contrast, when a gangster disguises himself as a gangster, he becomes a gangster—which he is already : he is at once a unity and a duality, at once true and false—and both truth and falsehood combine to establish his authenticity; his appearance (which is necessarily false) for once coincides, or seems to coincide, with his reality, which is a Void except in terms of his appearance . . . he is-what-he-is.

Theatre, then, is an inseparable part of real life—'you dramatize everything', complains Robert to Madame Lysiane in a scene which is almost entirely described in terms of a stage-production[13]; while Lt Seblon continues 'playing a part in his own private comedy'.[14] In real life—that is, with actors who are largely unconscious of their role, who are compelled to act their own appearances by force of inner necessity—this dichotomy between mask and face is itself a symbol of the highest significance : the symbol of symbols, of life itself. Because of this, it is invested with ritualistic grandeur, with religious solemnity, with all the aura of great tragedy. Genet's novels are all tragedies in the fullest sense of the word, even though the tragic is often embedded deep in the grotesque, the obscene or even in the farcical. '*Il suffit d'un très léger décalage,*' notes Genet in *Pompes Funèbres,*

par les mots le débarrasser de l'ironie, pour que l'humour nous révèle le tragique et la beauté d'un fait ou d'une âme[15];

Mettray and Fontevrault are tragedies of spiritual despair[16]; even Genet's murderers are essentially tragic figures, in that they give significance to the absurdity of death by voluntarily assuming responsibility for the death of another, and thus ultimately for their own.

This vision of life as a ritualistic tragedy, whose symbolism creates a higher meaning for death, and so redeems existence from absurdity, permeates every page that Genet has written : and naturally, in the theatre, he expects to find these attitudes heightened through art. For him, the ultimate perfection of the drama was attained when Christ spoke to the Disciples at the Last Supper—'Theatrically, I know of nothing more effective than the Elevation'[17]—and any profane drama which falls short of this unforgettable ritual is unsatisfactory. Or, to be more precise, for Genet there is no such thing as profane drama. All drama, by its very essence which is symbolic imposture, is sacred, ritualistic and 'grave'.

The trouble is that, even if there is no such thing as profane drama, there are all too many profane actors, Ideally, the actor should be a dedicated priest performing a ceremony of initiation into a world beyond reality; in point of fact, he (or she) is a prosaic professional exercising a trade. The priest can be tragic because he is conscious, not only of his part, but of its gravity and significance; every gesture that he makes in the performance of his pagan sacrifice or Christian Mass is a means to an end, and the end is transcendental. On the other hand, the ordinary mortal whose life is a ritualistic tragedy, goes towards his destiny unconscious of his part in the solemn sacrifice of life that ends in death. *His* tragedy, in effect, is his failure to recognize his own part in it : he searches for happiness, and his smile is the mask which hides his own reality, which he can never know. Mask and face here fail to correspond, not from any conscious effort at imposture or deception, but because man is the passive victim of an uncomprehended fatality:

> The hero is unaware of the seriousness of a tragic theme. [. . . .] If it be to death that he goes—a necessary end—unless it be to happiness, he does so as if to the most perfect, therefore most happy, self-fulfilment. He goes off with joyous heart.[18]

Harcamone is just such an unconscious actor,[19] and thus a true symbol of tragedy. But what of the professional? Genet's diatribes against the typical actor are directly inspired by his metaphysical preoccupations. The very profession of actor—in the normal sense of the word, the paid and trained illusionist—is intolerable to Genet (just as, for not dissimilar reasons, it is intolerable to Ionesco), because the actor is consciously creating for himself, with his gestures, his voice, and all the other properties of the stage, an appearance *in which he himself does not believe*, and whose sacred significance he does not appreciate. He is a parody of the priest: he uses the transcendental phenomenon of appearance for his own glory, and for the vain *amusement* of his audience. Instead of concentrating the mysterious forces which surround us into a solemn ritual, he disperses them and annihilates their significance; he transforms the gravity of the celebrant into triviality or *une triste frivolité*, and the symbolic communion of drama becomes a *'divertissement'*.[20]

It is essentially a progressive series of attempts to overcome the exhibitionism of the traditional naturalistic actor which—in part at least—dictates the evolution of Genet's dramatic technique. Not all the principles of drama which I have outlined here were worked out from the beginning; on the contrary, *Deathwatch*, Genet's first play, still follows most of the traditions of naturalism; it is not even, in Genet's most elementary sense, a symbol-in-itself, but a play-containing-symbols, like Claudel's *La Ville*, or Maeterlinck's *Pelléas et Mélisande*. Little of the later dramatic technique is apparent, even in embryo, save perhaps in the ritualistic or incantatory nature of the dialogue in the closing scenes. But with *The Maids*, the destruction of the primary element which constitutes the actor's exhibitionism— his creation of a perfect illusion, or in other words of an appearance (a symbol) *detached from reality*—begins. The actresses are still actresses-acting-maids (a perfect illusion); but the maids then act Madame, or each other, while simultaneously remaining themselves; and his second stage of deliberately broken illusion throws doubt on the reality of the first. The same process of dislocation is continued in *The Balcony*, but reaches its climax in *The Blacks*, where the interchange of reality and appearance, the disintegration of illusion, is taken much further—with the added but essential complication, that the Mask (the fake) alternately contradicts, and is identical with, the reality that it conceals, or rather half-conceals, for at no stage is there any attempt at perfect concealment. Thus we find a group of professional negro actors (a reality) acting the part of a group of amateur negro actors (an illusion) acting the part, either of negroes (a reality, or alternatively, an illusion concealing a reality identical with itself), or else of negroes-acting-the-part-of-whites (an imperfect illusion superimposed on an illusion-identical-with-reality). Here, the relationship between face and mask, between being and acting, is so delicate and so complex—particularly after the entry of Ville de Saint-Nazaire—that it is quite evident why Genet refuses to allow *The Blacks* to be performed, except by a negro cast; a performance by a cast of disguised white actors would destroy the whole balance of reality and illusion which constitutes the essential symbolism of the play.

However, to shatter the perfect illusion is only one aspect of Genet's plan for the systematic destruction of the actor's frivolity and exhibitionism. If the function of the actor is to correspond to that of the priest at a ritual, he must not only *know* himself to be at the same time both an individual and a symbol, but he must also have an equal faith in the significance of both—and so must the audience. 'Any performance,' writes Genet, 'is a failure unless I believe in what I see—which will cease to be, which will never have been, as soon as the curtain falls.'[21] In terms of a naturalistic (or frivolous) theatre, this is an impossibility; for, where the essence of drama is illusion, we either believe in it, or we do not. We cannot do both simultaneously. But as soon as illusion is transformed into symbol, then the impossible becomes possible. The officiating priest at communion is *both* Father *** handling a bit of wafer, *and* the Vicar of Christ offering the Body of Christ. His faith, or belief in both is simultaneous. He *is* both actor and the part acted. In *Deathwatch*, *The Maids* and *The Balcony*, in spite of the dramatic and symbolic intensities of these plays, the problem remains unsolved; for Genet's private mysticism cannot command the faith, either among his actors, or still less among his audience, with which the Demoiselles de Saint-Cyr performed *Athalie* to a congregation still under the sway of a Bossuet. It is the weakness of all modern dramatists who have tried to return to the classical concept of the drama as religious ritual, that religion no longer exercises sufficient influence on the life of the average European to make the symbolism seem more important than the play itself—and this alone would solve Genet's dilemma.

But as soon as Genet turns to *politics*, the problem is solved, for politics are our religion. A play about the colour-bar, acted by negroes to a white audience, or a play about the Algerian war acted by Arabs to an audience of French middle-class capitalists or *colons*, will raise the status of every movement to that of an arche-typal gesture, and every gesture to that of a symbol, in which both actor and audience will have absolute belief; and this belief (and its ensuing reactions) will be independent of illusion. Ultimately, al-though in a different sense from Brecht's, Genet's drama is a theatre of provocation, whose objective is 'to establish a kind of uneasiness in the auditorium'[22]—for, to provoke effectively and dramatically, you must first abandon the world of illusion for the world of living symbols. In the words of Antonin Artaud, the function of the drama is 'not to define thoughts, but to *cause thinking*'.[23]

To what extent Genet's concept of the drama and its technique is dominated by Artaud is uncertain, for Genet's first allusion to the great theorist does not occur until the *Lettre à Pauvert sur Les Bonnes*, which was first published in 1954. This *Lettre à Pauvert*[24] is shot through and through with the ideas of Artaud, as they appear in *Le Théâtre et son Double*—the contempt for all traditional Western drama, of which even the finest productions, Genet declares, are 'masquerades not ceremonies',[25] the idealization of the Oriental stage-spectacle, and in particular of the Balinese dance-drama, the deliberate reduction of the verbal element in the theatre to the profit of other means of theatrical communication, and in particular the whole concept of the drama as heavily-stylised symbolism, to the extent that even the individual actor becomes 'a symbol laden with symbols', the metaphor of a metaphor.[26]

One suspects that Genet in fact came upon Artaud fairly late; but that the technique and the ideal which he had already formu-lated for himself in the period between *The Maids* and *The Balcony* corresponded so closely with Artaud's theoretical formulation of a *théâtre de la cruauté* that he was able retrospectively to adopt Artaud's principles as though they had been his own from the be-ginning. On the other hand, we can trace also in some of these later writings—not only in the *Lettre à Pauvert*, but also in *The Funam-bulists*, and to a lesser extent in the *Atelier d'Alberto Giacometti*—suggestions of a different attitude towards art in general, and the drama in particular, which have perhaps more in common with the eighteenth-century aesthetician, Jean-Baptiste du Bos, than with the surrealist author of *La Coquille et le Clergyman*. Du Bos, in his *Réflexions Critiques sur la Poésie et sur la Peinture* (1719), saw art essentially as a comparatively harmless substitute for the more violent passions of man (the notion is taken up again by Freud in his analysis of the Farce, and echoed, for instance, by Eric Bentley in his 'Psychology of Farce'[27]), by which the full intensity of an emotion could be experienced in the abstract, without the dire consequences which would normally ensue from the identical emotion experienced in reality. For Genet, the purpose of art is similar, except that the experience of the sacred world which is condensed and transmuted through art has no intention whatsoever of being harmless. 'Unquestionably one of the functions of art is to substitute the efficacy of beauty for religious faith'[28]—but the emphasis is on the word *efficacy*, while beauty, by definition, implies both violence and destruction. The gradual discovery of the secret processes by which the now defunct efficacy of religion can be replaced by a more effective emotionalism, and then condensed through the medium of beauty so as to engender violence, represents the whole history of Genet's ventures into the drama, from *Deathwatch* to *The Screens*.

Once we accept Genet's definition of the drama as a symbolic ritual, wherein the breaking (or rather, the reduplication) of illusion is a fundamental part of the ceremony, requiring both actors and audience to believe simultaneously in two contradictory aspects of reality, then the rest of Genet's otherwise puzzling and controversial dramatic technique falls into place. As early as *Our Lady of the Flowers*, he was suggesting that the basis of drama should be the imperfect disguise, the broken *travesti* :

> If I were to put on a play in which women had roles, I would insist that these roles be performed by adolescent boys, and I would so inform the audience by means of a placard which would remain nailed to the right or left of the sets throughout the performance.[29]

and that the actors should speak with 'the voice of an image'[30]— an ecclesiastical incantation rather than a naturalistic representation of emotion. By the time of *Deathwatch*, the principle that the only way to act, and at the same time to reveal the fact that one is acting, is to act *unnaturally*, has been extended to all aspects of the performance, and this in spite of the still basically naturalistic structure of the play. No ingenious chiaroscuro, simply 'as much light as possible'[31]; no realistic *décor*; above all, no *subtleties* of any kind : 'We are acting tragically but we are *acting*.'[32]

It is a measure of Genet's brilliant technical ability that he has been able to make first-class drama out of such arid principles, the more so as, in one respect at least, it has meant a complete reversal of his earlier procedures. In the novels, the relationship between dialogue and description was essentially that which Nathalie Sarraute has described as sub-conversations—that is, a constant intervention by the narrator who reveals the thousand infinitely subtle threads of emotion, hostility, suspicion, poetry and dream

which form the secret links *(les tropismes)* between banal statement
and even more banal rejoinder in the dreariest of social dialogues.[33]
Genet replaces Nathalie Sarraute's tea-table commonplaces by the
vulgar, obscene, but equally commonplace exchanges between criminals and convicts; but otherwise the principle is the same.[34] In
writing for the stage, however, the narrator has to be sacrificed.[35]
Promptly, therefore, Genet shifts his ground. Part of the tension
of the plays, as well as of the novels, arises from this violent contrast
between the ingeniously subtle and the brutally banal (yet another
manifestation of the feminine/masculine conflict in Genet's imagination); but in the plays, it is the situation, the *décor*, and the whole
technique of the performance which embodies the crudity and
the banality, whereas the dialogue itself becomes poetic, subtle or
complex in a manner that is totally foreign to the novels.

There are three principles which govern Genet's dramatic technique, other than those of the Mask and the Symbol which we have
already discussed. The first is that which David Grossvogel has
christened 'the self-conscious stage'; the second, that of continuity
reduced to contiguity; the third, that of the circus.

The first dictates that the characters shall never lose sight, nor
allow the audience to lose sight, of the fact that they are, from beginning to end, actors performing in a play, with a set script that
they have learnt by heart. This is an ancient device, whose principle goes back to the mediaeval theatre; yet not until the present
century has it been used outside the domain of farce. 'Danger is
my halo, Claire,' says Claire herself addressing Solange in *The Maids*,
'and you, you dwell in darkness.' 'But the darkness is dangerous,' recites Solange, completing the speech that Genet has written
for Claire; whereupon, to make her point quite clear, she continues—'I know. I've heard all that before'—only to muddle up the
whole issue immediately after by giving an alternative explanation,
this time *within* the context of the illusion : 'I can tell by your face
what I'm supposed to answer.'[36] In this fairly typical instance, if the
borderline between the two realities is already sufficiently disturbed
by the first intrusion, it is irremediably annihilated by Solange's (or
Genet's) apparently ingenuous attempt to restore the original dimension.

The second principle defines Genet's attitude towards the use of
the dramatic gesture. As we have seen, all movement in space is also
movement in time : and as the continuity of time disintegrates into
contiguity (as it does in Genet's vision of the world, just as effectively
in the plays as in the novels), so every movement tends to resolve
itself into a series of static poses : the ballet-dancer's *entrechat* is
seen as a series of statues, each offering an infinitesimally small

variation on the attitude of its predecessor.[37] It is this same doubt
cast upon the inherent reality of movement that causes Genet to
disrupt the natural sequences of gestures in the play. Not that he
ever actually calls a halt in the action, producing static *tableaux* of
the kind so dear to the heart of Diderot or the perpetrators of the
nineteenth-century melodrama. Rather, his characters tend to move
at erratic speeds, now slow, now fast, as though the normal steady
flow of continuity had to be reconstituted artificially out of static
elements, and the result was a series of inaccuracies and hesitations—
as though marionettes were being made to move like living beings.
This is the type of movement that Genet, in *Comment jouer Les
Bonnes*, describes as furtive : 'The acting will be furtive, in order
that an over-ponderous diction should grow lighter and carry across
the footlights.'[38]

It is interesting to notice here how this type of broken movement, in Genet's dramatic imagination, suggests a return to the
levitation of *Our Lady of the Flowers*. Again—but now in a reverse
order—a phenomenon in time produces its equivalent in space. The
suspension of a continuity-in-time produces a parallel suspension in
mid-air : words, heavy with the burden of the sacred, or 'weighed
down with precise ideas,'[39] gravitate downwards; gestures, and
above all broken gestures, act as compensation and pull in the
opposite direction—a seemingly abstract and mystical idea which
nevertheless embodies a very practical dramatic reality, for it is
precisely these incongruities of speech and action which serve to
alleviate what might otherwise be the intolerable gravity of symbol
and content, and thus contribute significantly to the effectiveness
of the plays *as plays*. Much of Genet's drama—but in particular
The Maids—corresponds to Ionesco's definition of the Tragic Farce :
but in this case, the weight of tragedy lies essentially in the words;
the alleviating balance of farce, in the techniques of the stage and
of the acting.

Finally, the Circus. Not only Genet, but Artaud, Beckett and
most of the *avant-garde* draw on the flamboyant techniques of the
circus-ring to combat the conventions of a naturalistic tradition.
Long before Genet had described *The Blacks* as *une clownerie*,
Beckett had *his* clowns, Estragon and Vladimir, rambling in the
arena while ring-master Pozzo cracked the whip. But for Genet,
the circus represents a positive symbolic value in itself. 'The reality
of the Circus,' he explains in *The Funambulists*—itself a glorification of the whole concept of the circus—'resides in this metamorphosis of dust into gold dust'[40] : precisely that same metamorphosis of dustbins into poetry, of murder into sanctity, which forms
the *leitmotif* of Genet's vision. But in addition, the circus is drama

as Artaud saw it, where the visual elements have precedence over words, and the senses over intellect. It is the sensual art *par excellence*, full of colour, violence and danger, the art of the lion-tamer, the weight-lifter and the trapeze-artist, of gleaming, half-naked male bodies—in effect, for Genet, the art wherein drama comes nearest to the sexual orgasm. 'You must love the Circus and scorn the world.'[41] Consequently it is not surprising to find the General, the Judge and the Bishop of *The Balcony* raised high above the floor on stilts, in the best, time-honoured, Bertram-Mills tradition; nor to discover that the Blacks use their stage like the arena of the Big Top, with the audience high up on both sides; nor to find the dead of *The Screens* leaping through paper screens into their new dimension, for all the world like the Horseback Fairy in the pink tutu who shatters the graceful paper barrier of her hoop twice nightly beneath the canvas of the Cirque Médrano. For one thing about the circus is certain : that it is real without being realistic; it is one of the great symbols of the childhood of the world, and yet it never perfects a single illusion.

Deathwatch

Apart from this gradual evolution in concept and technique which I have attempted to describe, the main difference which separates Genet's two early plays, *Deathwatch (Haute Surveillance)* and *The Maids*, from the later plays, *The Balcony*, *The Blacks* and *The Screens*, is one of structure. The first two have the economy of means, the tightness of construction, the close interdependence of characters and the concentration within the rigid discipline of the unities which is characteristic of all that is best in French classical and neo-classical drama; and their model and inspiration is probably Sartre's most effective play, *No Exit*. Moreover, they are still fundamentally addressed to the intellect. The later plays, by contrast, depend at least as much upon visual effects as upon language; they are broad, flamboyant canvases of loosely-related episodes, panoramic rather than conventionally dramatic in structure—or rather, to use the term favoured by the great dramatist who was probably their inspiration, epic, in the exact sense in which *Mother Courage* or the *Caucasian Chalk Circle* are epics designed for representation in the theatre.

   Deathwatch was probably written about 1944-5, but not performed until February 1949—three years after the first performance of *The Maids*.[42] It takes us straight back into the world of *Miracle of the Rose* : the world of prisons and symbols, flowers and criminals, with the condemned murderer who was once called Harcamone or Clément Village, but who is now known as Snowball, imprisoned somewhere in his death-cell on some remote upper storey, yet— again like Harcamone—dominating by his invisible presence the action of the play. The French title *Haute Surveillance* is one of Genet's most ingenious ambiguities, resuming in itself the main significance of the action on three different levels : for if *'haute surveillance'* is the technical name for the peculiarly sadistic form of detention that French criminal law prescribes for its condemned prisoners awaiting execution, it also suggests the watch kept from above by Snowball, in his transcendental state of death-in-life, over the rest of the gaol and all its myriad inmates—a watch symbolized by the cigarettes which he sends downstairs to Green Eyes[43]— yet at the same time, and most important of all, it suggests the watch kept by God who, from the high mansions of Heaven, looks down on the tragedies of man and makes or mars (preferably mars) his destiny.

In the cell that is opened up before us on the stage are confined three men : Lefranc, a burglar, shortly due for release; Maurice, a delinquent, who, had he been only a few months younger, would probably have been packed off to Mettray; and Green Eyes, another murderer, but, unlike Snowball, awaiting trial and not yet condemned. Between these three men, with only occasional interruptions from a Warder, the entire action takes place : in one cell, and in the course of a single afternoon.

The hierarchy of transgression, running from the profane to the sacred, which was implicit in *Miracle of the Rose*, becomes explicit in *Deathwatch*. At the bottom of the scale is Lefranc—in some ways the incarnation of Genet himself—a minor criminal who has violated the laws of society but none of the major taboos of the race; next comes Maurice who, although still young, already possesses the *dureté*, the inhumanity which promises great crimes in the future; then Green Eyes, the murderer who has violated the most sacred of all taboos, that which decrees the sanctity of human life; and finally, at the summit, Snowball, in whom the cycle of crime and punishment, transgression and retribution, is complete. Far more clearly than in *Miracle of the Rose*, or even in *Our Lady of the Flowers*, the characters are aware of this hierarchy and its implications, and of the ideal of sanctity, of bearing on one's shoulders all the sins of the world. Green Eyes (he is never referred to except by this nickname) is aware of his own inferiority to Snowball; not only because Snowball is already condemned, but because there was a fundamental difference in the nature of their respective crimes.

Snowball gained some profit from his murder and thus avoided the trap of the *acte gratuit*; Green Eyes, who, like Clément Village, like Harcamone, strangled a girl, gained nothing :

> *Green Eyes:* Maybe I'm not as strong as Snowball because his crime was a little more necessary than mine. Because he killed in order to rob and loot, but, like him, I killed in order to live, and now I'm smiling.[44]

At the same time, Green Eyes recognizes his potential disciple and successor in Maurice (much as Querelle does in Gil Turko), and offers him a specific chance to join the élite of murderers when he leaves the prison : 'Will it be you? Are we going to make a little killer of you?'[45]; but he is equally aware of the fact that Lefranc is not of the stuff of which murderers are made :

> *Green Eyes:* Your robberies, your burglaries, it's not that sort of thing that's going to take you very far. It's not that that's going to bring you up as far as us.[46]

The difference between Lefranc and Genet himself is that Genet discovered an alternative route to sanctity, the route which lay downwards, through the morass of total abjection; Lefranc on the other hand has no knowledge of this alternative, nor have any of the other characters. The immediate problem of the play is whether an essentially passive character like Lefranc, or like Genet himself, *could* have taken the alternative route; whether, having accepted the fact that the Absolute, in his own case, can never be an Absolute Good, and therefore must necessarily be an Absolute Evil, he could have chosen, instead of his own Calvary of despair, degradation and betrayal, the more violent and glorious assault upon the Totality which is murder : '*Tuer un homme est le symbole du mal . . . c'est le Mal, Mal absolu*',[47] as Genet had already concluded in *Pompes Funèbres*. In relation to Green Eyes, Lefranc is perfectly clear as to what are the necessary attributes of sanctity : the transgressor must not only have had experience of Absolute Evil, but he must further experience his despair in total isolation. Thus, by substituting his own intelligence and personality for that of Green Eyes—who, being illiterate, cannot write his own letters to his wife, nor read those she sends him, and is therefore dependent on Lefranc, just as Estelle is dependent on Inès in *No Exit*—Lefranc manages to cause a break between the murderer and the one person who still kept him from the awareness of his own irremediable solitude.

In relation to himself, however, he is less clear-sighted. In spite of innumerable warnings from Green Eyes about the metaphysical conditions necessary before a straightforward murder can be transformed into a gateway to sanctity, Lefranc fails to understand, before it is too late, the trap that he is setting for himself. Deliberately and gratuitously he strangles the helpless Maurice, while Green Eyes looks on, smiling sardonically—and then turns to Green Eyes, believing that at last he also has escaped his ignominious destiny of abjection and failure, and has earned his place among the élite. But Green Eyes rejects him out of hand; and Lefranc discovers that it is *not* enough merely to be a murderer to shatter the walls that guard the transcendency of the spirit. His gratuitous crime is but once more failure added to the list of failures that constitute his life. He achieves his solitude, but it is Genet's solitude of degradation, not Harcamone's solitude of glory; the other path is closed to him for ever.

'*Salaud!*' is the final word of consolation that Green Eyes addresses to him; and he is forced to recognize that Green Eyes, in spite of everything, is right : 'I really am all alone'.[48]

The reason for Lefranc's failure, and the essential and underlying theme of the whole play, lies in the nature of Fatality, together with a purely Jansenistic concept of the operation of Divine Grace. The word Jansenistic is used here advisedly. Not only does *Death-watch* reflect the classicism of seventeenth-century French drama in its structure, but also in its basic preoccupations. Structurally, it has the economy, the interiority, the skilfully-controlled development of the most typical seventeenth-century tragedy : the exposition contains all the material necessary for the catastrophe, and Racine himself would probably have approved of the way in which the *dénouement* is foreshadowed in the opening line of the play, even if he did not immediately recognize the self-frustrating relationships between Lefranc and Maurice, Green Eyes and Snowball as a kind of grotesque and distorted reflection of those between Oreste, Hermione, Pyrrhus and Andromaque. On the other hand, the scene in which Green Eyes finally offers his wife to the Warder holds an echo of Corneille's *Polyeucte*, and the suggestion is perhaps not fortuitous. For *Polyeucte*, like *Deathwatch*, is similarly a play concerning the nature of Divine Grace; and the argument between Lefranc and Green Eyes is at bottom the argument between Corneille and Racine, between Molinists and Jansenists, between those who believe that man, by his own will and his own acts, can merit the Grace of God, and so eventually fashion his own salvation, and those who believe that God, from the beginning of all things, has predetermined the pattern of our lives, both now and hereafter, and that our will is no more than a handful of dust let fall unless the gift of Grace shall accompany it—nor shall we ever known whether our destiny was one of Paradise or damnation until it is too late, and the irrevocable act has been committed. Thus it is only *after* Phèdre has made her irremediable choice of action that she realises, not only that she was predestined to damnation, but predestined also to bring about her own downfall; in precisely similar manner, Lefranc also realizes, too late, that his attempt to take the fortress of transcendentalism by assault has excluded him for ever from the Absolute, and as the direct result of his own will and his own conscious act. Admittedly, the hoped-for operation of Grace in *Deathwatch* is the reversed image of its expected operation in *Phèdre* or *Andromaque*; but the end—the attainment of the Absolute—is identical; only the means are different, evil instead of good. The Grace of *Deathwatch* is a Black Grace, in exactly the same sense as one talks about a Black Mass. Genet's Jansenism is Jansenism-in-a-mirror.

Fully to grasp the implications of *Deathwatch*, it is necessary to return to some of our earlier discussions, and to consider the whole notion of Fatality as it appears in Genet's novels, and particularly in *Querelle of Brest*. That there is a mysterious and irremediable pattern of predestination in the universe is something that Genet has never doubted—a pattern embracing inanimate objects as well as human beings on an identical level and without distinction, so that the life of man is dominated by a series of meetings, apparently coincidental, but in fact the expression of a higher Purpose—meetings, not only between individuals[49] but, more significantly still, between men and objects. The revolver, the phial of poison, comes forward to meet the hand that will use it as ineluctably as the hand is advanced to grasp its opportunity. Our Lady already recognized that 'in short, everything occurred according to an order with only one possibility'[50]; and Culafroy, musing on suicide, realizes equally clearly that it is no matter for decision, but merely one of waiting for the fatal meeting between animate and inanimate, when events will follow their inevitable course.[51]

Given the essential fact, then, that there appears to be in the universe a sort of pre-established harmony, a deterministic pattern of Fatality, the problem remains, what is to be done about it—rebel against it, submit to it, or dominate it by *willing* to accept it as it is? All in all, Genet's heroes, at least in his later works, decide in favour of a voluntary acceptance of the inevitable : even so, they continue to recognize, with fear and superstitious reverence, the influence that Fatality may have on their ultimate destinies. This determinism takes innumerable forms : Bulkaen, the jewel-thief, takes on, even to his nickname ('Bijoux') the characteristic of his jewels[52]; Genet himself begins his emotional change from passive to active on account of the manner of walking forced on him by the peculiar cut of the pockets in the trousers of his prison-uniform.[53] Erik's whole mentality, his life itself, is determined by the accident of his physical beauty—'*Sa vie devait avoir la forme de son corps, sa complexion intime et délicate*'[54]—while Gil, like Culafroy, is determined in the present by the weight of that inanimate and irremovable millstone round his neck : his past.

Yet none of Genet's characters are merely passive fatalists. Their victimisation by powers outside their control constitutes, not their weakness, but their strength. For most of them realize from the start, and all of them, including Lefranc, come to realize by the end, that in dealing with predestination they are dealing with a force greater than any of the natural laws which control the normal behaviour of objects or of beings; and that, if they can harness, or exploit, this force, they become gods rather than men. Harcamone realizes this : by his act of murder, he has set in operation the laws of an inevitable destiny which make him stronger, alone, than the rest of the prison, warders and convicts, all together.[55] By accepting and exploiting the inevitable, he becomes himself the incarnation of this irresistible and supernatural power.

The problem lies with the future. The power of the irretrievable past can be harnessed and assimilated by acceptance : so also can that of the present, by recognizing and exploiting the unchangeable conditions of existence, by being-what-one-is. But the future is less easily mastered, because it offers a series of contradictions : on the one hand, the temptation of choice, of liberty, of contradicting the determination of destiny by willing events in the past to produce the opposite of those results which, by the normal laws of cause and effect, they *should* produce (*e.g.* as in *Pompes Funèbres*, by willing that evil should produce love instead of hate); on the other, the recognition of Fatality, of an inevitable and predestined pattern of events which, if harnessed, can give their seeming victim a power which is literally superhuman. In the event, who is stronger: the man who defeats destiny or the man who accepts it?

This problem, which is implicitly a criticism—a valid and significant one—of Sartre and of the existentialist doctrine of total freedom in the *angoisse* of ceaseless choice, comes to the surface in *Querelle of Brest*. Here, the protagonist of free choice is Mario—yet Mario realizes, with an intensity which escapes Sartre altogether, that the total liberty of the existentialist is in fact an invitation, either to perpetual indecision, or else to anarchy; for, in order to *remain* free, not in the abstract, but in specific instances, Mario must avoid all choice, and specifically all action. As soon as the choice is made or the act completed, then it ceases to be a freedom. At once more mystic and more realistic than Sartre, Mario realizes that there is no such thing as infinite choice in the abstract. Infinite choice is merely an unnumbered series of positive and practical decisions; and each choice made is a sacrifice to the power of an irresistible Fatality. The only *real* freedom is perpetual indecision :

> [Mario] made no movement, being at a loss to know how first to move, but chiefly because he was fascinated by his moment of victory, which inevitably would be destroyed by and for one possibly less intense, one less happy, he couldn't tell, but one that would certainly be irremediable. Once he had realised his ultimate potential, no further choice would be possible. Yet Mario was aware that a choice was hanging in the balance. He was at the ultimate centre of freedom of choice. He was ready to . . . except that he couldn't remain in this position for long. To lie down on his side, to stretch this or that muscle, would already be to make a choice; that is to say, to limit himself. He must therefore keep up this state of suspense.[56]

For Querelle, and even for Madame Lysiane, this anarchic existentialist freedom is not a strength, but a weakness. Querelle also refers to it as 'instability'. Liberty achieves nothing for him; it merely leaves him at the mercy of the actions of others who, less punctilious about their so-called freedom, continue to act, and thus escape his will and finally dominate him. Querelle is only the complete master of his own destiny if he is the master of that of others also; and he can only become this by willing *their* acts as well as his own, and thus doubly renouncing an ideal but impossible 'freedom of the infinite choice'.[57]

For Querelle, the *act* of willing is more important than the freedom to choose; his freedom is not the anarchic liberty of untrammelled decision, but rather the freedom of the Stoic who has simply conquered this anarchy within himself. In the case of the past, the process is simple : the act exists first, as an inescapable determinism; it *becomes* freedom when it is retrospectively willed to be what it is. In the case of the future, the problem is more complex : for here, freedom is the willing of an act to be what it is in the context of a Fatality which is willed in advance to be what it must be, and *then* believed in as an inescapable determinism. It is this elusive notion of a destiny which is created by willing, and yet which simultaneously decrees the context in which that will must be exercised, that Querelle describes as his faith in his star. 'Every sailor has a star', goes the popular song[58]; and Querelle elaborates the notion :

> Querelle placed absolute confidence in his guiding star. This star owed its existence to the trust the sailor put in it. It was, if you like, as if his confidence in his absolute trust sent out a beam that swept the skies till it reached to his star. Then for the star to preserve its size and splendour, its full power, Querelle had to preserve his trust in it—that is to say his trust in himself.[59]

Querelle, with his careful balance between a subjective and an objective Fatality, is none the less the most rationalistic of Genet's creatures; the others—Our Lady, Riton, Bulkaen, Green Eyes—are more mystically inclined, and consider their destiny simply as the working-out of inexplicable and supernatural forces. Yet all of them are agreed in their fear of an anarchic human independence, and in the sense of security and even joy which comes to them from knowing themselves bounded by a framework of inevitability.

In all the novels, then, destiny is considered as a force to be welcomed and if possible exploited. Querelle is alone in exploiting it as a source of power over man; his fellow-heroes consider it rather as a force that may carry them towards their own salvation. It will destroy them; but, by lucidly accepting the higher purpose of their own destruction, they can use it to their own ultimate spiritual advantage. In this sense, the destiny of Our Lady or of Bulkaen is already very close to the concept of Divine Grace. However, as with the idea of Grace in its more Jansenistic interpretation, the role of the individual will is limited to willing in advance to accept this total concept of a destiny, and to willing retrospectively that the acts that such a destiny has brought about should in fact be-what-they-are; it does not permit the willing in advance of a specific fatal act, for this is set up the individual will in anarchic revolt against God. In the same way the Christian, or Cornelian, martyr may willingly submit in advance to God's purpose, whatever it may be, and may accept the prospect of his own death; but he may not commit suicide. Adapting this same belief to Genet's peculiar context, Green Eyes is the martyr, the predestined Chosen-of-God; Lefranc is the suicide who, in all variations of Christian doctrine, is condemned to eternal damnation.

This Fatality of divine predestination works in two ways: either by making men commit acts which they have not consciously willed; or else by imposing on them an obligation to 'will' these same acts by hedging them about by a semblance of necessity. In *Deathwatch*, Green Eyes represents the first of these alternatives, Snowball the second. Green Eyes kills the girl without even realizing what he is doing[60]; and afterwards, like Gil, he would give all he has to undo the murder that he has committed:

> *Green Eyes:* I ran in all directions. I shifted. I tried every form and shape so as not to be a murderer. [. . . .] I squirmed and twisted. People thought I had convulsions. I wanted to turn back the clock, to undo what I'd done, to live my life over until before the crime.[61]

It is only towards the end that he accepts his act for what it was: the operation of a Divine Grace in and through him which constitutes at the same time his destruction (his martyrdom) and his transcendence. Snowball, on the other hand—although we are told no details about his crime—was driven to it by necessity. In straightforward legal terms, it was not a *crime passionnel*, but murder accompanied by robbery. Thus Snowball profited from his murder in a way that Green Eyes did not; and the fact of this profit is, for Genet, evidence of those obscure laws of necessity by which the Grace operated in this particular case. Characteristically, Green Eyes admits that this is a higher form of Grace than had been bestowed upon himself, and he pays homage to Snowball in consequence. This is not merely the same argument as that which we have examined already, concerning the respective merits of gratuitous and non-gratuitous acts in their approximation to Absolute Evil; rather, it is the same sort of distinction as that which operated between Polyeucte and Pauline, where the former profits from a more imperious or efficacious form of Grace specifically aimed at his own destruction (and therefore salvation), whereas Pauline, less favoured, benefits only from a more general working out of the Divine purpose. But both cases are rigorously contrasted with that of Lefranc, who deliberately *wills* his act with the idea of playing substitute for a destiny, or a Grace, which has not been granted to him. It is as though Querelle should have willed *outside* the context of his star. To return to an earlier argument, he who would bear on his shoulders the sins of the world must also take on himself the crimes of the world. But—and here *Deathwatch* goes beyond *Querelle of Brest*—the crimes committed have their full metaphysical value *only* if they are experienced in their full horror *as crimes committed for their own sake*; for only then will they contain their full quota of evil, despair and transcendency. To commit a crime in the good intention of bearing the sins of others (or even of achieving one's own salvation) is as stupid and as ineffectual as Saint Vincent de Paul who tried to accept the punishment without having done anything to deserve it. The good cancels out the evil, the evil counterbalances the good, and the result is a void—a nothingness, a simple annihilation.

All this is argued out between Green Eyes and Lefranc in the last few pages of *Deathwatch*, after the murder of Maurice. Green Eyes accuses Lefranc of having willed the good—of having murdered 'for nothing. For the glory of it'[62]—in fact, of having totally misunderstood both Green Eyes himself, and God, and destiny (and Genet!) :

> Green Eyes: You fool, don't you realize it's impossible to overshadow me? I didn't want anything—you hear me? I didn't want what happened to me to happen. It was all given to me. A gift from God, or the Devil, but something I didn't want.[63]

To this Lefranc replies—as Querelle might have replied—that to will an act to be-what-it-is, whether in the past or in the future,

is the highest form of authenticity, the completest acceptance of
destiny. *His* act, he argues, was doubly authentic, in that, firstly,
he had willed it to be what it was; and also in that, secondly, he had
deliberately imagined himself at that point in the future when he
would be looking *back* on this same act in the past, and had contrived the act in such a way that he could be *sure* that he would
continue to accept it retrospectively. But this, according to Green
Eyes (and to Genet) is bad theology. God's Grace is a *gift,* it cannot
be provided for in advance : Lefranc was, as it were, taking out
insurance with a non-existent company. Acceptance can *only* be
retrospective. Or perhaps, in terms of a different theology, Nirvana
is that which cannot be desired because, once desired, it becomes
an object instead of a subject, a concept instead of a Totality beyond
all particular concepts, and so ceases to be itself : it is no longer
Nirvana once it is an object of desire. So also with Grace : to desire
Grace is to pervert the very nature of Grace itself, to transform
it into a fake, a false-Grace, an illusion. For the true Saint, the
absolute ascetic, is he who, like Divine-Culafroy, must all his days
do that which is most repugnant to him. If that which is repugnant
is *desired,* it is no longer utterly repugnant, and so the Saint becomes
a mere common-or-garden sinner.

In much the same vein, Querelle at one point explains that he
does not murder in order to rob, but robs *because* he has murdered,
thus providing a *retrospective* necessity for an act which otherwise
might threaten to dissolve into its own gratuitousness. But Lefranc
and Green Eyes immediately take the problem back on to the level of
theology. Even assuming that Saint Vincent de Paul had committed
the same crime as the *galérien* before being able to take his place
at the oar, the fact remains that Saint Vincent would have committed *his* crime, not the *galérien*'s. Identities—as we shall see in
The Maids—may be interchangeable; crimes possess an absolute
reality of their own, which admits of no substitution.[64] In other
words, the criminal is defined—both existentially and theologically—
by the crime he has committed; to substitute a different crime is
not to bear away the sins of the Other, but merely to create another
(different) criminal. How then could Christ bear away the sins of
the world (since men are defined by their acts, and above all by their
criminal acts, their transgressions) without annihilating the whole
race of mankind in the process? 'You !' yells Green Eyes, 'you tried
to get there by fraud'.

> *Lefranc:* I wanted to take your place. . . .
> *Green Eyes:* And what about our crimes?
> *Lefranc:* Including the crimes.
> *Green Eyes:* Not ours.[65]

The problem seems insoluble—it *is* insoluble, in fact, on any level—and Genet makes no attempt to reach a final answer. In any case, there is no conceivable answer in rationalistic terms; and it is a rational answer that Lefranc seems to be requiring. *Deathwatch* is the most purely mystical work that Genet has written—a point which is brought out strongly in the *dénouement*, which might almost (making allowances for the unlikely *moral* context) be borrowed from a Jansenistic manual of instruction demonstrating the all-powerfulness of God and the impotence of man. For Lefranc, rejecting Green Eyes' arguments, yet finding himself without the Grace of God, while his acts have failed in their purpose and merely left him nearer to annihilation than he was before, rises up in opposition against God, rejects God's Grace, and determines—again like Svidrigaïlov—to manufacture his own Grace and to become his own Absolute.[66]

But the twist is that Lefranc's ultimate *malheur*—his suffering, his despair—comes, not as he willed it, from the murder of Maurice, but in a way that he had completely failed to foresee, from his rejection by Green Eyes. Thus, in so far as the Grace which is salvation springs from an act which is a plunge into despair, and thence into the sacred, yet which by definition cannot be desired or deliberately sought for, the Grace comes to Lefranc all the same, and in spite of himself, through his unforeseen rejection; just as, in Polyeucte, it comes to Félix, although every one of his acts hitherto seems to have rendered it impossible. God's will is all, the will of man is nought.

The ending of the play, then, can be interpreted in two different ways : either as the despair of total failure, or else as the unexpected and undeserved gift of Grace which is present, unrealized, in that despair itself. Whichever way we take it, *Deathwatch* is a strange and an effective drama which throws a great deal of light on Genet's theological preoccupations. Whether it is actually acceptable in the theatre is a different matter. Its symbolism is highly personal and, unless interpreted in the light of the novels, obscure; and the effect, on the stage, of Genet's concept of sanctity in reverse, of a Divine Grace which operates through the gift, not of good, but of evil, is so unexpected as to seem grotesque, perhaps, rather than provocative. The ritualistic *Ecce Homo* applied, not to Christ, but to Green Eyes, the illiterate and foul-mouthed murderer of a prostitute,[67] is anomalous rather than scandalizing; the play *has* depth and complexity, but the audience has to supply too many missing elements before these qualities can become fully apparent. Its dramatic structure, on the other hand, is almost perfect; and possibly, as Genet's novels come gradually to reach a wider public, the play which is their *envoi*, and which constitutes Genet's final word on so many of the problems first raised by Divine and Our Lady, may come to be appreciated in the way that has not been possible before.

The Maids

By contrast with *Deathwatch*, Genet's second play, *The Maids* *(Les Bonnes)*, excited considerable interest even in its primitive version (Théâtre de l'Athénée, 1946); and in its revised form (Théâtre de la Huchette, 1954) immediately laid the foundations of Genet's international reputation.

The Maids is based on a real episode. In September 1933, two sisters, Christine and Léa Papin, in service with a wealthy middle-class family at Le Mans, conspired to murder their mistress and her daughter; and the ensuing trial, which uncovered a seething mass of cruelties, injustices and passionate emotions, became a *cause célèbre* in pre-war France—a scandal which, on account of the way in which all the evidence was deliberately biased in favour of the ruling *bourgeoisie* and against the servants, produced a wave of disgust among the younger generation of left-wing intellectuals— including Sartre himself.[68] Whether in fact the original Papin sisters deserved to be considered as proletarian martyrs in the crusade against a vicious and insensitive *bourgeoisie* is more than doubtful; such evidence as is reliable suggests that the elder was an advanced paranoiac, the younger a case of severe hysteria, and that both were intellectually subnormal, scarcely better than morons. The elder, in fact, although sentenced, was never executed, but declared insane two days after the trial—to the disgust and disillusionment of her more idealistic supporters. Be that as it may, this is the factual story that lies behind *The Maids*; and the very fact that Genet used such material—much as Stendhal used the case of Antoine Berthet, or Flaubert, that of Delphine Couturier—reveals a progress towards objectivity which lay still unsuspected in *Deathwatch*.

The sisters Christine and Léa become the sisters Claire and Solange : and these names alone, with their suggestions of light and darkness, sun and angels, suffice already to lift them out of the sordid reality of Le Mans, and to elevate them to the very centre of Genet's mythology :

> *Solange:* Ah! Yes, Claire, Claire says, to hell with you! Claire is here, more dazzling than ever. Radiant![69]

However, from the very first line of the dialogue, this secondary symbolism contained within the play is supplemented by a far more

radical symbolism which is rooted in the nature of the drama itself :
the simultaneous awareness, for the audience, of illusion and reality,
presented in such a way that the two opposites, far from either
merging or cancelling each other out, subsist together in all their
irreconcilable hostility, each a dynamic and irreducible force in its
own right. For, as the curtain rises, we discover Claire and Solange,
both, within the general context of dramatic illusion, having a degree
of reality as Maids. But, within this general context, they themselves
have created a domain of secondary illusion, a play-within-a-play,
in which Claire plays the part of Madame—a deliberately incomplete and faulty illusion in her grotesque and borrowed dresses, and
with her gruesomely padded body that parodies the sexual attributes
of the opulent woman—whereas Solange, perfectly disguised as
Solange, plays the part of Claire.

In this opening scene, in which the two Maids play at an exchange of personalities which, in the end, effectively reduces *all*
appearances to the status of a game *(un jeu)*, the more significant
part is that of Solange. Claire merely assumes the appearance, the
gestures and the language of Madame, the mistress insulting and
degrading the servant—any servant—and engendering an atmosphere of hatred and intolerable abjection, much as the earlier
Madame of *Pompes Funèbres* had hurled the unspeakable filth of
her abuse at Juliette, the Little Skivvy :

> Claire [*disguised as Madame, to Solange, disguised as Claire*]: I've told
> you, Claire, without spit. Let it sleep in you, my child, let it stagnate.
> Ah! Ah! (*She giggles nervously*). May the lost wayfarer drown in
> it. Ah! Ah! You are hideous.[70]

The main interest in Claire's role lies in the way in which she has
created and developed the illusion of her own double. As in *Querelle of Brest*, Claire and Solange—sisters, but not twins, for Solange
deliberately insists that she is the elder—are already to some extent
doubles in relation to each other; but, unlike Querelle and Robert,
who are above all conscious of their inner unity, the Maids owe
much more to their outward appearance : their identical grey hair,
withered faces and domestic aprons, than to their spiritual or
psychological consciousness of being two simultaneous aspects of a
single identity—in other words, the unity-in-duality of the sisters
is more the result of a deliberate and artificial trick of costume than
was the case with the earlier brothers. On the other hand, on the
level of the game, when Solange plays the part, and therefore takes
on the character, of Claire, the real Claire addresses the pseudo-
Claire as Claire, even when she herself has temporarily slipped back
out of her stage character as Madame, and resumed her own reality
as herself. The complexity of this doubling, of course, is further in-

creased by Solange, who also slips back and forth from her role as
Claire (in which case she is THE Maid, insulting and working her
self up to a fury of hatred and vengeance against THE Mistress) to
her reality as Solange; for in reality, Solange is jealous of her sister,
and accuses her of having alienated the affections of her (Solange's)
lover—the Milkman. Of both levels—reality and game—the *hatred*
alone remains identical; but the transition from one level to the
other sometimes takes place within a single speech, so that the
duality Claire/Solange, and the duality real-Claire/pseudo-Claire,
merge into each other, and produce now a sort of four-fold mirror-
reflection of a single identity :

> Solange [*disguised as Claire, walks up to Claire, disguised as Madame*]:
> Yes, my proud beauty. You think you can always do just as you like.
> You think you can deprive me forever of the beauty of the sky, that
> you can choose your perfumes and powders, your nail-polish and silk
> and velvet and lace, and deprive *me* of them? That you can steal the
> milkman from me? Admit it! Admit about the milkman. His youth
> and vigour excite you, don't they? Admit about the milkman. For
> Solange says: to hell with you!"[71]

On the other hand, if Claire incarnates the whole concept of the
mirror and the double, Solange embodies that phenomenon which,
for Genet, is the supreme symbol of the whole mystery of truth and
illusion : a reality deliberately, and for preference crudely, disguised
in such a way that disguise and reality are identical—the beggar's
sore covered over with a fake sore identical in appearance. Solange,
who is a maid, disguises herself deliberately and carefully as . . . a
maid; and the only clue that reveals the distinction between true
and false is the name : Solange, or, as the case may be, Claire. Thus
Genet has taken his initial principle, that the ultimate reality of the
Self is a Void which may be given any shape, consequently any
reality, by appearance, a stage further : for in the case of Solange,
the only final distinction between her true and false identities—even
for herself—lies in the *name* which she chooses to give them at any
precise moment. The *word* is the final arbiter of reality, and Jean
Genet, the Poet, is master of the word. In this way, finally, Genet
carries out his revenge on the world which originally condemned
him and rejected him from among the society of men; for he has
reduced all reality to the symbol of itself, and left himself, the Lord
of Symbols, sole and divine dictator of what shall or shall not be
acknowledged to be real. 'My victory is verbal,'[72] he declares in the
The Thief's Journal; in words lie all authority, all treachery, all
fear—and ultimately all the irresistible power and secret dynamism
of those supernatural forces which rule the pattern of the world.[73]

Nightly, in their ritual-sacrificial game of exchanged identities,

Claire and Solange ceremonially act the murder of Madame. Dream or reality? As always in Genet, the contents of the dream spill over into waking life : for there *is* a real Madame, and the Maids have planned her real murder—with gardenal, dissolved into her evening potion of lime-tea. But the plan goes wrong. Madame has a lover, Monsieur, whom Claire, no less involved in the metaphysics of betrayal than is Divine, or Riton, or Stilitano, has denounced to the police for some nameless felony, having first collected, or manufactured, sufficient evidence to ensure that he will be convicted. But the police are hesitant and, just before Madame returns home, a telephone-call informs the Maids that Monsieur has been released on bail. Certain now that their treachery will be discovered, the Maids realize, not only that their dream of murdering Madame must become a reality if they themselves are to escape the consequences of their denunciation, but also that it must be realized immediately. Madame returns, the gardenal is ready; but then Claire and Solange, human beings who have betrayed another human being, are in their turn betrayed by the active malevolence of the inanimate world :

> *Claire:* You know perfectly well that objects are deserting us.
> *Solange:* Do you think that objects worry about us?
> *Claire:* They never do anything else. They are betraying us.[74]

It begins when Madame spots traces of her own rouge on Claire's face, then the displaced receiver on the telephone, finally the kitchen alarm-clock which has wandered into the drawing-room; the whole of the ritual is on the point of discovery, would indeed have been discovered then and there, had not Claire revealed that it was Monsieur who had telephoned. Delirious with excitement, Madame rushes off to meet him, leaving her lime-tea untasted—and Claire and Solange remain alone once more, their dream of murder having evaporated, now doomed themselves, with one final sacrificial ritual for their only consolation. For the last time, they go through the exchange of identities; this time, however, Solange *dresses* as Madame, but, by her words and gestures, *acts* the part of Claire-the-Maid; while Claire remains dressed as Claire (or perhaps Solange), but acts the part of Madame—double-identities which they will retain until the end of the play, except that at one point—the final dissolution of reality into dream—Solange, still dressed as Madame, acts the part of a Maid acting the part of her Mistress.[75] As the curtain falls, however, reality take its revenge, and it is Claire—whose gestures, in spite of her Maid's appearance, have given her at last the identity of Madame—who shifts this reality out of time into eternity by herself drinking the lime-tea-and-gardenal. Thus truth and falsehood become for ever indistinguishable in the wordlessness of death; for the poison was intended for Madame; Claire *is* Madame, and, now she can no longer speak her name, will remain so for all eternity:

> *Claire:* Don't interrupt again. I repeat. Are you listening? Are you obeying? I repeat. My tea!
> *Solange:* But. . . .
> *Claire:* I say: my tea.
> *Solange:* But, Madame. . . .
> *Claire:* Good. Continue.
> *Solange:* But, Madame, it's cold.
> *Claire:* I'll drink it anyway. Let me have it. And you've poured it into the best, the finest tea-set. . . .
> [*She takes the cup and drinks, while Solange, facing the audience, remains motionless, her wrists crossed as though fastened by handcuffs.*][76]

This extraordinary play, with its perfect one-act structure, its overwhelming dramatic tension and its density of thought and symbolism, is rightly considered as one of the masterpieces of the contemporary theatre. But, because of its stress on fluctuating identities, it has also served to link Genet's drama irrevocably with the Theatre of the Absurd, for not all critics have realized that the interchangeable identities of Claire and Solange have their origins in a series of metaphysical concepts which are very different from those, say, of Ionesco; and their coincidence with the shifting identities of Choubert in *Victims of Duty*, or of the Smiths and the Martins in *The Bald Prima-Donna* is more apparent than real.

The interchangeability of identity in Ionesco results from the breakdown of the laws of cause-and-effect, the disruption of Aristotelian logic,[77] leading to the denial of the concept of time as an absolute continuum, and to the assertion that all apparently causal relationships are in fact the result of pure coincidence. Where there is no certitude of cause-and-effect, still less of First or Final Causes, then our world is, in the most literal sense, absurd, and all related concepts: personality, psychology, purpose, significance, etc., become utterly meaningless. But in Genet, as we have seen, *all* aspects of existence have significance—and that, not merely in terms of human logic, but of a superhuman reality, a Divine Plan, an unfathomable Fatality. If anything, it is the very multiplicity of significance on different, incompatible levels, which produces the breakdown of normal logic, rather than any *lack* of meaning, or the failure of that logic in itself. For Genet, every phenomenon, every identity, has *at least* a double significance: the problem is that each half of the double can be aware of itself only in terms of the other. Solange can be aware of herself only in terms of Claire. 'It will be your task, yours alone, to keep us both alive',[78] says Claire to Solange just before she dies; but an earlier exchange has made the relationship clearer :

> *Solange:* When slaves love one another, it's not love.
> *Claire:* And me, I'm sick of seeing my image thrown back at me by a mirror, like a bad smell. You're my bad smell.[79]

Genet's problem, in other words, is much closer to that of Beckett's *Unnamable*, than to that of Camus, Arrabal or Ionesco. There *is* a significance, even in identity; the difficulty is to define it, except in terms of something, or somebody, else. For Beckett, the Absolute Self takes on the name of Worm :

> Worm, to say that he does not know what he is, where he is, what is happening, is to underestimate him. What he does not know is that there is anything to know. His senses tell him nothing, nothing about himself, nothing about the rest, and this distinction is beyond him. Feeling nothing, knowing nothing, he exists nevertheless, but not for himself, for others, others conceive him and say, Worm is, since we conceive him, *as if there could be no being but being conceived*, if only by the beer.[80]

The difference between Beckett and Genet, on the one hand, and Ionesco on the other, lies in the confident assertion (which I have italicized) in the last sentence. For Ionesco (at least, in the early plays) there is *no* permanent basis to identity; for Beckett there is, but it is mystic, inconceivable—or rather, it can only define itself in accordance with its reflection in the Other. For Beckett, this Other is called Mahood. Worm and Mahood constitute a double, negative and positive, not merely interchangeable, but constituting, by their very existence, a perpetual and inevitable interchange. So it is also with Querelle and Robert; and so it is with Claire and Solange.

Madame, characteristically, cannot tell the difference at all between Claire and Solange—since both wear the same uniform, both *appear* the same.[81] Given the instability of the real Self, its permanent identity for others is constituted, either by its appearance, or else by their emotion. Erik Seiler *thinks* that he knows his own identity. (' "*Je suis seul à être Erik Seiler*". *Cette certitude l'exaltait*'[82])—but the validity of this belief is immediately questioned by Genet himself, who simply takes his place as *I* and proceeds to relive *his* childhood in his place. By contrast, Stilitano surrenders his identity to his clothes; and, when he hangs them up at night, this identity remains with them, and not with him.[83] A mistaken identity—the favourite device of the French farce, the *quiproquo*—implies, not merely a failure in communication, as it does in Molière or Labiche, but an actual substitution of identity. The emotions aroused by the false appearance (the *shadow* of Charlot's hand resting on Bulkaen[84]) are identical with those evoked by a reality; the emotions aroused in Solange by Claire's appearance as Madame are identical with those aroused by Madame herself— therefore it is only logical that the consequences should be identical and that Claire-as-Madame should die as though Claire *were* Madame. All emotions in Genet, in fact, are directly dependent, not on reality, but on appearance; and since the reality beneath the appearance can shift and change continuously, the emotions— love or hate—appear to constitute an independent entity. Love— in Genet as in Proust—is independent of its specific object. Genet's love for Divers is transferred to Bulkaen and back again to Divers, as a continuity of emotion, without Genet even being consciously aware that its apparent cause has changed.[85] So also with hate. It is irrelevant whether Solange hates Claire-as-Madame or Madame herself : the appearance alone, regardless of the identity, is sufficient to constitute the reality of the hatred.

But if there is an independent stability in the emotions, this only serves to emphasize the terrifying instability of the Self. For, on the one hand, if the Ego can only know itself—and therefore *be* itself— in others, it will vary to infinity according to whatever shape the Other may chance to take. 'A catastrophe is always possible', con- fesses Genet in *The Thief's Journal*. 'Metamorphosis lies in wait for us [. . . .]. I have lived in fear of metamorphoses.'[86] On the other hand, even if the Ego does not actually *become* the Other, it can- not know itself except in terms of what the Other *says* about it. The Other—the double—is the mirror in which it sees itself; but it is a *speaking* mirror, and, unlike Snow-White's version, it can and probably will tell lies. 'I have never been able to see myself,' com- plains Lt Seblon[87]; and symbolically, all Genet's prison-cells are mirrorless. The Figure cannot tell lies to its Image, for, not know- ing what it is, it cannot make statements, but only ask questions; the Image, on the other hand, can and will tell lies to the Figure. Once again, it is the Figure, the reality, which is at a disadvantage; the initiative lies with the reflection.

Where a third person is involved, moreover, the mutual rela- tionship of the Ego and the double becomes more complex still. Since any powerful emotion—love or hate—exists as an Absolute in the subject, regardless of its specific object, it cannot hope to be aware of itself, and therefore cannot realize itself *directly*. It must pass indirectly through a third person, a mirror reflecting, as it were, in both directions. Strictly speaking, it is only the mirror (the third person) who can appreciate to the full the intensity of the emotion. Thus Roger, when he is go-between in the relationship between Gil

Turko and Querelle, feels more urgently than either the emotion that unites them.[88] Similarly Genet himself reveals that the most overwhelming experience of his life is to feel himself 'decomposed'[89] as the glance from one lover to another passes through him and is realized *in* him.[90] By contrast, Lefranc, who is emotionally less generous than Genet himself, feels his position as a mirror between Maurice and Green Eyes as an insupportable torture—again an emotion stronger than that experienced by either of the principals :

> *Lefranc:* I'm fed up being between you, fed up feeling your gestures pass through me when you talk to each other. I'm fed up with the sight of your little mugs. I know all about your winks [. . . .] You wear me out.[91]

Lefranc gets his revenge by deliberately distorting Green Eyes' reflection of himself and by substituting his own identity for what should be, by rights, a straightforward mirror-image of Green Eyes himself.[92] Change love into hatred, and we have the underlying theme of *The Maids*. *The Maids* is a play about hatred, or rather, about the same interchangeability of love and hatred as Absolutes that we examined in *Pompes Funèbres*; only, in this case, it is the hatred which is predominent. Claire and Solange are physical, Lesbian, incestuous lovers (just as Christine and Léa Papin were shown to be in real life), with Solange as the dominant partner; and as the love shades off into hate, so it is Solange's hatred of Claire (or of herself in Claire) that is the dynamic force behind the action. *The Maids*, we should never forget, is a play about the relationship between the Maids, to which Madame is only incidental—which is the reason why, in the play as opposed to real life, Madame survives, while it is Claire who dies. Madame (or Claire-as-Madame) is the mirror in which Solange's hatred of Claire is reflected and intensified—a fact which Claire herself realizes only too well :

> *Claire:* Through her, it was me you were aiming at. I'm the one who's in danger.[93]

Without Madame, Claire could never be more than the identical mirror-image of Solange. Lefranc, in revenge for being forced to be a mirror, deliberately distorts the image thrown by Green Eyes; Solange, employing a similar procedure but with a different technique, uses Madame as a distorting-mirror in which the image of Claire shall be differentiated from the original reality of Claire, and thus enable her hatred to be realized.

Does this mean, then, that Madame has no specific significance—dramatic, social or political—in herself? Knowing Genet's hatred of the *bourgeois*, and more especially of the *bourgeoise*, and remembering the prototype of Madame who appeared in *Pompes Funèbres*, with her lucubrations about the loathesomeness of servants,[94] it is difficult not to feel something of the playwright's passionate anger on a social plane. On the one hand, there is the theme of revolt that runs all the way through the play, *'la révolte des bonnes'*[95]—on the other, there is Genet's sympathy for all the outcasts and the under-privileged members of society, among whom the French domestic servant, even as recently as 1950, remained a striking and an anom-alous specimen in a society which, in other respects, had done away with much of its slavery. As an ex-convict, he sees all servants as fellow-sufferers, plunged like himself into the depths of humilia-tion . . . for waiters in particular he has a special affection and, in *Our Lady of the Flowers,* he credits them with that special vision which comes to those whose lives verge upon that absolute darkness of despair which opens the gates of the sacred and the transcen-dental. Like Querelle, like all murderers, all waiters and all poets, Claire and Solange are *'des monstres',*[96] and share in the dream-world of other monsters, but does this make them also symbols in our time—as Léa and Christine were in theirs—of an oppressed and victimized proletariat?

Specifically, in his introduction, Genet warns us against such an interpretation :

> One thing must be written : there is no question here of pleading a case on behalf of the lot of domestic servants. I presume that house-servants have a trade-union—that is none of our concern.[97]

—but this is something of an over-simplification. Genet, whether he likes it or not, has been assimilated into the ranks of the com-mitted dramatists. Or rather, as we shall see, he has written major plays in political settings about the problems of commitment; and the flamboyant effect of these dramas, considered as works of art for the theatre, has tended to obscure the tentative, even negative, conclusions of the dramatist. Inevitably, it is in the context of *The Balcony, The Blacks* and *The Screens*—of revolution, the colour-bar and colonial exploitation—that any contemporary audience is likely to judge *The Maids.* That hatred and politics should go to-gether is, unhappily, one of the basic laws of man-in-society; and so powerfully does this hatred emerge from the dialogues of Claire and Solange, that it is almost impossible not to feel it as an expres-sion of social violence and a symbol of protest against injustice. None the less, the relationship between politics and metaphysics, in Genet's later plays, is complex and anything but easy to unravel. In the last analysis, his fundamental preoccupations remain the same : identity, transcendence and art. But a transcendence which is sought for in the middle of a massacre is liable to take on a col-our different from that which is sought for among the peace-time cafés of Montmartre; and even problems of identity acquire a nuance of violence and militancy when they are argued out in the heat of a race-riot, or pondered over behind the barbed wire of a concentration camp in Algeria. *The Maids* is first and foremost a play of masks and doubles, illusions and unrealities and symbols; but it is also, if only marginally, a play about hatred and injustice in a social context. In Genet's original parable, the outcome of the battle is not known; but it is perhaps not without significance that the Small Boy who was Night was *also* specifically playing soldiers.

NOTES

1 Omitted in the English version of *The Maids*. '. . . la description de gestes quotidiens vus de l'extérieur.' (*Bonnes—C.J.L.B.*, p. 10)

2 Omitted in the English version of *The Maids*. 'Il faut à la fois y croire et refuser d'y croire; mais afin qu'on puisse croire, il faut que les actrices ne jouent pas selon un mode réaliste.' (*Bonnes—C.J.L.B.*, p 10)

3 'Un jeune écrivain m'a raconté avoir vu dans un jardin public cinq ou six gamins jouant à la guerre. Divisés en deux troupes, ils s'apprêtaient à l'attaque. La nuit, disaient-ils, allait venir. Mais il était midi dans le ciel. Ils décidèrent donc que l'un d'eux serait la Nuit. Le plus jeune et le plus frêle, devenu élémentaire, fut alors le maître des Combats. "Il" était l'Heure, le Moment, l'Inéluctable. De très loin, paraît-il, il venait, avec le calme d'un cycle, mais alourdi par la tristesse et la pompe crépusculaires. A mesure de son approche, les autres, les Hommes, devenaient nerveux, inquiets. . . . Mais l'enfant, à leur gré, venait trop tôt. Il était en avance sur lui-même: d'un commun accord les Troupes et les Chefs décidèrent de supprimer la Nuit, qui redevint soldat d'un camp. . . . C'est à partir de cette seule formule qu'un théâtre saurait me ravir.' (*Pauvert*, pp. 147-148)

4 'La morne tristesse d'un théâtre qui réflète trop exactement le monde visible, les actions des hommes et non les Dieux.' (*Pauvert*, p. 144)

5 A technique probably borrowed from certain Parisian floor-shows— *e.g.* from *La Lune Rousse*—where it has long been popular.

6 *Screens*, p. 7. 'Auprès du paravent, il devra toujours y avoir au moins un objet réel (brouette, seau, bicyclette, etc.), destiné à confronter sa propre réalité avec les objets dessinés.' (*Paravents—Q.I.*, p. 10)

7 Omitted in the English version of *The Maids*. 'Si possible les fleurs seront des fleurs réelles, le lit un vrai lit. Le metteur en scène doit comprendre, car je ne peux tout de même pas tout expliquer, pourquoi la chambre doit être la copie à peu près exacte d'une chambre féminine, les fleurs vraies, mais les robes monstrueuses et le jeu des actrices un peu titubant.' (*Bonnes—C.J.L.B.*, p. 12)

8 *Our Lady*, p. 64. 'Tu jouais à jouir, peut-être.' (*Notre-Dame*, p.11)

9 *Ibid.*, p. 71. '. . . de se libérer, par un désespoir extérieur, par un deuil visible fait de larmes, de fleurs, de crêpe, des cent grands rôles qui la possédaient.' (*Notre-Dame*, p. 16)

10 Text omitted in the English translation of *The Maids*. '. . . mes toilettes noires pour mes visites au parloir.' (*Bonnes*, p. 62)

11 *Thief*, pp. 47-8. (*Journal*, p. 57)

12 *Ibid.*, p. 112. (*Journal*, pp. 132-3)
13 *Q. of B.*, pp. 200-213. 'La scène était morte . . .' etc. (*Querelle*, pp. 287-95)
14 *Ibid.*, p. 235. (*Querelle*, p. 308)
15 *Pompes Funèbres*, p. 101.
16 *Rose*, pp. 69, 92, etc; (*Miracle*, pp. 235, 252)
17 'Théâtralement, je ne sais rien de plus efficace que l'élévation.' (*Pauvert*, pp. 145-6)
18 *Thief*, p. 187. 'Le héros ne connaît pas le sérieux d'un thème tragique. [. . . .] Si c'est à la mort qu'il va—dénouement nécessaire—à moins que ce soit au bonheur, c'est comme à la plus parfaite réalisation, donc la plus heureuse, de soi, il y va d'un coeur joyeux.' (*Journal*, pp. 222-223)
19 See *Rose*, pp. 44, 58; (*Miracle*, pp. 217, 227)
20 *Pauvert*, pp. 142-3, 145.
21 '. . . est vaine si je ne crois pas à ce que je vois qui cessera—qui n'aura jamais été—quand le rideau tombera.' (*Pauvert*, p. 146)
22 Omitted in the English version of *The Maids*. '. . . établir une espèce de malaise dans la salle.' (*Bonnes—C.J.L.B.*, p. 10)
23 Artaud, A., *Le Théâtre et son Double*. In *Oeuvres Complètes*, Paris (Gallimard) 1964, vol. IV, p. 83. 'Ne pas préciser des pensées, mais faire penser.'
24 J.-J. Pauvert is an *avant-garde* French publisher who, in 1954, produced an edition, in one single volume, of the two versions of *Les Bonnes*. See *Bibliography*, Section I, No 64.
25 *Pauvert*, p. 143.
26 *Ibid.*, p. 144.
27 Bentley, Eric, 'The Psychology of Farce', in *Let's get a Divorce and other Plays*, N.Y., 1958.
28 'Sans doute une des fonctions de l'art est-elle de substituer à la foi religieuse l'efficace de la beauté.' (*Pauvert*, p. 146)
29 *Our Lady*, p. 231. 'S'il me fallait faire représenter une pièce théâtrale, où des femmes auraient un rôle, j'exigerais que ce rôle fût tenu par des adolescents, et j'en avertirais le public, grâce à une pancarte qui resterait clouée à droite ou à gauche des décors durant toute la représentation.' (*Notre-Dame*, p. 119)
30 *Ibid.*, p. 305. '. . . une voix d'image, voix plate.' (*Notre-Dame*, p. 167)
31 *Deathwatch*, p. 7. '. . le plus de lumière possible.' (*Haute Surveillance*, p. 10)
32 Omitted in the English version of *Deathwatch*. 'Nous jouons tragiquement mais nous jouons.' (*Haute Surveillance*, p. 10)
33 See Nathalie Sarraute, 'Conversation et Sous-Conversation', in *L'Ere du Soupçon*, Paris (Gallimard: Collection Idées) 1956, pp. 95-147.
34 For a good example of this technique, see *Rose*, pp. 47 *et seq.* (*Miracle*, p. 219)
35 An elementary fact which, none the less, some novelists who later take to the drama fail dismally to learn. *E.g.* Robert Pinget.
36 *Maids*, p. 13; the English text corresponds only approximately to the French original, and loses the effect:
'*Claire:* Le danger m'auréole, Claire; et toi tu n'est que ténèbres. . . .
Solange: . . . infernales! Je sais. Je connais la tirade. Je lis sur votre visage ce qu'il faut vous répondre.' (*Bonnes*, pp. 25-6)
37 It is interesting to observe contemporary writers, at grips with the prob-

lem of *le néant,* following the same paths as their seventeenth-century predecessors in their attempt to elucidate the concept of the Infinite (Descartes, Leibniz, Newton, Malebranche, etc.), and stumbling on similar conclusions: a sort of dramatised infinitesimal calculus.

38 Omitted in the English version of *The Maids.* 'Le jeu sera furtif afin qu'une phraséologie trop pesante s'allège et passe la rampe.' (*Bonnes—C.J.L.B.,* pp. 7-8)

39 *Our Lady,* p. 80. '. . . lourds d'idées précises.' (*Notre-Dame,* p. 21)

40 *Funambulists* in *E.R.,* p. 46. 'La réalité du cirque tient dans cette métamorphose de poussière en poudre d'or.' (*Funambule,* p. 183)

41 *Ibid.,* p. 49. 'Il faut aimer le Cirque, et mépriser le monde.' (*Funambule,* p. 201)

42 In *L'Enfant Criminel,* Genet comments ironically, when he was refused permission to talk on the radio: 'Les journaux déjà s'étonnent qu'un théâtre fût à la disposition d'un cambrioleur et d'un pédéraste.' (p. 151)

43 *Deathwatch,* pp. 29-30. (*Haute Surveillance,* p. 104)

44 *Ibid.,* p. 30.
   '*Yeux-Verts:* Je suis peut-être moins fort que Boule-de-Neige parce que son crime était un peu plus nécessaire que le mien, parce qu'il a tué pour piller et pour voler, mais comme lui j'ai tué pour vivre et j'ai déjà le sourire.' (*Haute Surveillance,* p. 105)

45 *Ibid,* p. 22. 'On va faire de toi un petit assassin? Un petit bagnard? Hein? Maurice.' (*Haute Surveillance,* p. 53)

46 Omitted in the English version of *Deathwatch.*
   '*Yeux-Verts:* Tes vols, tes cambriolages, ce n'est pas cela qui peut te mener loin. Ce n'est pas cela qui peut te mener jusqu'à nous.'

47 See above, p. 154.

48 *Deathwatch,* p. 40. '*Lefranc:* Tu as raison. Je suis vraiment tout seul.' (*Haute Surveillance,* pp. 134-5)

49 See *Our Lady,* p. 156. (*Notre-Dame,* p. 70). The Austrian poet, Hugo von Hofmannsthal, likewise evolved a 'mystique of meetings'. See his essay: 'Die Wege und die Begegnungen' (1907)

50 *Our Lady,* p. 193. 'Tout, enfin, se passait selon un ordre à possibilité unique.' (*Notre-Dame,* p. 93)

51 *Ibid.,* p. 105. (*Notre-Dame,* p. 37)

52 *Rose,* p. 114. (*Miracle,* p. 267)

53 *Ibid.,* p. 12. (*Miracle,* p. 194)

54 *Pompes Funèbres,* p. 44.

55 *Rose,* p. 172. (*Miracle,* p. 309)

56 *Q. of B.,* pp. 222-3. '[Mario] ne faisait aucun mouvement faute de savoir lequel d'abord, mais surtout il était fasciné par cet instant victorieux qu'il fallait détruire par et pour il ne savait quel autre de moindre intensité peut-être, de moindre bonheur, et qui serait irrémédiable. Il ne pourrait plus choisir, s'étant accompli. En soi-même Mario sentait un équilibre de choix. Il était au centre enfin de la liberté. Il était prêt à . . . sauf que cette attitude ne pouvait durer longtemps. Se reposer sur la cuisse, détendre tel ou tel muscle sera déjà choisir, c'est-à-dire se limiter. Il devait donc garder son instabilité longtemps. . . .' (*Querelle,* p. 301)

57 *Ibid.,* p. 312. (*Querelle,* p. 346)

58 In real life, Général Boulanger seems to have shared Querelle's idea, if in a rather more rudimentary form.

59 *Q. of B.*, p. 266. 'Querelle à son étoile accordera une confiance absolue. Cette étoile devait son existence à la confiance qu'avait en elle le matelot—elle était si l'on veut l'écrasement sur sa nuit du rayon de sa confiance en, justement, sa confiance, et pour que l'étoile conserve sa grandeur et son éclat, c'est-à-dire son efficacité, Querelle devait conserver sa confiance en elle—qui était sa confiance en soi.' (*Querelle*, p. 326)

60 *Deathwatch*, p. 24. (*Haute Surveillance*, p. 66)

61 *Ibid.*, p. 23.
'*Yeux-Verts:* Je courais à droite et à gauche. Je me tortillais. J'essayais toutes les formes pour ne pas devenir un assassin. [. . . .] Je me contortionnais. On m'aurait cru en caoutchouc. Les gens disaient que j'étais convulsionnaire. Mais je voulais remonter le temps, défaire mon travail, revivre jusqu'avant le crime.' (*Haute Surveillance*, pp. 56-7)

62 *Ibid.*, p. 39. '. . . pour rien. Pour la gloire.' (*Haute Surveillance*, p. 130)

63 *Ibid.*
'*Yeux-Verts:* Mais, malheureux, tu ne sais pas qu'on ne peut plus me dépasser? Je n'ai rien voulu. Tu m'entends? Je n'ai rien voulu de ce qui m'est arrivé. Tout m'a été donné. Un cadeau. Du bon dieu ou du diable, mais quelque chose que je n'ai pas voulu.' (*Haute Surveillance*, pp. 130-1)

64 Or at any rate, not a *voluntary* substitution. Gil Turko's acceptance of Querelle's murder is involuntary.

65 *Deathwatch*, pp. 39-40.
'*Yeux-Verts:* Mais toi, toi, salaud, tu as triché pour venir. [. . . .]
Lefranc: J'ai voulu prendre ta place. . . .
Yeux-Verts: Et mon crime?
Lefranc: Jusqu'au crime.
Yeux-Verts: Pas jusqu'au mien.' (*Haute Surveillance*, p. 132)

66 *Ibid.*, p. 40. (*Haute Surveillance*, p. 133)

67 *Ibid.*, p. 30. (*Haute Surveillance*, p. 104; see also pp. 77, 101, 102, 105, 112)

68 Simone de Beauvoir, *La Force de L'Âge*, pp. 136-138. See also the film, *Les Abysses*, directed by Nico Papatakis, scenario by the dramatist Jean Vauthier. Reviewed in *Les Temps Modernes*, Apr. 1963, pp. 1911-1920. It is interesting to compare Vauthier's use of the theme with Genet's.

69 *Maids*, p. 12.
'*Solange:* Claire! Claire vous emmerde! Claire est là, plus Claire que jamais. Lumineuse!' (*Bonnes*, p. 25)

70 *Ibid.*, p. 8.
'*Claire:* Je vous ai dit, Claire, d'éviter les crachats. Qu'ils dorment en vous, ma fille, qu'ils y croupissent. Ah! ah! Que le promeneur égaré s'y noie. Ah! ah! vous êtes hideuse, ma belle.' (*Bonnes*, p. 15)

71 *Ibid.*, p. 12.
'*Solange:* Oui Madame, ma belle Madame. Vous croyez que tout vous sera permis jusqu'au bout? Vous croyez pouvoir dérober la beauté du ciel et m'en priver? Choisir vos parfums, vos poudres, vos rouges à ongles, la soie, le velours, la dentelle, et m'en priver? Et me prendre le laitier? Avouez! Avouez le laitier! Sa jeunesse, sa fraîcheur vous troublent, n'est-ce pas? Avouez le laitier. Car Solange vous emmerde.' (*Bonnes*, p. 24)

72 *Thief*, p. 52. 'Ma victoire est verbale.' (*Journal*, p. 62)

73 *Our Lady*, pp. 145-6. (*Notre-Dame*, p. 63)
74 Omitted in the English version of *The Maids*.
'*Claire:* Tu sais bien que les objets nous abandonnent.
Solange: Crois-tu que les objets s'occupent de nous?
Claire: Ils ne font que cela. Ils nous trahissent.' (*Bonnes*, pp. 76-77)
75 *Maids*, p. 37. (*Bonnes*, p. 87)
76 *Ibid.*, p. 42.
'*Claire:* Je répète. Ne m'interromps plus. Tu m'écoutes? Tu m'obéis?
Je répète! Mon tilleul!
Solange: Mais....
Claire: Je dis! mon tilleul.
Solange: Mais Madame....
Claire: Bien. Continue.
Solange: Mais Madame, il est froid.
Claire: Je le boirai quand même. Donne. Et tu l'as versé dans le service
le plus riche, le plus précieux. . . . *(Elle prend la tasse et boit cepen-
dant que˚Solange, face au public, reste immobile, les mains croisées
comme par des menottes).*' (*Bonnes*, p. 93)
In the definitive text of the play, the curtain falls on this line, with
this stage-direction. In the earlier version, however, Solange is given
a long, concluding monologue; and it is on this variant that the
English translation is based.
77 See the author's: 'Eugène Ionesco: the Meaning of Un-meaning', in
Aspects of Drama and the Theatre, Sydney U. P., 1965.
78 *Maids*, p. 41.
'*Claire:* Tu seras seule pour assumer nos deux existences.' (*Bonnes*,
p. 91)
79 *Ibid.*, p. 21.
'*Solange:* S'aimer dans la servitude, ce n'est pas s'aimer.
Claire: C'est trop s'aimer. Mais j'en ai assez de ce miroir effrayant
qui me renvoie mon image comme une mauvaise odeur. Tu es ma
mauvaise odeur.' (*Bonnes*, p. 48)
80 S. Beckett, *The Unnamable*, in *Three Novels*, London (Calder); N.Y.
(Grove Press) 1959, p. 349.
81 Omitted in the English version of *The Maids*. (*Bonnes*, p. 72)
82 *Pompes Funèbres*, p. 123.
83 *Thief*, p. 56 *note*. (*Journal*, p. 67 *note*)
84 *Rose*, p. 120. (*Miracle*, p. 272)
85 *Ibid.*, pp. 72-83. (*Miracle*, pp. 237-41)
86 *Thief*, p. 30. 'Une catastrophe est toujours possible. La métamorphose
nous guette. [....] J'ai vécu dans la peur des métamorphoses.'
(*Journal*, p. 37)
87 *Q. of B.*, p. 106. 'Je ne me suis jamais vu.' (*Querelle*, p. 233)
88 *Ibid.*, pp. 186-7. (*Querelle*, pp. 279-80)
89 *Our Lady*, p. 265. (*Notre-Dame*, p. 141)
90 *Ibid.*, p. 249. (*Notre-Dame*, p. 130)
91 *Deathwatch*, p. 14. The English translation differs slightly from the
original French.
'*Lefranc:* J'en ai assez, d'être entre vous deux, d'être traversé par les
gestes de l'un qui cause avec l'autre. J'en ai assez de regarder vos
petites gueules. Je les connais vos coups de paupières!
Maurice: On a le droit.
Lefranc: Vous m'épuisez'. (*Haute Surveillance*, p. 30)

92 *Ibid.*, pp. 10-11. (*Haute Surveillance*, pp. 18-22, 45)

93 *Maids*, p. 18.
   '*Claire:* C'est moi que tu vises à travers Madame, c'est moi qui suis
   en danger.' (*Bonnes*, p. 40)

94 *Pompes Funèbres*, p. 113.

95 *Maids*, p. 12. (*Bonnes*, p. 25)

96 *Bonnes—C.J.L.B.*, p. 10. Omitted from English version of the play.

97 Omitted in the English edition of *The Maids*. 'Une chose doit être écrite :
   il ne s'agit pas d'un plaidoyer sur le sort des domestiques. Je suppose
   qu'il existe un syndicat des gens de maison—cela ne nous regarde
   pas.' (*Bonnes—C.J.L.B.*, p. 11)

8

ANARCHY IN THE BROTHEL

(The Balcony)

A thought expressed is a lie.
Tyutchev

Les journaux sont les cimetières des idées.
Proudhon

The contrast between *The Maids* (definitive version, 1954) and *The Balcony* (first version, 1956), is about as great as any that can be imagined in the case of a dramatist who, in spite of a total renovation of technique, has abandoned none of his original ideas. The transformation is above all one of structure. The neat neo-classicism of the early plays has been swept into limbo, to be replaced by the open-plan vistas of the Brechtian epic theatre, accompanied by all the typical paraphernalia of the Berliner Ensemble, itself heir to the German Expressionistic drama of the 'twenties : tableaux instead of unified acts or scenes in the French tradition; grotesque masks; *Verfremdungseffekte*; satire, parody and distortion; scenes of political or revolutionary action—and a new kind of dramatic effectiveness, in which, progressively, the spoken word (and consequently all forms of normal dramatic psychology) comes to play an ever-diminishing part, while its place is taken by the violent impact of colour, movement and pure sound.

None the less, thoroughly Brechtian as these later plays appear on the surface (especially *The Screens*), it is important to distinguish between form and content. If Genet has adopted a Brechtian technique, this does not necessarily imply a conversion to Brechtian political, or even dramatic principles. Most of the characteristic features of the epic theatre—the shattering of illusion, the deliberate artificialities, the symbolism verging on caricature—were already implicit in Genet's own dramatic ideology; and in so far as he has exploited Brecht's *schema* of production and Brecht's mannerisms, it is because these seem to have offered a ready-made, a God-sent answer to his own specific problems. They also suggest—in theory at least—a change of audience. A play such as *The Maids*, with its complex ideas and closely-argued dialogue full of allusions and implications, can only hope to appeal to an intellectual élite; *The Screens*—to take the extreme contrast—with its simplified dialogue and its arguments either stylized into folk-tales or else flattened out into slogans, is clearly designed to appeal to the mass. It is one of Genet's most remarkable achievements to have produced a major contribution to the *avant-garde* theatre in both idioms; and if *The Maids* is still read and acted a hundred years hence, there is a fair chance that it may have at least *The Blacks* to keep it company.

A truly Brechtian drama is, of course, a committed drama, a *théâtre engagé*. One of the oddest features of Genet's later evolution is that he seems somehow to have become *engagé malré lui*. Both implicitly and explicitly, Genet has spent his life denying any form of commitment. When society exiled him, he remained *alone* in the face of society. His cult of solitude and ascetic isolation, his impenitent individualism raised to the mystic status of sanctity, his awareness of his own *singularité* as a freak, a monster or a poet— all these are radically opposed to the traditional ideals of social solidarity, of revolutionary mass-action. Even those of his heroes who wear uniform—the soldier Gabriel, the sailor Querelle—remain essentially alone within the disciplined groups of which, theoretically, they form a part; and in fact they go further, and actually contrive to exploit the power of the mass, as symbolized in their respective uniforms, to increase their own force and virility as individuals, rather than adding their individual energies to the group. They take from the community all that it has to offer; they contribute nothing.

All Genet's heroes, considered in a social context, are fundamentally *negative*. They are not merely outlaws, that is, individuals in opposition to the laws and conventions of established society; they instinctively reject the very concepts of law and discipline as positive phenomena, and therefore as fundamentally alien and unacceptable to their own negativity. The organized band of criminals—as we have heard Genet argue already—is not merely an illusion, a burglar's daydream : it is a logical impossibility.[1] It follows that Genet has no sympathy for the Workers; for work—in a twentieth-century context at any rate—is rarely individualistic. It is a positive and disciplined activity of the mass; and the worker therefore belongs as inseparably to the organized totality of society as does the capitalist who employs or exploits him. There may be *beauty* in the sight of this co-ordinated activity—as there is among the dock-labourers of Brest :

> All through the long day they have toiled . . . in the multiple confusion of co-operative enterprise, dovetailing their respective ploys, each performing his allotted task towards the completion of a job which visibly unites them in close affinity.[2]

—but it is a beauty to be contemplated from afar, as a pattern of gestures, as a thing of abstract aesthetic delight, never emulated. Genet's characters, almost without exception, are those who never work : they are the parasites of society, either official ('you servicemen,' observes Querelle, 'soldiers or sailors never have the feeling that you have toiled'[3]), or unofficial—the pickpockets, pimps and prostitutes of the underworld. Although, as I have argued, there is a great deal of mystic Jansenism in Genet's own philosophy, the only time that he actually uses the word, he takes it in its popular and derogatory sense, meaning harsh, puritanical, dreary, ungenerous and interfering . . . and applies it to the industrial proletariat!

> . . . the whole world—and the most terribly dismal part of it, the blackest, most charred, dry to the point of Jansenism, the severe, naked world of factory workers—is entwined [with marvels : the popular songs lost in the wind. . . .][4]

In a sense, Genet's vision has less in common with the puritanical earnestness of our own time than with the more sybaritic traditions of the sixteenth and seventeenth centuries, where manual labour was considered a defilement, and where the intricate analysis of emotional, ethical and philosophical questions was the prerogative of a leisured and aristocratic élite, from which the wretch who actually had to earn his living was more-or-less automatically excluded. In our century, the élite has changed in appearance, but the principle still holds good; for only the criminal, the down-and-out, the convict or the member of the Armed Forces can afford to be permanently idle, and thus allow his mind to disentangle itself from the relative and the provisional, and range at liberty among the Absolutes. Or such, at least, is the opinion of Jean Genet.

But convicts and criminals are normally anything but Left-inclined. It is invariably Fascism, not Communism, which appeals to the criminal element in an industrial society—a fact which Genet

notes with unerring accuracy in *Pompes Funèbres*,[5] just as he
observes the inherent conformism of Darling, who 'loved his mother
just as he was a patriot and a catholic',[6] or is conscious in himself
of his taste for sumptuous furnishings in the bourgeois-reactionary
style-Rothschild, or his Proustian passion for the ritual and prestige of an ancient and aristocratic lineage.

More revealing still, Genet, in the heat of his search for an
Absolute of evil and negativity, specifically rejects those concepts
of humanism, humanitarianism, brotherhood, etc., on which all
socialistically inclined movements for proletarian solidarity and revolution are ultimately based. In place of the rationalistic, Voltairian
ideal of justice, he prefers a mystic doctrine of love and sacrifice—
and he is prepared to develop these thoroughly irrational principles,
implicit in the death of Christ (for, as many Christian theologians
have realized, love and sacrifice are *not* compatible with justice : it
was most decidedly *not* just that Christ should be crucified) to their
logical, if paradoxical, conclusion : the exaltation of *injustice*. It is
not humanity, but a cold and marble-sculpted inhumanity that he
seeks for among his lovers[7]; he daydreams of the cruelty of Mettray;
and when Mettray, as the result of a long campaign waged in the
press, is eventually disbanded, he protests violently, both in *Miracle
of the Rose* and in *L'Enfant Criminel*, against those well-intentioned
but incorrigibly stupid humanitarians who have razed a thing of
beauty to the ground and so 'destroyed a miracle'[8] no less effectively
than Cromwell's companies of reforming Ironsides destroyed those
other miracles of superstition and perfection : a monarchy and a
church. For Genet, all men are *not* brothers—even Robert and
Querelle fight almost to the death—and his hypersensitive feeling
for his own uniqueness is nauseated by a word and a concept whose
sentimentality implies a physical and an emotional relationship
which is as second-rate as it is uncalled-for, while its literal meaning
implies a common origin in that most detestable of all symbolic
figures in Genet's world : the Mother. 'I loathe the brotherhood
that establishes bodily contacts.'[9]

From this it follows that Genet makes a radical distinction between negative and positive social protest, between individual and
organized revolt, between the absolute refusal of an accepted ethic
and the active propagation of a political programme. He does not—
as the true socialist does—allow his sympathy for any individual
to be determined, or at least influenced, by the fact that this individual is the victim of oppression; but if he *is* the victim of oppression, then Genet expects him to react in the same way as himself :
by a negative, isolated and absolute rejection of all that the oppressor
stands for. 'I do not love the oppressed,' he states categorically in

Miracle of the Rose, 'I love those whom I love, who are always handsome, and sometimes oppressed, but who stand up and rebel.'[10]

The explanation of this assertion, which is essential to the understanding of Jean Genet, and which—even under the later influence of Sartre and Brecht—he will never retract, is that, of all the major writers of our time, he is perhaps the least materialistic. His values are never, at bottom, those of wealth, possessions, or even food—characteristically, he describes even the war-time famine among the prisoners of Fontevrault in aesthetic, not material terms:

> This hunger which at first helped to disenchant the jail, has now become so great that it is a tragic element which finally crowns the prison with a savage baroque motif, with a ringing song which is wilder than the others. . . .[11]

And precisely the impact—and the shock—of Genet on our time is that he makes us realise how intrinsically materialistic are the values even of our *avant-garde* and revolutionary idealisms. In this sense, of course, he is a reactionary, as Sartre realized only too well . . . which leaves us with the somewhat prickly dilemma, that either we must cultivate the values of the spirit and therefore be labelled social reactionaries, or else we must turn our backs on reaction and adopt the materialistic values of revolution, which means in fact joining in the rat-race for packed-sliced-loaves and TV sets on a massive proletarian and international scale. Or else, as the only alternative, succumb to the time-honoured illogicality of history, which has decreed that, time and time again, devoted and selfless ascetics have led the revolutions whose aim has been selfish, crude and materialistic.

For Genet himself, the problem is different. Both reactionaries and revolutionaries are equally unacceptable to him intellectually, for both represent the disciplined forces of anti-individualism which are repugnant to him—the only difference being that the first represent a society which has already excluded him, whereas the second represent a movement from which he would rather exclude himself. Emotionally, on the other hand, he is strongly attracted by the archaic mysticism of reaction, yet repelled by the individuals who incarnate it; whereas he is on the whole attracted by individual revolutionaries, yet disgusted by their materialistic ambitions and disciplinarian methods.

In a word, Genet is an anarchist of the most classical variety. He has defined his own intrinsic attitude again and again : he is not in revolt against any particular society; he has simply opted out of *all* societies—which, in the long run, is a far more difficult attitude to maintain, and perhaps a more courageous rebellion to attempt. Lt Seblon, typically, describes his adventures as taking place 'in the

most a-social recesses of our soul'[12]; and the Lieutenant's adventure
is a spiritual Odyssey of the same type as that which Genet, speaking
now in his own name, categorises as being 'never governed by rebellion or a feeling of injustice.'[13] Yet once this attitude becomes
the basic material of literature—above all, when it is transmuted into
the comparative objectivity of drama, where the reactions of the
audience are much more independent, much less easily controlled
or swayed by the writer's interpolated comments—then willy-nilly
it takes on a new dimension, a new meaning. Genet diligently
abstracts his heroes from their social context, shows them as negative,
individualistic and concerned only with sanctity and transcendental
Absolutes; equally diligently, the audience replaces them where
they came from, and persists in interpreting them as positive heroes
or victims in a relative social or political setting. In other words,
a negative hero as an individual *may* become a positive hero in a
social context—and a social context is what the theatre, almost
inevitably, provides. This is the essence of Genet's dilemma as a
dramatist : he refuses to create a socialist theatre, yet inescapably
his negative revolt will be interpreted as some sort of socialism.

Beginning with *The Balcony*, Genet's later plays are all attempts
to resolve this dilemma, with greater or lesser degrees of success.
The Balcony is perhaps the least satisfactory, or at any rate the
most muddled, from this point of view. On the one hand, the arguments in favour of anarchic or negative individualism are developed
to an unprecedented degree of complexity; yet on the other, strongly
influenced by Brecht and perhaps by Sartre *(Les Mains Sales)*, he
feel under compulsion to produce some sort of attempt at a positive
hero in the strictest Zhdanovist tradition. The result is confusion. The
most hopeful solution would appear to be that of *The Maids* or *The
Blacks* : to create individually negative characters, and to invite
or allow the audience to make a socially positive interpretation if it
wishes. By contrast the positive hero in a socialist context is a death-
trap, above all for a writer whose whole cast of mind is negative, or
at the most satirically ironical, as Gogol discovered when, in response to acrid criticism, he started on a second (positive) part of
Dead Souls. Like Gogol, Genet can handle satire, although not
entirely happily, since even satire implies that the victim, viewed
negatively on the stage—the General, for instance, 'with his starred
or oak-leaf encircled military cap'[14]—is criticized from a strongly
positive point of view in the author or at least in the audience;
but he fails lamentably in depicting his positive heroes and heroines :
his Chantal, his Roger—

> *Irma:* I let the plumber come. How do you imagine him? Young and
> handsome? No. He's forty. Thick-set. Serious, with ironic eyes.[15]

—his revolutionary troops and leaders. Not that we can accuse him of any lack of lucidity here. Only too well he realizes himself that Sartre's Brunet and Hoederer, or the barricade-heroes of Brecht, Gorky and Toller, are outside his range, not only because they have no reality for him, but because he dislikes them so intensely, and all they stand for metaphysically and ideologically :

> It will be necessary to invent the typical revolutionary, then to paint him, or model him on a mask, since I can see no one, not even among the Protestant communities of Lyons, with a face long enough, dismal enough and savage enough to play this part.[16]

Hitherto, Genet's talent, and much of his effectiveness, sprang from his almost unique ability to present negative, anti-social heroes from a negative and equally anti-social viewpoint. In this instance, quite literally, two negatives combined to make a positive : in *Pompes Funèbres*, he had no need to satirise Riton and the Fascist gangsters of the *Milice*. It was sufficient that the social outcast Genet should present the social outcast Riton in all gravity as the hero-of-heroes. Any additional element of satire could only have detracted from the overwhelming effect of nausea; the presence of a positive criterion of social or moral values would merely have reduced Riton to the status of a piece of melodramatic propaganda. But the Brechtian theatre insists on a conventionally positive attitude in the dramatist, and Genet has done his best to conform— but only with partial success. The caricatures of the Judge, the General and the Bishop in *The Balcony*, like those of the French troops and the colonial planters in *The Screens*, are effective propaganda for a moment, but, in the long run, unconvincing; and even in *The Blacks*, the masked figures of the five whites tend towards banality, and rob the play of the unquestioned power that it possesses when the Blacks alone hold the centre of the stage.

Luckily, even in *The Balcony*, these conventionally positive attitudes and heroes play only a comparatively small part in the drama as a whole. Characters such as Chantal and Roger-the-Plumber, or Ville de Saint-Nazaire, are destined eventually to be eclipsed by Saïd, of *The Screens*, a strange and complex figure, whose social-dramatic *function* as a positive hero is carefully offset by his negativity as an individual harking right back to the anti-heroes, the unheroic roughnecks of *Our Lady of the Flowers*.[17]

Saïd is precisely one such 'voyou de la pire espèce'; he belongs to the same race as Darling and Our Lady himself. What has changed in *The Screens* is not his own character, but the context in which he is required to act. War and revolution require qualities which, in a peaceful, middle-class milieu, are considered as intolerable vices. Thus both Saïd and Genet can remain negative in outlook, yet the over-all emotional effect produced by the play is very different from that of the earlier novel. In this sense, Saïd promises a solution to the dilemma of Roger-the-Plumber; but it is a solution which will only be arrived at gradually.

Yet even this is perhaps an over-simplification. Saïd suggests an answer to the problem : How is the dramatist to prevent a positive social hero from becoming a negative literary bore? But this answer presupposes that the audience should *want* to interpret the play as a positive political statement. What in fact Genet achieves in the sequence of plays running from *The Balcony* to *The Screens* is something rather more subtle and very much more characteristic. It is pure sleight-of-hand. For these three social dramas are in reality fakes, most dexterous illusions—just like the illusions in *The Balcony*. They are not political plays; they are plays which deliberately, cunningly and carefully set out to exploit, for arcane metaphysical purposes of the dramatist's own devising, the audience's *wish to believe* that they are political plays. In all probability, if Roger and Chantal, or Saïd, or Village and Virtue, were actually to spark off a revolution, Genet would not openly object, provided that it left him free to go his own way—which it almost certainly would not. But in actual fact, politics are the means, not the end; in these plays, the real end is *hatred*.

To return to Genet's basic definition of the drama. The highest, most compelling form of experience—the experience which Genet describes as sacred and which forms the basis of all his mysticism— occurs when the human consciousness becomes simultaneously aware of two co-existent dimensions of existence : the real and the transcendental. This, as Genet sees it, is the underlying miracle of the Christian Eucharist; and it is also the principle of all true theatre. The spectator who sees only Mr *** the actor, is like the communicant who sees only a scrap of wafer in the hands of the priest; the spectator for whom the illusion is perfect, who forgets Mr *** the actor and sees only King Lear or Dr Astrov, is like the communicant who sees *only* the Body of Christ. Neither of these experiences is complete; for each lies still within the normal limits of logic, each is confined to its own dimension. The truly mystic experience is to be aware of both realities at the same time, and to have an absolute belief in each.

One cannot believe (religious sense) in what one knows to be a pure illusion. To become the object of a Faith, the illusion must be transformed into a symbol—that is, it must owe its transmutation, not to anything in itself (disguise, etc.), but entirely to the *wish to believe* in the mind of the believer. There is no *illusion* in the Communion-wafer; it is neither disguised nor modelled nor painted; it does not even try to look like a lump of bread. If it is felt to be the Body of Christ, this is exclusively because the believer desires that it should be so.

But obviously this transmutation by Faith can only take place in a context of extreme, violent and irrational emotion—intense love, intense fear or intense hatred : and of these three, in Genet's analysis, the last is by far the strongest, the most effective. While Christianity continued to be more a religion of hate than of love, as it was during the sixteenth and seventeenth centuries, then it was the perfect medium for inspiring the intensity of irrational belief in a symbol that the drama requires. But now, to the average European, doctrinal disputes have become rather marginal. Religious heresy no longer shocks us—only deliberate sacrilege still produces a few faint stirrings of the old subconscious resentments.[18] But these hidden reserves of violence and hatred are by no means exhausted : it is merely that, in our minds, they are released by a different set of stimuli. And, according to Genet, the three most powerful of these stimuli, whose function is to release vast nuclear forces of hatred—and therefore of potential mystic-dramatic experience—are sex, racial antagonism, and politics. To produce a maximum of intensity, all three should act concurrently. In extremely simplified form, what Genet proposes is that the stage should present, ideally to a white audience of episcopalian Goldwaterites from Arkansas, the spectacle of a communist negro raping the wife of the State Governor. Given this context, Genet argues, the degree of *illusion* created by the acting becomes irrelevant; the audience will provide all the hatred, and consequently all the belief, that is necessary. The actor will become a *symbol*.

This is the principle on which Genet's last three plays are built. In *The Balcony*, the technique is still hesitant and uncertain; the erotic element is developed, and combined with the provocation of sacrilege (a whore disguised as the Virgin Mary); but the political element is weak, abstract and unconvincing, while the racial element is absent altogether. *The Blacks*, by contrast, is brilliantly effective—here, it is the racial hatred which provides the main component, from which the two others, sex and politics, naturally derive. And in *The Screens*, the three elements again combine, although in this case they owe at least part of their dynamic impact to what may prove to be the fairly ephemeral context of the Algerian War. But in all cases, the politics of these so-called political plays is subservient to the main design. Genet has transformed Artaud's Theatre of Cruelty and Brecht's Theatre of Provocation into a highly disquieting *Theatre of Hatred*.

These are the primary concepts underlying Genet's later drama—concepts which he sums up succinctly in the *Lettre à Pauvert*:

> I have no idea what the drama will be like in a socialist world: I have a much better notion what it would be like under the Mau-Mau.[19]

In other words, Genet deliberately adopts and exploits the techniques of Brechtian political drama; but whereas Brecht shows the evil of a given political situation in order to provoke his audience into a reaction which will lead eventually to a revolution and substitute a better society for that which has been satirized on the stage, Genet uses his political situations exclusively for the violently negative emotions which they have the power to excite in his audience, and then directs this concentration of audience-emotion straight back at the play itself, which now acquires, by virtue of the hysterical atmosphere in which it is performed, a new symbolic and transcendental dimension. Brecht uses the drama for the sake of its repercussions in the outside world; Genet exploits the outside world wholly for the sake of its repercussions in the drama. Brecht knows his enemies, and guides his audience accordingly; Genet is hesitant to recognize any specific enemy:

> If one has chosen to watch oneself deliciously dying, it is essential to carry out with strict precision, and to organize, the symbolic funerary ritual. Otherwise one must choose rather to live and discover the Enemy. For my part, the Enemy will never be anywhere.[20]

It is not the presence of *an* enemy which generates hatred; it is the simultaneous confrontation of two irreconcilable opposites: Black and White, French and Arabs, Generals and Communists. Monsieur Blankensee is as much an enemy to the Arab as the Arab is to Monsieur Blankensee; Genet (in theory at any rate) is not concerned to say that one is good, the other bad—which is the reason why he deliberately makes Saïd, his Arab hero in *The Screens*, a creature of abjection and evil. On the contrary: the responsibility of deciding which is good and which is bad remains with the audience; and the audience will have made up its mind, irrationally and immutably, long before it comes into the theatre. It does not require an evening at *The Blacks* to make Blacks hate Whites and Whites hate Blacks; Genet is only concerned to intensify an already existing emotion or prejudice, and to underline its irrationality by causing it to submerge all other social, moral or intellectual principles. The power of *The Blacks* comes from the fact that the White-hater will find his hatred of Whites increased by the play, regardless of the fact that the Black hero, Village, is a sadistic ritual murderer; and the Black-hater will continue to abominate Blacks, despite the inescapable lunacy and degradation of the protagonists of his own cause, the Court of Whites. Or at least, this is the theory. In practice, and perhaps despite himself, Genet's sympathies, as we have seen, go to the oppressed. He *does* choose his enemies, even though he hesitates to designate his enemies' enemies as his friends. In fact, he allows his heroes one advantage, and one only, over their opponents : they are a degree nearer reality, a degree further removed from caricature. The *grands bourgeois* of *The Balcony*, the Whites of *The Blacks*, the planters and *légionnaires* of *The Screens* are masked and caricatured in a way which makes their evil apparent; by contrast, the evil and abjection of the whores, the Blacks or the Arabs has to be looked for, excavated from its partially-hidden depths. By a final and supremely ingenious twist of the theory of appearances, Genet, in these later plays, reverses the role of masks and faces : for the mask reveals more clearly than any face the moral or political reality beneath, while the very reality of the face is the most impenetrable and perfect of masks, disguising evil as good, abjection as heroism, and even the game[21] of politics and revolution as a serious pursuit of noble minds. It is by taking masks *off* his heroes that Genet manages to disguise himself as Brecht.

The Balcony is a transitional play, occupying much the same position in relation to the general development of Genet's drama as did *Pompes Funèbres* in relation to that of the novel. It is probably his best-known work for the theatre after *The Maids* : it is spectacular, startling, titillating and *avant-garde*; it is, to audiences brought up in a naturalistic tradition, an abrupt revelation of the whole range of anti-naturalistic or Brechtian techniques, yet stripped of many of the irritating platitudes of Brechtian didacticism. It is set in a brothel. It has been filmed. In a word, it is a play ideally conceived '*pour épater le bourgeois*'.

Yet it is plainly the least satisfactory of all the dramas that Genet has so far written. Its essential weakness is that it uses a technique designed to create an intense dramatic atmosphere—in this case of hatred—but that, instead of presenting situations specially conceived so as to stir up this hatred to a maximum, it argues intellectually about the causes and nature of emotion. This seems to be because Genet himself is extremely uncertain how to handle his own material. As the initial situation, that of Revolutionary-versus-Bourgeois, develops, Genet finds himself more and more on the side of the Bourgeois—not for any political reasons, still less for economic ones, but on account of what seems, to him, the intolerable element of *bonté*—of humanitarian justice and rationalism—implied

in the anti-bourgeois ideology. Riton was an enemy of the bourgeoisie, but he sustained his opposition without for one second having recourse to noble or humanitarian principles; and, characteristically, it is Madame's 'kindness' which excites Claire and Solange
to their final paroxysms of hysteria. But, in *The Balcony*, it is the
Establishment which incarnates that hardness, cruelty and inhumanity which Genet instinctively opposes to the intolerable and
(to him) sentimental womanliness of brotherly love; it is the Bishop
who asserts that

> In truth, the mark of a prelate is not mildness or unction, but the most
> rigorous intelligence. Our heart is our undoing. We think we are master
> of our kindness; we are the slaves of a serene laxity.[22]

—and who develops the same theme in typically Genetian fashion a
few lines later :

> It is something quite other than intelligence that is involved. . . . It may
> be cruelty. And beyond that cruelty—and through it—a skilful, vigorous
> course towards absence. Towards Death?[23]

—whereas Chantal, the only one among the whores who is involved
with the revolutionary Left, has to work herself up to a state of
hatred by exciting herself with her own words : and even so, all
she achieves is a kind of *bonté* which has turned sour—'*une adorable
bonté empoisonnée*'.[24]

This uncertainty of objective, which in its turn occasions some
uncertainty in technique, mars the whole structure of the play. After
three medium-length *tableaux* (i—iii), in which visual effects and
arguments are carefully balanced, there comes a brief *tableau* iv which
is entirely visual; but this is followed by an inordinately long *tableau* v, which by itself occupies at least a quarter of the entire play,
and which is given over to the elaboration of a very difficult and
abstract dialectic—in the form of a dialogue between Madame Irma,
the prostitute Carmen and the Chief of Police—a dialectic which
is at least as complex as any of the arguments in *Querelle of Brest*,
and almost impossible to follow in a stage performance. This argument, the theory of functions, is both fascinating and important in
itself; but it is drastically out of place in a play whose simplified
and stylized forms require a simplified and stylized content to complete the aesthetic unity. Not that the arguments should necessarily
be simple in reality; but at least they must *appear* simple. In *The
Blacks*, the dialectic at bottom is just as complex as in *The Balcony*;
but its complexity is hidden and is only revealed by implication. In
The Balcony, every step in the dialectic is argued out stage by stage
between the characters, and the result is as though Brecht and
Gabriel Marcel had taken a hand in writing alternate scenes in the

same production : an unevenness, a lack of balance which destroys precisely that element to which Genet attaches most importance— the absolute *belief* which the audience should accord to the symbolic dramatic figures who dominate the action.

Essentially, then, whereas *Deathwatch* was a play that *used* symbols, and *The Maids* a play that *was* a symbol, *The Balcony* is a play *about* the use of symbols—or rather, a play that uses symbolism to explain the functioning of symbols—and which is, consequently, non-dramatic. Again and again it collapses into static abstractions, and has to be rescued by some of the more spectacular expressionist or *avant-garde* gimmicks which, since their function is simply to restore dramatic interest to a basically undramatic core of argument, tend to seem purely gratuitous—in any case, they are never properly integrated into the initial conception or into the basic structure of the play. None the less, *The Balcony* does have qualities; and if the foregoing criticism seems harsh, the fault is largely that of Genet himself. For had he not, in *The Blacks*, so convincingly shown that the very problems that defeated him in *The Balcony* were capable of a brilliant solution, we should have no standard by which to judge him so severely.

The setting of *The Balcony*, a number of its characters and many of its arguments are developed from *Querelle of Brest*. The sailors' brothel in Brest, La Féria becomes *Le Grand Balcon*, while Madame Lysiane develops into Madame Irma, and Robert Querelle into Madame Irma's lover, Arthur. The erotic atmosphere of La Féria is diluted in *Le Grand Balcon*, partly for obvious reasons of dramatic censorship, but partly also in obedience to one of Genet's dramatic theories, which is that the true drama is in itself a mystic-transcendental, and therefore a primarily erotic experience; and consequently, that the isolated eroticism of specific characters merely damages the over-all effect : 'Individual eroticism in the theatre debases the performance.'[25] On the other hand, the *style Rothschild* ideal of luxury remains; and the iron spikes on the door, which symbolized the isolation of La Féria from the rest of the world, are transformed into the bayonets or rifles of the revolutionaries. For *Le Grand Balcon* is a universe apart, an island in the midst of a city in turmoil; the Workers have risen against the Government, the Ministers, the Church and the Establishment—all symbolized in the figure of the Queen.

At this point, the initial similarity with La Féria ends. The Balcony (another of Genet's symbolic-suggestive titles, reminiscent of *Haute Surveillance* : the throne—Heaven, altar or condemned cell—from which an isolated consciousness looks down on the rest of humanity and bears away the weight of its sins)—the Balcony is a brothel of a special type. It is 'the most artful, yet the most decent house of illusions'.[26] It is the microcosm; or rather, it is the mirror-reflection of the real world, where all appearances become reality. It provides costumes, props, accessories and endless mirrors; and each customer acts out, in an erotic ritual of pure appearances, the part in which he would like to see himself. Bank-clerks and commercial travellers realize themselves as judges, generals or bishops; a cashier from the Crédit Lyonnais finds himself in the presence of Our Lady of the Immaculate Conception, the miraculous vision of Lourdes[27]; each of the countless salons is dedicated to an illusion: tortures, rustic idylls, royalty, ritual ceremonies; there is a 'Studio of Mirrors', a 'Studio of Scented Fountains'; there is a 'Moonlight Studio', for the romantic and a 'Urinal Studio' for the pornographic; there is (inevitably) an 'Amphitrite Studio' for those whose vision is of sailors and the sea, and a 'Studio of Tramps, where filth and poverty are magnified'. And finally, there is a 'Studio of Solemn Death, decorated with marble urns . . . the tomb! The Mausoleum Studio'.[28]

Inside the elaborate *décor* of these tiny closed worlds of absolute illusion, whores and customers together enact the rituals of make-belief—'the liturgies of the whore-house'—ranging from the coronation-ceremonies of the Kings of France, by way of 'a housewife returning from market', to a missionary dying on the cross, and Christ in person.[29]

Building from this foundation, the *prima-facie* subject of the play is that which, by now, we will have come to expect from Genet, given such material: the interpenetration of dream and reality, the total determination of inner truth by outward appearance. The clerk dressed up as a General (his whore meanwhile metamorphosed into a cavalry charger, his *'beau genet d'Espagne'*) becomes a general even to his death on the field of battle, and without irony watches, from the high balcony of his enthralled imagination, the progress of his own State Funeral. But not the customers alone are involved in these hallucinatory masquerades: Carmen, the whore who plays the Immaculate Conception for the cashier from the Crédit Lyonnais, is transmuted by the illusion into the diametrical opposite of her own reality: the common whore *becomes* the Purest of Virgins, the Mother of God; and the dynamic tension between these two simultaneous opposites, the positive and negative of reality, constitutes her own extreme of mystic experience. When Madame Irma takes the role away from her, her transcendental reality is destroyed, and the offer of the part of Saint Theresa as an alternative is but the poorest of consolations.[30] And when, ultimately, the barrier between the two worlds, brothel and revolution, is shattered, when the

Queen is killed and Madame Irma is offered the privilege of playing the part of the Queen (whilst at the same time her mirror-world Bishop, Judge and General replace their now-liquidated namesakes in the real world), she, and they, *become* the beings whose appearance they have assumed and, helped by the ambiguous figure of the Chief of Police, stamp out the insurrection with much greater swiftness and efficiency than the erstwhile realities whose mere reflection they are. The Image-in-the-Mirror is more *real* than the Figure, argued Genet in *Our Lady of the Flowers*, since that which can be perceived has greater substantiality than that which must for ever remain unperceived and unknown : the Self is a *Néant*, the appearance is all. In *Querelle of Brest*, Genet takes his analysis further : perceiver and perceived constitute at once an existentialist and a mystic double, a positive Totality which is at the same time a Void, an unreality. Now finally, in *The Balcony*, he takes this theme to its furthest and most abstract point of development, no longer considering Figure and Image as the constituent elements of the isolated individual, but relating both to their function in society. Already we have seen how Genet's theory of archetypes was leading him gradually from the individuality of Culafroy and Divine, Bulkaen or Botchako, towards a vision of universals : *the* Thief, *the* Sailor, *the* Murderer. *The* Murderer was the figure of an individual murderer reflected in the mirror. But what if one takes an already existing universal (revealed as such by his anonymity, his robes, his ritual gestures, his uniform), stands him in front of the mirror, and watches the reflection . . . what then? What will be reflected?

> *The Bishop:* Now answer, mirror, answer me. Do I come here to discover evil and innocence? And in your gilt-edged glass, what was I? Never— I affirm it before God Who sees me—I never desired the episcopal throne. To become bishop, to work my way up—by means of virtue, or vices—would have been to turn away from the ultimate dignity of bishop. I shall explain : in order to become a bishop, I should have had to make a zealous effort not to be one, but to do what would have resulted in my being one. Having become a bishop, in order to be one I should have had—in order to be one for myself, of course !—I should have had to be constantly aware of being one so as to perform my function.[31]

This is the answer, given in the opening scene of *The Balcony* : a universal reflected in a mirror shows a function. And beneath all its flamboyancy and Brechtian bravado, this is the real and serious purpose of *The Balcony* : it is an anatomy of functions.

The Self as seen by the Other corresponds to the mirror-Image as seen by the Figure; in both cases, that which is *known* is the appearance, not the reality. But in any social context, the Other, looking at the Self-as-appearance. inevitably sees in it the symbol of a given

degree of power or weakness. Every purely social relationship involves an awareness of other individuals within the society as specific
incarnations of the distribution of social power—that is, in terms
of the *functions* accorded to them by society—and necessarily, the
recognition of a given degree of power in the Other entails an
adjustment of the Self in relation to it. If Mr *** is superior or
senior to me, then I am inferior or junior to Mr ***. Socially, in
Donne's words, 'no man is an island'; *I*—as a social animal—am
irremediably defined by my functional relationships with others; yet
at the same time, the Other, even when he is my superior, is defined
by his functional relationship to me, since it is only by virtue of
the fact that I am his junior that he is my senior. Did I not exist,
his function in relation to me would cease to exist in the same
instant.

It is this latter aspect that interests Genet. That the junior should
exist only as a function of the senior (the mirror-image as a function
of the Figure) is a platitude not worth discussing, until it becomes
apparent that the reverse is inseparable from it. Until there is a
victim, there is no murderer; and the murderer, in his function *as a
murderer*, exists only '*grâce à l'autre*'.[32] Claire and Solange exist
as Maids in a functional relationship to Madame; but Madame likewise owes her present status, as a mistress, exclusively to the existence of Claire and Solange. Each, therefore, is responsible for the
other, each carries, in his or her function, a total and absolute responsibility for the existence of the other : 'It is thanks to me alone
that you exist [. . . .]. It would need so little effort on my part, and
you would exist no more'.[33]

Part of the 'kindness' of Madame, then, is to continue to allow her
Maids to exist; and if the Maids kill Madame, in the same instant
they destroy themselves as Maids. Transpose this into political terms,
and the conclusion is that any revolt by the oppressed against the
oppressor destroys, at the same time as the existence of the oppressor, the fundamental social identity of the oppressed. Hobbes, three
hundred years earlier, was arguing in a similar manner when he
demonstrated, in the *Leviathan*, that any rebellion against the
legitimate Authority of itself destroyed the whole social identity of
the rebels, and the very concept of society disintegrated into an
identity-less State of Nature. But, to revert to *The Maids*, in the
scene referred to above, Madame is not Madame : the speaker is
Claire acting the part (*i.e.* taking on the appearance, gestures, etc.)
of Madame. The function of Madame, therefore, is seen to be
detachable from Madame as an individual; her *appearance* alone
constitutes her social identity, her function, whereas her Self is a
Void, an elusive and insubstantial unreality.

In a social context, then, power is pure appearance; every social force—as Pascal demonstrates in *Les Pensées*—is essentially a symbol of power which depends for its efficacy exclusively on its being recognized as such by others. It follows, therefore, that an unadulterated symbol—for example, a simple robe-of-office, uncontaminated by the ambiguous element of a Void-Identity inside it—will be more effective than the combination : Lord-***-in-his-robe-of-office. And since, as we have seen from *The Maids*, power-symbols and identities *are* separable, it follows that the purest source of authority within a society will be, not the office-holder in person, but his reflection in a mirror.

But : the reflection-in-a-mirror is dead, and therefore cannot itself be a source of power. Whence, then, comes the origin of its power? In this case, as in the case of all other symbols and archetypal gestures, answers Genet, from the past. The power of a Bishop lies, not in the individual identity of the man, nor in the mirror-image of the vestments and the mitre, but in the scores and hundreds of episcopal predecessors who have endowed the ritual appearance with its symbolic significance, and who are therefore more positively present in every act which is an exercise of power than is the unfortunate (or importunate) current incumbent. This is the dilemma of the Bishop—and of all the other Figures—in *The Balcony* : the wretched man wants to *be* a Bishop. But he cannot. He is a Bishop only in so far as his appearance is recognized as such by Others; and the symbolic force of this recognition depends not on himself, but on the eclipsing of himself by the army of his predecessors. Only in one circumstance can he persuade identity and function to coincide : by eliminating all the Others, and by considering his own reflection in the mirror. For the Others, his function is his appearance, detached from himself; for himself alone, in intimate tête-à-tête with his mirror, he *is* his own appearance—and since he *is* it, its efficacy will for once cease to depend on the archetypal influence of his predecessors. When the Others vanish, the predecessors vanish with them : he and his Image are alone, and at long last he is-what-he-is : a Bishop. This is the erotic-mystic manner in which The Balcony performs its task and satisfies its clients : it allows them to retain (or to acquire) their functions, and yet to be what they are. In Genet's words, the whole play is 'the glorification of the Image and of the Reflection'[34]; and almost every speech in the drama is an amplification of this fundamental definition :

> *The Bishop:* . . . a function is a function. It's not a mode of being. But a bishop—that's a mode of being. It's a trust. A burden. Mitres, lace, gold-cloth and glass trinkets, genuflexions. . . . To hell with the function ! [. . . .] I wish to be a bishop in solitude, for appearance alone. . . . And

> in order to destroy all function, I want to cause a scandal and feel
> you up, you slut, you bitch, you trollop, you tramp. . . .[35]

From this initial theme spring innumerable minor developments.
Ethically, Genet begins to argue that, since all functions are interdependent, then 'good' and 'bad' functions are mutually dependent
on each other, and therefore that the good depends for its existence
on the bad, just as much as the existence of the bad is defined by
what we choose to call good.[36] And then, he continues, if one of these
two functions should prove to be a fake, or an illusion, what then
are its relations to the other which depends on it?

> *The Judge:* Look here: you've got to be a model thief, if I'm to be a
> model judge. If you're a fake thief, I become a fake judge. Is that
> clear?[37]

However, since *The Balcony* is primarily a political play, the
main problems are those of the inter-relationship of functions within
the power-hierarchy of society. For the *power* of a function is not
exclusively due to its identification with an archetype, that is, to its
permeation by the delegated powers of the dead. The living can
also delegate their own powers, transferring them, or a part of them,
in such a way as to give life to the symbolic functions of others.
Thus the Chief of Police owes his power to the Queen . . . and the
Queen to whom? To God. And God to whom? To the Bishop. And
the Bishop to whom? To the mass, the proletariat, who lend efficacy
to his symbolism by recognizing it as an image of power, yet who,
at the moment, are in rebellion against the Queen.[38] Or, to take another problem: when two equal-status power-symbols meet and
recognize each other, what is their reciprocal reaction? Madame
Irma and the Queen are both independent summits of power in their
own domain, both exercise a classic authority of functions in relation
to their own dependents (Carmen for Madame Irma, the Chief of
Police for the Queen); both, by their existence, confer reality, or
authenticity, on those who exist as a function of themselves. But in
relation to each other? Genet asks the question,[39] but does not answer
it—yet one suspects the outcome is annihilation. Equal functions are
interchangeable (Irma becomes the Queen) and eliminate each
other: Irma-as-Queen is no longer Irma-as-Madame; but Irma-as-
Queen destroys the Queen-as-Queen. Like two snakes, two equal
functions eat each other by the tail, until nothing is left of either
but the ultimate Nothingness whose ever-present terror it is the
comforting role of functions to conceal.

If we tie up this with Genet's perennial search for *la singularité*,
for an absolute identity that is-what-it-is independently of every
other animate and inanimate being, then *The Balcony* is a confession

of total failure. No man in society can be-what-he-is, neither the highest not the lowest, let alone those in between. The Sovereign is only Sovereign thanks to the existence of his or her subjects; the thief is defined in terms of his victims and, until he has found some-one to rob, cannot, without absurdity, define himself as a thief. At bottom, the problem remains unchanged since the beginning. If the individual can only *be* himself—that is, possess an authentic iden-tity—by first knowing himself for what he *is*, he must at all times be both himself and his own double. And in society, he can only have an absolute or singular existence by being simultaneously both himself and that other creature, whose function constitutes his defini-tion. The criminal can only be totally himself if he is at the same time his own victim : 'My excitement seems to be due to my assum-ing within me the role of both victim and criminal.'[40]

In the novels—but above all in *Querelle of Brest*—the problem takes on a special symbolical form. As a criminal, Genet perceives his diametrical, functional opposite in the Police; and so he con-ceives the image of the absolute and authentic individual identity as a being who is simultaneously policeman and criminal. Thus Darling, the pimp, shop-lifter and dope-smuggler, establishes his identity by becoming a police-informer.[41] 'I secretly love, yes, I love the police',[42] Genet himself confides to us in *The Thief's Journal*—for, just as there is a special aura of mysticism that surrounds the murderer, so, by virtue of their complementary functions in society, a similar aura of transcendency will surround the policeman whose function it is to arrest him and thus to re-affirm the sacred but violated taboos of the community. 'The world of the police,' Genet explains, is

> a formless, moving, hazy universe, constantly self-creating, elementary and fabulous [. . . .] a sacred power, acting directly upon my soul and troubling me.[43]

In Genet's strange and penetrating vision, the most characteristic functional relationships of society are not those of tyrant and slave, or Field-Marshal and private soldier, but those of law-breaker and detective; and the metaphysical hero-of-our-time is he in whom these two functions interpenetrate, and who consequently is depend-ent for his identity only on his own double. In *Pompes Funèbres*, it is the Nazi SS men, or the minions of the Gestapo, who embody this ideal, for never has Europe witnessed a more efficient combina-tion of the *Polizeistaat* and the criminal mentality than that dis-played by Himmler's bravos. But in *Querelle of Brest*, the whole subsidiary development of the novel—the relationship between Mario, the 'Chief of Police', and Nono, the brothel-keeper—is a working-out of this characteristically obsessive idea. Mario has all the features of the criminal, Nono all those of a policeman : together, as the complementary aspects of a single being, as a self-sufficient Total Function, they become god-like, a *'personnage fabuleux'*,[44] the very 'quintessence of value'.[45] When either of them is alone, he is less than half himself, he is a reflection without a figure, or a figure without a reflection; he is inauthentic :

> Mario was no longer simply a member of the police force, but something less than a policeman in that he had no direct contrary, that is to say the direct contrary against which, as a policeman, he was opposed. He could be one only in outward appearance by being opposed to the world he fought against.[46]

Thus the complex philosophy of social identity which forms the main theme of *The Balcony* depends on a number of interrelated propositions, most of which are developed in other works. (i) That the identity of the individual and his function are independent and separable concepts; (ii) that identity as such is an indefinable Void until it is defined by function, which, however, is an appearance and not a reality; (iii) that all functions are interdependent, and consequently that the definition of an identity depends upon the operation of a complex network of social relationships; (iv) that authenticity—the definition of an absolute and independent identity—can only be achieved by isolating one's function from those in relation to whom it has its *raison d'être*—i.e. by looking at one's own robes in a mirror; or else (v), by conjuring up out of one's own imagination a purely illusory Other for it to function on (the whore dressed up as *une voleuse*); or finally (vi), by absorbing into oneself both one's own function and that of the Other with whom it exists in reciprocal relationship. The purpose of *Le Grand Balcon*—the brothel, the House of Illusions—is primarily, by means of its multiple mirrors, to enable the individual to perceive his function as separate from himself—a feat of which the Revolutionaries in the outer world are incapable—and thus to enable its original possessor to re-assume it lucidly and consciously, by act of will. So finally he may be permitted to establish at the last his own identity : his absoluteness, his sanctity.

These arguments, however, are no more than a small part of the tangle of metaphysical dialectic which weaves its way in and out of the various tableaux in *The Balcony*. The bulk of the play is in fact concerned mainly with two subsidiary issues, the first of which determines the evolution of that enigmatical, and in places downright obscure, symbolic figure, the Chief of Police, while the second constitutes Genet's most categorical statement about the nature of politics—*all* politics, not excluding the socialist or revolutionary variety—and explains his attitude towards them.

In the first, Genet argues that a function is not detachable, and therefore cannot be consciously re-assumed in such a way as to form an authentic identity, until it has been granted the status of a symbol in popular imagination. (It is because the major functions of society have the status of symbols that they are sacred, consequently erotic, and thus finally come to constitute the dream-situations of the Brothel.) Furthermore, Genet argues, any such symbol of a function, by virtue of the very fact that it *is* eventually detached from the living, if negative, identity that gives it reality, is *dead*. The Grand Balcony, in Madame Irma's definition, is a House of Illusions; but, much more pertinently, it is also a Mausoleum; it is Hell, Hades, the buried Underworld[47]; it is the dwelling of the Dead 'I dragged you . . .' begins Roger to Chantal after he has rescued her from the Brothel to lead the Revolution; and Chantal herself completes the sentence : '. . . from the grave'.[48]

The struggles of the Chief of Police to detach his functional image from his own identity, and to give it independent status as a symbol in one of the Salons of the Grand Balcony form the main theme of the latter part of the play—with what purpose it is not particularly clear, since there is no evident reason why the functions of the Police should be less easily detachable, as a separate entity, than are those of General, or Fireman, or for that matter Housewife, all of which have been granted their special Salons, their ritual and their devotees in the Brothel already; nor is it at all clear how, or for what reason, the Chief of Police finally succeeds in his ambition. Admittedly, by crushing the insurrection, he becomes the image of Death, and thus more in keeping with the atmosphere of the Brothel, that house of dead symbols—'I'll have my tomb, Irma !'[49]—but the dialectic is specious and unconvincing, and in places even trite in its rather unimaginative symbolism, reminiscent of the duller necrological passages in *Pompes Funèbres*.

By contrast, the argument which presents the function-symbol itself as the image of Death is of a different quality altogether, and shows Genet's dialectic taking the same resentfully anti-committed and anti-political direction as that of Orwell or Ionesco.

In the background, we must always remember the poet's insoluble dilemma in the twentieth century : he is first and foremost an artist in words, words are the means by which he has learned to communicate the most intimate truths of his heart and his experience, his convictions and beliefs, his vision of creation. But communication is one thing, mass-communication is another. Mass-communication debases, vulgarises, simplifies, distorts, corrodes, corrupts and eventually—if the propaganda-machine is efficient enough, and the situation favourable—kills; yet all the time, it uses nothing but words, the same words as the poet is using to fashion his unique and crystalline dream of perfection. There are, in fact, two languages, with a single vocabulary between them : the language of the poet and the language of the mass-persuaders. And more and more frequently, we shall find the poet recoiling in horror, not so much from the vulgarization of his language by the mass, as from its deliberate abuse and distortion by the politicians, the journalists and the ad-men.

This fact alone is enough to suggest why so many serious poets and writers of our time tend to opt out of politics—it certainly explains why Genet, who adores the individualistic and highly-coloured *argot* of the masses, is repelled by the jargon of socialism. It is senseless to argue that the poet should not make social and political judgements in terms of aesthetics; if he did not make them in terms of aesthetics, he would not be a poet—unless he were sufficiently objective, sufficiently master of his own reactions, to keep his politics and his art a world apart and, like Alain Robbe-Grillet, live a committed life while writing uncommitted literature. Or else, like the pop artists of recent years, deliberately exploit the slogans of the ad-mass with a full, wry and sardonic perception of their bogus blatancy.

No such degree of sophisticated objectivity is to be expected from Jean Genet. For him, the dead language of politics and the living language of poetry are mortal enemies, and the latter can only survive if it rejects the former. (This attitude will perhaps be modified slightly, but only slightly, in *The Screens*.) And the obsessive death-theme of *The Balcony* is, at bottom, a carefully-argued case for the poet's right to reject propaganda, even in the most deserving of political causes.

For Genet, as we have seen, the most vital and living of all experiences are those which are symbolic; yet the Grand Balcony, that house of symbols, is designated as the House of the Dead. The reason is that the symbols which form the substance of Madame Irma's pageantry are the product of a *mass*-imagination. They are *functional* symbols, the emblem, not of man, but of man-in-society. They are the end-product of a series of acts, each one of which is designed, not to accomplish an object, but to produce an image for mass-consumption. As the Chief of Police puts it to the three Grotesques : '. . . You've never performed an act for its own sake, but always so that, when linked with other acts, it would make you a bishop, a judge, a general. . . .'[50] To some extent, of course, the same criticism could be made of Divine; but Divine, when she performed the ritualistic and purposeless gestures that gave her the appearance of a boxer or a cyclist, did it for her own satisfaction or salvation; never for mass-communication, power or profit. And between the individual and the mass lies all the difference between life and death. The symbolism of the individual lies in the gesture, and the gesture itself, even in *The Balcony*, is equated with life; the symbol of the mass, by contrast, is the Uniform.

Recalling that Genet, for the greater part of his early life, was obliged to wear uniforms of one sort of another, his preoccupation with the subject becomes understandable. In fact, however, it is not until *Querelle of Brest* that the theme is worked out in any detail. At least five of the characters in *Querelle of Brest*—Querelle himself, Mario, Gil, Dédé and Lt Seblon—are at one time or another deeply puzzled by the implications of wearing a uniform, whether it is their own or somebody else's. Here, the uniform itself becomes a symbol of power, the organized power of the mass which can envelop and protect the individual. At first, this power seems friendly. Dédé shelters behind the power symbolized in the police-uniform worn by Mario,[51] Lt Seblon finds, in his naval épaulettes, some evidence of his own authenticity[52]; Gil finds both invisibility and a new personality in the blue trousers and red-pompom'd beret stolen for him by Querelle.[53] But at the same time, the wearing of a uniform submerges the individual in a ritual—a complex and inhuman ceremonial. It transforms him from an individual into a symbol, it abolishes his singularity and makes him a *personnage fabuleux*, endowed with all the secret force of the Great Universals. Lt Seblon sees Querelle as THE Sailor; but Querelle himself goes further, and thinks of himself, no longer as a human being, but as a ship, the very incarnation of the whole function of the Navy :

> His body was fitted with guns, iron-clad, armed with torpedoes, easy to manœuvre though heavy enough in all conscience, bristling and bellicose. He was now LE QUERELLE, a huge destroyer, a greyhound of the ocean, a vast, intelligent, thrusting mass of metal.[54]

Gil, who is fleeing from the police, welcomes the chance which his uniform gives him, both to 'become invisible' to the eyes of his trackers, and also, more signficantly, 'to know all the pleasures and consolations, that the habitual wearing of it provides by way of assurance and the resulting abolition of self-consciousness.'[55] But, by the time of writing *The Balcony*, Genet's attitude has changed. The function of the robe or uniform is still the same : to permit the individual to 'abolish himself', and to dissolve into the *'fascinating image'* of some traditional symbol of power.[56] However, the emphasis is now very different. The individual and his symbolic function (his uniform) still correspond to Figure and mirror-Image; but the mirror-Image is now seen to be detachable, and to take its reality exclusively from the *mass*, observing it and giving it significance. In other words, the original double (Figure + Image) that composed the Total Man is now destroyed, and a new and this time wholly abstract double is created in its place : Image (uniform) + anonymous mass. But the anonymous mass is itself an unreality, an abstract concept. The new double, therefore, is composed of two unrealities, and together they make up a new totality : the Totality of Death.

Moreover, the Image-symbol which is observed and given meaning by the mass is *static*. When the individual gestured into the mirror, the mirror-image responded : it moved, it was—in appearance at least—alive. But the power-symbol is immutable and dead. The mirror is temporary in its reflections; the function is permanent. Thus, in *The Balcony*, the mirrors which had dominated the opening tableaux gradually give way to the Photographers, who fix their images on film for all eternity : emblematic, unchanging, outside time.[57] Consequently, in so far as the uniform bears any real relationship to the individual who has abolished himself within it, this relationship can only become authentic when the individual himself is outside time and static . . . that is, yet once again, when he has left the living and finally joined the dead :

> *The General:* If I went through wars without dying [. . . .] it was for this minute close to death [. . . .] where I shall be nothing, though reflected *ad infinitum* in these mirrors, nothing but my image [. . . .] It is indeed a descent into the grave. . . .
> *The Girl:* But, Sir, you've been dead since yesterday.
> *The General:* I know . . . but a formal and picturesque descent, by unexpected stairways. . . .
> *The Girl:* You are a dead general, but an eloquent one.
> *The General: Because* I'm dead, prating horse. What is now speaking, and so beautifully, is Example. I am now only the image of my former self. . . .[58]

It is significant that this passage which I have quoted occurs still fairly near the beginning of the play. As the drama progresses, so does the argument, and the later scenes deal with a different aspect of the problem altogether.

The function-symbol, as we have seen, cannot change, cannot move as the mirror-image can move; none the less, it can operate—that is, like a motion-picture opposed to a still, it can go through a series of photographically-stereotyped gestures, repeatable *ad infinitum* and without meaning in themselves; unalterable, unless the film itself is changed. It operates, in the fullest sense of the word, as a ritual, a sacred and immutable series of ceremonial gestures. But at the same time, since it is the embodiment of a *power*, it must transmit or exercise that power; it is not enough that, by the effect of an illusion, it should create out of static poses an appearance of movement, of life; it must, quite literally, function. This means that such ritual acts will and must eventually become political acts. And so, in the latter scenes of the play, the symbolic Bishop, Judge and General become active political figures in reality, wielding power and dominating the lives of others. Yet they are still dead, still essentially *unreal*, for all that :

> *The Bishop:* ... We're going to have to act.
> *The Queen:* Act? You? You mean to say you're going to strip him of his power? [*Variant*]
> *The Judge:* We have to fulfil our functions, don't we?[59]

In other words, he who takes on the appearance of a function-symbol is trapped. For, as the Bishop puts it, the symbol is power, and power *will* act. As with the Sorcerer's Apprentice, the obedient fetish, once set in action, cannot be stopped until it is finally broken, and this will happen only when the mass ceases to believe in it, and thus dissolves its reality. Even the Queen, who called the symbols into being originally, cannot now call them back into limbo by an act of will.[60] The only choice, then, is whether the function-symbol acts to the advantage or to the detriment of the *status quo*. This is the '*question très sérieuse*' which the Bishop asks the Queen :

> *The Bishop:* . . . are you going to use what we represent, or are we going to use you to serve what we represent?[61]

The only possible retreat from the dangerous power of a mass-symbol which has begun to function with terrifying automatism in reality is to attempt to make it revert to its original status as a pure symbol—that is, to withdraw it from the eyes of the political mass, and to place it immutably in front of the mirror, where, to all eternity, it can observe and realize itself. This is the nostalgia for a lost paradise which haunts the three Grotesques all through their active political career. The ultimate perfection of a function-symbol is one which has only the *appearance* of a purpose, and has finally abandoned its vocation to function in reality. It is a power-symbol which is *sterile* . . . which brings us back to the Grand Balcony, the Brothel, with its sterile whores and its sterile mirrors, to which, amid the devastation of the play's end, the various characters return.

Thus, even in *The Balcony*, Genet's aestheticism, his search for the Absolute, triumphs. Politics are the domain of dead symbols, of incomplete realities, which degrade the Absolute Beauty of their pure appearance by galvanizing themselves artificially into acts; and even these acts lead one and all to death. The Judge delivers to the Executioner, the General kills and is killed in battle, the Bishop assigns his sinners straight to Hell. Chantal, the most living of the whores, is killed; and only when she is thoroughly and irrevocably dead does

she appear on the insurrectionary banners, and 'wave in the Heaven
of the Revolt'. 'Tomorrow,' says the Envoy, 'they'll be ready to die
for Chantal alone'[62]; and in a later scene, he has no consolation to
offer the Queen in her complaint that it is she, not Chantal, who
should have filled the Heavens with her Image :

> *The Envoy:* You're on the postage-stamps, on the bank-notes, on the seals
> in the government offices [. . . .] Your Majesty can only be represented by
> an abstraction.
> *The Queen:* Will I therefore never be who I am?
> *The Envoy:* Never again. [. . . .]
> *The Queen:* Every event of my life—my blood that trickles if I scratch
> myself. . . .
> *The Envoy:* Quite, Madame. Each event will be written with a capital.
> And now. . . .
> *The Queen:* But that's Death?
> *The Envoy:* It is indeed.[63]

Ultimately, for Genet, the choice between the individual and the
mass is a choice between life and death; between beauty and horror,
between perfection and imperfection. The most abstract symbol of
beauty that Genet uses, both in the plays and in the novels, is the
Song. In *The Balcony*, both Chantal and Carmen are names with a
peculiar significance. 'In every revolution,' says Madame Irma, 'there
is a fanatical whore singing a *Marseillaise* and turning virgin
again.'[64] In spite of this, however, politics and art (the Song) are
incompatible. The insurgents, notes Irma again, 'are threatening,
but they no longer sing'.[65] Roger, the insurgent leader, confesses even
to Chantal that he cannot sing his love for her.[66] The *Marseillaise*,
in this context, is not a song, but a mass-symbol. When art and
politics come into contact, one or the other is doomed. For Genet,
there is no hesitation. It is politics which is doomed. Even the Chief
of Police, for all his insensitivity, understands this :

> *The Chief of Police:* The rebellion's riding high, it's moving out of this
> world. If it gives its sectors the names of constellations, it'll evaporate
> in no time, and be metamorphosed into song. Let's hope the songs are
> beautiful.
> *Irma:* And what if their songs give the rebels courage? What if they're
> willing to die for them?
> *The Chief of Police:* The beauty of their songs will make them soft. Un-
> fortunately, they haven't yet reached the point of either beauty or
> softness.[67]

In a political context, beauty—or poetry, or art—is impermissible.
Politics are concerned with relative situations and provisional solutions, never with the Absolute, the perfect. And for Genet, as we
have seen, only the Absolute has any value. Even in *The Maids*, the
essential injustice of the situation is aesthetic rather than social or

even moral : the conflict lies between the inherent ugliness of Claire and Solange, and the *'beauté des gestes de Madame'*. The final conclusion of *The Balcony*, then, is an indictment of political activity, a fundamental assertion of non-commitment. And yet—and this is the inescapable paradox that runs all through Genet's work—not only is *The Balcony* an undeniably political play, but both the dramas which follow it belong to the ranks of committed literature. Which brings us to the very core of Genet's disconcerting programme of committed anarchy : his refusal to accept any form of *categories*. All organized political activity—the sort of activity that invites commitment—is based on categories : on simplifications, slogans, groupings; there are left-categories, right-categories, revolutionary, reactionary, Stalinist, Trotskyist categories. And the slogan-categories of Socialism are, if possible, even more intractable, sweeping and unreal than those of the bourgeoisie. Genet's instinctive sympathies go to the oppressed; but only so long as they remain individuals. If Genet eschews commitment, it is because any party-programme transforms the individuals whom he loves into ad-mass-symbols which, as a poet, he despises and detests. It transforms the living into the dead. And so, for Genet, there is all the difference in the world between those who formulate the slogans of the revolution, and those who are *'debout dans la révolte'*—between the spiritual independence of the artist and the spiritual enslavement of the well-disciplined Party-Member.

NOTES

1 *Thief*, pp. 87-8. (*Journal*, p. 105)
2 *Q. of B.*, p. 11. 'Toute la journée ils ont vraiment travaillé [. . . .], confondant leurs gestes, les enchevêtrant, les complétant l'un par l'autre aux fins d'une oeuvre qui en sera le noeud visible et serré.' (*Querelle*, p. 175)
3 *Ibid.*, p. 11. 'Le soldat, qu'il soit matelot ou fantassin, n'a jamais le sentiment d'avoir travaillé.' (*Querelle*, p. 175)
4 *Our Lady*, p. 215. '. . . le monde entier—et le plus terriblement morne de lui-même, le plus noir, calciné, sec jusqu'au jansénisme, le monde sévère et nu des ouvriers d'usine—est entortillé [de ces merveilles qui sont les chansons populaires. . . .].' (*Notre-Dame*, p. 108)
5 This is confirmed by the historical records of Inspector Bony's French-recruited Gestapo during the Occupation.
6 *Our Lady*, p. 309. '. . . qui aimait sa mère comme il était patriote et catholique.' (*Notre-Dame*, p. 169)
7 *Rose*, p. 106. (*Miracle*, p. 262)
8 *Ibid.*, p. 170-1. (*Miracle*, p. 308)
9 *Ibid.*, p. 114. 'J'ai horreur de la fraternité qui établit des contacts peau à peau.' (*Miracle*, p. 268)

10 *Ibid.*, p. 246. 'Je n'aime pas les opprimés. J'aime ceux que j'aime, qui sont toujours beaux et quelquefois opprimés mais debout dans la révolte'.

  In the *Journal*, Genet goes further still and describes how, now that he is no longer poor, he dreams of deliberately taunting with his wealth the riff-raff of beggars and down-and-outs whom he has left behind. *Thief*, p. 80. (*Journal*, p. 95)

11 *Rose*, pp. 32-3. 'Or, cette faim, qui d'abord aida au désenchantement de la prison, voici qu'elle devient si grande qu'elle est un élément tragique qui achève de couronner la Centrale d'un motif baroque et sauvage, d'un chant sonore plus fou que les autres.' (*Miracle*, p. 209; see also pp. 234-235, 325)

12 *Q. of B.*, p. 107. '. . . dans la région la plus asociale de notre âme.' (*Querelle*, p. 233)

13 *Thief*, p. 8. '. . . par la révolte ni la revendication jamais commandée.' (*Journal*, p. 10. Cf. pp. 13, 174)

14 Omitted in the English edition of *The Balcony*. '. . . son képi étoilé ou cerclé de feuilles de chênes.' (*Balcon*—*C.J.L. Bal.*, p. 9)

15 *Balcony*, p. 50. 'Roger. Le plombier. Tu l'imagines comment? Jeune, beau? Non. Quarante ans. Trapu. L'oeil ironique et grave.' (*Balcon*, p. 109)

16 Omitted in the English edition of *The Balcony*. 'Il faudra inventer le type révolutionnaire, puis le peindre ou modeler sur un masque, car je ne vois personne, même parmi les protestants lyonnais, ayant le visage assez long, assez triste et assez farouche pour jouer ce rôle.' (*Balcon*—*C. J. L. Bal.*, p. 9)

17 *Our Lady*, p. 134. (*Notre-Dame*, p. 56)

18 *Cf.*, for instance, the controversy raised here and there by John Antrobus' play: *You'll come to love your sperm-test*.

19 'Je ne sais ce que sera le théâtre dans un monde socialiste, je comprends mieux ce qu'il serait chez les Mau-Mau.' (*Pauvert*, p. 147)

20 *Ibid.*, 'Si l'on a choisi de se regarder mourir délicieusement, il faut poursuivre avec rigueur, et les ordonner, les symboles funèbres. Ou choisir de vivre et découvrir l'Ennemi. Pour moi, l'Ennemi ne sera jamais nulle part.'

21 *Balcony*, pp. 49-50. (*Balcon*, pp. 106-7)

22 *Ibid*, p. 7: the opening speech of the play. 'Ce n'est pas tant la douceur ni l'onction qui devraient définir un prélat, mais la plus rigoureuse intelligence. Le coeur nous perd. Nous croyons être maître de notre bonté : nous sommes l'esclave d'une sereine mollesse.' (*Balcon*, pp. 12-13)

23 *Ibid.*, 'C'est même d'autre chose encore que d'intelligence qu'il s'agit. . . . Ce serait de cruauté. Et par delà cette cruauté—et par elle—une démarche habile, vigoureuse, vers l'Absence. Vers la Mort. Dieu?' (*Balcon*, p. 13)

24 *Ibid.*, p. 61. (*Balcon*, p. 120): 'A sweet and deadly kindness.'

25 Omitted in English version of *The Maids*. 'L'érotisme individuel, au théâtre, ravale la représentation.' (*Bonnes*—*C.J.L.B.*, p. 9)

26 *Balcony*, p. 33. 'La plus savante, mais la plus honnête maison d'illusions.' (*Balcon*, p. 71)

27 *Ibid.*, p. 31. (*Balcon*, p. 67)

28 *Ibid.*, p. 36. (*Balcon*, pp. 78-9) (The last item is omitted in the English version.)

29 *Ibid.*, p. 46. (*Balcon*, pp. 100-101)

30 *Ibid.*, p. 37. (*Balcon*, pp. 80-81)
31 *Ibid.*, p. 11.
    '*L'Evêque:* . . . Répondez donc, miroir, répondez-moi. Est-ce je viens ici découvrir le mal et l'innocence? Et dans vos glaces dorées, qu'étais-je? Je n'ai jamais, je l'atteste devant Dieu qui me voit, je n'ai jamais désiré le trône épiscopal. Devenir évêque, monter les échelons—à force de vertus ou de vices—c'eût été m'éloigner de la dignité définitive d'évêque. Je m'explique : pour devenir évêque, il eût fallu que je m'acharne à ne l'être pas, mais à faire ce qui m'y eût conduit. Devenu évêque, afin de l'être, il eût fallu—afin de l'être pour moi, bien sûr—il eût fallu que je ne cesse de me savoir l'être pour remplir ma fonction.' (*Balcon*, p. 21)
32 *Our Lady*, p. 130. (*Notre-Dame*, p. 53)
33 The text is altered almost unrecognizably in the English translation. (*Bonnes*, p. 23)
34 Omitted in English version of *The Balcony*. '. . . la glorification de l'Image et du Reflet.' (*Balcon— C. J. L. Bal.*, p. 10)
35 *Balcony*, pp. 11-12.
    '*L'Evêque:* . . . une fonction est une fonction. Elle n'est pas un mode d'être. Or, évêque, c'est un mode d'être. C'est une charge. Un fardeau. Mitres, dentelles, tissus d'or et de verroteries, génuflexions. . . . Aux chiottes la fonction! [. . . .] Je veux être évêque dans la solitude, pour la seule apparence. . . . Et pour détruire toute fonction, je veux apporter le scandale, et te trousser, putain, putasse, pétasse et poufiasse.' (*Balcon*, pp. 21-22)
36 This also seems as though it might be a direct reply to Sartre, who, in *Saint Genet*, had argued that the good was a reflection of *l'Etre*, and therefore preceded the bad, which was a reflection of *le Néant*.
37 *Balcony*. pp. 15.
    '*Le Juge:* Ecoute : il faut que tu sois une voleuse modèle, si tu veux que je sois un juge modèle. Fausse voleuse, je deviens faux juge. C'est clair?' (*Balcon*, p. 30)
38 *Ibid.*, p. 97. (*Balcon*, pp. 176-7) (Abbreviated in the English version.)
39 *Ibid.*, pp. 72-3. (*Balcon*, p. 142)
40 *Thief*, p. 12. 'Mon trouble semble naître de ce qu'en moi j'assume à la fois le rôle de victime et de criminel.' (*Journal*, p. 16)
41 *Our Lady*, p. 92. (*Notre-Dame*, p. 29)
42 *Thief*, p. 194. 'J'aime secrètement, oui j'aime la police.' (*Journal*, p. 231)
43 *Ibid.*, pp. 168-9. 'Le monde des policiers est un univers informe, mouvant, vaporeux, sans cesse se créant, élémentaire et fabuleux [. . . .] une puissance sacrée, agissant directement sur mon âme, me troublant.' (*Journal*, p. 200)
44 *Q. of B.*, p. 42. (*Querelle*, p. 192)
45 *Ibid.*, p. 45. (*Querelle*, p. 194)
46 *Ibid.*, p. 289. 'Mario n'était plus qu'un policier, mais l'étant sans son contraire (c'est-à-dire sans ce contre quoi le policier luttait) il l'était moins. Il ne pouvait l'être qu'à l'extérieur de soi, en s'opposant au monde qu'il combattait.' (*Querelle*, pp. 331-2)
47 *Balcony*, pp. 17, 20, 31, etc. (*Balcon*, pp. 35, 41, 66, etc.)
48 *Ibid.*, p. 64. The whole of Scene VI is radically different in the English version.
    '*Chantal:* Je sais : tirée d'un tombeau.' (*Balcon*, p. 118)
49 *Ibid.*, p. 47. 'J'aurai mon tombeau, Irma !' (*Balcon*, p. 103)

50 *Ibid.*, p. 97.
 '*Le Chef de Police:* Vous n'avez donc jamais accompli un acte pour l'acte lui-même, mais toujours pour que cet acte, accroché à d'autres, fasse un évêque, un juge, un général. . . .' (*Balcon*, p. 176)

51 *Q. of B.*, p. 64. (*Querelle*, p. 206)

52 *Ibid.*, p. 314. 'Son sentiment d'avoir une réalité grâce à la rigueur d'un ordre sans lequel son grade ni son autorité n'agiraient.' (*Querelle*, p. 347) (The English text gives a quite different sense to this passage.)

53 *Ibid.*, p. 254. (*Querelle*, p. 319)

54 *Ibid.*, p. 41. 'Son corps s'armait de canons, de coques d'acier, de torpilles, d'un équipage agile et lourd, belliqueux et précis. Querelle devenait *le Querelle*, destroyer géant, écumeur de mer, masse métallique, intelligente et butée.' (*Querelle*, p. 192)

55 *Ibid.*, p. 256. '. . . de s'abolir dans une profonde quiétude par le charme d'un appareil rituel.' (*Querelle*, p. 320)

56 *Balcony*, p. 91. (*Balcon*, p. 166)

57 *Ibid.*, pp. 85-88. (*Balcon*, pp. 157-173)

58 *Ibid.*, pp. 25-6.
 '*Le Général:* Si j'ai traversé des guerres sans mourir [. . . .] c'était pour cette minute proche de la mort [. . . .] où je ne serai rien, mais reflétée à l'infini dans ces miroirs, que mon image [. . . .] C'est bien d'une descente au tombeau qu'il s'agit.
 La Fille: Mais mon général, vous êtes mort depuis hier.
 Le Général: Je sais . . . mais d'une descente solennelle, et pittoresque, par d'inattendus escaliers. . . .
 La Fille: Vous êtes un général mort, mais éloquent.
 Le Général: Parce que mort, cheval bavard. Ce qui parle, et d'une si belle voix, c'est l'Exemple. Je ne suis plus que l'image de celui que je fus.' (*Balcon,* pp. 54-5)

59 *Ibid.*, p. 90.
 '*L'Evêque:* Il va falloir agir.
 La Reine: Agir? Vous? Vous voulez dire que vous allez nous déposséder de notre pouvoir?
 Le Juge: Il faut bien que nous remplissions nos fonctions.' (*Balcon*, pp. 164-5)

60 *Ibid.*, pp. 93-4. (*Balcon*, p. 170)

61 *Ibid.*, p. 93.
 '*L'Evêque* . . . allez-vous vous servir de ce que nous représentons, ou bien nous . . . allons-nous vous faire servir ce que nous représentons?' (*Balcon*, p. 169)

62 *Ibid.*, p. 76.
 '*L'Envoyé:* Demain, c'est pour Chantal qu'on se fera tuer.' (*Balcon*, p. 146)

63 *Ibid.*, pp. 99-101. This section of the text contains important variants.
 '*L'Envoyé:* Vous êtes déjà sur les timbres-poste, sur les billets de banque, sur les cachets des commissariats.
 La Reine: Je ne serai donc jamais qui je suis?
 L'Envoyé: Jamais plus.
 Le Reine: Chaque événement de ma vie: mon sang qui perle si je m'égratigne. . . .
 L'Envoyé: Tout s'écrira pour vous avec une majuscule.
 La Reine: Mais c'est la Mort?
 L'Envoyé: C'est Elle.' (*Balcon*, pp. 174-5)

64 Omitted in the English version of *The Balcony*. 'Dans toute révolution il y a la putain exaltée qui chante une *Marseillaise* et se virginise.' (*Balcon*, p. 83)

65 *Balcony*, p. 49. '. . . sont menaçants mais ils ne chantent pas.' (*Balcon*, p. 107)

66 *Balcon*, p. 124. Omitted in English text.

67 *Balcony*, p. 50.

> '*Le Chef de Police:* La révolte s'exalte et s'exile ici-bas. Si elle donne à ses secteurs des noms de constellations, elle va vite s'évaporer et se métamorphoser en chants. Souhaitons-les beaux.
>
> *Irma:* Et si leurs chants donnent aux révoltés du courage? Et qu'ils veuillent mourir pour eux?
>
> *Le Chef de Police:* La beauté de leurs chants les amollira. Malheureusement, ils n'en sont pas à ce stade, ni de la beauté, ni de la mollesse.' (*Balcon*, p. 109)

9

POLITICS WITHOUT PLATITUDES

(*The Blacks* and *The Screens*)

> *Quand la vérité n'est pas libre, la*
> *liberté n'est pas vraie.*
> Jacques Prévert

> *Il n'est pas permis, de notre temps,*
> *de ne pas haïr; toute charité est*
> *interdite. La pire des fautes est de*
> *succomber à la tentation de la bonté.*
> Eugène Ionesco

Genet's aestheticism emerges victorious from *The Balcony*. His rejection of politics is a refusal to accept the abuse of language, however progressive the cause in which the abuse is perpetrated. The mass-symbolism of propaganda is the dead, the *ersatz* replica of symbolism in the individual, which is the gateway to the eternal. The imagery of the mass is always false : there is no essential difference in this respect between the Swastika and the Croix-de-Lorraine, between Judas and Joan of Arc, between Madame Irma and Chantal. In politics there is neither good nor bad, right nor wrong; there are merely death and lies. The Envoy does his best to justify the inevitable lies of the professional politician, on the traditional ground that the end justifies the means : 'It is a true representation of a fake incident,' he argues. But Genet's own opinion is clear enough from the reply of the First Photographer, who is only too eager to agree :

First Photographer: That's common practice, your Majesty. When some rebels were captured, we paid a militiaman to bump off a man I'd just sent to buy me a packet of cigarettes. The photo shows a rebel shot down while trying to escape.

The Queen: Monstrous!

The Envoy: But have things ever happened otherwise? History was lived so that a glorious page might be written, and then read. It's reading that counts.[1]

Genet's attitude, then, as defined in *The Balcony*, is one of belligerent non-commitment. Yet one has only to compare his plays with those of another belligerent in the same cause, Eugène Ionesco, to realize that something is very wrong with this definition. There is a 'right-wing anarchism' (Ionesco's own phrase[2]), and an anarchism of the left—and it is to the latter that Genet seems to belong. It is to the conventional *platitudes* of politics that Genet objects, not to politics in themselves. Were it possible to present a political and social ideology other than in terms of a dead or moribund mass-symbolism, the case might appear very different. Politics deal in goodies and baddies; art, with truth only, irrespective of moral categories. If it were possible to present a revolutionary political programme in terms of individual realities, instead of an ideology compounded of abstractions and categorical imperatives—in brief, a socialism without slogans, without platitudes and without heroes—then Genet might adhere. Or rather, not adhere, for there would be nothing positive enough to adhere to. But, as an individual and an artist, take part. And this in fact seems to be the aim of Genet's last two plays, *Les Nègres (The Blacks)* and *Les Paravents (The Screens)* : to present, by purely emotional and artistic means, a case against society on behalf of the outcasts and the oppressed, in which the conventional role of goodies and baddies is reversed. Mass-symbols—the functional platitudes of politics—are composed of mass moral judgements, above all on the left. 'Often, alas,' laments Ionesco, 'the most detestable kind of bourgeois is the anti-bourgeois kind of bourgeois'[3]; similarly, there is no puritanism more obstinately puritanical than that of the traditional anti-puritan, or thorough-going militant marxist. Reverse this traditional pattern, and there is a chance—a remote one, perhaps, but it appears to be the only possibility—of abstracting the ideal of Revolution from the dead hand of an *a-priori* mass-morality. And so Genet carefully allocates the Good (such as it is) to the Right, and Evil to the Left—and then places all his art and all his sympathy in the service of the latter. It is the Missionary who preaches goodness, Sir Harold who personifies order and prosperity, Monsieur Blankensee whose life is dedicated to beauty. It is Saïd who is abject and treacherous, Village who is murderous, Malika and Warda and Virtue (a touching misnomer) who are whores. In this topsy-turvydom of values, the banality and boredom which are the hall-marks of so much of the right-thinking Left disintegrate, and Art and Revolution are perhaps, for an instant, reconciled. This is the apotheosis of the anti-hero.

The Blacks

To turn to *The Blacks* (1958) after the metaphysical jigsaw-puzzles of *The Balcony* is a refreshing experience. Explicit metaphysical argumentation rarely has a place in the drama because, as we have seen, it is fundamentally undramatic, in form if not in content. The genius of Paul Claudel managed to find a place for it, but only by refashioning his whole dramatic structure to correspond to the intricate and fluctuating patterns of his dialectic. But if there is one type of drama which, more than any other, is inappropriate for working out themes as complex as that of the theory of reciprocal functions, it is surely any drama in the tradition of Brecht or Artaud, where the aim is precisely to diminish the significance of rational language. *The Blacks* makes no such mistake. Its structure is that of a total theatre—that is, of a theatre employing *all* media which can contribute to the dramatic impact of the spectacle : it uses music, dance, rhythm and ritual; it contrasts masks and faces, illusion and reality; it employs different levels, exploiting a multiplicity of stage-dimensions—it is perhaps the finest realization to date of that ideal which Artaud referred to as 'poetry in space'. It borrows its techniques from the jazz-band and the jam-session, from the church service, from the music-hall (Archibald's role as compère to his troupe is practically a parody of the traditional Mister Interlocutor who accompanied the Edwardian Nigger Minstrel shows), from the circus, and even, in the episodes of orchestrated laughter, from some nightmarish Albert Hall, in which the rehearsal of the Hoffnung Festival Choir has got mixed up with the stylized, cadenced mockery of an Aristophanic chorus. In such a context, the chief function and dramatic value of language is as a medium of incantation; the words sway and pulsate like African dancers, and their very sound is hypnotic, hallucinatory and cruel. Their meaning is rarely more than a contributory factor to their physical impact : it is the simple *motif*—perhaps only three or four notes of a scale—on which a Miles Davis, a Bix Beiderbecke, will weave his patterns of primitive colour and sophisticated violence. The theme 'Livid . . .' for instance : Virtue's *Litany of the Livid*—

Livid as a t.b. death-rattle,
Livid as the droppings of a man with jaundice,
Livid as the belly of a cobra,
Livid as their convicts,
Livid as the god they nibble in the morning,
Livid as a knife in the night,
Livid . . . except: the English, Germans and Belgians,
    who are red . . . livid as jealousy.
Hail, the livid![4]

—or the old, familiar theme of abjection, as it is transformed when Snow pours out her whole pent-up frenzy of contempt for Village:

If I were sure that Village bumped the woman off in order to heighten the fact that he's a scarred, smelly, thick-lipped, snub-nosed negro, an eater and guzzler of Whites and all other colours, a drooling, sweating, belching, spitting, coughing, farting goat-f——r, a licker of white boots, a good-for-nothing, sick, oozing oil and sweat, limp and submissive, if I were sure he killed her in order to merge with the night. . . . But I know he loved her.[5]

The comparison between *The Blacks* and the improvisations of a negro jazz-band is not merely suggested by the common racial origins of the performers. Genet has rejected the whole traditional structure, intellectual, logical and conceptual, of the European theatre—the time-honoured techniques that Artaud refers to as 'a theatre of idiots, madmen, inverts, grammarians, grocers, anti-poets and positivists—in short, Westerners!'[6] and which Ionesco has dubbed a detective-story drama:

Choubert: Every play that has ever been written, from ancient times to the present day, has never been anything else but a detective story. The theatre has never been anything but realistic and detectivistic. Every play is a police-enquiry leading to a satisfactory solution. There is a puzzle, which is solved for us in the closing scene. Sometimes earlier. One searches . . . one discovers.[7]

Instead, Genet has constructed a play which has much more in common with music than with normal drama, where representation has given way to abstraction, and the aim of convincing an audience assumed to be intellectual has been replaced by that of rousing it to a state of mystical or hysterical delirium by means which the High-Priest shares with the demagogue, and the jazz-band with the snake-charmer. Yet the final effectiveness of the play lies in the fact that it is not by any means devoid of ideas. The dialectic is there, as ingenious as in everything else that Genet has written, but it is conveyed by implication rather than by statement: it can be thought about, argued about after the performance is over; but not while it is in progress.

Given such a concept of the play as a whole, it is obviously not to be expected that *The Blacks* should tell a coherent story in the manner of *Deathwatch* or *The Maids*. It has a theme, the theme of Black and White, and this theme is worked out in an intricate series of variations, constantly changing in tone and tempo, but never in mood, for the mood is hatred. Only when Black and White, for a few fleeting instants, are not directly confronted is the all-permeating hatred transformed into its identical-opposite : love. But when this does happen, when Village and Virtue come together in the interludes between more serious matters, Genet reveals a strain of lyrical tenderness and deeply-moving intimacy which, coming as it does between man and woman, and replacing the sexual brutalities and the symbolic idealisms of Mettray or Fontevrault, is perhaps the greatest surprise of the play :

> *Village:* But if I take your hands in mine? If I put my arms around your shoulders—let me—if I hug you?
> *Virtue:* All men are like you : they imitate. Can't you invent something else?
> *Village:* For you I could invent anything : fruits, brighter words, a two-wheeled wheelbarrow, cherries without pits, a bed for three, a needle that doesn't prick. But gestures of love, that's harder . . . still, if you really want me to. . . .
> *Virtue:* I'll help you.[8]

This particular surprise, however, is reserved for the specialist or the student of Genet. For the audience, the element of surprise implicit in the normal sources of dramatic tension, the *enigma* as Choubert calls it, is replaced by a structure which gradually reveals itself as having significance on different and unsuspected levels. The actors, of course, are basically Negro actors—in the original Paris production, a troupe called Les Griots. Compèred by Archibald, they are introduced as a group of Negroes with ordinary, everyday backgrounds, but now come together to produce an entertainment—*une clownerie* :

> *Archibald:* When we leave this stage, we are involved in your life. I am a cook, this lady is a sewing-maid, this gentleman is a medical student, this gentleman is a curate at St Anne's, this lady . . . skip it. Tonight, our sole concern will be to entertain you. So we have killed this white woman.[9]

The murdered White Woman lies entombed on the stage in a white draped, flower-covered catafalque, and around this, the third dimension of illusion is developed : the rhythms, rituals and ceremonies of hatred and murder. Meanwhile, high up in their gallery, five Negroes masked as Whites : the Queen, the Missionary, the Valet, the Governor and the Judge, provide a fourth dimension—

an audience for the *clownerie* of the others. But what, precisely, *is* this audience? For those below them on the stage, Archibald, Village and Virtue, Snow and Bobo and Diouf, the Court both is and is not an audience : it watches them, listens to them, applauds them, yet it is composed of actors *acting* an audience. It is also a chorus. It is also, in symbolic form, the Enemy. And so the play develops for over half its length, working out permutations and combinations with the elusive material of dimensions, of plays-within-plays and audiences-within-audiences, until suddenly, with the dramatic entry of Ville de Saint-Nazaire,[10] the whole delicate structure collapses with the revelation of a new dimension still : this time, a play-*outside*-the-play. Ville de Saint-Nazaire is not concerned with any dream of love or murdered Whites; he is a *real* political agitator (but what in Heaven's name, by this time, *is* real?) who has been attending a secret meeting just up the street, at which, not a White, but another Negro, has been condemned to be liquidated for having betrayed the clandestine Society for Negro Rights. And meanwhile all the rest—actors, audience true or false, dimensions one to four, disintegrate into dreams : for the whole evening's *clownerie* was merely a deliberate diversion (as Archibald warned us at the beginning), a smoke-screen to keep our attention fixed while the Executive Committee got on with the job. The White Court strips off its masks, the rest strip off their personalities, and for an instant, they are any group of real Negroes having an urgent political discussion, with the ex-Valet, that erstwhile masked caricature of the bourgeois intellectual or artist in capitalist society, now revealed as the cell-leader, whose orders are obeyed instantaneously and without question. Eventually he commands the members of his cell or combat-section to take up their parts again, and to resume the *clownerie*—and we are back in the dimensions of illusion. But of course, the victory lies with Genet. For in the closing scenes, when we know that all that we are watching is merely an illusion, we forget, or half-forget, that the hard, political play-outside-the-play is even further from reality than the actors-acting-actors of the play itself. Or . . . is it? For in yet another dimension, there is more reality—immediate political reality this time—in the idea of an armed and organized Direct Action Committee of a Society for Negro Rights than there is in ritualistic dances about the imaginary catafalque of an imaginary murdered White. Which is real and which is illusion? Compared with *The Blacks*, Pirandello's experiments with the same problem seem almost childish. Ultimately— since there must be an end—the whole masked Court of Whites makes its way not unreluctantly towards the Infernal Regions, enveloped in a glittering rain of muddled colonialistic platitudes :

The Queen: Governor, lead off!

The Governor: Very well! Colonially speaking, I've served my country well *(He takes a swig of rum)*. I've been given a thousand nicknames, which proved the Queen's esteem and the savage's fear. [. . . .] Well, all right, take aim at this indomitable heart. I die childless . . . but I'm counting on your sense of honour to donate my bloodstained uniform to the Army Museum.[11]

Heaven forbid, of course, that we should take all this too seriously. After all, the idea that Black might conquer White is simply . . . ludicrous. It is, as Genet assures us so consolingly, only a *clownerie*. Perhaps. Or perhaps not. Not by accident does Genet arrange his fairy-tale so that the symbolic murder of the White Woman takes place to the strains of *Dies Irae*.[12]

Another parallel to the structure of *The Blacks*, with its fragmentation, its deliberate distortion, its semi-abstraction, its violence, above all its ferocity, is to be found in Picasso's *Guernica*. One should add also, in the intensity of its political implications and in the limited range of its colour. *The Blacks* is a *Guernica* in black-and-white. The emphasis, however, is on the black. Genet's sympathy for Negroes, as the scapegoats of *les salauds*—the dominant white bourgeoisie—goes back to *Our Lady of the Flowers*. On the one hand, he sees them as bearing the sacred stigma of all 'expiatory victims, whether goat, ox or child, and which kings and Jews still have today'[13]; on the other, he explains the traditional anti-social behaviour of the Negro in a White society as being, not innate, nor even an expression of resentment, but rather as an imitation of the Whites. Seck Gorgui, for instance, 'was naturally modest,' writes Genet in the early novel, 'but the whites had taught him immodesty, and in his zeal to be like them, he outdid them.'[14] In *Our Lady of the Flowers*, however, the barrier is not so much between Blacks and Whites, as between Establishment and outcasts; and among the latter, Blacks and Whites constitute an almost homogeneous community. But in *The Blacks*, Genet's symbolical two-worlds have become less personal, more specifically political. The characteristic of the Black is not his social status (there are at least two bourgeois occupations named among Archibald's troupe : preacher and medical student), but precisely his *blackness*. As Genet's thought develops, he comes more and more to visualize blackness and whiteness as contending Absolutes : individual Blacks may be coffee-coloured—*café nature, café turc, café au lait* or even *Nescafé* : 'But what exactly *is* a black? First of all, what's his colour?'[15]—but THE Black is black with an unqualified, undiluted, uncompromising blackness. His blackness is his function, just as the Bishop's mitre is his function in *The Balcony*. It is his symbol, his reality as it is designated by the Others. 'A Jew', maintains Sartre, dealing with a similar problem, 'is a man whom *other men* think of as a Jew'[16]; and elsewhere, in the same remarkable essay, he develops the theme : 'Anti-semitism [. . . .] is simultaneously a passion and a way of conceiving the world.'[17]

And just as the Jew, in an anti-semitic society, may insist upon and emphasize his Jewishness, as his only defence, his ultimate guarantee of authenticity, so Genet's Negroes blacken their already black faces with black boot-polish,[18] thus raising their status from the particular to the universal. 'My colour!' exclaims Snow (her antithetical name, like that of Virtue, merely emphasising her identity), 'Why, you're my very self!'[19] 'When I beheld you,' says Village of his first meeting with Virtue, 'you were wearing a black silk dress, black stockings, patent-leather pumps and were carrying a black umbrella.'[20] 'The tragedy will lie in the colour black,' proclaims Archibald,[21] thus summarizing the whole drama; and gradually the theme develops. Blackness becomes not merely one symbol among others; it determines the whole polarity of the play. 'I order you to be black,' intones Archibald, gravely, to Village, 'I order you to be black to your very veins. Pump black blood through them. Let Africa circulate in them'[22]—and with their colour, the Blacks, in their incantations, summon up and claim eternally as their own, all that goes with it : their savagery, their cruelty, their *odeurs* and their *oeil jaune*, their past of slavery, their heritage of Africa, culminating in a superb and terrifying tirade by Felicity, the goddess, the fertility-symbol, the Mother-Earth that has been and again shall be when all the earth is Black :

> Dahomey! Dahomey! To my rescue, Negroes, all of you! Gentlemen of Timbuctoo, come in, under your white parasols! Stand over there. Tribes covered with gold and mud, rise up from my body, emerge! [. . . .] Are you there, Africa with the bulging chest and oblong thigh? Sulking Africa, wrought of iron, in the fire, Africa of the millions of royal slaves, deported Africa, drifting continent, are you there?[23]

The corollary of this is the absolute, total and uncompromising rejection of all that is White. Whiteness, for Genet—to return to the specific and intuitive symbolism which we have discussed earlier[24]— is never associated with light. Likewise, in *The Blacks*, light, with all that it implies, aesthetically and mystically, is the product of darkness; for the dark precedes the light and contains its possibility, just as the darkness of Chaos covered the Waters and preceded the Creation, just as the night sky contains and makes visible the stars. 'We were Darkness in person,' declaims Felicity, 'Not the darkness which is absence of light, but the kindly and terrible Mother who contains light and deeds'.[25] The opposite of Black, therefore, is not just White, but White-without-radiance : pallor, absence; the colourlessness of Death and of the Void. Black is virility, white is effeminacy—a symbolism which probably enables Genet for the first time to dissociate the effeminate from the feminine, and to create such unforgettable female characters as Snow and Felicity, Bobo and Virtue.

White, then, is Death; and into the category of Death fall all the virtues of the Whites : civilization, politeness, culture, beauty, objectivity, humanitarianism . . . all the *'bonté des blancs'*; Archibald even refuses to allow Village to use the words 'my father', on the grounds that the very act of pronouncing the word veiled the cutting edge of his voice with 'a shade of tenderness'.[26] When Felicity summons up her cruel hordes of Africa, the White Queen replies with an invocation to all the Arts—all the products, past and present, of a pale-faced civilization :

> *The Queen:* To the rescue, angel of the flaming sword, virgins of the Parthenon, stained-glass of Chartres, Lord Byron, Chopin, French cooking, the Unknown Soldier, Tyrolean songs, heroic couplets, poppies, sunflowers, Aristotelian principles, a touch of coquetry; vicarage gardens. . . .[27]

Obviously, however, this clear-cut distinction, which pushes all beauty and all culture, all poetry even, resolutely into the arms of Death, poses something of a problem. Felicity, in spite of being Black and alive, has all the inspiration of a poetess, and it is interesting to note that perhaps the only memorable lines of formal verse that Genet has written in his life are those chanted by the Blacks during the scene of the ritual murder :

> 'Neige : *Expire, expire doucement,*
> *Notre-Dame des Pélicans,*
> *Jolie mouette, poliment,*
> *Galamment, laisse-toi torturer. . . .'*[28]

Above all, the lovers, Village and Virtue, find in each others' beauty an inescapable temptation. In every other respect, the Blacks reject the very concept of Beauty, as an alien convention, a gift as cruel as all other charity, condescendingly granted from above : a pretty disguise to hide the iron reality of economic slavery and exploitation. When Village describes the blackness of Virtue in poetic terms, Bobo objects; he is betraying his race, she argues, he has heard the siren-call of a White culture, he is the fifth-columnist by whose agency all will be lost. Not beauty, but vulgarity—a deliberate, defiant and hate-inspired vulgarity—is the symbol of the Blacks[29]; lilies and roses belong to the colonial oppressor; for themselves, 'soot and blacking, coal and tar'[30] are more appropriate emblems. Even Genet's obsessive colour-symbolism at last suffers a change under pressure

from this impulsive rejection of White beauty, and the many hues
of blue which had dominated the novels—from the blue of angels'
wings to the blue of Querelle's trousers—are now identified with the
effete, the intolerable, the dead or dying beauty that a white civilization imposes on its dark-skinned victims. The murdered 'White
Woman' is wearing 'a blue dress'; Snow, in the opening scene,
symbolizes the vindictiveness of the troupe by eating a blue iris off
the coffin; and in one of the strangest episodes of the play, Village,
making love to Virtue, against his will betrays the strength of the
temptation of beauty—*white* beauty—in his own soul, by addressing
her in a poetry where blue has taken the place of black :

> *Village:* The limpidity of your blue eyes, that tear gleaming at the corner,
> your heaven-blue bosom. . . .
> *Virtue:* You're raving. Whom are you talking to?
> *Village:* I love you and I can't bear it any longer.[31]

And yet . . . the fact, the *force* of love is there. 'I'm handsome,
you're beautiful, and we love each other',[32] says Village to Virtue.
This is perhaps the most poignant contradiction in *The Blacks* : that
it was the White man who invented love and the Black man who
now feels it; and consequently, that every stirring of the Black
man's heart must either remain silent, or else allow itself to be con-
taminated at source with a White vocabulary, a White imagery. This
is the cruellest domination of all, far crueller than an overt slavery.
The White man has not only stolen the Black man's land and his
liberty; he has stolen his poetry, stolen his power to love. Village
at first is afraid even to look at Virtue, in case she should be beautiful. . . . 'I fear you may be.'[33] But gradually he begins to see the
glimmerings of a solution. If it were possible to replace a 'White'
beauty by a specifically 'Black' beauty—even a beauty which, in
White eyes and in White words, was ugliness, even if it meant reversing the very order of a White-ordered universe—then the miracle
might be achieved, and freedom regained. At the end of the play,
Felicity takes up the same theme, in her reproaches to the Queen.
To the White man, all things white are beautiful; but to the
Black. . . .

> Whatever is gentle and kind and good and tender will be black. Milk
> will be black, sugar, rice, the sky, doves, hope, will be black.[34]

The love-idyll of Village and Virtue has a sound psychological
basis, as well as a political and metaphysical significance. All evidence points to the fact that the very concept of romantic love is a
European invention, and a comparatively recent one at that. It
originated in eleventh-century Provence; and even today, any
literature which is based on such a concept is to all intents and

purposes totally meaningless, say, to the Buganda tribesman, or in the remoter villages of Ghana. Thus the very fact that Village feels love for Virtue is the beginning of a betrayal.

But Genet, inevitably, works out the theme, not so much in terms of African psychology, as in terms of his own preoccupations. The dominant society of our time is still White; the Black, therefore, is its opposite, its mirror-image. 'But we—you and I,' says Village to Virtue, 'were moving along the edge of the world, out of bounds.'[35] The Black, then, *cannot* love : for love-in-the-mirror is the mirror-image of itself, its own opposite which is still itself—hate. A positive force such as love is impossible in a negative context. At first, Village refuses to accept this; his immediate reaction to being in love is violently to reject *both* worlds, Black and White, and to let his love flourish in absolute isolation.[36] But the strength required to reject all social pressures is superhuman, and Village is only human after all. Gradually, he comes to accept his own blackness, and with it, the realization that, to love Virtue, he must start by hating her absolutely, and see what comes of it :

> *Village:* I was unable to bear the weight of the world's condemnation. And I began to hate you [. . . .] The fact is, I hate you.[37]

In relation to each other, Village and Virtue are powerless; both are Black and their Blackness is negation, is nothing but a function of White. Its only chance of self-realization is to reverse the roles of Figure and Reflection. Only by destroying—conquering, dominating or absorbing—White, by asserting its *own* values against those of the conquerors, will Black become the Figure, and White be reduced to the part of Image-in-the-Mirror. Here, Virtue is better-placed than Village. As a prostitute whose customers are White, she has power over them, Delilah-power, the destructive power of woman's body over man's desire. 'She has powers that you haven't' comments Archibald to Village, 'there are times when she dominates the Whites'[38]—but Village is still tempted by his vision. Infuriated by this incipient betrayal of Blackness, Archibald—in a superbly dramatic scene—exiles both the lovers 'among the Whites' . . . that is, simply down among the audience, where they belong. In this crisis, it is Virtue again who takes the lead. If love is the very core and symbol of Whiteness, then she and Village have only two alternatives : either to go away and lose themselves for ever among the alien race; or else to 'love blackly', inventing a new love, a new language and formula of love, in spite of all the power, poetry and beauty of Europe. If they can achieve this, then not only will they realize themselves, but the secret power of the White world will be destroyed. Black victories, Black freedom, Black territorial gains are nothing while the key to the mysteries of the relationship between man and women remains White. For it is not the Missionaries who hold the key of Heaven, but those who have discovered the difference between *das ewig Weibliche* and a wife worth twenty head of cattle. Romeo, Tristan, Faust, Don Rodrigue, Swann . . . not a touch of the tar-brush among the pack of them.

That the realization of a Black love would constitute a fatal threat to the White man's supremacy, the Court realizes only too well. 'Damn it, they're going to gum up the works!' blusters the Governor[39]; and the Missionary chimes in : 'They've got to be prevented from continuing.'[40] But their fears, as yet, are premature. To create a Black love is not easy. Virtue tries, and fails . . . word by word, as she whispers her love to Village, a change comes over her : it is not love which is growing Black, but she who is growing White :

> Virtue: Oh noble pallor, colour my temples, my fingers, my belly! [. . . .]
> I am white, it's milk that symbolizes me, the lily, the dove, quicklime and the clear conscience, Poland with its Eagle and snow! Snow. . . .[41]

Village struggles on, but all in vain. Syllable by syllable he builds up his language of a Black beauty, and Felicity helps him with her 'Dahomey! . . . Dahomey! . . .'—but the pull of the other world is too great. As Village hesitates, Archibald and Snow come to him with a challenge : to overcome love with hate 'for the last time'. And, on condition that it is 'this evening, for the last time', Village agrees. The White world must *first* be destroyed with hate; then, and then only, Black Village can love Black Virtue. Which is what happens at the play's end. One by one the Whites descend towards obliteration; and as they die, the great lyric of Black Love rises into the air, its incantations haunting the theatre as this ferocious *clownerie* closes :

> Virtue: I too, for a long time, didn't dare love you. . . .
> Village: You love me?
> Virtue: I would listen. I would hear you striding along. I would run to the window and from behind the curtain would watch you go by. . . .
> Village: You were wasting your time. I strolled by like an indifferent male, without a glance . . . but at night I would come and capture a beam of light from between your shutters. I would carry it off between my shirt and skin.[42]

The moral to be drawn from the tale of Village and Virtue is the same as that which emerges from every other episode in the play : that Black and White are irreconcilable. There is no middle way. And to make the moral clear in different terms, there wanders in and out among the other figures of the action the strangest being of them all : Samba Graham Diouf. Diouf is the half-way house : a Negro by blood, a Christian by faith (he is variously referred to as 'Curate at St Anne's', as 'His Reverence the Canon', as 'my dear

Curate', as 'Mr Vicar-General, for whom Christ died on the Cross', and as 'Our Grand-Vicar'; moreover, the Graham allusion in his name is unmistakable), he is the humanist, the compromiser, the arbiter, the half-and-half. When a symbolic White Woman is required for the ritual murder, it is Diouf who dons a White mask and flaxen curls and plays the part. It is he who preaches 'meekness' (la douceur)[43] and aspires to Heaven. What the blue angels were to Divine, so the White Woman is to Diouf. When the Missionary objects that the Holy Eucharist must be either white or black, it is Diouf who proposes the most sweetly reasonable compromise : 'White on one side, black on the other.'[44] And it is Diouf whose doctrine of tempering hate with love, antagonisms by diplomacy, is sharply criticized by Archibald, and its author called to order :

> *Archibald:* Sir, if you have any intention of presenting even the most trivial of their ideas without caricaturing it, then get out! Beat it![45]

If there is something of the Reverend Billy Graham in Diouf's doggedly optimistic cross-breeding of God and politics, there is a great deal more of the late Dr Albert Schweitzer—a far more dangerous individual, from Genet's point of view. In one sense, one might argue that the whole of *The Blacks* was a direct warning to the coloured populations of the world to reject the temptation of the Schweitzerian solution. Schweitzer at Lambarene; Schweitzer building hospitals, dedicating his life and his knowledge to the regeneration of a Black community; Schweitzer bringing his organ to the swamps of the Gabon, playing Bach fugues under the tropical stars; Schweitzer the humanist, the theologian, the musicologist, the scholar, the doctor, the intellectual Christian; Schweitzer the Saint, the Hero of our Time . . . and Schweitzer, the man who, more than any other, has contributed to blur the political issues in Africa, and to damage the cause of the Blacks. Or so Genet believes, and in this he is not alone. Many of the more enlightened Africans believe it also.

For, while the enemy was the Trader or the big capitalist combine, the Governor with his whip, his ceremonies and his squad of Senegalese or Gurkha troops, the Bible-bashing Missionary, the objective was unmistakable. The White man was the oppressor, and must be evicted or destroyed. But when the White Man comes with University Education in one hand and penicillin in the other, when he comes veiled in disinterested generosity, then the simple-minded Black Man may be deceived into thinking that he is not the enemy after all. Or even the not-so-simple-minded Black Man, like Diouf. Diouf is as well aware as any of his fellows of the poison that is called charity :

Diouf: The kindness of the whites settled upon my head, as it did upon upon yours. Though it rested there lightly, it was unbearable, Their intelligence descended on my right shoulder, and a whole flock of virtues on my left. And at times, when I opened my hands, I would find their charity nestling there.[46]

Never the less, in Christ's words, 'He that is not with me, is against me'—and Genet provides the echo and the application. He who is not with the Blacks, sharing the totality of their hatred of all things White, is against them. And although Diouf is not taken in by the charity of the alien race, he is infected with their rationalism no less than Village is infected with their love. Perhaps, in the end, the natives of Dahomey or of the Gabon will give the world a Black Descartes . . . why not? But this is still in the future. As yet, there is no specifically Black rationalism, there is only White rationalism adapted—and disastrously adapted, since it saps the very foundations of an African liberation: the cult of unadulterated hatred. When Diouf calls Bobo 'a technician of hatred',[47] he pays her the greatest compliment that Genet can imagine; and if *The Blacks* belongs technically to a Theatre of Hatred, the practical political need for this emotion informs the content of the play just as clearly as it dictates its form. And so poor Diouf, for all his good intentions, is the villain. Dramatically speaking, he is doomed. After a welter of high-flown, humanistic phrases, in which he almost loses himself, he senses the weakness of his cause, and begins to apologize: '. . . but I'm old, and I think. . . .' Bobo, however, cuts brutally across the end of his excuses with yet another restatement of the central theme of the play:

Bobo: Who's asking you to? What we need is hatred. Our ideas will spring from hatred.[48]

And over and above the dramatic statement that the day of compromise is over in racial conflict, and that the only conclusion that could have been drawn from Dr Albert Schweitzer's patriarchal age was that his ideas had been out of date for even longer than one would have suspected, there lies another assumption which is fundamental to *The Blacks*: namely, that in spite of the metaphysical and linguistic struggles of Virtue and Village, the outcome of the battle is already known. The supremacy of White over Black is already a thing of the past; and indeed, the reactions of the Court to the insults aimed at them from below are more of nostalgia for a vanished age than fury or even mild anger. Moreover, if the Blacks have no pity for the vanquished Whites, the reason, paradoxically, is that there is no need for it. Romantic chivalry is not part of Genet's creed—nor of Archibald's. The Whites are finished anyway; and so the Blacks propose to finish them off, scientifically and objectively, yet without either fear or malice, as though they were simply rather unpleasant insects. Not scorpions, which are still dangerous; merely silverfish. The only possible victory left to the Whites, as the Queen observes, is to anticipate by suicide the inevitable execution.[49]

It is these basic assumptions which account, in part at least, for the power and originality of the play. Different in this from almost every other play or novel on a similar subject, the Blacks are shown entirely without fear. They have already won. They are even now the equals, if not the superiors, of the Whites. Such fear as there is (mainly concealed), is on the side of the Whites—an analysis which corresponds, not only to political reality in Africa, but also to Norman Mailer's striking analysis (in *Advertisements for Myself*, London, 1961, p. 278) of the causes of racial hatred in the Southern States. It is a measure of Genet's stature as a dramatist that he was able, in *The Blacks*, to show a conflict of equal contempt on both sides of an argument, and yet to have distinguished, by infinitely subtle gradations, between the contempt that is based on fear in the Gallery, and the contempt that has conquered fear in the centre of the stage. And it is also his supreme boldness as a political commentator to have put the case for the oppressed by showing the oppressed triumphant and utterly remorseless in their victory.

The Screens

After *The Blacks*, *The Screens* (1961) seems at first something of an anti-climax. It is the most purely Brechtian of all Genet's plays : explicit argument is reduced to a minimum, traditional psychology has dwindled to vanishing-point; instead, the dramatic effect is created by a series of brilliant visual images, stylized and simplified almost to the point of primitivism, by violence, slogans, caricature, deliberate vulgarity, and by the overwhelming impression of hatred that remains in the atmosphere long after the actors of each individual scene have vanished. Yet in a sense, it is as though Genet, for all his involvement in revolutionary dramatic techniques, had never wholly forgotten his classical heritage. There is at least a hint of *Bajazet* in *The Blacks*, for in both plays the essential fact is that the battle, on which the fate of all the characters depends, has been fought and decided long before the first curtain rises, and consequently, that all the seemingly free acts which constitute the tragedy appear in the outcome to be no more than the senseless gestures of marionettes, ineluctably determined by a will or an event whose fatal immensity embraces and envelops them all. In a less specific way, *The Screens* also suggests a dramatic concept not so alien to Racinian tragedy as might at first appear : for just as Racine deliberately eliminated, or reduced, all those aspects of a normal dramatic technique—décor, gesture, surprise, even striking forms of language—in order to emphasize his one central dramatic concept, the lucid human intelligence at grips with a fatality which was destined to destroy it, so also Genet seems deliberately to blur or weaken every image that could permit the individual scene or character to encroach upon the central situation—the War in Algeria—and the emotion, hatred, that is engendered by it.

The feeling of anti-climax has worried a number of critics who have read the play before seeing it on the stage. 'The play is not an easy one,' writes Tom Milne. 'On paper it tends to look like an inchoate mass of epic-Brechtian scenes, a mixture of crude polemics and visionary insights, vulgar humour and extraordinary beauty of language'.[50] In the theatre—or rather, in performance, for Genet has designed the play for out-of-door production—the effect is different, although, even so, it is marred by the worst defect of Genet's political plays : it is far too long, and consequently tends to drag in the later scenes. Most of the more obsessive themes and problems of Genet's earlier dramas are now reduced to their visual equivalents, or else simplified into straight caricature. The multiple dimensions of illusion and reality, for instance, of *The Maids* or *The Blacks*, are translated visually in terms of the four levels of screens on the stage in front of which the action takes place; the dreams are acted out rather than argued about; the theme of the mirror-image, after its development into the notion of the symbolic mass-function which we examined in *The Balcony*, is here reduced to a veritable caricature of itself : the function of a militaristic patriotism, the image of a political cause :

> *The Lieutenant:* France is watching us. She's sending us out to die. . . . comb your hair. [. . . .] It's not a matter of intelligence, but of perpetuating an image that's more than ten centuries old.[51]

None the less, beneath this camouflage of primitivism, parody and pure dramatic spectacle, we can discover traces of ideas which show that Genet's complex vision of the world has by no means ceased to evolve; only they have to be sought for with some perseverance. They are no longer on the surface for all to see.

The first of these major themes is inherent in the very structure and subject of the play itself : the reality of politics, or, in Sartrian terms, the question of the writer and commitment. In *The Balcony*, Genet explicitly rejected the concept of commitment, on the grounds that all political affiliations, parties, ideologies, etc., deal with dead symbols, while the artist, by the fact of his very vocation, can *only* work with living words and individual images. As if to contradict himself, Genet then wrote *The Blacks*, a most uncompromisingly committed play, in which he attempted, by eliminating the symbolic platitudes that cling to the positive hero, and by reversing the traditional associations of good with the positive cause and evil with the negative one, to create the vision of a world in which progressive politics were not inevitably decked about with platitudinous and even reactionary values, whether moral or aesthetic. But it says a great deal for Genet's relentless honesty with himself that, in spite of the brilliant achievement of *The Blacks,* he remained dissatisfied with his own conclusions. The snag of *The Blacks* is Ville de Saint-Nazaire. In *The Balcony*, whose conclusions are fundamentally anti-political, the positive hero, Roger, is admitted only on sufferance; the active and organized, positive type of political activity is rejected and, in the end, Roger himself is absorbed back into the non-committed, aesthetic world of the Brothel. But Ville de Saint-Nazaire is a different matter. His appearance in the action— one almost suspects—is independent of his creator's intentions : he enters not so much because Genet wanted him, as because the forces of political reality demanded his presence; and worse still, having come, he dominates the play, and relegates the rest of the action to the paper domain of clownery. Yet this clownery embodied all Genet's laborious heart-searchings, his desperate attempt to create a socialism without platitudes in which he, as an artist, might participate without 'selling his birthright for a pot of message'— a world of negatives which might somehow add up to positive action. Ville de Saint-Nazaire knocks all that flat. Positive political action needs positive heroes, and positive heroes need platitudes. Genet's attempt to create a political idealism based on negatives is revealed for what it is : straightforward anarchism.

In *The Blacks*, Genet was obviously reluctant to accept this conclusion; at the end of the play, Ville de Saint-Nazaire, with his unpalatable reminders of reality, has vanished, and Village and Virtue realize their Utopian dreams of a Black and independent love. But *The Screens* brings the question up once more, and answers it very differently. Beneath the conflict of French and Arabs which forms the obvious subject of the play lies a much profounder and, for Genet, more immediately relevant conflict : that between anarchy and organization. If the main division of the characters is into White and Brown, there is also a secondary division which cuts right across the first : on the one hand the anarchists, the reversers of conventional values so dear to Genet's heart : Saïd, his Mother,

Leïla his wife, Kadidja and Ommu; on the other, the orthodox forces of political reality, which include not only the Colonials and the Légionnaires, but also the disciplined Arab combatants themselves who, in the final moments of the play, execute Saïd, and in so doing relegate Genet's dreams where they belong . . . to the world of poetry which, in political terms, is the world of Death. Thus are the values of *The Balcony* reversed completely. In *The Balcony*, Genet had rejected political reality because it was incompatible with beauty—with Carmen, Chantal and the symbolic miracle of the Song. In *The Screens*, Ommu takes up the same argument with one of the Arab combatants; but now it is the Soldier—significantly anonymous, not an individual, but an uncharacterized member of the Mass—who wins. And consequently Saïd dies :

> *Ommu:* Certain truths are not applicable, otherwise they'd die. . . . They mustn't die, but live through the song they've become. . . . Long live the song !
> *The Combatant:* Neither I nor my friends fought so that it would sing in you, Caroline.[52]

In a sense, the ending of the drama is ambiguous. Saïd is defeated, and with him, all Genet's belief and hope that it may be possible, even in the domain of politics, to envisage and to formulate a truth uncontaminated by the half-truths and slogans born of necessity. But now even Ommu, who argues out the case, pronounces her own condemnation : 'Certain truths just *cannot* be applied'. Truth—the Absolute Truth which alone is of any concern to the poet or the artist—has literally no place in politics. It is, literally, 'inapplicable'; for either it destroys the whole positive organization on which effective politics are based, or else it becomes tainted with this alien positivism, and ceases to be itself : ceases to be either true or absolute :

> *Ommu:* Soldier ! [. . . .] There are truths that must never be applied, those that must be made to live through the song they've become.[53]

Of the outcome of the argument, there is no doubt. In *The Balcony*, the insurgents are defeated by the Brothel; in *The Screens*, symbolically, it is from the Brothel that the combatants emerge, to capture and execute Saïd. The ambiguity lies in Genet's own attitude.[54] All the way through the play, his sympathies lie with Saïd and Leïla, with Kadidja and the Mother, and more specifically with Ommu; the Combatants are presented unsympathetically, and, in an earlier scene, the argument that poetry is an impermissible luxury in times of political crisis is placed in the mouths of two of the more revolting characters on the Colonialist side : the Vamp and the Son of Sir Harold.[55] Yet in the end, Genet admits himself defeated—

one of the most fascinating aspects, incidentally, of the drama, for it must in all conscience be rare enough for a dramatist to use his art in order to demonstrate the failure of his own most intimate convictions. The death of Saïd places Genet himself in the position of having to abandon either politics or poetry, having failed in his attempt to reconcile the two. The only question is, which? Either alternative, now, is almost equally inconceivable. To retreat from commitment would be to betray, not only Sartre and all the progressive Left who, in the long run, have made his reputation, but also his own inherent sympathy for the victim and the underdog. To retreat from poetry would be to betray himself.

It is not, however, until the closing scene of the play that this dilemma becomes apparent. Until then, Genet deliberately tricks us into believing that the solution presented in *The Blacks* will work again. Moreover, the breakdown of his abstract theory of non-committed commitment does not mean that, in itself, *The Screens* is not a most effectively committed play. When we first meet Saïd, he is on his way to his wedding, accompanied by his Mother. Saïd is the negative hero, who simultaneously embodies the rejection of an orthodox and right-thinking society—in this case, the well-bred and civilized society of the Colonials—by a deliberate rejection of its values, and at the same time the rejection of *all* political categories and generalizations, French and Arab alike, by his indomitable individualism. Like Genet himself, his authenticity resides in his abjection. He plunges downwards into sanctity through his experiences of degradation and evil. His poverty implies his rejection of any ideal of economic prosperity; his marriage, an equally categorical rejection of the conventional notion of beauty. Leïla (the Arabic word means night—a direct link with the darkness of the Negroes in *The Blacks*) has only one outstanding individual characteristic : her ugliness. She is 'the ugliest woman in the next town and all the towns around'[56]; and progressively her ugliness becomes, for herself, for Saïd and for his Mother, the symbol of a total Negativity :

> *The Mother:* Since you're ugly, be idiotic.
> *Leïla:* According to you, I should try and become more and more of a stupid cow?
> *The Mother:* Have a shot, anyway. We'll see if it does any good.[57]

Meanwhile, Saïd progresses through further stages of negation. From an outcast he becomes a thief (and Leïla, now his inseparable shadow, the symbol of his *malheur*, becomes a thief likewise, so as not to be separated from him); from a thief, a gaolbird; from a gaolbird, a traitor, and his treachery is his final negation of positive values, since he is betraying his (and Genet's) own committed cause. And yet, parallel with this descent through abjection, his emblem rises, like that of Chantal, and 'bespangles the Heaven of the Revolution', so that. in the end, he is no longer even himself : his search for the solitude and sanctity of Total Abjection is defeated by the action of the masses, who detach his image from his reality and use it as a 'function-symbol', thus plunging him into the world of death and unreality, even while he is still alive :

Ommu: It's dead that we want you, dead, but it's alive not dead. . . .
Saïd: That's leaving me dead alive !
Ommu: It's neither dead nor alive ![58]

Around this central narrative, the epic progress of Saïd from individual to Universal, from life to death, from poverty to sanctity (it is as though Divine had got mixed up with Chantal and Roger-the-Plumber), Genet builds up an abstract picture of the War : a kaleidoscope of dreams, visions and unrealities, from the Brothel— once again, the home of Illusions—to the battlefield, from the plantations where the Arabs set fire to the orange-groves to the cemetery where Si Slimane, the legendary hero of the Arab cause, returns momentarily and grudgingly from the dead. The colour and variety of these scenes is impressive : their import, in the long run, identical—for no man, in Genet's final analysis, can commit herself to a cause, however admirable, and still remain, in the fullest sense, alive. And so, one by one, heroes and villlains alike burst through the barrier of Death, and find themselves, to their mild surprise, in the regions beyond : French and Arabs together, united for ever in their unreality. For even the supreme and sacred individualism of Evil is powerless against the deadly abstractions of commitment, and the victory of the Cause is only procured at the cost of the annihilation of the spirit.

The Screens is assuredly the most pessimistic play that Genet has so far written; its conclusions, however, were already implicit in *Our Lady of the Flowers.* Divine's 'salvation through despair' was only conceivable in a totally a-social context; Divine was the outcast, the scapegoat, and her rejection of society was conditional upon her acceptance of a total isolation, a total negativity. The concept of an organized community of outcasts is no more feasible in a political than it is in a social or ethical context : it runs counter to Genet's whole understanding of the nature and function of evil, his whole vision of transcendence. Divine was the isolated negation of the spirit, whose existence relegated the whole remainder of society to the limbo of a positive materialism. She was the Not-Being who *defined* Being, but who could not merge with it unless she first destroyed herself. And the artist also, for Genet, is precisely such another dynamic negative.

But in politics, it is not merely a question of the Not-Being of the

artist attempting to merge with the Being of society; it is much
more a question of the urgent and positive forces of Being enveloping and destroying the artist against his will, should he so much
as seem to recognize their existence. His only hope is to cut himself
off completely, as Divine once did. It is not sufficient to reject the
values of society in the hope of destroying the society that incarnates these values : if they are to be rejected, they must be rejected
for the sake of the act of rejection itself. The unspoken hope that,
out of a negative act or attitude, there may grow a positive result
is the final temptation that Genet's anti-heroes have to overcome.

In other words, Saïd's search for an Absolute of evil fails in that,
unlike Divine, or unlike Genet himself, he uses it as a means to an
end—the end of *hatred*, and therefore, ultimately, of political idealism, of Revolution, of Socialism and the new society. Or, worse still,
even if he himself does not use it, he ensures, by placing himself
in a political context, that others will use it for him. This is the
symbolic difference between Leïla and Kadidja. Leïla, in her Divine-
like simplicity, cultivates her abjection for its own sake.[59] Kadidja,
by contrast, cannot distinguish between ends and means. For her,
the function of evil is to produce hatred, the function of hatred
to engender more evil, more acts of terrorism, and the final purpose
of terrorism is to bring about the Victory of the Cause. At first sight,
Kadidja's incantations to the Forces of Evil seem to belong to the
same category as Felicity's summons to the spirits of Africa in *The
Blacks*; but in fact there is an important distinction. Felicity loves
her Africa and its evil for its own sake; Kadidja (and before her,
Malika, one of the Whores in the Brothel) recites her Litany of
Hatred with an ulterior motive. Kadidja's invocation :

> Evil, wonderful evil, you who remain when everything buggers off,
> miraculous evil, you're going to help us. I beg of you, evil, and I beg
> you standing upright, impregnate my people.[60]

produces an immediate political result, as one after the other the
Arabs rush in and, in one of the most dramatic scenes of the play,
draw on a screen the images of their acts. 'And don't be ashamed,
my sons!' encourages Kadidja, 'Merit the world's contempt. Slit
throats, my sons . . . .'[61] and so they continue, until the screen is
filled with horrifying scribbles. Then another screen is brought in,
and then another. . . . As a political manifesto, a justification of
terrorism, the impact is frightening. None the less, the brilliant
success of the drama as such still leaves the crucial problem unsolved.

Something of the same hesitation shows in Genet's attitude to
Beauty in *The Screens*. Just as culture was the symbol of the Whites
in *The Blacks*, so Beauty becomes the symbol of the oppressors, the

colons, in *The Screens.* It is the emblem of the Légionnaires, with their handsome profiles and their spotless uniforms; it is the symbol of order, civilization and economic prosperity. In Monsieur Blankensee's garden, the rose acquires yet another degree of symbolic value : its orderly beauty is identified with the whole of French culture, from Descartes to Mallarmé.

> *Monsieur Blankensee:* We're the lords of language. To tamper with roses is to tamper with language.
> *Sir Harold:* And to tamper with language is sacrilegious.[62]

It follows logically, then, that the Arabs should adopt ugliness as the emblem of their reality—an emblem which the extremists, Saïd, Leïla and Ommu recognize unhesitatingly as their own. But, once again, the problem is not so clear-cut in a political context as in an individual one. To begin with, Beauty—in its specifically French sense, as an emanation of Cartesian logic, order and the discipline of form—is not easily dissociated from other forms of discipline and efficiency. It may be the symbol of an effete and moribund culture; it is also synonymous, as all old-fashioned corps-commanders realized, with the competence of an army in the field. 'Beauty, beauty! Brick-and-mortar of armies!' announces the General in the course of his Litany of Platitudes; and even in spite of its somewhat strange development—

> One *has* to go. Armed, in boots and helmets, right, but also powdered, cosmeticked, made-up, the thing that kills is grease-paint on a skeleton of precise gestures. . . .[63]

—the idea contains an element of truth. Gradually, even the Arabs, beginning with Bachir, begin to have doubts, whether the anarchy of 'ugliness'—physical or moral—is the most effective reply to the discipline of beauty. Ommu and Nedjma take up the negative side of the argument, while the same anonymous Combatants who later carry out the murder of Saïd proceed to identify beauty with efficiency and with *law* : for the precise and beautiful motions of the machine depend on the stability of laws, just as much as does the behaviour of the individual in society.

> *The Soldier:* War has its laws.
> *Ommu:* But not its moral laws.
> *The Soldier:* Yes, it has. War teaches us what peace will be. Neither killing nor getting killed, no, we want to be the stronger. We need armour.[64]

During this argument, the rain comes down. The Soldier tries to move under shelter, and Ommu starts to jeer at him : 'You're worrying about your nice uniform . . .?' but this time the Soldier really knows his mind :

The Soldier: **That** too. One fights less well in rags. And one fights less well when one has an ugly mug and is less attractive to women.[65]

—and he even remains impervious to Ommu's much more serious accusation that, just as Village became White as soon as he started to talk of love, so the Arabs become French as soon as they abandon their own prerogatives of ugliness and anarchy :

Ommu: You boys have now reached the stage of uniforms, discipline, jaunty marches and bare arms, parades and heroic death while singing *Madelon* and the *Marseillaise* and martial beauty. . . .
The Soldier: Why not? There are other things than shit and filth. . . .
Ommu: You lousy little stinker, you snot-nose, go join the other side where there's stately beauty, you little snot-nose! But maybe you've done it, you're joining them, and copying them excites you. To be their reflection is already to be one of them. . . .[66]

At this point, Genet suspends the argument. Plainly, his sympathies as an individual, a poet, an outcast, a seeker-after-Absolutes, are all on the side of Ommu; yet his practical intelligence tells him that the Soldier is right, and, once again, that positive commitment cannot be reconciled with the anarchy of total negation. As a last resort, however, he takes up an idea, originally developed in *Miracle of the Rose* but half-forgotten since : that beauty, which is merely an idealized form of appearance, is as detachable from the object which displays it as indeed are all other forms of Mirror-Image from the Figures that give rise to their existence. Originally, Genet developed this theory in relation to the physical beauty of his lovers— Bulkaen for instance. It seemed to him that the fatal power of Bulkaen's beauty had nothing to do with Bulkaen himself, but represented an independent and devastating force by which he, Jean Genet, was destroyed, without the young burglar even being so much as aware of what was taking place. In *The Screens*, the Cadi takes up the same argument, but applies it to beauty in general—including the abstract, Cartesian beauty of Justice, or the economic efficiency of French agricultural development in North Africa. Beauty, suggests the Cadi, is not a part of the reality of things : it is an abstract, it cannot be possessed; but as an independent force of its own, it renders the object, whose disguise it is, equally unpossessable. Applied to human relationships, or even to art, this argument sounds plausible enough[67]; the artist can no longer possess the sculpture that he has made in the same way as he once possessed the block of stone from which it came; for he, by his own act, has taken it out of the domains of time and space and placed it irrevocably in the elusive timelessness of eternity. And as an Eternal, it has a symbolic, abstract and sacred reality of its own : it escapes from the materiality of possession.

Apply this to the domain of Colonialist economic exploitation, however—which is what the Cadi proceeds to do—and the conclusions are disturbing. As opposed to the usual Colonialist argument, that the original natives no longer have a right to the land in their own country, because all its real value lies in the improvements which the Europeans have brought to it, the Cadi maintains that Monsieur Blankensee's famous rose-gardens no longer belong to him, precisely *because* he has made them beautiful. 'Things cease to belong to those who've been able to make them more beautiful', he maintains to the assembled Arabs :

> . . . better and more beautiful, light-footed, winged, they gratefully abandon the one who made them better. When they've gone, nothing left, not a particle, zero, pfft ! [68]

One might almost suspect that Genet, in a last, desperate attempt to reconcile his artist's aestheticism with politics, is trying to use the conventional concept of Beauty—which he himself now identifies unhesitatingly with the enemy society—as an argument in favour of the outcast. But, in spite of the ingenious twists of logic involved (and this passage is very typical of Genet's later use of paradox), in the long run the argument defeats itself. For if beauty is sufficient to invalidate the claim of Monsieur Blankensee to so many square kilometres of Algerian countryside, unfortunately it invalidates the claims of the Arabs simultaneously. What remains is not an Arab-owned economy, but simply a Void, a *zero*. Discreetly, the Cadi lets the argument drop, the scene ends, and Genet is back where he started. The absolute, anarchic beauty of the poet is doomed in any political context; whereas the social beauty of a disciplined and organized community will be exploited for utilitarian purposes just as ruthlessly and freely by the new, Utopian society as by the old.

As the final screen is dragged off the stage in *The Screens*, Genet is no nearer to a solution of the antagonism between himself and society than he was when he wrote the first page of *Our Lady of the Flowers*. *He* is on one side, isolated and alone for ever; society—even the splendid Socialist society of Sartrian dreams—is on the other. It is not that he seeks to exclude himself from politics (these last three plays are sufficient to disprove straight away any such accusation); it is rather that politics, because of their very nature, exclude him. At the beginning of *Our Lady of the Flowers*, he *felt* he was excluded, condemned for ever to solitude and isolation; by the end of *The Screens*, he *knows* that this is so. The loneliness of the orphan changed into the loneliness of the thief; the loneliness of the thief into that of the convict, that of the convict into that of the artist—but it is always the same loneliness. It is interesting to see how this theme of solitude comes to the surface again in his later works : in the *Atelier d'Alberto Giacometti* and in the brothel-scenes of *The Screens*. The little essay on the Swiss sculptor Giacometti is of no great value considered as art-criticism; but it is a fascinating prose-poem on the subject of solitude, or rather, to use the term which took its place in *Querelle of Brest*, '*la singularité*'.

The aim of the politician is to eliminate the individual, and to dissolve him into the Universal; he constructs his practical-minded visions, not out of identities, but out of functions. The artist, on the contrary, is concerned only to reduce the Universal to the particular; to bring out the absolute and unique identity, not only of living beings, but also of rocks, landscapes, lumps of marble—even bottles or tightrope wires. 'The work of Giacometti,' asserts Genet, 'communicates the knowledge of the solitude of every being and of every object, together with the fact that this solitude is our most certain title to glory.'[69] Even in a context of *time*, the artist's task is to reduce the myriad-peopled world of continuity to the isolated, blinding realization of the present instant. Politics—and not only Marxist politics—is a function of history; art is the elimination of history. Relationships in time become meaningless; the object organises all time exclusively and eternally about itself :

> This ability to isolate an object and to enable it to be filled with its own, its unique, significances, can be achieved only through the abolition of the historical reality of him who contemplates it.[70]

—and the same is true of other physical dimensions : 'Each object creates its own infinite space.'[71]

With every argument in *Giacometti*, the gap between the artist and the politician widens. Politics deals in continuity, art in contiguity. Politics is the science of organized relationships—which, admittedly, constitute one sort of beauty. Art is the awareness of the Absolute which remains when all relationships have been discarded. . . . Beauty again, but of a very different sort. Two incompatible worlds, which Genet would desperately wish to reconcile, yet which admit only of the most tenuous link between them : the link which Genet symbolizes in the Brothel.

It is not merely because of her traditional degradation that Genet, when at last he finds a positive role for woman to play in the world of his poetic vision, incarnates her in the figure of the Whore. It is because she reflects his own position as a solitary, an artist, flung willy-nilly into a world of relationships. His conscience, amid the agitated injustices of this mid-century period, thrusts him forth against his will and better judgement into the battles between Socialism and Fascism, Colonialism and Self-Determination, reaction and

revolt. He blunders, still armoured in his isolation, into a mêlée
of relationships, attempts to find common causes, to discover a
society which not only will accept him, but which he also can accept.
And each encounter with the Others leaves him more isolated, more
definitely outcast, and perhaps more wounded, than before. Such
also is the life of the prostitute : precariously balanced between the
inner and the outer worlds, she belongs absolutely to neither, yet
cannot encompass the exigencies of both. Her needs, her profession,
drive her out to seek relationships; yet each new relationship drives
her back further into her wounded isolation : 'Is it not in the Brothel
that woman might take pride in the wound which never more
will set her free from solitude ?'[72]

The Whore, like the artist, belongs to the mystery of the night.
Like him, she is non-utilitarian. She is not a mother, she is not a
housewife. She is sterile. 'What I like about whores,' said Giacometti once to Genet, 'is that they don't serve any purpose. They are
just there. That's all.'[73] Like him, she is sacred—she is the very
symbol of transgression, just as art itself is, at bottom, a transgression that stinks in the nostrils of all right-thinking people.

And at the same time, she is herself a work of art. She is all
appearance, all illusion. *'Le style est l'homme même,'* wrote Buffon;
'I *am* my style,' counters Warda in *The Screens* :

> Poor golden petticoats! I'd always hoped that one day, instead of being
> an adornment, you'd be, by yourselves, the whore in all her glory.[74]

But when politics intervene, when war destroys the serenity of the
Brothel, it is her style which is the first thing to go. Her style is her
identity, her authenticity—just as it is that of Genet himself. 'One
must want to be a total whore, right down to the skeleton,' says
Warda to Malika, who has let herself be absorbed in dreams of a
liberated Algeria[75]—just as Genet knows that he must will himself
to be a total poet, and yet is forever tempted to step out of his reality
and reform the world. The Whore's choice is his own : either to go
out into the world and be destroyed; or else to retreat into the
Brothel and build a dream-world of Image and Reflection that is
more real than reality. Only one of Genet's whores escapes into another dimension altogether : Virtue, who finds herself in her love
for Village, who makes herself a new identity in which the 'total
whore' is transformed into the 'total negress'. But for Jean Genet
himself, any such escape now seems unlikely. The ending of *The
Screens* suggests a retreat into the Brothel of Illusions that is Art-
for-Art's-sake. Self-contemplation in the Mirror. At least, until the
next temptation comes, to look outside the door and see what is
going on.

Conclusion

Jean Genet is one of the supreme artists of negation. He is, in the plainest sense of the word, a nihilist—an annihilator, destroying, by shock, argument and paradox, the whole code of values and habits of mind by which, conventionally, we live.

Yet Nihilism, in the mid-twentieth century, holds a significance rather different from that which it did a hundred years ago. When Turgenev, in his novel *Fathers and Sons*, conceived the character of Bazarov, and thus drew the first portrait of the authentic Nihilist, he saw him as a rationalistic disbeliever, a herald of the new, cynical, disillusioned age of science, rejecting everything—monarchy, orthodoxy, morality—that failed to survive the cold test of critical objectivity. For the Russian critic Pisarev, who acknowledged himself to be Bazarov's equivalent in real life, the conventional values which did survive this test were few indeed : to him, even the great geniuses of the past were so many fakes and delusions, mere men of straw. Shakespeare, Goethe, Pushkin were so many idols, whose worship was no more than yet another meaningless tradition (or simple vested-interest) handed down from generation to generation. And, as he realized, to question the intrinsic reality of their greatness— or that of any other sacred convention—was not merely eccentricity, but sacrilege.

At the height of the Victorian epoch, whether in France, in England or in Russia, the sheer, solid weight of positive, right-thinking opinion was overwhelming; and the only reply to an immutable and divinely-inspired 'yes' was a categoric and daemonically-inspired 'no!' In every code, from the ethics of the pulpit to the etiquette of the drawing-room, there reigned an aura of known certainty, and whosoever proclaimed with due assurance, 'this is so', spoke with the conviction of undisputed authority. In the Beginning was the Word, and the Word was Truth.

But since the days of Pisarev, much has changed, and above all our reaction to those who proclaim what they choose to announce as being the Truth. The Word of God has become the verbiage of mass-communication, the shining weapon of Truth has become the ingenious trickery of publicity and propaganda. 'Politicians seek to blur issues,' says Lord Chandos, 'as well as to define them; P.R. people want to create favourable responses; preachers hope to arouse emotion; official spokesmen of all sorts seek the security of clichés.' And no form of language has suffered so much from distortion as the positive, universal proposition. Montaigne, that gentlest of seekers after knowledge, so revered the positive statement of a universal truth, in the manner of Senecan *sententiae*, that he had a series of them painted on the roof-beams of his library, so that they might always be present to his mind. But for us, the positive, all-embracing truth or injunction is tainted with the corruption of uncertainty. We live, argued Nathalie Sarraute, in an era of *suspicion*. How true are positive truths when they are enunciated by Hitler or by Stalin, by the glossies or by commercial TV? 'All Slavs are racially inferior to the Germans.' 'All Trotskyists are bourgeois reactionaries.' 'All children love Choxicles.' 'Gutrot is Good for You'—these, and a million other dicta of a similar type, are the *sententiae* of the age of mass-communication.

Not that they *necessarily* embody untruths : more often, they belong to a domain of half-truths, to a remote, irrelevant, twilight world, where such archaic, non-commercial concepts as Truth or Lies have no precise or verifiable meaning. The universal positive proposition no longer opens up a realm of significant certainties, but leads rather to the disquieting penumbra of platitudes and slogans. Wherever Truth may reside, there is the uncomfortable feeling that it is clearly not in the sweeping, generalized assertion : 'this is so'—at least in the realm of ethics. It is all but impossible to be a moralist in the present age; to say anything significant about ethics, it is necessary to be an anti-moralist. Hence the phenomenon of Jean Genet.

That truth—if such a thing exists at all—lies, not in the conventional formulae of assertion, but in the dynamic forces that may be generated by negation, is the discovery, the vital and guiding principle, of the Existentialist generation. The positive is seen as false, misleading and dangerous; or else, simply, as vacant, insipid and meaningless. Sartre establishes the whole of his philosophy, and even of his psychology, on a basis of *le Néant*—the ultimate negativity of the Self which is the source of all perception, all awareness. Simone de Beauvoir envisages the negativity of death as the only force strong enough to create positive significance in life. Ionesco contrasts the dynamism of negation—the Absurd—with the vapid nonsensicality of assertion and (again like Sartre) generates hope exclusively from hopelessness : 'Human life begins on the farther side of despair'. Negation, likewise, is the key to Beckett's tormented world of irrational numbers and circles without centres. When a character is positive enough to bear a name, he is a dream, an unreality; the only ultimate truth lies in that undefinable Void who is the Unnamable. In the past, it was the East which based its philosophy on the dynamic negative, the inconceivable, the plenum void; the West preferred its lucid concepts, its clear and distinct ideas, its positive logic, its logical positivism. But propaganda and publicity are chang-

ing this : there is one language for the politician, another for the
poet. Assertion stands for lies; negation, or something near to it, for
truth. And Genet, being a poet, and therefore desperately concerned
with truth, is forced to use the language of negation.

'In order to speak the truth, it is necessary to tell lies', argued
Cocteau; and Genet, his disciple in this as in so much else, echoes
him word for word. It is only by lying that one can hope to grasp
at the truth; it is only by dint of being an anti-moralist that
one may hope to be a moralist at all. Thus Genet's nihilism, unlike
that of Bazarov, is rooted in an essential ambiguity. When positive
truths have been so over-stated that they lose all their significance,
then the only remaining form of significant statement would seem
to be negation. This is not to say that Genet's paradoxes are merely
right-thinking platitudes turned inside out, designed to imply their
contrary by inversion, as is the case with Fielding in *Jonathan Wild*.
By and large, it would seem that they are to be taken at their face
value; rather the essence of Genet's ambiguity lies in the fact that
his moral nihilism crystallizes for the reader the very substance
of ethics—just as his fictions (his lies) symbolize the very substance
of truth—with a clarity, a forcefulness and an urgency which no
more positive attitude could hope to achieve. There is, in fact, a
kid of Hegelian dialectic at work, although the ultimate synthesis
of positive and negative is in the nature of a force rather than a
resolution. The thesis of conventional morality is assailed by the
antithesis of Genet's anti-ethic; the conflict generates both heat
and energy; and, as in Ionesco's theory of dynamic contradiction, the
result is a turbulent void or *Néant*, from which is destined to emerge,
perhaps a new logic, conceivably a new morality, unquestionably
a new poetry.

This is Genet's somewhat idiosyncratic version of Simone de
Beauvoir's *Morale de l'Ambiguïté*. And indeed, this thread of ambiguity runs through every aspect of his work. He is nothing if not
ambiguous. His symbol of the Figure and its simultaneous Image-
in-the-Mirror, which informs almost every page that he has written,
is at the same time the most characteristic symbol of that ineradicable ambiguity which lies within himself. He is both positive and
negative, male and female, committed and uncommitted; and each
time we ask ourselves which is the *real* Genet, the only conceivable
answer is : both. Provided only that they are sufficiently antithetical,
almost all the obvious definitions are equally true—on condition
that one bears always in mind that *the* truth of any answer depends
upon the simultaneous assertion of its opposite.

Pornographer or philosopher? Both. To deny that Genet's novels
are pornographic (or, more specifically, to use a distinction which we

have discussed earlier, erotic) would be as absurd as to insist that they were *only* pornographic. It would also reveal that one had not read *The Thief's Journal*. Recalling that crudest of 'positive heroes' who ever came to haunt nightmares of a poet, Genet writes :

> As for Armand's immodest attitudes, I cannot quite say that they were the cause of my decision to write pornographic books, but I was certainly flabbergasted. . . .[76]

But it is equally true that a conscious decision to write pornography implies a philosophic attitude. Pornography, or extreme verbal eroticism, is the deliberate use, in literature, of certain aspects of sexual experience in order to shock, horrify and disgust. Any so-called pornography which fails to shock, disgust or horrify—the breast-sellers of the Charing-Cross Road bookstalls—is not pornography at all, but a dim sub-species of sentimental sexual idealism, the poor, debased and bloodless progeny of Lancelot and Guinevere, of Paul and Virginie, of earnest Werther and his dreamy-eyed Charlotte. True pornography is distinguished by the fact that it takes sex, not sentimentally, but seriously (too seriously, perhaps), as an experience which may be celestial, or destructive, or diabolic, but which cannot be catered for by Groups for Pre-Marital Instruction, no matter whether these are held in the Town Hall or the Church Institute. Whether, in reality, the sexual act between civilized Western couples ever attains to these extremes of superhuman ecstasy is doubtful. Many interesting features emerge from the Kinsey Report; but an awareness of coitus as a divine or diabolical communion is not one of them. The human being has no more than a given amount of physical, emotional and spiritual energy to spend in the process of existing; and, in a modern democratic community, he is forced to spend most of it on work. Only leisure gives man the chance to realize himself as something more than a social animal, a wage-earner or an integrated statistic : the leisure of the aristocrat, or the leisure of the spiv. De Sade chose his disquieting heroes from among the first of these two classes; Genet selects his from among the second. Yet both share the essential privilege of the saintly mystic : his leisure.

And if by any chance we are on the move towards a more leisured society, then the problem may become extremely urgent. At present, there is only literature to remind us that, beyond the borders of the physical and the material, there lies (so one suspects) a terrifying region, where the brightest sunlight is but shadow cast by the inconceivable brightness beyond; or at least, that by pushing the body to the furthest limits of its capacity and endurance, it may be possible to catch a glimpse of something else. Not that this something else is necessarily pleasant—but neither, for that matter, is any other

form of mystic experience, in the sense that pleasant means comfortable or cosy; in fact, as the Saints have often told us, it can
be decidedly unsettling. As it is in Genet. Which is one good reason,
among others, why the Censor should begin to have his doubts. For
the Censor, after all, is only the voice of Society, and Society is first
and foremost concerned with its own preservation. In the eyes of
Society, sex may safely be identified with love, moonlight and silver
roses; or else, more profitably and still more safely, with maternity
clinics and increases in population. But as soon as it approaches the
mysteries of the Black Mass, then the danger-signals must be flown.
And long may they fly; for when they cease to do so, it might mean
that neither sex nor literature will any more be taken seriously. And
that will be the real dawning of Huxley's Brave New World.

Genet, then, in his avowed hostility to society, is an out-and-out,
avowed pornographer. Yet this alone is only a single facet of the
truth. For every sexual act and every sexual reaction is only the introduction to a vast panorama of symbolism and metaphysical
imagery, beneath which the original act is buried almost to the
point of obliteration. The sexual act lies at the very centre of the
mystery of identity : for when two are as one, what happens to the
original two? Were there originally two separate identities, or only
an unreality of Self reflected in the mirror of the Other? Is the
total-identity a Double, or is the reality of the individual only a
Void, a Nothing reflected in a Something-not-Itself? From the
lasciviousness of the Queen,

> Stew'd in corruption, honeying and making love
> Over the nasty sty,

to the abstractions of *Being and Nothingness* is but a step; and
from *Being and Nothingness* to the *Critique de la Raison Dialectique*
only a step further. For the man who is but a Negative in relation
to his own Double (or lover) is also the Individual of whom societies
are composed, the Average Man of the statisticians, the enlightened
Proletarian of progressive committee-rooms, the cannon-fodder of
a *Realpolitik*. But can there be a *Real*-politik (in the broader sense)
without real citizens for the politicians to be realistic about? A society,
argued Rousseau, is *not* the same as the mere sum-total of the individuals who compose it—and all the more recent ideologies of the
State have tended to agree. But if man-the-citizen is different from
man-the-individual, then he has another identity. He is a Double
of himself. He is his own image; or else the image that the politician
sees is his reality—in which case, he himself is not real at all. Another Void. . . ? Metaphysical conundrums, perhaps. And yet, in
our society where, year by year, every individual act and thought

is evaluated more and more in terms of its political significance, such questions are anything but frivolous. Not that they are the obvious questions that everyone would ask. But Genet's function is precisely to burst through the barrier of the obvious, and to grope with the elusive intangibilities beyond. And if he can only shatter our philosophical *idées fixes* by first of all demolishing our moral prejudices and presuppositions, he is quite prepared to do so. He is himself a social function; and to the symbolic functionaries of *The Balcony*— the Bishop, the Judge, the General, the Chief-of-Police—he should perhaps have added yet one more : the Pornographer.

In this vein, one could go on asking many antithetical questions. Revolutionary or reactionary? Both. Realist or mystic? Both. Symbolist or existentialist? Both. Traditionalist or *avant-garde*? Here, even more disquietingly, the answer seems once more to be the inevitable : both. Certainly few writers of the *avant-garde*, at any time, have belonged more inexplicably to the last *arrière-garde* but one.

Divine's technique of moving backwards into the past by standing still in the present and letting time flow on into the future is almost a period-piece of anti-logic; it is, in fact, exactly what would have happened to the White Queen and Alice if they had stopped running. Yet curiously, it is almost exactly what seems to have happened to Genet himself. By what singular reversal in the normally smooth-running mechanism of time did Genet, merely by standing still in the middle years of the twentieth century, find himself, apparently all unawares, back in the closing years of the nineteenth . . . and to have lived through them steadily, emerging on the further side in about the year 1905? It is almost as though his actual memories stemmed from a period some twenty years before he was (in reality) born. When he seeks a comparison for Our Lady's hair-style, he remembers those long-forgotten *cocottes*, Emilienne d'Alençon and Eugénie Buffet; and when he writes poetry, he remembers the muddled lyricism of Jammes and the jewelled obscurities of Mallarmé. His cult of evil would have been familiar to Baudelaire; his satanism belongs by rights to the epoch of Huysmans and Lautréamont; his metaphysic is an echo of Dostoievsky. In the circles of Wilde and 'Bosie', he would have felt himself at home; it was Wilde who brought to the fore that underworld of homosexual *voyous* who later come to haunt the pages of *Our Lady of the Flowers* and *The Thief's Journal*; it was Wilde and Whistler who preached Genet's own doctrines of aestheticism; and if it was also Wilde who wrote an essay called *The Truth of Masks*, it was Max Beerbohm who capped it (like Stilitano) by going to a fancy-dress party with his face disguised in a mask exactly reproducing his own features underneath. In the *Yellow Book*, Genet could have published *The Funambulists* without a qualm; and how admirably it would have been illustrated by Aubrey Beardsley!

If the characteristic of the nineties is to be decadent, precious and anarchic, no writer is more blatantly ninety-ish than Genet. When the murderer Ravachol was caught and tried, it was the *fin-de-siècle* novelist Paul Adam (and not Genet) who cried out: 'A saint is born among us!'; and less than a decade later it was the young Marinetti (and not Genet) who argued that 'art can only be violence, cruelty and injustice'. Genet's symbolism is as *fin-de-siècle* as his politics; it was in the nineties that that woolly-minded demicharlatan, Joséphin (Sâr) Péladan, exalted the sacred image of the Mystic Rose above all other symbols; it was in the nineties that the French workers as a whole chose to reject the harsh disciplines of organized socialism in favour of the more poetic violence of anarchy. Somewhere between the gilded bedrooms of *Nana* and the dilapidated garrets of *L'Assommoir*, between the Looking-Glass paradoxes of Lewis Carroll and the gestures-into-reality of the *Happy Hypocrite*, Genet seems to have his spiritual home. His ideal of sanctity—as Sartre has argued—fairly reeks of the effluvia of an over-ripe capitalist society. 'Saint Genet' would undoubtedly be taken in as a fellow-lodger by that other morbid martyr whose voice we hear in the *Notes from Underground*; he is pretty incongruous among the clinics and cafeterias of the Welfare State.

And yet, in spite of this, he belongs unquestionably to our own time. It is *because* we are one and all, willy-nilly, docile citizens of the Welfare State that his protest becomes significant. In a *laissez-faire* society, however degenerate, his arrogant abjection loses half its point. For he is the One against Society; and his rebellion through degradation, futile though it may be, is in itself a far more effective threat to our self-complacency than Orwell's more positive anti-Utopias. The danger of the Welfare-State mentality is that it feeds on, and then engenders, a socialistic idealism which, being always projected into the almost-immediate future, yet never quite realized, becomes uncritical: 'You never had it so good'. Its values acquire the status of categorical imperatives, for there is no conflict between the real and the ideal, between the here-and-now and Utopia itself: the ultimate Socialist State is merely a bigger and better Welfare State. Whereas, for Genet, Utopia is the opposite, and not the intensification, of what exists already. Genet is the last of the old, genuine anarchists—or perhaps the first of the new: for he is an anarchist who has forged his final convictions, not simply in opposition to a Socialism which he detests, but reluctantly, and in spite of almost overwhelming temptations, in defiance of a Socialism which he admires. Yet there are platitudes on the Left as well as on the Right; and the antediluvian moral code by which we try and live is perhaps even more strongly entrenched among Marxists than among McCarthyites. Not that Genet's anti-ethic offers much of a practical solution. But at least it may serve to remind us of something which we forget too easily : namely, that Revolution is a total concept; and that the New Society, unless it is based on some sort of New Ethic, is liable to lead directly to the concentration camps : 'La Révolution sera morale, ou elle ne sera pas.'

In the last analysis, however, to state new social values is the task of the revolutionary moralist; the poet's duty is confined to stating his own. But for Genet, to state his own values implies a most violent criticism of those which are currently accepted. He does not formulate a new morality; but he most emphatically questions the old. And to question values is the very birthright of the artist.

NOTES

1 *Balcony*, pp. 87-88.
  '*Le 1er Photographe:* C'est dans les habitudes, Majesté. Quand les révoltés furent faits prisonniers, nous avons payé un gendarme pour qu'il abatte devant nous un homme qui allait me chercher un paquet de cigarettes. La photo représentait un révolté descendu alors qu'il tentait de s'évader.
  La Reine: Monstrueux !
  L'Envoyé: Ce qui compte, c'est la lecture. L'Histoire fut vécue afin qu'une page glorieuse soit écrite puis lue.' (*Balcon*, pp. 161-162)
2 Ionesco describes himself as 'un anarchiste de droite'. Half a century earlier, however, Max Beerbohm had coined the identical phrase to describe himself : 'I am a Tory anarchist'.
3 Ionesco, Eugène, 'Depuis dix ans je me bats contre l'esprit bourgeois et les tyrannies politiques', in *Arts*, No. 758, 20-26 Jan. 1960, p. 5.
4 *Blacks*, p. 46. *Litanie des Blêmes*
  'Blêmes comme le râle d'un tubar,
  Blêmes comme ce que lâche le cul d'un homme atteint de jaunisse,
  Blêmes comme le ventre d'un cobra,
  Blêmes comme leurs condamnés à mort,
  Blêmes comme le dieu qu'ils grignotent le matin,
  Blêmes comme un couteau dans la nuit,
  Blêmes . . . sauf : les Anglais, les Allemands et les Belges qui sont rouges . . . Blêmes comme la Jalousie,
  Je vous salue, Blêmes !' (*Nègres*, p. 86)
5 *Ibid.*, p. 23.
  '*Neige:* Si j'étais sûre que Village eût descendu cette femme afin de devenir avec plus d'éclat un nègre balafré, puant, lippu, camus, mangeur, bouffeur, bâfreur de Blancs et de toutes les couleurs, bavant, suant, rôtant, crachant, baiseur de boucs, toussant, pétant, lècheur de pieds blancs, feignant, malade, dégoulinant d'huile et de sueur, flasque et soumis, si j'étais sûre qu'il l'ait tuée pour se confondre avec la nuit. . . . Mais je sais qu'il l'aimait.' (*Nègres*, p. 42)

6 Artaud, Antonin, *Le Théâtre et son Double*, in *Oeuvres Complètes*, vol. IV, Paris (Gallimard) 1964, p. 50.
'Un théâtre d'idiot, de fou, d'inverti, de grammairien, d'épicier, d'anti-poète et de positiviste, c'est-à-dire d'Occidental'.

7 Ionesco, Eugène, *Victimes du Devoir*. In *Théâtre Complet*, vol. I, Paris (Gallimard) 1954, p. 179.
'*Choubert:* Toutes les pièces qui ont été écrites, depuis l'antiquité jusqu'à nos jours, n'ont jamais été que policières. Le théâtre n'a jamais été que réaliste et policier. Toute pièce est une enquête menée à bonne fin. Il y a une énigme, qui nous est révélée à la dernière scène. Quelquefois avant. On cherche, on trouve.' *Cf.* Ionesco. *Plays*, vol. II, London, Calder & Boyars, 1958, p. 269.

8 *Blacks*, p. 96.
'*Village:* Mais si je prends tes mains dans les miennes? Si je t'entoure les épaules—laisse-moi faire—si je te serre dans mes bras?
Vertu: Tous les hommes sont comme toi: ils imitent. Tu ne peux pas inventer autre chose?
Village: Pour toi, je pourrais tout inventer: des fruits, des paroles plus fraîches, une brouette à deux roues, des oranges sans pépins, un lit à trois places, une aiguille qui ne pique pas, mais des gestes d'amour, c'est plus difficile . . . enfin, si tu y tiens. . . .
Vertu: Je t'aiderai.'
(*Nègres*, p. 180)

9 *Ibid*, pp. 13-14.
'*Archibald:* Quittée cette scène, nous sommes mêlés à votre vie: je suis cuisinier, madame est lingère, monsieur étudie la médecine, monsieur est vicaire à Sainte-Clotilde, madame . . . passons. Ce soir, nous ne songerons qu'à vous divertir: nous avons donc tué une blanche.'
(*Nègres*, pp. 24-25)

10 Saint-Nazaire, like Brest, is a French naval dockyard. Echoes of Querelle!

11 *Blacks*, pp. 89-90. This passage of the text contains a number of variants.
'*La Reine:* Gouverneur, en route!
Le Gouverneur: Soit! Colonialement parlant, j'ai bien servi ma patrie. J'ai reçu mille surnoms qui prouvaient l'estime de la Reine et la trouille du sauvage [. . . .] Eh bien, soit, visez donc ce coeur indomptable. Je meurs sans enfants. . . . Mais je compte sur votre sens de l'honneur pour remettre mon uniforme, taché de sang, au musée de l'Armée.'
(*Nègres*, pp. 170-171)

12 *Ibid.*, pp. 60-61. (*Nègres*, pp. 112-3)

13 *Our Lady*, p. 302. '. . . victimes expiatoires, qu'elles fussent bouc, boeuf, enfant, et qu'ont encore aujourd'hui les rois et les Juifs.' (*Notre-Dame*, p. 164)

14 *Ibid.*, p. 191. [Seck Gorgui 'était pudique naturellement mais les Blancs lui avaient enseigné l'impudeur, et dans sa rage à vouloir leur ressembler, il les dépassait.' (*Notre-Dame*, p. 92)

15 *Blacks*, p. 5. 'Qu'est-ce que c'est qu'un noir? et d'abord de quelle couleur?' (*Nègres*, p. 12)

16 Sartre, Jean-Paul, *Réflexions sur la question juive*, Paris (Gallimard: Collection Idées) 1954, p. 83:
'Un Juif est un homme que les autres hommes tiennent pour Juif.'

17 *Ibid.*, pp. 18-19. 'L'anti-sémitisme [. . . .] est à la fois une passion et une conception du monde.'

18 *Blacks*, pp. 11, 45. (*Nègres*, pp. 18, 84)

19 *Ibid.*, p. 16. 'Ma couleur! Mais vous êtes moi-même!' (*Nègres*, p. 29)

20 *Ibid.*, p. 29. 'Quand je vous vis, vous aviez une robe de soie noire, des bas noirs, un parapluie noir et des souliers vernis.' (*Nègres*, p. 53)

21 *Ibid.*, p. 16. 'Le tragique sera dans les couleurs noires.' (*Nègres*, p. 28)

22 *Ibid.*, p. 42. 'Je vous ordonne d'être noir jusque dans vos veines et d'y charrier du sang noir. Que l'Afrique y circule.' (*Nègres*, p. 76)

23 *Ibid.*, pp. 59-60. 'Dahomey! . . . Dahomey! . . . A mon secours, Nègres! Tous. Sous vos blancs parasols, messieurs de Tombouctou, entrez. Mettez-vous là. Tribus couvertes d'or et de boue, remontez de mon corps, sortez! [. . . .] Tu es là, Afrique aux reins cambrés, à la cuisse oblongue? Afrique boudeuse, Afrique travaillée dans le feu, dans le fer, Afrique aux millions d'esclaves royaux, Afrique déportée, continent à la dérive, tu es là?' (*Nègres*, pp. 110-111)

The rhythms and the rhetoric of this magnificent passage suggest that, by this date, Genet was not unfamiliar with Claudel. *Cf.* the speech of Saint James of Compostella in *Le Soulier de Satin*, or, more particularly, Amalric's outburst at the end of Act I of *Partage de Midi*, beginning:

'A gauche, Babylone et tout le bazar, les fleuves
qui descendent de l'Arménie,
A droite, l'Equateur, l'Afrique. . . .'

24 See above, p. 146.

25 *Blacks*, p. 80. 'Nous étions la nuit en personne. Non celle qui est absence de lumière, mais la mère généreuse et terrible qui contient la lumière et les actes.' (*Nègres*, p. 154)

26 *Ibid.*, p. 22. (*Nègres*, p. 38)

27 *Ibid.*, p. 38.

'*La Reine:* A moi, vierges du Parthénon, ange du portail de Reims, colonnes valériennes, Musset, Chopin, Vincent d'Indy, cuisine française, Soldat Inconnu, chansons tyroliennes, principes cartésiens, ordonnance de Le Nôtre, coquelicots, bleuets, un brin de coquetterie, jardins de curés. . . .

Toute la Cour: Madame, nous sommes là.'

(*Nègres*, p. 69)

28 *Ibid.*, p. 61.

'*Snow:* Expire, expire gently,
Our Lady of the Pelicans,
Pretty seagull, politely,
Gallantly, let yourself be tortured. . . .'

(*Nègres*, p. 113)

29 By contrast, a sure sign of Genet's sympathy for—and tact towards—the Blacks is that, without exception, one and all speak a perfectly classical language. There is no dialect, no *argot*, not a hint of pidgin French.

30 *Blacks*, p. 30. 'La suie, le cirage, le charbon, le goudron suffisent.' (*Nègres*, p. 55)

31 *Ibid.*, pp. 52-3.

'*Village:* La limpidité de votre oeil bleu, cette larme qui brille au coin, votre gorge de ciel. . . .

Vertu: Tu délires, à qui parles-tu?

Village: Je vous aime et je n'en puis plus.'

(*Nègres*, p. 98)

32 *Ibid.*, p. 35. 'Je suis beau, tu es belle, et nous nous aimons.' (*Nègres*, p. 63)

33 *Ibid.*, p. 30. 'J'ai peur que vous ne le soyez.' (*Nègres*, p. 54)

34 *Ibid.*, p. 81. '. . . ce qui est doux, bon, aimable et tendra sera noir. Le lait sera noir, le sucre, le riz, le ciel, les colombes, l'espérance.' (*Nègres*, p. 155)

35 *Ibid.*, p. 29. 'Nous nous déplacions, vous et moi, à côté du monde, dans sa marge.' (*Nègres*, p. 53)

36 *Ibid.*

37 *Ibid.*, p. 29.
'*Village:* Je ne pus supporter la condamnation du monde. Et je me suis mis à vous haïr [. . . .] Exactement, je vous hais.'
(*Nègres*, pp. 53-54)

38 *Ibid.*, p. 32. 'Elle a plus de pouvoirs que toi. Il lui arrive de dominer les Blancs.' (*Nègres*, p. 58)

39 *Ibid.*, p. 35. 'Ils vont tout foutre par terre, nom de Dieu !' (*Nègres*, p. 62)

40 *Ibid.*, p. 35. 'Il faut les empêcher de continuer.' (*Nègres*, p. 63)

41 *Ibid.*, p. 36.
'*Vertu:* O nobles pâleurs, colorez mes tempes, mes doigts, mon ventre !
[. . . .] Blanche, c'est le lait qui m'indique, c'est le lys, la colombe, la chaux vive et la claire conscience, c'est la Pologne et son aigle et sa neige ! Neige. . . .' (*Nègres*, pp. 64-5)

42 *Ibid.*, pp. 91-2.
'*Vertu:* Moi aussi, il y a longtemps que je n'osais t'aimer. . . .
Village: Tu m'aimes?
Vertu: J'écoutais. Je t'entendais venir à grandes enjambées. Je courais à la fenêtre et derrière les rideaux je te regardais passer. . . .
Village: Peine perdue : je passais, mâle indifférent, sans jeter un coup d'oeil. . . . Mais la nuit je venais surprendre un rayon de lumière entre tes volets. Entre ma chemise et ma peau je l'emportais. . . .'
(*Nègres*, pp. 173-4)

43 *Ibid.*, p. 28. (*Nègres*, p. 51)

44 *Ibid.*, p. 27. 'Blanche d'un côté, noire de l'autre'. (*Nègres*, p. 48)

45 *Ibid.*, p. 28.
'*Archibald:* Si vous deviez, monsieur, apporter parmi nous la moindre, la plus banale de leurs idées qui ne soit caricaturale, allez-vous-en ! Barrez-vous.'
(*Nègres*, p. 52)

46 *Ibid.*, p. 28.
'*Diouf:* Sur ma tête comme sur la vôtre, légère et insupportable, est descendue se poser la bonté des Blancs. Sur mon épaule droite leur intelligence, sur la gauche tout un vol de vertus, et quelquefois, dans ma main, en l'ouvrant, je découvrais blottie leur charité.'
(*Nègres*, p. 51)

47 *Ibid.* 'Une technicienne de la haine.' (*Nègres*, p. 51)

48 *Ibid.*
'*Diouf:* Je suis vieux et je pense. . . .
Bobo: Qui vous le demande? Ce qu'il nous faut, c'est la haine. D'elle naîtront nos idées.'
(*Nègres*, p. 51)

49 *Ibid.*, p. 88. (*Nègres*, pp. 168-9)

50 Milne, Tom, 'Reflections on the Screens', in *Encore*, No. 50 (vol. xi, No. 4), July-Aug. 1964, p. 25. In performance at the *Théâtre de l'Odéon* (1966) many cuts were in fact made in the text.

51 *Screens*, pp. 104 and 106.

'*Le Lieutenant* [*to a group of Légionnaires*]: La France nous regarde. Elle nous envoie mourir. . . . Peignez vos cheveux. [. . . .] Ce n'est pas d'intelligence qu'il s'agit : mais de perpétuer une image qui a plus de dix siècles. . . .'

(*Paravents*, pp. 155 and 157)

52 *Ibid.*, pp. 171-2. In this scene, both living and dead characters are present.

'*Ommou:* Certaines vérités sont inapplicables, sinon elles mourraient. . . . Elles ne doivent pas mourir, mais vivre par le chant qu'elles sont devenues. . . . Vive le chant !

Le Combattant: Ni moi ni mes amis on ne s'est battu pour que ça chante en toi, Caroline.'

(*Paravents*, pp. 254-5)

53 *Ibid.*, p. 171.

'*Ommou:* Soldat ! . . . il y a des vérités qui ne doivent jamais être appliquées. C'est celles-là qu'il faut faire vivre par le chant qu'elles sont devenues.'

(*Paravents*, p. 254)

54 It is likely that this attitude was developed in conversation with Sartre, and more particularly with Simone de Beauvoir, who was preoccupied with problems of an individualist socialism, especially during the period 1943-1950. It is interesting to compare Genet's treatment of the theme with that of Simone de Beauvoir, especially in *Le Sang des Autres* (1945).

55 *Screens*, p. 99. (*Paravents*, p. 148)

56 *Ibid.*, p. 12. 'La plus laide femme du pays d'à côté et de tous les pays d'alentour.' (*Paravents*, p. 14)

57 *Ibid.*, p. 24. The latter part of this passage is cut out in the English version.

La Mère: Puisque tu es laide, sois idiote.

Leïla: D'après vous je dois chercher à devenir de plus en plus con?

La Mère: Essaye toujours, on verra ce que ça donnera.

(*Paravents*, p. 33)

58 *Ibid.*, pp. 169-170.

Ommou: C'est mort qu'on te veut mort mais c'est vivant pas mort. . . .

Saïd: C'est me laisser mort pour vivant !

Ommou: C'est ni mort ni vivant !

(*Paravents*, pp. 251-2)

59 *Ibid.*, pp. 97-8. (*Paravents*, pp, 145-6)

60 *Ibid.*, p. 86. 'Mal, merveilleux mal, toi qui nous reste quand tout a foutu le camp, mal miraculeux tu vas nous aider. Je t'en prie, et je t'en prie debout, mal, viens féconder mon peuple.' (*Paravents*, p. 130)

61 *Ibid.*, p. 90. 'Et n'ayez pas honte, mes fils. Méritez le mépris du monde. Egorgez, mes fils.' (*Paravents*, p. 134)

62 *Ibid.*, p. 67.

'*Monsieur Blankensee:* Nous sommes les maîtres du langage. Toucher aux roses, c'est toucher à la langue.

Sir Harold: Et toucher à la langue est sacrilège.'

(*Paravents*, p. 97)

63 *Ibid.*, p. 113. 'La beauté, ciment de l'armée [. . . .] On doit y aller. Armés, bottés, casqués, oui, mais aussi poudrés, cosmétiqués, fardés ce qui tue c'est un fond de teint sur un squelette de gestes précis.' (*Paravents*, p. 167)

64 *Ibid.*, p. 121.
'*Le Soldat:* La guerre a ses lois.
Ommou: Mais pas de lois morales.
Le Soldat: Si. Elle nous apprend ce que sera la paix. On ne veut plus tuer ni être tués, on veut être les plus forts. Il faut une armure.'
(*Paravents*, p. 178)

65 *Ibid.*, p. 121.
'*Ommou:* Tu crains pour ton bel uniforme?
Le Soldat: On se bat moins bien quand on est en loques. Et on se bat moins bien quand on a une sale gueule et qu'on plaît moins aux filles.' (*Paravents*, p. 179)

66 *Ibid.*, p. 119.
'*Ommou:* . . . vous autres, vous êtes déjà au stade de la tenue, de la discipline, des jolies marches et des bras nus, des parades et de la mort héroïque en chantant *Madelon, Marseillaise* et la beauté guerrière. . . .
Le Soldat: Pourquoi pas? Il y a autre chose que merde et crasse. . . .
Ommou: Espèce de petit voyou, morveux, passe de l'autre côté, où est la beauté digne, voyou morveux! Mais c'est peut-être fait, vous y passez, et ça vous excite de vous calquer sur eux, être leur reflet c'est déjà être eux. . . .' (*Paravents*, p. 176)

67 It is, in fact, an argument developed at considerable length in Proust's *In Remembrance of Things Past*.

68 *Screens*, p. 124.
'*Le Cadi:* Les choses cessent d'appartenir à ceux qui ont su les rendre plus belles. Meilleures et plus belles, agiles, ailées, elles abandonnent avec gratitude celui qui les a rendues meilleures. Elles parties, plus rien, que dalle, zéro, foutu.' (*Paravents*, p. 183)

69 *Giacometti*, p. 25. 'L'oeuvre de Giacometti communique la connaissance de la solitude de chaque être et de chaque chose, et que cette solitude est notre gloire la plus sûre.'

70 *Ibid.*, p. 47. 'Cette capacité d'isoler un objet et de faire affluer en lui ses propres, ses seules significations n'est possible que par l'abolition historique de celui qui regarde.'

71 *Ibid.*, p. 26. 'Chaque objet crée son espace infini.'

72 *Ibid.*, p. 53. 'N'est-ce pas au bordel que la femme pourrait s'enorgueillir d'une blessure qui ne la délivrera plus jamais de la solitude?'

73 *Ibid.*, p. 71. 'Ce qui me plaît dans les poules c'est qu'elles ne servent à rien. Elles sont là. C'est tout.'

74 *Screens*, p. 114. 'Pauvres jupons d'or! J'ai cherché qu'un jour, au lieu d'être parure, vous soyez à vous seuls la putain dans sa gloire!' (*Paravents*, p. 169)

75 *Ibid.*, p. 21. 'Il faut se vouloir une putain totale.' (*Paravents*, p. 28)

76 *Thief*, p. 128. 'Ses impudiques attitudes je ne puis dire qu'elles sont à l'origine de ma décision d'écrire des livres pornographiques mais [j'en] fus certainement bouleversé. . . .' (*Journal*, p. 150)

BIBLIOGRAPHY

NOTE: Many of the early (clandestine or semi-clandestine) editions of Genet's works are very difficult to trace, even where they are known with certainty to exist. This list, therefore, is merely a guide, and makes no claim to be complete. Its shortcomings, moreover, would have been far greater than they are, had it not been for the wealth of information so generously provided by that knowledgeable bibliophile and collector, Mr Arthur Uphill; by Dr T. V. Benn, of the University of Leeds; by Dr Peter Hoy, of the University of Leicester; by Dr R. W. F. Wilcocks, of the University of Khartoum; and by Mr Edwin Morgan, poet and scholar, of the University of Glasgow. I should like to take this occasion to record my gratitude to them for their invaluable co-operation in compiling this bibliography.

Editions from which most of the quotations in the text have been taken are marked with an asterisk.

SECTION I

Works by Jean Genet

(a) POEMS

1. *Le Condamné à Mort*
   Fresnes, September 1942. 11 pp., unsewn, in loose board covers, octavo. Copy with author's MS corrections in Bibliothèque Nationale, Rés. p. Ye. 1561.

2. —*Le Condamné à Mort: suivi de Poèmes, l'Enfant Criminel, le Funambule.* Décines (L'Arbalète) 1966. Trade edition.

3. —*The Man Condemned to Death/Le Condamné à Mort.* N.Y. [no date, no publisher: probably pirated edition, 1965] Edition limited to 300 copies. Octavo, stiff puce wrappers, lettered in black. Illustrated with two 'mauvais-Cocteau' style drawings. Parallel text in French and English. English translation by Diane di Prima, Alan Marlowe, Harriet and Bret Rohmer.

4. *Chants Secrets*
   L'Arbalète, n.p., n.d. [=Lyon, 20 March 1945]. Large octavo, 47 pp. Cover lithograph by Emile Picq. Printed by Marc Barbezat, 8 rue Godefroy, Lyon. B.N. 4° Ye. 898 and Rés. m. Ye. 529
   Contains: 'Le Condamné à Mort' (pp. 13-26)
   　　　　　'Dédicace' (to Maurice Pilorge) (pp. 27-28)
   　　　　　'Marche Funèbre' (pp. 31-45)

5. *La Galère*
   In *La Table Ronde*, 3e Cahier, 1945, pp. 155-168. Dedicated to Nico Dakis.

6. —Paris (J. Loyau), July 1947. Quarto, collectors' edition, with six engravings by Léonor Fini. Limited to 80 copies. B.N. Enfer, 1612.

7. —MS variants of *La Galère*. Genet made 15 numbered autograph copies of this poem, 7 pp., octavo, written in ink on Rives paper. These versions, of which one is signed and dated 'Paris 19 août 1944', contain significant variants. Compare the following:

> 'Harcamone aux bras verts haute reine qui vole
> Sur ton odeur nocturne et les bois éveillés
> Par l'horreur de son nom ce bagnard endeuillé
> Sur ma galère chante et son chant me désole.'
>
>   (*Poèmes*, p. 53),

with the version in MS No. 8:

> 'Harcamone aux yeux verts haute reine qui vole
> Sur ton odeur nocturne et les bois éveillés
> laisse-moi retrouver la galère. Endeuillé
> par l'amour qu'il te garde un forçat s'y désole.'

8. *Poèmes*

Lyon (L'Arbalète) 1948. Quarto, bound with spiral binding. Cover illustrated with a polyphoto-series of the author. 107 pp., limited edition on 'pur fil Lana'. B.N. Rés. m. Ye. 529.

Contains: 'Le Condamné à Mort'
            'La Galère'
            'La Parade'
            'Un Chant d'Amour'
            'Le Pêcheur du Suquet'

9. —'Un Chant d'Amour'. French text, accompanied by a photograph of Genet. *View* (Paris), vol. vi, Nos. 2-3, March-April 1946, p. 11. (This is the earliest printed version of the poem that I have been able to trace).

10. —'A Love Song'. English translation of 'Un Chant d'Amour', by James Kirkup. *The Window*, Feb. 1954 (French Number, edited by Philip Inman), pp. 26-30.

11. —['Le Pêcheur du Suquet']. English translation by Edwin Morgan of an extract (Gallimard version), under the title: 'Jean Genet— from: le pecheur du suquet'. *The Outsider* (New Orleans), vol I, No. 2, Summer 1962, pp. 52-53.

12. —['Le Pêcheur du Suquet']. English translation by Edwin Morgan of an extract (Gallimard version), under the title: 'A Colloquy . . from *Le Pêcheur du Suquet*'. *The Outsider* (New Orleans), vol, I, No. 3, Spring 1963, pp. 44-45.

13. —['Le Pêcheur du Suquet']. English translation by Edwin Morgan of two extracts, under the titles: 'In the death cell' and 'Purple flowers'. *The Insect Trust Gazette* (Philadelphia), No. 1, 1964, pp. 59-60.

14. *Poèmes*

*Décines (L'Arbalète) 1962. Octavo, wrappers. Various numbered collectors' sub-editions on special paper. Similar to 1948 edition, but lacking cover-photographs and including 'Marche Funèbre'. Trade edition.

15. —Décines (L'Arbalète) 1966. Reprinted together with *Le Condamné à Mort*, *L'Enfant Criminel* and *Le Funambule*. See No. 2.

16. *Oeuvres Complètes de Jean Genet*
Paris (Gallimard) 1951-1953. 3 vols.
Contain: 'Le Condamné à Mort' (II, 177-186)
'Un Chant d'Amour' (II, 399-402)
'Le Pêcheur du Suquet' (III, 163-169)
(Some modifications in the text)

(b) NOVELS

17. *Notre-Dame des Fleurs*
Fragment [cf. Gallimard text, pp. 144-165] originally published in the literary review *L'Arbalète*, No. 8, April 1944, pp. 5-36, under the title *Notre-Dame-des-Fleurs* [hyphenated *sic*]. Edition limited to 1100 numbered copies on vélin pur fil. This remarkable volume also contains the original edition of Sartre's *Huis Clos* (under the title : *Les Autres*), and writings by Leiris, Queneau, Claudel and Mouloudji. Bibl. de l'Arsenal, 8° Jo. 22705.

18. —[Complete text, original version]. Monte Carlo, 'aux dépens d'un Amateur', Sept. 1944. Quarto, 267 pp., edition limited to 350 copies, none of which was on special paper. B.N. Enfer 1401.

19. —[Original version]. Lyon (L'Arbalète), 30 Aug. 1948. Limited edition, in-16°, hand-printed on pur fil Lana, watermarked 'L'Arbalète'. Bodoni 12-point, red and black. 411 pp. Available to subscribers only. B.N. Enfer 1672.

20. —[Revised version]. *Paris (Gallimard) 1951. In *Oeuvres Complètes de Jean Genet*, II, 7-175. Dated 'Prison de Fresnes, 1942'. Numerous reprints.

21. —Décines (L'Arbalète) 1966. Octavo, 109 pp., printed on double-columns. Trade edition.

22. —*Our Lady of the Flowers*. Paris (Paul Morihien) 30 Apr. 1949. Original version, English translation by Bernard Frechtman. In-16°, 396 pp. Edition limited to 500 copies, publisher's leather, lettered in gilt, design by Cocteau on front cover, marbled endpapers. Available to subscribers only. Collectors' sub-edition, 25 numbered copies on Rives paper. B.N. Enfer 1402.

23. —Extract from the preceding, under title : 'The Game'. *Tiger's Eye* (New York), No. 8, 1949, p. 99 ff.

24. —Extract from No. 22, under the title : 'The Night's Children'. *Tiger's Eye* (New York), No. 9, 1949, p.1 ff.

25. —Extract from No. 22, in *New Directions Anthology*, No. 11, 1949-50.

26. —Complete text, English translation as for No. 22. Paris (Olympia Press) 1957. In-16°, pp. 269. 'Traveller's Companion Series', No. 36. B.N. Rés. p. y² 1000.

27. —Extract from No. 26, under the title : 'Jean Genet: from *Our Lady of the Flowers*'. *Evergreen Review* (New York), No. 18, May-June 1961, pp. 33-58.

28. —English translation of revised (Gallimard) text, by Bernard Frechtman. Introduction translated from J.-P. Sartre, *Saint-Genet Comédien et Martyr*. N.Y. (Grove Press) 1963. *London (Blond) 1964.

29. —Extract from *Notre-Dame des Fleurs*, English translation by Harry Goldgar. *Western Review* (State University of Iowa), vol. xiv, No. 3, 1950, p. 183 ff. Preceded by 'A Note on Jean Genet', by H. Goldgar, pp. 181-182.

30. —Extract from *Notre-Dame des Fleurs*, in an anonymous English translation. *New Story* (New York), No. 1, 1951, p. 5 ff.

31. —*Gutter in the Sky*. Anonymous, pirated English translation of *Notre-Dame des Fleurs*. Accompanied by 'Preparatory notes on an unknown sexuality', by Jean Cocteau. Philadelphia. (André Levy) 1956.

32. *Miracle de la Rose*
Fragment [cf. Gallimard text, pp. 189-214] originally published in the literary review *L'Arbalète*, No. 10, May 1945, pp. 7-40. The issue was published 'à un nombre limité d'exemplaires sur Johannot.' This volume also contains poems by Olivier Larronde, seemingly an imitator of Genet.

33. —Lyon (L'Arbalète), 30 March 1946, collectors' edition, quarto, set in Bodoni 12-point, 537 pp., publisher's binding, edition limited to 475 copies. B.N. Rés. 4° Ln. 27. 83466; also in Baillieu Library, Melbourne.

34. —Décines, Isère (L'Arbalète), n.d. [1957?]. In-16°, 484 pp. Edition limited to 2,200 copies. B.N. Rés. 16° Ln. 27. 83466. A. Baillieu Library, Melbourne.

35. —*Paris (Gallimard) 1951. In *Oeuvres Complètes de Jean Genet*, II, 187-397. Dated: 'La Santé. Prison des Tourelles. 1943'. Numerous reprints.

36. —*Miracle of the Rose* English translation (of Gallimard text) by Bernard Frechtman. N.Y. (Grove Press) 1965; *London (Blond) 1965.

37. *Pompes Funèbres*
Extracts published in an anonymous English translation, under the title 'It's Your Funeral', in *View* (Paris), vol. vi, Nos. 2-3, March-April 1946, pp. 24, 36-37, 46-47, 49-51.

38. —[Complete text, original version]. 'Bikini', n.p., n.d. [1947]. Large octavo, 313 pp., B.N. Enfer 1543.

39. —[Complete text, original version]. Paris [? Paul Morihien] April 1948. Edition based on No. 38, but with numerous minor corrections. In-12°, wrappers, cover-photograph showing baldaquin of a hearse, title-page design in the manner of Cocteau, 375 pp. Edition limited to 1,500 numbered copies on Vergé paper. Described as 'strictement hors commerce'. Baillieu Library, Melbourne.

40. —[Revised version]. *Paris (Gallimard) 1953. In *Oeuvres Complètes de Jean Genet*, III, 7-162. Numerous reprints.

41. —*Pompes Funèbres—Das Totenfest*. German tr. by Marion Luckow. Hamburg (Merlin-Verlag) 1967.

42. *Querelle de Brest*
'Milan', November 1947. 4°, 251 pp. Original edition, 'hors commerce', limited to 525 copies, of which 40, 'numérotés sur vélin', are inscribed 'pour les amis de Querelle', and signed by

the author. Luxury edition, quarto, illustrated wrappers, containing 29 lithographs by Cocteau. In addition, 15 special copies were printed 'sur vélin de Lana', each including an original drawing by Cocteau. Libr. Congress, 58-32034. B.N. Enfer, 1671.

43. —[? Paris, Morihien] December 1947. Edition limited to 1850 copies. White wrappers, lettered in blue on spine; front wrapper, white lettering on blue background, with device of two anchors crossed, in red. No illustrations, but contains author's note about his plans for the revised edition, *Capable du Fait*. Large octavo, pp. 250. Baillieu Library, Melbourne.

44. —*Paris (Gallimard) 1953 [revised edition]. In *Oeuvres Complètes de Jean Genet*, III, 171-350. Numerous reprints.

45. —*Querelle*. Roman. Aus dem Französischen von Ruth Vecker-Lutz. Reineck bei Hamburg (Rowohlt-Verlag), 1955.

46. —*Querelle*. German translation, as for preceding. Paris (Olympia Press) 1958. In-16°, 400 pp., portrait on cover. B.N. 16° Y² 21045.

47. —*Querelle*. German translation, as for No. 45. Published jointly by Rowohlt-Verlag (Reineck) and Olympia Press (Paris), 1962.

48. —*Querelle*. German translation, as for No. 45. Rowohlt-Verlag, Reineck bei Hamburg, 1965. 372 pp. Trade edition. *Cf. Frankfurter Allgemeine Zeitung*, 10 July 1965.

49. —*Querelle of Brest*, complete English text, translated by Roger Senhouse. N.Y. (Grove Press) 1967; *London (Blond) 1966.

(c) AUTOBIOGRAPHY

50. *Journal du Voleur*
'Aux dépens d'un Ami', n.p., n.d. [1948?]. Quarto, in sheets, 312 pp. Edition limited to 400 copies. B.N. Enfer, 1614.

51. —*Paris (Gallimard) 1949. Slight modification of the preceding. The second volume, which is announced on p. 286 of this edition, has never appeared. Numerous reprints.

52. —*The Thief's Journal*. English translation of the original version by Bernard Frechtman. Published as an extract in *Transition Forty-Eight* (Paris) [dated 15 Jan. 1949], No. 4, pp. 66-75. See also p. 155.

53. —Extract (tr. Frechtman, as for preceding). *New World Writing*, vol. ii, pp. 285-291. N.Y. (New American Library: 'Second Mentor Selection') 1952.

54. —Extract (tr. Frechtman, as for No. 52), together with an introduction by Jean-Paul Sartre: 'A Note on Genet'; *Merlin* (Paris), vol. ii, No. I, Spring-Summer 1953, pp. 4-14.

55. —Complete English text, tr. Frechtman, with additional footnotes; also Sartre, 'A Note on Genet' (see No. 54). Paris (Olympia Press: 'Collection Merlin') 1954, in-16°, 291 pp. Wrappers, design of hands, white on black.

56. —[re-issue of preceding]. Paris (Olympia Press: 'Traveller's Companion Series', No. 78) 1959. Including Sartre: 'A Note on Genet' (see No. 54). B.N. Rés. p. Y² 1000.

57. —Complete English text, tr. Frechtman, based on revised Gallimard text, and omitting Sartre 'A Note on Genet'. N.Y. (Grove Press) 1964; *London (Blond) 1965; N.Y. (Bantam Books) 1965 (Paperback).

58. —*Confessions of a Thief*. Anon. English translation, published as an extract in *World Review*, n.s., No. 10. Dec. 1949, p. 28 ff.

59. —*A Thief's Journal*. Anon. English translation, published as an extract in *Paris Review*, No. 13, Summer 1956, pp. 45-49.

60. —*The Beggars of Barcelona*. English translation by Raymond Federman, published as an extract in *The Big Table* (Chicago), vol. i, No. 3, 1959, pp. 111-115.

(d) PLAYS

60a. *Haute Surveillance*
One-act, Théâtre des Maturins, 24 Feb. 1949. Produced by Jean Genet. *La Nef* (Paris), March-April 1947.

61 —*Paris (Gallimard) 1949. Numerous reprints. A variant text, which was used in performance, has remained in MS. It is this text, however, which is employed in the English translation.

62. —*Deathwatch*. English translation by Bernard Frechtman, based on prompt-copy version. Contained in *The Maids and Deathwatch*, N.Y. (Grove Press) 1954; *Deathwatch*, London (Faber) 1961. Various reprints.

63. *Les Bonnes*
One-Act, Théâtre de l'Athénée, 17th April 1946, produced by Louis Jouvet [original version], Théâtre de la Huchette, 1954 [revised version]. First published [original version] in the review *L'Arbalète*, No. 12, May 1947, pp. 47-92, in a limited edition 'sur Johannot.' B.N. 4° Z. 3698.

64. —'Les deux versions précédées d'une Lettre de l'Auteur' [i.e., the 'Lettre à Pauvert sur *Les Bonnes*']. In-16°, pp. 155. Sceaux (J. J. Pauvert) 1954.

65. —[Revised version]. In *Les Bonnes et l'Atelier d'Alberto Giacometti*. Décines (L'Arbalète), 20 May 1958. [Also in this volume: *L'Enfant Criminel*; *Le Funambule*; *Lettre à Pauvert*]. Edition limited to 3,000 numbered copies, including 250 'hors commerce, in-16°, sur Lana Jésus', watermarked 'L'Arbalète', and other special collectors' copies.

66. —[Revised version]. *Les Bonnes, précédé de Comment jouer les Bonnes*. Décines (L'Arbalète) 1963. Numerous reprints.

67. —*The Maids*. English translation by Bernard Frechtman, based on the original version; preceded by a translation of Jean-Paul Sartre's Appendix on *Les Bonnes* from *Saint-Genet*, and followed by a 'Note on Genet'. N.Y. (Grove Press) 1954, in *The Maids and Deathwatch* (see No. 62), 166 pp. Various reprints. *London (Faber) 1957 (contains *The Maids* only, without the introduction or concluding note). Reprints including paperback.

68. *Le Balcon*
Full-length play in 9 scenes. First performed in English at the Arts Theatre, London, April 1957. Décines (L'Arbalète) 10 June

1956 [original version, 9 scenes in 2 acts]. In-16°, wrappers illustrated with a lithograph by Giacometti, 'réalisée par Mourlot', 195 pp. Edition limited to 3,000 numbered copies, set in Bodoni d'Hubert-Denous, on Lana-Jésus watermarked 'L'Arbalète'; also 32 numbered copies on Japon nacré impérial, 30 stamped by the author 'J.G.', and various 'hors commerce'. This edition is dedicated to Pierre Joly. B.N. 16° Yth 1809.

69. —[Version in 15 scenes.] Décines (M. Barbezat: Editions de l'Arbalète) 1956. 244 pp. (Senate House Library, University of London.)

70. —[Revised version, 9 scenes]. Preceded by 'Un Avertissement: Comment Jouer *Le Balcon*'. Décines (L'Arbalète) 1960.

71. —['Version définitive', 9 scenes]. Includes 'Comment jouer *Le Balcon*'. *Décines (L'Arbalète) 1961, numerous reprints.

72. —*The Balcony*. English translation by Bernard Frechtman. Version in 9 scenes, but with some textual variants. N.Y. (Grove Press) 1958 (also in Evergreen Books and in Evergreen Originals); *London (Faber) 1957.

73. *Les Nègres*
Full-length 'clownerie'. First performed at the Théâtre de Lutèce, 28 Oct. 1959, produced by Roger Blin. Décines (L'Arbalète) 2 Jan. 1958. In-16°, wrappers, cover-design by Jean Genet, lithographed by Mourlot, 154 pp. Edition limited to 3,200 numbered copies, set in Bodoni d'Hubert-Denous on Lana-Jésus; also 32 on Japon nacré impérial, 50 with Author's stamp 'J.G.' and 250 'hors commerce'.

74. —Edition with 33 photographs by Ernest Scheidegger of the Théâtre de Lutèce production (see No. 73). Preceded by 'Pour jouer *Les Nègres*'. *Décines (L'Arbalète) 1960. Various reprints.

75. —*The Blacks: A Clown Show*. English translation by Bernard Frechtman, revealing some textual variants. N.Y. (Grove Press) 1960; *London (Faber) 1960. Reprints.

76. *Les Paravents*
Full-length play in 17 scenes. Schlosspark Theatre, Berlin, May 1961. Original title: *Ça Bouge Encore* (see *Express*, 28 Feb. 1960, p. 28; *Lettres Nouvelles*, 28 Oct. 1959, pp. 24-6). Preceded by 'Quelques Indications'. *Décines (Marc Barbezat: L'Arbalète) 1961. Of the various collectors' editions, that of 150 numbered copies on watermarked Lana contains 10 additional drawings.

77. —*The Screens*. English translation by Bernard Frechtman. N.Y. (Grove Press) 1962; *London (Faber) 1963.

(e) ARTICLES, ESSAYS, CRITICISM, etc.

78. *'Adame Miroir*
Ballet-scenario, music by Darius Milhaud, choreography by Janine Charrat. Performed by the Ballets Roland Petit, Théâtre Marigny, 1946. Paris (Hengel) 1948, incl. piano score. 27 pp.

79. —Text reprinted, together with *L'Enfant Criminel*. *Paris (Paul Morihien) 1949, pp. 37-58. (For details of this edition, see No. 86).

80. *Atelier d'Alberto Giacometti, l'* In *Les Lettres Nouvelles*, V, No. 52, Sept. 1957, pp. 199-218.

81. —Décines (L'Arbalète) 1958. For details of this edition, see under *Les Bonnes* (No. 65). The Giacometti essay, in this volume, is slightly longer than in the subsequent version.

82. —(With numerous photographs by Ernest Scheidegger) *Décines (L'Arbalète) 1963. Reprints.

83. —*Giacometti's Studio*. English translation by Terence Kilmartin. *The Observer Colour Supplement*, 11 July 1965, pp. 27-30.

84. *Comment jouer le Balcon*. 1960, See above, under: Plays—*Le Balcon* (Nos. 70-71).

85. *Comment jouer Les Bonnes*. 1963. See above, under: Plays— *Les Bonnes* (No. 66).

86. *Enfant Criminel, l'*
Script for a radio-talk which was never given. *Paris (Paul Morihien) Feb. 1949, pp. 7-33 of a volume which also contains *'Adame Miroir* (see above, No. 78). 60 pp. in-12°, including a limited edition of 50 numbered copies on Marais-Crèvecoeur. White wrappers, lettered up spine in red. Front wrapper photograph [? of Genet] as a juvenile delinquent, standing in the doorway of a cell. First page of text also has a photograph of Genet as adolescent. Baillieu Library, Melbourne.

87. —Reprinted in *L'Atelier d'Alberto Giacometti* (see above, No. 65), Décines (L'Arbalète) 1958, pp. 149-172.

88. —Reprinted in *Le Condamné à Mort* (see above, No. 2), Décines (L'Arbalète) 1966.

89. *Funambule, le*
*Décines (L'Arbalète) 1958; in *L'Atelier d'Alberto Giacometti* (see above, No. 65), 1958, pp. 173-204.

90. —Reprinted in *Le Condamné à Mort* (see above, No. 2), Décines (L'Arbalète) 1966.

91. —*The Funambulists*. English translation by Bernard Frechtman. *Evergreen Review*, No. 32, Apr.-May. 1964, pp. 45-49. Illustration by Jerome Martin.

91a. *Grèce! . . .*
Article on Jean Cocteau. *Empreintes* (Brussels), May 1950, pp. 23 *ff*.

91b. *J'ai été victime d'une tentative d'assassinat. Arts* (Paris), 1 May 1957.

92. *Lettre à J.-J. Pauvert sur Les Bonnes*
1954. See above under: Plays—*Les Bonnes* (No. 64).

93. —Reprinted in *L'Atelier d'Alberto Giacometti* (see above, No. 65), 1958, pp. 142-148.

94. —*A Note on Theatre*. English translation by Bernard Frechtman, in *Tulane Drama Review*, vol. vii, No. 3, Spring 1963, pp. 37-41.

95. *Lettre à Léonor Fini*
    Paris (J. Loyau) 1950. Octavo, pp. 10, with 8 plates, all of paintings by Léonor Fini. B.N. 8° V. pièce 31512.

96. —*Mademoiselle: A Letter to Léonor Fini.* English translation by Bernard Frechtman, in *Nimbus*, vol. iii, No. 1. [? 1955], pp. 30-37, together with one reproduction of a painting of Genet by Léonor Fini, p. 31.

97. *Lettres à Roger Blin.*
    Series of notes and letters concerning the production of *Les Paravents* at the Théâtre de France, 21 Apr. 1966. Illustrated with photographs of the production. Paris (Gallimard/N.R.F.) 1966. 69 pp.

98. *Pour jouer les Nègres.* 1960. See above, under : Plays—*Les Nègres* (No. 74).

99. *Secret de Rembrandt, le*
    Illustrated. *Express,* No. 377, 4 Sept. 1958, pp. 14-15. According to Simone de Beauvoir, the editors insisted on making heavy cuts in the original MS of this article before publication. The 'Essai sur Rembrandt,' announced as being in preparation with Gallimard (1958), has not materialized. Cf., however, No. 100.

100. *Something which seems to resemble decay. . . .*
    Published in an English translation by Bernard Frechtman, in *Art and Literature : An International Review* (Lausanne), No. 1, March 1964, pp. 77-86. [Contains additional material on Rembrandt : cf. No. 99].

101. *To a would-be producer.*
    Letter written to the Polish poet, Jerzy Lizowski, explaining Genet's refusal to allow *Les Nègres* to be performed in Warsaw. First published in English translation by Bernard Frechtman, *Tulane Drama Review*, vol. vii, No. 3, Spring 1963, pp. 80-81, followed by two photographs of the Théâtre de Lutèce production of *Les Nègres*, by Sandra Lousada and André Acquart

102. *What I like about the English is that they are such liars. . . .*
    Published in an anonymous English translation in *The Sunday Times Colour Supplement*, 24 Feb. 1963, p. 11, together with photograph of Jean Genet.

(f) UNTRACEABLE, OR OF UNCERTAIN ATTRIBUTION

103. *Bagne, le*
    Announced in 1963 as being 'in preparation'. According to an unconfirmed report (Sept. 1965), Genet had then 'recently burnt' the MS. However, in No. 21 (1966), it is again announced as being 'in preparation'.

104. *Beaux Gars, les*
    Illustrated with 27 drawings by Jean Boullet. 1951, published 'par une société d'Imprimerie Méditerranéenne'. Untraceable.

105. *Elle*
    As for No. 103.

106. *Fée, la*
    As for No. 103.

107. *Football*
    Announced in 1958. No subsequent references.

108. *Fous, les*
    As for No. 103.

109. *Rembrandt*
    See Nos. 99-100.

110. *Splendid's*
    Play in two acts, described in a checklist published by Paul
    Morihien in 1949 (*L'Enfant Criminel:* see No. 86) as already
    being in print. Never performed and now untraceable. In Sept.
    1965, Genet is reported to have said that 'the play had never
    been published and that the MS had recently been destroyed;'
    none the less, in No. 21 (1966), it is again announced as being
    'in preparation,' and is now given an alternative title: *La
    Rafale.*

(g) ADDENDA

    The following works of Genet have recently appeared in German
    translation:

111. *Balkon (der)*. Schauspiel. German tr. by Georg Schulte-Frohlinde.
    Hamburg (Merlin-Verlag) 1967. 139 pp.

112. *Briefe an Roger Blin*. German tr. by Gerald and Uta Szyszkowitz.
    In one volume together with *Der Seiltänzer (Le Funambule)*.
    Hamburg (Merlin-Verlag) 1967, pp. 1-60.

113. *Neger (die)*. Clownerie. German tr. by Katarina Hock and Ben
    Poller. Stage adaptation by Hans-Joachim Weitz. 500 numbered
    copies with illustrations by Ali Schindehütte and Arno Wald-
    schmidt. Hamburg (Merlin-Verlag) 1967. 112 pp.

114. *Notre-Dame-des-Fleurs*. German tr. by Gerhard Hock. Hamburg
    (Merlin-Verlag) 1967. 268 pp.

115. *Pompes Funèbres—Das Totenfest*. German tr. by Marion Luckow.
    Hamburg (Merlin-Verlag) 1967. 240 pp.

116. *Seiltänzer (der)*. German tr. by Manon Grisebach. In one volume
    together with *Briefe an Roger Blin*. Hamburg (Merlin-Verlag)
    1967, pp. 61-91.

117. *Tagebuch eines Diebes*. Roman. German tr. by Gerhard Hock
    and Helmut Vosskämper; introduction by Max Bense. Hamburg
    (Merlin-Verlag) 1967. 278 pp.

118. *Wände Überall (Les Paravents)*. Scenenfolge. German tr. by Hans
    Georg Brenner. Hamburg (Merlin-Verlag) 1967. 220 pp.

SECTION II

Criticism

ABEL, Lionel. 'Metatheater: *Le Balcon*', *Partisan Review* (N.Y.), vol. xxvii, No. 2, 1960, pp. 324-330.

ARMSTRONG, W. A. *Experimental Drama*. London (Bell) 1963.

Aspetti di Jean Genet. Studi di Letteratura francese, I. *Biblioteca dell' Archivum Romanicum*, Serie I, Vol. 89. Florence (Olschki) 1967. xvi + 175 pp.

ATTINELLI, Lucio. 'Genet et l'Italie', *Cahiers des Saisons*, No. 21, Spring 1960, pp. 50-51.

BACHMANN, Claus Henning. 'Die Passion des unbarmherzigen Genet. Anmerkungen zu der deutschen Erstaufführung des *Balkon* und zu den *Zofen*' [*Le Balcon* and *Les Bonnes*], *Antares 7* (1959), pp. 246-248.

Balcon, Le (some minor reviews):
   DUSSANE. *Mercure*, No. 339 (1960), pp. 511-512.
   LEMARCHAND, J. *Figaro Littéraire*, 21 May 1960, p. 16.
   MARCEL, Gabriel. *Nouvelles Littéraires*, 26 May 1960, p. 10.
   POIROT-DELPECH, B. *Le Monde*, 19 May 1960.

BARTHES, Roland. 'Jean Genet: *Le Balcon* (mise-en-scène de Peter Brook)', *Théâtre Populaire*, No. 38, 1960, pp. 96-98.

BATAILLE, Georges. *L'Erotisme*, Paris (Minuit) 1957. Tr. Mary Dalwood, *Eroticism*, London (Calder) 1962.

— *La Littérature et le Mal*, Paris (Gallimard) 1957. 'Genet', pp. 185-226.

BEIGBEDER, Marc. *Le Théâtre en France depuis la Libération*, Paris (Bordas) 1959. 'Genet', pp. 158-160, etc.

BLÖCKER, Günther. 'Ein Vertrauter der Nacht', *Frankfurter Allgemeine Zeitung*, No. 157, 10 July 1965.

BOISDEFFRE, Pierre de. *Une Histoire vivante de la Littérature d'aujourd'hui*, Paris (Le Livre Contemporain) 1957. 'Genet', pp. 277-280; 661-662; etc.

BOLLE, L. 'Saint-Genet, ou la Théologie du Voyou', in his *Les Lettres et l'Absolu*, Genève, 1959, pp. 107-119.

BONNEFOY, Claude. *Genet*, Paris (Classiques du XXe Siècle) 1965. 126 pp.

BORY, J.-L. 'Strick a frôlé le chef-d'oeuvre', *Arts*, 1 Jan, 1964, p. 7 [review of film of *Le Balcon*].

BROPHY, Brigid. 'Notre-Dame des Fleurs', *London Magazine*, June 1964, pp. 89-94.

BRUSTEIN, Robert. 'The Brothel of the Western World', *The New Republic*, vol. cxliii, No. 3, 28 March 1960, pp. 21-22.

— *The Theatre of Revolt*, London (Methuen) 1965.

CAILLOIS, Roger. *L'Homme et le Sacré*, 2nd ed., Paris (Gallimard) 1950.

CHAIGNE, Louis *Les Lettres Contemporaines*, Paris (Del Duca) 1964. 'Genet', p. 599.

CHAMPIGNY, Robert. *Le Genre dramatique*. Monte Carlo (Regain) 1965.

CHESTER, Alfred. 'Looking for Genet', *Commonweal*, vol. xxxvii, 1964, pp. 63-67.

CHIARAMONTE, Nicola. 'Jean Genet: White and Black', *Partisan Review* (N.Y.), vol. xxviii, Nos. 5-6, 1961, pp. 662-668.
— 'Le Cérémonial de Jean Genet', *Tempo Presente*, An. XII, 1967.

CISMARU, Alfred. 'The Antitheism of Jean Genet', *Antioch Review*, vol. xxiv, 1964, pp. 387-401.

CLARK, Eleanor. 'The World of Jean Genet', *Partisan Review*, vol. xvi, No. 4, Apr. 1949, pp. 442-448. See also the special French number of the same journal, Spring 1946.

CODIGNOLA, Luciano. 'Jean Genet, o l'illusione dello scandalo', *Tempo Presente*, An. II, Nos. 9-10, Sept-Oct. 1957, pp. 773-775.

CRUICKSHANK, John. 'Jean Genet: the Aesthetics of Crime', *Critical Quarterly*, vol. vi, 1964, pp. 202-210.

DORT, Bernard. 'Le Jeu de Genet: *Les Nègres*', *Temps Modernes*, vol. xv, 1959/60, pp. 1875-1884.
— *Genet*. Paris (Seghers: Series 'Théâtre de tous les Temps'). In preparation.

DRIVER, T. F. *Jean Genet*. Columbia Essays on Modern Writers. 48 pp. 1966.

DURAND, G. *Les Structures anthropologiques de l'Imaginaire*, Paris (P.U.F.), 2nd ed., 1963.

DURET, P. 'Nègreries', *Le Temps des Hommes*, No. 9, Jan-Mar. 1960. pp. 101-104.

DUVIGNAUD, Jean. 'Roger Blin aux prises avec *Les Nègres* de Genet', *Les Lettres Nouvelles*, 28 Oct. 1959, pp. 24-26.

EHRMANN, Jacques. 'Genet's dramatic metamorphosis: from appearance to freedom', *Yale French Studies*, No. 29, Spring-Summer 1962, pp. 33-42.
— 'Of Rats and Men' [on Sartre's *Saint-Genet*], *Yale French Studies*, No. 30, Winter 1962-3, pp. 78-85.

ELEVITCH, B. 'Sartre and Genet', *The Massachussetts Review*, vol. v, 1963-4, pp. 408-413.

ELSEN, Claude. 'Mythologie de Jean Genet', *Cahiers de la Pléiade*, Spring 1950, pp. 51-57.

ELSON, J. 'Genet and the sadistic society', *London Magazine*, Aug. 1963, pp. 61-67.

'Entretien avec Peter Brook' [*Le Balcon*, first French production at the Théâtre du Gymnase], *L'Express*, No. 466, 19 May 1960, pp. 44-45.

ESKIN, Stanley. 'Theatricality in the avant-garde drama: a Reconsideration of a theme in the light of *The Balcony* and *The Connection*', *Modern Drama*, vol. vii, 1964, pp. 213-222.

ESSLIN, Martin. *The Theatre of the Absurd*, N.Y. (Doubleday Anchor) 1961; London (Eyre & Spottiswoode) 1962. Ch. 4: 'Jean Genet—A Hall of Mirrors', pp. 140-167.

FERNANDEZ, Dominique. 'Genet', in *Ecrivains d'Aujourd'hui*, ed. Bernard Pingaud, Paris (Grasset) 1960, pp. 255-262.
— 'Claudel et Genet', *Nouvelle Revue Française*, vol. viii, 1960, pp. 119-123.

FOWLIE, Wallace. *Dionysus in Paris*, N.Y. (Meridian Books) 1958. 'Genet', pp. 218-222.
— 'The New French Theater: Artaud, Beckett, Genet, Ionesco', *Sewanee Review*, vol. lxvii, 1959, pp. 643-657.

— 'The Case of Jean Genet', *Commonweal*, vol. lxxiii, No. 5, 28 Oct. 1960, pp. 111-113.

— 'The Art and Conscience of Jean Genet', *Sewanee Review*, vol. lxxii, 1964, pp. 342-348.

FRANZEN, E. *Formen des modernen Dramas von der Illusionsbühne zum Antitheater.* Munich (C. H. Bock) 1961.

GASCOIGNE, Bamber. *Twentieth Century Drama*, London (Hutchinson's University Library), revised ed., 1963. 'Genet', pp. 191-192 and *passim*.

GOLDMANN, Lucien. 'Une pièce réaliste: *Le Balcon* de Genet', *Temps Modernes*, vol. xv, No. 171, June 1960, pp. 1885-1896.

GOZZI, Luigi, 'L'Orizonte drammatico di Jean Genet', *Il Verri*, An. IV, No. 6, Dec. 1960, pp. 76-90.

GROSSVOGEL, David I. *Four Playwrights and a Postscript*, Ithaca (Cornell U.P.) 1962. 'Genet: the Difficulty of Defining', pp. 133-174.

GUICHARNAUD, Jacques. 'An Existential Analysis of Genet' [on English translation of Sartre, *Saint-Genet*] *Yale Review*, vol. liii, 1963-4, pp. 435-440.

— *Modern French Drama from Giraudoux to Beckett*, Yale U.P., 1961. 'Genet', pp. 168-172.

HEIST, Walter. 'Die faschistische Komponente. Randbemerkungen zum Werk von Genet', *Frankfurter Hefte*, jahrg. xvii, Jan. 1962, pp. 29-39.

HILLARD, Gustav. 'Das Drama von Jean Genet', *Merkur*, jahrg. xvi, Heft 6, No. 172, pp. 596-600.

KARSCH, W. 'Genet, poète maudit, siegt in Berlin. Sein neues Stück, *Wände* [*Les Paravents*], in Berlin uraufgeführt', *Theater Heute*, vol. ii, No. 6, June 1960, pp. 8-10.

KESTING, M. 'Das Drama als Inferno: über Genets Theaterstücke', *Theater Heute*, vol. iii, No. 5, May 1962, pp. 22-23.

— *Panorma des zeitgenössischen Theaters*, Munich 1962. 'Genet', pp. 126-131.

KNAPP, Bettina. 'An interview with Roger Blin', *Tulane Drama Review*, vol. vii, No. 3, 1963, pp. 111-124.

LEBESQUE, Morvan. 'Jean Genet, ou le rebelle aux miroirs', *Carrefour*, No. 833, 31 Aug. 1960, p. 26.

LUCCIONI, G. 'De Somptueuses Funérailles', *Méditations* 4, Winter 1961-2, pp. 149-153.

LUCKOW, M. *Die Homosexualität in der literarischen Tradition; Studien zu den Romanen von Genet*, Stuttgart (Enke) 1962 (*Beiträge zur Sexualforschung*, No. xxvi).

McMAHON, Joseph H. *The Imagination of Jean Genet*, Yale U.P. and Paris (P.U.F.), 1963.

— 'Keeping faith and holding firm', *Yale French Studies*, No. 29, Spring/Summer 1962, pp. 26-36.

MAGNAN, J.-M. 'Genet ou la Beauté indigne', *Cahiers du Sud*, vol. lvii, 1963-4, pp. 150-152.

— 'Sur Genet', *L'Arc*, No. 14, Feb. 1962, pp. 60-62.

— *Essai sur Jean Genet.* Paris (Seghers: Series 'Poètes d'Aujourd'hui') 1966.

MARCEL, Gabriel. '*Les Nègres*: une scandaleuse exploitation des thèmes à la mode', *Nouvelles Littéraires*, 17 Dec. 1959, p. 10.

MARKUS, Thomas B. 'Genet, the theatre of the perverse', *Educational Theatre Journal*, vol. xiv, 1962, pp. 209-214.

— 'The psychological universe of Jean Genet', *Drama Survey* (Minneapolis), vol. iii, 1964, pp. 386-392.

MAURIAC, Claude. *'Le Balcon'* [film], *Figaro Littéraire*, 9 Jan. 1964, p. 20.

MAURIAC, François. 'Le cas Jean Genet', *Figaro Littéraire*, 26 March 1949.

MELCHER, Edith. 'The Pirandellism of Genet', *French Review*, vol. xxxvi, Oct. 1962, pp. 32-36.

MENNEMEIER, Fr. N. 'Genet: die Magische Realität des Invertierten. Maskenspiele und Aufstand zum Tode', in his *Das Moderne Drama des Auslandes,* Düsseldorf 1961, pp. 327-337.

MILNE, Tom. 'Reflections on the Screens', *Encore*, No. 50, Jul.-Aug. 1964, pp. 21-25.

MORGAN, Edwin. 'Jean Genet: a life and its legend', *Sidewalk*, (Edinburgh), vol. I, No. 1, 1960, pp. 53-66. Recast under the title: 'Jean Genet: "A legend to be legible" ', *The Outsider* (New Orleans), vol. ii, No. 2 (Summer 1962), pp. 35-40.

— *Nègres, les* (some minor reviews):
CLAIR, A. *Présence Africaine*, xxx, Feb.-Mar. 1960, pp. 118-119.
FOWLIE, W. *Tulane Drama Review*, vol. v, No. 1, Sept. 1960, pp. 46-48.
GOUHIER, H. *La Table Ronde*, No. 146, Feb. 1960, pp. 186-188.
LEMARCHAND, J. *Figaro Littéraire*, 7 Nov. 1959, p. 16.

NELSON, Benjamin. 'Sartre and *Notre-Dame des Fleurs'*, *The Psychoanalytical Review*, Fall 1963, vol. 1, No. 3 (Special issue: 'Psychoanalysis and Literature').

— *'The Balcony* and Parisian existentialism', *Tulane Drama Review*, vol. vii, No. 3, 1963, pp. 60-79.

NIMIER, Roger. *Journées de Lectures*, Paris (Gallimard) 1965. 'Genet', pp. 122-124.

NOULET, Madame E. *'Le Balcon'*, *Les Lettres Nouvelles*, vol. iv, No. 2, 1956, pp. 313-316.

NUGENT, Robert. 'Sculpture into drama: Giacometti's influence on Genet', *Drama Survey*, vol. iii, 1964, pp. 378-385.

PAOLANTONIO, José-Maria. 'Nuestro Teatro de Flagelación'. *Teatro XX*, No. 18, 1965.

PIERRET, Marc, 'A propos des *Nègres'*, *Lettres Nouvelles*, vol. vii, No. 32, 2 Dec. 1959, p. 35.

PIWINSKA, Marta. *'Parawany*—misterium makabryczne', *Dialog*, 1964, No. 5.

PORTAL, Georges. 'Genet: Celui par qui le scandale n'arrive pas', *Ecrits de Paris*, No. 185, Sept. 1960, pp. 96-102.

POULET, Robert. 'Genet, ou l'ennemi', in his *Aveux Spontanés*, Paris, 1963. pp. 109-114.

— *La Lanterne magique*, Paris (Debresse) 1956. 'Genet', pp. 160-166.

PRONKO, Leonard C. *Avant-Garde: The Experimental Theatre in France*, Berkeley and Los Angeles (California U.P.), 1962. 'Genet', pp. 140-154.

— 'Genet's *Les Paravents'*, *L'Esprit Créateur* (Minneapolis), vol. ii, No. 4, Winter 1962, pp. 181-188.

PUCCIANI, Oreste. 'Tragedy, Genet and *The Maids'*, *Tulane Drama Review*, vol. vii, No. 3, 1963, pp. 42-59.

RECK, Rima D. 'Appearance and reality in Genet's *Le Balcon*', *Yale French Studies*, No. 29, Spring/Summer 1962, pp. 20-25.

REGNAUT, M. '*Les Nègres* au Théâtre de Lutèce', *Théâtre Populaire*, No. 36, 4e trimestre 1959, pp. 50-53.

RINIERI, J. J. 'Journal du Voleur', *Temps Modernes*, No. 43, May 1949, pp. 943-945.

— 'Genet: *Les Bonnes*', *La Nef*, No. 30, May 1947, pp. 156-160.

ROY, Claude. 'Sur Genet et Duras', *Nouvelle Revue Française*, vol. ix, No. 104, Aug. 1961, pp. 311-314.

St AUBYN, F. C. 'Jean Genet: a scandalous success', *Hopkins Review*, vol. v. 1951, pp. 45-53.

SARTRE, Jean-Paul. *Saint-Genet Comédien et Martyr*, Paris (Gallimard) 1952, 573 pp. (Vol. i of the *Oeuvres Complètes de Jean Genet*). Various sections of this work appeared earlier in numbers of *Les Temps Modernes*. Tr. Bernard Frechtman, *Saint-Genet*, N.Y. (Braziller) 1963. London (W. H. Allen) 1963. The section on *Les Bonnes* reproduced separately in BOGARD, T., and OLIVER, W. I., *Modern Drama: Essays in Criticism*, N.Y. and O.U.P. (Galaxy), 1965, pp. 152-167. Various other sections of this work have also been extracted and used in English translation as introduction to plays and novels by Genet. See above, Section I, Nos. 28 and 67.

SCHULZE-VELLINGHAUSEN, Albert. *Theaterkritik, 1952-1960*, Hannover 1961. Genet, *Die Dienstmädchen*, pp. 217-219.

SELZ, Jean. '*Les Nègres*: tragédie ou exorcisme?' *Les Lettres Nouvelles*, 11 Nov. 1959, pp. 37-38.

SERREAU, Geneviève. *Histoire du 'Nouveau Théâtre'*. Paris (N.R.F. Collection 'Idées') 1966.

SIMON, Alfred. 'Genet, le nègre et la réprobation', *Esprit*, année xxviii, No. 280, Jan. 1960, pp. 170-173.

SORDO, Enrique. 'Jean Genet, o el escandalo', *El Noticiero Universal* (Barcelona), 5 Nov. 1965.

STREM, George C. 'The theater of Jean Genet: Facets of illusion—the Anti-Christ and the Underdog', *Minnesota Review*, vol. iv, 1964, pp. 226-236.

SVENDSEN, J. M. '*Corydon* revisited: a reminder on Genet', *Tulane Drama Review*, vol. vii, No. 3, 1963, pp. 98-110.

SYPHER, W. *Loss of the Self in modern French Literature and Art*, N.Y. (Random House) 1962.

TAUBES, Susan. 'The white mask falls', *Tulane Drama Review*, vol. vii, No. 3, 1963, pp. 85-92.

TAYLOR, John R. *Anger and After*. Penguin Books, 1963.

THODY, Philip. *Jean Genet: A Study of his Work*, London (Hamish Hamilton), in preparation.

TIEDEMANN, Rolf. 'Entzauberte Metaphorik der Dignität: über Jean Genet', *Zeugnisse*, 45, 1964, pp. 257-277.

Tulane Drama Review, vol. vii, No. 3, 1963. Special Genet/Ionesco number.

WALTHER, E., and BENSE, M. 'Sartre und Genet', *Augenblick*, 3/4, Sept.-Oct. 1958, pp. 13-18.

WELLWARTH, George E. *The Theater of Protest and Paradox*, New York, U.P., 1964. 'Genet: The Theater of Disillusion', pp. 113-133 and *passim*.

— 'The new dramatists (3): Jean Genet', *Drama Survey* (Minneapolis), vol. i, No. 3, Winter 1962, pp. 308-320.

WILCOCKS, R. W. F. *Jean Genet: A Study of his Drama*. Ph.D. Thesis, University of Khartoum, 1966 (unpublished).

Yale French Studies, No. 29, Spring/Summer 1962. Special issue devoted to *The New Dramatists*.

YEAGER, Henry J. 'The uncompromising morality of Jean Genet', *French Review*, vol. xxxix, No. 2, Nov. 1965, pp. 214-219.

YERLÈS, P. 'Réflexions sur le théâtre de Genet', *Revue Nouvelle*, (Tournai/ Paris), vol. xxxiv, 1961, pp. 340-345.

ZADEK, Peter. 'Acts of Violence', *New Statesman*, 4 May 1957, pp. 568-570.

ZAND, Nicole. 'Entretien avec Roger Blin' [*Les Paravents*], *Le Monde*, 15 April 1966.

— 'Fiche documentaire I: *Les Nègres*, de Jean Genet', *Théâtre de Demain*, nouv. sér., No. 11, Oct.-Nov. 1960, pp. 29-30.

THEMATIC INDEX

NOTE: Genet's works are listed under the original French titles. Figures in italics denote unbroken references.

Abjection, 31-32, 36, 39-40, 59, 99, *106-9*, 165, 172, 227-28, 285, 300-302

Absolute, search for, 6, 14, 32-35, 39, 46, 48-49, 53, 55, 57, 59, 70, 107, 109, 126-27, 145-49, *150-65*, 175, 177-78, 181, 186-87, 216-17, 227, 229, 235, 242, 253-54, 275-76, 288, 299, 306

Absurd, 112, *143-45*, 149, 176, 181-82, 189, 213-14, 218, 240, 309

Abysses, les, 248

'Acte gratuit', 154, 194-95, 227, 233-34

Actor, *218-21*, 222-23, 237-38, 258, 286-88

'ADAME MIROIR, 9-11, 26, 196

Aesthetics, aestheticism, 78, 85, *88-93*, 113-14, 127, 151-52, 173, 195, 253, 255, *273-77*, 282, 298, 305, 307, 313

Alençon, E. d', 313

Algeria (Arabs), 22, 163, 221, 259-60, *296-307*

Ambiguity, 47, 111, 176, *202-4*, 226, *310-15*

Anarchism, 115, 151, 163, 175-76, 230-32, *255-58*, 277, 283-84, *298-99*, 303-4, 314

Angels, 33, *47-48*, 49, 111, 116, 126-27, 141, 175, 236

Animism, 15, 25, 40, *141-45*

Antrobus, J., 278

Apollinaire, G., 130

Arbalète, l', 103

Archetypes, 43, 45-46, 70-71, 113, 116-17, 192, 221, 265, *267-68*

Argot, 9, 107, 129, 136, 163-64, 272, 317

Art, artist, 39, 71, 78, 86, 113, 121, 124-26, 142-43, 145, 221-22, 276-77, 283-84, 287, 290, 301-2, 304-5, *306-7*

Artaud, A., 71, 94, 125, 213, 217,

221-22, 224-25, 246, 259, 284, 316

Asceticism, 107, 127, 159, 161, 179, 234

ATELIER D'ALBERTO GIACOMETTI, 62, 90, 98, 105, 145, 166, 171, 221, *306-7*, 320

Aubert, M., 157-58

Auriol, V., 104

Authenticity, 14, 20-24, 33, 43-45, 47, 49-51, 59, 88, 100, 114, 116, 145, 159, *194-96*, 217, 234, 267-70, 289, 300

Autumn, 76-77, 81

BALCON, 14-16, 20, 25, 76, 81, 96, 105, 116, 130, 137-38, 140, 145, 150, 171, 199, 219-21, 225, 244, *251-81*, 282-84, 288, 297-99, 313, 315

Ballet, 9-11, 41, 44, 46, 92, 113, 125, 223-24

Barbezat, M., 103

Barbezat, O., 103

Bataille, G., 25, 28, 37, 61, 97, 203, 208

Baudelaire, C., 72, 93, 124, 152, 313

Beardsley, A., 92, 314

Beauty, 17, 24-25, 39, 45, 48, 78, 83, *84-85*, 86, *88-93*, *125-27*, 151, 158, 222, *290-93*, 300, *302-5*

Beauty/ugliness, 80, 83, *89-92*, 107, 126-27, 276-77, 291, 300, 303-4

Beauvoir, S. de, 28, 76, 95, 104, 124, 129-30, 134, 168, 202, 248, 309-10, 319

Beckett, S., 11, 34, 51, 56, 61, 64, 105, 130, 148-49, 183-84, 191, 206, 224, 241, 249, 309

Becoming, 83

Beerbohm, M., 202, 313, 315

Bergson, H., 83, 206

Black/white, 260, *286-95*

Blake, W., 69, 146, 214

Blue, 32, 46, 55, 81, 87, 127, 152, 291

BONNES, 14-15, 20, 48, 60, 82, 105, 124, 129, 140, 143, 165-66, 171, 179-80, 213-14, 216-17, 219-21, 223-25, 234, *236-45*, 246-52, 256, 261, 263, 266-67, 276-79, 286, 297

'Bonté' (charity), 179-80, *261-62*, 266, 290, *294-95*

Bourgeoisie, 22, 35, 38, 56, 77, 93, 104, 107, 132, 152, 156, 161, *162-65*, 236, 243-44, 254, *261-62*, 277, 283, 287-88

Brecht, B., 117, 215, 221, 225, *251-52*, 255-57, 259, *260-61*, 262, 265, 284, 296-97

Brothel, 172, 174, 261, 263-64, 270-71, 275, 298-99, 301, *306-7*

Brotherhood, 254, 262

Buddhism, 11, 58

Buffet, E., 313

Burglary, 21, 36, 41, 86, 101, 103-4, *111-16*, 137, 175

Camus, A., 104, 143, 181-82, 189, 241

Cannibalism, 139-40

CAPABLE DU FAIT, 170

Catherine, Saint (of Siena), 108, 187

Chambers, R., 63

Chamisso, A. von, 22, 26, 196

CHANT D'AMOUR, 129

Characterization, 116-19, 172-73

Christ, Christianity, 23-24, 33, 36, 38-40, 42-43, 51-56, 58, 80, 82, 149, *178-79*, *182-83*, *187-89*, 193, 198, 218, 220, *230-35*, 254, 258-59, 264, 293-95

Circus, 224-25, 284

Classicism, 225, 228, 251

Claudel, P., 215, 219, 284, 317

Cocteau, J., 93, 103-4, 129, 132, 203, 310

Collaborators, 129-30, 138

Colonialism, 287-88, 303, 305-6,

Colour-symbolism, 42, *81-82*, 289-93

Commitment, 137, 145, 244-45, *251-61*, *271-77*, 282-84, 297-98, 300-301, 304

Communism, 253-54, 260

CONDAMNÉ À MORT, 25, 28, 61, 67, 93, *101-2*

Convict-galley, 70, 80, *82*, 135-36, 188

Coppée, F., 67, 78, 93

Corneille, P., 24, 54, 99-100, 117, 167, 194, 228, 232-33

Cowardice, 83-84, 147, 157, 159

Crime/punishment, 21, 35, 75, *185-89*, 226-27

Cruelty, 90, 139, 158, 161, 221, 254, 259, 262,

Curtain-symbol, 32, 87

Dagger-symbol, 71

Death, 7, 9, 15, 17, 21, 25, 37, 41-42, 48, 53, 58, 67, 77, 86-89, 105-6, 112, 124, 126, 139, 182, 218, 262, 264, *271-76*, 290, 299-300

Descartes, 18, 96, 151, 247, 295, 303-4,

Despair, 111-13, 146, 161, 216-17, 244, 309

Devil's-Island, 82, 86

Dialogue, 222-23

Dostoievsky, F., 23, 32-33, 53, 130, 141, 155, *181-82*, 185-86, 197, 205, 235, 313-14,

Double-symbol, 6, 14, 17-18, 126, 146-48, 159, *173-74*, *196-202*, 213, *237-38*, 240-41, 265, 269, 273-74, 312

'Douceur', 55, 83, 142, 147, 160, 294

Drama (theory and technique), 19, 82, 101, 129, *213-25*, *251-52*, *258-61*, 262, 284-86, 296-97

Dreams, 82, 102, 109, 115, 118, 121, 239

Duality, 197-202, 214-15, 217

Du Bos, J.-B., 221-22

Durand, G., 63

ENFANT CRIMINEL, 164, 209, 247, 254

'En-soi', 5, 12-13, 19, 124, 184, 200-201, 217

Eroticism, 10-11, 25, 36, 41, 80, 87, 146, 160, 175, 225, 259, *263*, 271, 311

Error, 193-96

Espionage, 47

Establishment, the, 163-64, 262-63, 288

Ethics, 45, 78, 92-93, 147, *175-80*, 268, 283, 309-10

Être (l') et le Néant, 5, 7, 11-13, 19, 25-26, *136-37*, 145, 165, 168, *201-2*, 301-2, 312

Eucharist, 51, *58-59*, 146, *258-59*, 294

Evil, absolute, 90, *150-60*, 165, 173, 180-86, 195, 227, 233, 302

Existentialism, *4-7, 11-14*, 19, 43, 48, 88, 100, 121, 129, 136-38, 159, 181, 183-84, 190-91, 196-97, *201-2*, 230-31, 265-66, 309

Expiation, 186-89

Fakes, 19-21, *51-53*, 203, 214, 258, 268

Fall, 32-33

Fascism, 253-54, 306

Fatalism, fatality, 15, 40, 49, 70, 99-100, *122-23*, 143, 146, 149, 152, 164, 226, *228-36*

Fear, 159-60, 259, 296

Figure/image, *12-14, 18-21*, 32, 43-44, 50, 57, 91, 126, 146-48, 196, 200, 203, 242-43, *265-75*, 292, 304, 307

Fissure-symbol, 44, *83-84*, 88-89, 112, 125, 158

Flowers, 17, 32, 42, 48, 50, 67, 73, *75-79*, 86, 93, 116, 152, 161, 192, 202, 214, 216, 290-91

Fontevrault, 18, 23, 40, 47, 50, 66, 70, 73, 75, 77, 81, 86-87, 95, 101, 116, 130, 191, 199, 218, 255, 286

Force de l'Âge, 22, 28, 76, 95, 104, 124, 129, 134, 168, 248

Force des Choses, 129-30

Fragmentation, 119, 135-36

France, 32, 103, *156-57*

Francis, Saint (of Assisi), 78

Frechtman, B., x, 130, 168

Freedom/determinism, 71, 100, 114, 123, 149, 155, 181, 194, *230-33*

Fresnes, 33, 87, 95, 116, 163

Freud, S. (Freudianism), 36, 56, 221-22

FUNAMBULE, 33, 89, *124-26*, 134, 142, 221, 224, 247

Functions, 3, 20, 24, 142-45, 199, 262, *265-75*, 288, 300, 306

GALÈRE, 67

Genet, Jean, ix-x
  Adolescence, 5, 14, 99-100, *102-3*;
  Childhood, 4-5, 93, 102, 106, 124;
  Legend, 102-7, *117-21*, 124, 127-28, 156, 202; *Manhood*, 101-5; *Name*, 78-79

Gestapo, 23, 163, 269, 277

Gestures, 41, *42-46*, 47-48, 53, 70-71, 87, 89, 92-93, 106, 113, 121, 124-25, 137, 142, 150, 184, 217, 221, *223-24*, 239, 253, *272-75*

Ghosts, 47

Giacometti, A., 89-90, 126, 130, 142-43, *306-7*

Gide, A., 108, 155, 181, 194-95, 207-8

Gilles de Rais, 151

Glass-symbol, 7, 33, 47, 86, 147, 160, 185

God, 6-7, 12-13, 15-16, 20, 23-24, 32-33, 37-40, 45, 48-51, 53-55, *56-60*, 78, 99, 117, *122-23*, 135, 143, 146, 150-51, 155-56, 159, 161, *181-83*, 185-86, 193-94, 196, 201, 226, 228, 232, 235, 294

Goethe, J. W. von, 66, 83, 84, 293, 308

Golden Legend, 99-134, 178, 187

Good/evil, 6-7, 20, 24, 35-36, 38, 91, *150-60*, 164, *178-79*

Grace (theological), 15-17, 33, 45, 150-51, 190, *228-36*

Graham, Rev. Billy, 293-94

Gravity, 40-41, 47, 86, 173, 218

Hatred, 18, 167, 238, 242-44, *258-61*, 262, 286, 293, 295-97, 302

HAUTE SURVEILLANCE, 15-16, 18, 21, 27, 129, 142, 151, 187, 219-20, 222, *225-36*, 246-50, 263, 286

Hedonism, 141

Hell, 32-33, 35, 38, 77, 116

Helvétius, 176, 179, 205

Hero, anti-, 283-84

Hero, positive/negative, *252-58*, 283-84, 298, 300

Hitler, A., 22-23, 103, 115, 136, 138, 140, 153-54, 161, 176, 309

Hobbes, T., 178-79, 266

Homosexuality, 11, 22, 37, 55, *79-81*, 84, 107, *110-11*, 112-13, 138, *139-41*, 145, 153, 160-61, 171, 173, 180, 197, 208, 313

Humanitarianism, 90, *254*, 261-62, 290, 294

Humiliation (shame, degradation), 22-25, 31-33, 49, *106-8*, 110, 172, 177, *182-83*, 244

Identity, *8-12*, 14, 17, 24, 45-46, 70, 88, 111, 119, 138, *139-40*, 141, *183-86*, 199, *200-202*, 216, *234-45*, *265-75*, 312

Illusion, 213-16, *219-21*, 237-38, *258-60*, 264-65, 286-88, 297

Imagery, 108-9, *160-61*

Imposture, 52-53, 217

Inanimate objects, 6-7, *71-73*, *124-26*, *139-45*, 171-72, 180, 191-92, 197, 229, 239

Incantation, 219, 222, 284-85, 290

Indifference, 48, 80, 125, *146-47*, 161

Infinite, 57-58

Inhumanity, 161, 180, 254, 262

Ionesco, E., 19-20, 47, 63, 78, 117, 143-44, 149, 162, 182-84, 213, 215, 219, 224, 240, 249, 271, 282-83, 285, 309-10, 315-16

Irony, 173

Jammes, F., 313

Jansenism, 159, 215, *228-36*, 253

Jealousy, 147-48, 167

Jewels, 195, 229

Jews, 288-89

Joan, Saint, 23, 282

Jouhandeau, M., 53, 130

JOURNAL DU VOLEUR, 7-8, 11, 15, 22, 26-28, 42, 47, 52, 56, 58, 60-65, 76, 79, 82, 87, 92-93, 95-98, *99-134*, 137, 144, 148, 153, 156-59, 166-70, 172, 177, 181, 204-6, 208-9, 238, 242, 245-46, 248-49, 269, 277-79, 311, 313, 320

Judas Iscariot, 24, 282

Justice, 254, 256

Lace-symbol, *86-87*, 214

Language, 238, 251, *271-73*, 282, 284, 303, 308-9

Lautréamont, Comte de, 108, 313

Lawrence, D. H., 76, 162, 182

Leduc, V., 129

Leiris, M., 104

LETTRE À PAUVERT, *214-15*, *218-22*, 245-46, 260, 278

Levitation, 44, 47, 75, 159, 224

Liberty, 71, 100, *114-16*, 121, 123, *180-81*, *185-86*, 230-35

Light/Darkness, 7, 77-78, 88, 146, 152, 236, 289-90, 300

Littérature (la) et le Mal, 25, 28, 61, 208

Love, 18, 39, 111-12, *145-50*, 158-59, 200, 242-43, 259, *290-93*

Love/hate, 139, *149-50*, 200, 243, 286, 292

Luxury, 76, 171-72, 254

Maeterlinck, M., 214, 219

Magic, 8, 45, 48, 70, 75-77, 79, 84, 87, 89, 121, 125, 171, 185, 195

Malevolence, 140, 143, *160-61*, 173, 180

Mallarmé, S., 68, 72, 78, 93, 303, 313

Manon Lescaut, 146

MARCHE FUNÈBRE, 67, 93

Mask (disguise), 11, 19, 48, 85, 88, 125, 203, *218-20*, 238, 261, 284, 286-88, 313-14

Masochism, 139

Mass, Holy, 40-41, 43, 51, 58, 146, *218-20*, 229

Mass-communication, *271-73*, 282, *308-10*

Mass/individual, 252, 268, *271-77*, *282-84*, 299, 303-4

Materialism, 255

Metamorphosis, 45, 224, 242-43

Mettray, 13, 17-19, 22, 40-42, 47, 66, 70, *73-74*, 75, 77, 81-82, 85-86, 89-90, 101-2, 109, 116, 122, 130, 131, 152, 161, 164, 191-92, 199, 218, 226, 254, 286

Michelangelo, 40, 43, 61-62, 89, 130

'Milice, la', 23, 42, 130, 138, *152-53*, 156-57, 161, 163-64, 257

Milne, T., 297, 318

MIRACLE DE LA ROSE, 14, 18, 22, 27-28, 34, 41-42, 48-49, 55, 57, 60-65, *66-98*, 99-104, 106, 109-110, 113, 118, 121, 124, 128-36, 152, 166-69, 175, 199, 206-8, 225-26, 229, 246-47, 249, 254-55, 277-78, 304

Miracles, 17, 21, 44, *48-53*, 59, 81, 106, 183, 198-99, 214, 254

Mirror-symbol, *7-25*, 31, 33, 42-43, 52-53, 55, 57, 68, 75, 77-78, 85, 91-92, 106, 112, 121, 124, 126, *146-50*, 151, 158-59, 161, 174, 178, 182, 192, 197, 199, 214, 229, 238, 241-43, *265-75*, 292, 297

Monastery, 73

Monsters, 112, *152-53*, 172-73, 191, 244

Mother-symbol, 32, 102, 105-6, 130, 254

Murder, 7, 11, 15-16, 21, 24, 35, 37, 39, 41-42, 48, 59, 69, 72, 112, 119-20, 143, 149, *154-56*, 160, *170-209*, 218, 226-28, 238, 266, 286

Mysticism, 47, 51, 58, 88, 111, 136, 146, 160, 176, 254

Names, *78-79*, 86, 95-96, 198, 236, 238, 276, 294

Naturalism, 215, 218-19, 222, 224

Nature, 76-77, 92

Nazis, 24, 32, 35, 71, 87, 95, 115, 130, 136, 138, 153, 156, 161, 163, 176, 269

NÈGRES, 14, 20, 23, 81, 85, 88, 96, 116, 124, 128, 137, 150, 164, 171, 213, *219-20*, 225, 244, 256-57, 259, *260-61*, 262-63, 283, *284-96*, 297-98, 300, 302, 315-18,

Negroes, 22, 88, 163, 219-21, 284-96, 300, 307

Nihilism, 308-9, 310

Nirvana, 234

NOTRE-DAME DES FLEURS, 5, 8, 14-16, 22, 26-27, *31-65*, 66-68, 78-79, 81, 87-88, 94-101, 103-4, 106, 111-12, 114, 118, 120, 122, 130-31, 133-35, 137, 146, 148, 150, 152, 157, 162, 166-69, 171-72, 175, 177, 191-92, 205-7, 222, 224, 226, 244-47, 249, 257, 265, 277-79, 288, 301, 305, 313, 316

Novel (techniques of), 116-24, 135-36, 170-75, 189

Objectivity, 100-101, 135, 137, 171

Opposites, 20-21, 24, 35-36, 78, 83-84, 91, 146, *148-50*, 160, *163-65*, 203, 222, 237-38, *258-59*, 264, *310-15*

Orwell, G., 53, 64, 95, 176, 271, 314

Others, *4-7*, *12-13*, 16, 18, 43, 71, 85, 88, 106, 117, 119, *139-40*, 146, 158-59, 184, 197, 200, 241-43, *265-75*, 288-89

Papatakis, N., 248

Papin sisters, 236, 243-44

PARAVENTS, 3, 14, 23, 48, 82, 88, 96, 105, 116, 124, 137, 142, 144-45, 166, 168, 171, 216, 222, 225, 244-45, 252, 257-61, 272, 283, *296-307*, 319-20

Pascal, B., 4, 207, 267

Passivity, 99, *109-116*, *139-41*, 160, 172

Patriotism, 19, *156-57*, 254

PÊCHEUR DU SUQUET, 104, 129, 153

Perception, 117-20, 144, 183-86, 200, 217

Pilorge, M., 35, 61, 103, 157

Platitudes, 283, 298, 303, 309

Plato, Platonism, 8, 43, 68, 92, 107, 121, 141, 146, 151

Pléiade, Prix de la, 129

POÈMES, 28, 67-68, 93, 100, 103, 114, 124, 129, 135

Poetry (poet), 20-21, 24-25, 38-39, 42-43, 48, 50-52, 71-73, 77-79, 83, 85, 101-3, 113, *124-28*, 137, 141-42, 159, 185, 189, 197, 202, 213-14, 216, 271-73, 276-77, *290*, 299-300, 305, 307, 309-10, 313

Police, 117, *269-71*

Politics, 145, 175, 221, 244-45, *251-60*, *266-77*, 282-83, 287, 294-96, *297-307*

POMPES FUNÈBRES, 4, 14, 16, 18-20, 23, 26-27, 34, 36, 41-42, 47-48, 55, 58, 60-63, 65, 74, 87, 89, 94-98, 100, 102, 104-5, 117, 128-33, *135-69*, 170-71, 177, 185, 188, 200, 205-6, 208, 218, 227, 230, 237, 241, 243, 246-47, 249-50, 254, 257, 261, 269, 271

Pornography, 36, 55, 136, 145, 204, *310-12*

'Pour-autrui', 12-13

'Pour-soi', 5, 12-13, 19, 124, 183-84, 200-201, 217

Power, *266-75*

Proletariat, 163, 236, 244, 253-54

Propaganda, 257, 272, 308-10

Prostitutes, 105, 171-72, 175, 292, *306-7*

Proust, M., ix, 46, *73-74*, 81, 90, 98, 106, 130, 146, 148, 162, 167, 204, 207, 242, 254, 320

342 INDEX

QUERELLE DE BREST, 11, 14, 16, 20,
26-28, 32, 45, 47, 60, 62-63, 72,
87-88, 94-98, 100, 102, 115-17,
120, 124, 131-34, 136-37, 140,
151-53, 165-68, *170-209*, *229-34*,
237, 242-43, 246-49, 262-63, 265,
269-70, 273, 277-80, 306

Racialism, 244-45, 259, *284-96*
Racine, J., 15, 23, 54, 117, 146,
158-59, 220, 228, 296-97
Realism, reality, 23, 32, 69, 117-18,
214-16, 225
Reality/imagination, 117-21, 215-16,
237-40, 286-88
Redemption, 102, *187-89*, 234
'Relègue, la', 103-6, 111
Religion, 15, 19, 33, 38-43, 58,
145, *187-89*, 220, 222, 259
Revolution, 162-63, 257-60, 263-65,
274-77, 284, 302, 315
Rimbaud, A., 78, 124
Ritual, *41-44*, 46, 71, 79, 139, 153,
159, 195, 218-19, 238-39, 260,
264, *273-75*, 286
Rose-symbol, 67, 73, *75-81*, 126-27,
175, 198, 202-3, 303, 314
Royalty, 116, 153, 254, 264, 268,
288

Sacred/profane, 16-17, *36-42*, 44-47,
50-53, 58-59, 69-70, 73-74, 78,
81, 89, 106, 108, 111, 121, 125,
141, 146, 158, 181, 187, 190,
198, 202, 218-19, 226-27, 258-59,
269, 307
Sadism (de Sade), 136, 139, 154, 160,
175-76, 311
Sailor-symbol, *9-11*, 25, 36, 81, 89,
171-209, 264
Saint-Genet Comédien et Matryr,
4, 11, 26, 28, 43, 51, 56-57, 62,
65, 93, 95, 128-29, *150-51*, 167,
205, **279**
Sanctity (saints), 15-16, 32-38, 48-49,
53-60, 75, 78, 81-82, 86-87, 92,
106-9, 127, 141, 146, 151, 158,
160, 165, 173, 175, 177-82,
187-89, 193, 197, 226-27, 234,
300-301
Santé, la, 116, 163
Sartre, J.-P., 4-7, 11, 13-14, 19,
24-28, 32, 43, 49, 51, 53, 56-57,
62, 65, 67, 71, 76, 78, 85, 88, 93,

95, 100-104, 109, 116, 124, 127-30,
136-38, 145, 150-51, 155, 157,
162-63, 167-68, 179, 181, 183-84,
200-202, 203, 205-6, 217, 225,
227, 230, 236, 255-57, 279, 288-89,
297, 305, 309, 316, 319
Satanism, 150, 152, 154
Satire, 40, 118, 176, 256-57
Schweitzer, A., 38, *294-95*
Sculpture, 7, 41, 125-26, 142, 193,
223-24
SECRET DE REMBRANDT, 129
Security, 114-16, 146, 232
Self-knowledge, 4-7, 10, 14, 18,
200-201, 242-43, *265-70*
Sénémaud, L., 104, 118, 147, 153
Servants, 138-39, 163-65, 171,
237-45
Sexuality, 19, 39, 41-42, 55, 71, 80,
111, 117, 139, 145, 259, 311-12
Simultaneity, 189-91, 199, 203
Singularity, 6, 22, 142, *152-53*, 164,
197, 252, 268-69, 273-74, *306-7*
Slogans, 252, 272, 277, 283, 296,
309
Socialism, 145, *164-65*, 243-45, 255,
272, 277, 283, 302, 305-6, 314,
319
Society/order, *161-65*, 173, 179-80,
252-55, 256, *303-4*
Solitude, 3-6, 15-16, 22-24, 26, 75,
87, 107, 126-27, 145-46, 152-55,
162, 164, 178-79, 227-28, 252,
305-7
Song, 83, 92, 107, 142, 147, 197,
276, 299
Spain, 79, 103, 127
Stephen, Saint, 54, 187
'Style-Rothschild', 76, 171-72, 254,
263
Subjectivity, 117-19, 127-28
Suffering, 146, 177
Superstition, 38, *40-41*, 48, 73, 79,
185, 254
Symbolism, 20, 38, 41-45, 50-53, 58,
66-93, 113, *125-27*, 160, 171-72,
174-75, 198-99, 202-3, *213-22*,
237-38, *258-61*, *263*, *267-75*, 282

Taboos, *36-41*, 58, 89, 106, 155,
158, 226-27
Tattooing, 87, 164
Théâtre (le) et son Double, 71, 94,
221, 246, 285, 316

Theresa, Saint (of Avila), 23, 38, 53-54, 108, 187, 264

Theresa, Saint (of Lisieux), 78

Time, 43-44, 73-74, 144, 183-84, *189-96*, 199, 224, 240, 306

Tragedy, 218-19

Traitors (betrayal), 19, 22, 24-25, 48, 147, *156-60*, 172, 174, 195, 203, 239, 300

Trinity, *13-16*, 197

Truth/lies, 19-20, 48, 52-53, 88, 127-28, *202-4*, 214, 217, 239-40, 282-83, 299, *308-10*

Uniform, 173, 252, *273-75*, 303-4

Unity (mystic), 10-11, 14-16, 21-22, 111-12, 199-200

Vauthier, J., 248

Veil-symbol, 42, *84-88*, 160, 214

Veni Creator, 40, 42, 85, 88

Vincent de Paul, Saint, 23, 38, *187-89*, 233-34

Violence, 90, 114-15, 140, 146-47, 161, 175, 221-22, 225, 244-45, 259-60, 288

Virgin Mary, 25, 36, 40, 52, 59, 81, 215, 259, 264

Virility, *109-16*, 139-41, 174, 180

Void ('le néant'), *5-19*, 22, 48, 57, 77, 84, 88, 111, 144, 151, *181-87*, 192, 194, 199-200, 216, 233, 238, 265-68, 301, 305, 309

Vulgarity, 81, 92, 107, 290, 296

Waiters, 163, 244

Wall-symbol, 116, *174-75*, 185, 192

Wedding-symbol, 41-42, 85, 87

Weidmann, 86, 157

Wilde, O., 92, 107, 114, 205, 313

Women, 32, *105-6*, 138-39, *171-72*

Work, 253-54